Questions and Answers on Conversations with God

Books by Neale Donald Walsch

Conversations with God, Book 1

Conversations with God, Book 1 Guidebook

Conversations with God, Book 2

Conversations with God, Book 3

Meditations from Conversations with God, Book 1

Meditations from Conversations with God, Book 2, A Personal Journal

The Little Soul and the Sun

Friendship with God

Neale Donald Walsch on Relationships

Neale Donald Walsch on Abundance and Right Livelihood

Neale Donald Walsch on Holistic Living

Questions and Answers on
Conversations with God

Neale Donald Walsch

Cover design by Marjoram Productions
Cover Painting by Louis Jones

For information write:

Hampton Roads Publishing Company, Inc.
134 Burgess Lane
Charlottesville, VA 22902

Or call: 804-296-2772
FAX: 804-296-5096
e-mail: hrpc@hrpub.com
Web site: http://www.hrpub.com

If you are unable to order this book from your local bookseller, you may order directly from the publisher. Quantity discounts for organizations are available. Call 1-800-766-8009, toll-free.

Library of Congress Catalog Card Number: 99-71610

ISBN 1-57174-140-2

10 9 8 7 6 5 4 3 2 1

Printed on acid-free paper in Canada

For

BRYAN L. WALSCH, SR.

My brother, and, during those wonderful
early years of childhood, often my protector,
sometimes my tormentor, but always
my best friend.

He encouraged me to ask the really big questions.
He showed me it was possible to know the answers.

Table Of Contents

Acknowledgments

My first word of thanks goes, as always, to my best friend, God. Life has become better and better since I began a real, honest-to-goodness conversation with God, and since I've had a friendship with God, it's been one miracle after the next.

My wife, Nancy, and my children come next, for giving me the space and granting me the time to continue these writings, allowing me to share with the world what had been a very private experience, and to turn our lives upside-down in the process.

I owe a debt of thanks, on this book in particular, to my wonderful friend and personal assistant for special projects, Rose Wolfenbarger, who has spent years filing, recording, and categorizing every answer I have ever written to the letters I have received, and many months culling through those answers to compile the material here.

Introduction

Everybody in the world has questions about life and how it works. Everybody in the world also has the answers. Not everybody in the world knows this.

I certainly didn't. I looked everywhere for answers—but within. I listened to parents, family, and friends, teachers, pastors, leaders, authors, philosophers—anyone and everyone I thought might have something to say.

Then I turned to God.

I asked a pile of questions. And I finally got answers. Those responses form the published trilogy known as *Conversations with God*. They've also led to more questions. Not just from me, but from many of the millions of readers of those books.

The most important answer I received was that I no longer had to ask questions. All of the answers, God said, are inside of me. All I have to do is go within. That's all that any of us have to do. Go within, and meet The Creator. For within us is where God resides.

It is okay, of course, to ask questions of others. Sometimes it is useful, and often it is very valuable, to get input from Another Part of God. It is good to remember, however, that no part of God hears the message that is meant for you more clearly than the part of God that is within you. So listen to advice, seek counsel, consider input, but always weigh it carefully against the guidance from your own Inner Voice. If you elevate outside input to the level of Absolute Truth, you announce and declare that you are not the source. This would be a lie about you.

These might seem to be strange things to say in a book of questions, but, actually, they are exactly the right things to say. I do not want you to think that the answers found here are any more authoritative than the answers found in your own heart. That is where the real wisdom lies. That is where the real truth resides.

Sometimes the greatest value of input from another source is that it opens you to your own truth. Certainly, that's the intention here. That's why I take the time in each issue of my personal newsletter to readers to answer a handful of the more than 300 letters a week that I receive from people all over the world asking about the *Conversations with God* material, and how to apply it in their lives. And that's why we've selected and placed in this book some of the most interesting "Q-and-A's" from five year's worth of those newsletters.

When you read these letters, don't be surprised if you find a bit of yourself here. All of us, after all, are asking the same questions. All of us are looking, in our own way and from our own perspective, at the same issues. So what you are holding in your hands right now is not a book at all, but a mirror.

I invite you to gaze deeply into it. Look to see what's being reflected here. It might just be the path to your own highest truth.

Neale Donald Walsch
August, 1999
Ashland, Oregon

Questions and Answers on
Conversations with God

CHAPTER 1

Complex Questions

I love questions. They make my mind expand. And the more difficult the questions, the better I like it. That's why I loved answering the questions in this book. They include some of the most challenging inquiries I've ever received on the *Conversations with God* material, reflecting the passions, frustrations, interests, and curiosities of some wonderfully engaging and courageous people.

Throughout the book, I've tried to categorize these inquires by topic. Some writers, however, clearly had no intention of limiting themselves to one subject per letter. I thought of taking these multiple-topic inquiries and breaking them into segments, putting the various sections into more definable categories, but, in the end, I felt that this would have taken a lot of the steam out of them. These questions are juicy precisely because they are compound and complex.

Life, of course, is like that, too. So here they are, questions that offer a slice of life. Real questions, about real life, from real people.

Why Do People Hurt Each Other?

My name is Penny and the only word that seems to sum up how I felt when I read your book was wow! Neale, these are the questions that your book has raised for me.

(1) 1 still don't understand why people in relationships, especially families, constantly hurt each other, and the relationships go up and down. Is it karma being worked out from past lives?

(2) In your book, God says the color white does not mean without color, it means color inclusive. Does this apply to race? Does this mean that a white person represents all of the other races combined? As an African-American, I'm curious why God created different races, and His/Her thoughts on the current race issues. I know that no one race is superior to another, but I just need to hear it from God . . . though I already know.

(3) Are you sure there is no devil? Who was Lucifer? There is evil in this world, but is the source solely man? Is there no bogeyman out there? Do you realize if we truly believe this, how much fear this releases—and what potential it shows we have?

(4) How do I release my great level of fear about everything?

(5) Is God a "he" or a "she?" Which is it? And what should we call her? Does she mind? Does she even care? I could never have asked such a facetious question before reading your book.

(6) Are there any good organized religions that incorporate most of God's true messages? I was raised a Catholic, but left the church when I started my search for truth. I don't know what to label myself now, except "Child of God." I totally believe in Jesus (because he answered me time and time again), so I suppose that makes me a Christian of sorts. I believe in a lot of New Age thought, but not all. So I might be a Christian New Age Mystic. (Smile)

And finally (7), how can I talk to the Goddess? Will She talk to me, even with all my fears and doubts? How do I connect with Her? This sounds crazy, but I want to hear Her say she loves me, too, and feel her love. I want to spend my life helping others that are less fortunate, but I need to ask Her what area I should help out in—AIDS, homelessness, kids? Where! Can you help me? I hope that you can feel the sincerity of my message, and I have faith that you will answer me. With much love and thanks. Penny.

My wonderful, wonderful Penny, of course I am going to answer you! And what a letter! I could write a book from this one! Let's take your questions in order.

(1) People hurt each other in relationships because they do. They do it because they do, Penny. There is no larger reason for it, such as "working out karma from past lives," etc. It's just something that happens. It's part of life. Nobody hurts another out of villainous intent. Remember these two important teachings, Penny:

- No one acts inappropriately, given their model of the world
- All attack is a call for help

People hurt each other because they want something they think they can't have, or have something they don't want. They are in one of the above two conditions, and they don't know what to do about it. They think that the only method of getting their way, having their desires met, etc., is to hurt another. They do not have to do this, but they do not know that. They do not understand how to "have what they want," or "not have what they don't want," without hurting one another.

The problem is education, not intent.

Greet each instance of hurt with compassion and love. Compassion for others' lack of understanding (we have all been there at one time or another), love for others' humanness, and their attempts—however apparently misguided—to solve their dilemmas and keep on trying to make their lives work.

We are engaged here in a process of becoming. Of creating. Of being. Some of us are "being" more than others. That's just how it Is. That's what I call "Isness." It's just what's true. Accept that with a smile. Embrace that with love in your heart. Understand, deeply, that no one wants to hurt you. They simply do it inadvertently, or perhaps, indeed, on purpose, because they know no other way to have the experience they desire. The next time someone hurts you, ignore the hurt and go to the only question which matters: What do you want or need so badly that you feel you have to hurt me to get it? You can ask this question silently, in your heart, or, if you have a particularly open and honest relationship with the other person, you can actually address the question verbally. Try it sometime. It is a terrific argument stopper. It is a terrific abuse ender.

What do you want or need so badly that you feel you have to hurt me to get it?

What is it you want to have, or feel, right now?

Is there a way I can help you to have that without giving up who I am?

Even asked silently, in your own heart, these questions can change the moment so dramatically, so immediately, so powerfully, that you won't even know what happened. And your "partner" in the dance will wonder what new level of mastery you've gone to! There's much more to say on this subject.

(2) I cannot speak for God here, Penny. And while I've said that, let me make that statement about everything that appears in these letters. These letters are not an extension of the book *Conversations with God.*

I am not presently at the level where I can sit down any time I wish and begin receiving the kind of information that came through me for that book at my whim. As I explained in *Book 1*, those writings took a year to come through. Another year for *Book 2*. And even longer for *Book 3*. So I do not claim the letter you are holding in your hand to be a direct channeling from God, or inspired writing, a term I do use to describe the *CWG* trilogy. These letters to readers reflect what I have gotten out of the trilogy myself. They are my understandings, based on over six years of "taking dictation" for the trilogy. I want to be clear on that. I want to get as far away as I can from any paradigm which suggests that "What Neale Says is What God Says." It would be a huge—I mean, monumental—mistake to create such a paradigm around me.

Now, to your questions on race, Penny. I do not believe that the so-called "white race" represents all other races combined, but rather, it is simply one more off-shoot of the Mother Race, with skin pigmentations and physical characteristics that are nothing more or less than the result of biological survival imperatives in the earliest stages of human development, based upon conditions existent for the various peoples on the planet at that time. These races continue to proliferate as a result of the hereditary gene pool which was formulated at that time and then passed on through succeeding generations.

As to "why God created different races," I do not think God sat down one pleasant morning and said, "I shall create many different races, each of a different color and characteristic." I think that God simply allows the process of life to exist, and that it is out of the process of life that all things are created. Not just races, but volcanoes. Hurricanes. Earthquakes. Human errors and mistakes. Travesties of justice. Goodness and mercy. You name it. I don't think that God sits up there somewhere and creates these "terms and conditions" of the human experience one by one, or even all at once with a single master stroke. I think that God simply created life itself, as we have defined it in the physical universe, with an extraordinary set of laws which govern the who, what, where and why of things. The discipline of science is man's attempt to uncover those laws, to understand them, and then to work with them to produce desired results. There is even a spiritual movement called Religious Science, which is based on the thought that God's laws are understandable by man, and may be used with predictable and consistent results.

As to God's "thoughts on the current race issues," I don't know about that. You'd have to ask Her. I do have an idea, however, of how God might answer that question. I believe God might say, "Human beings have exhibited an extraordinary penchant for taking anything which renders them different, and allowing that to separate them. You have created a species which does not tolerate differences very well. It is this single human failing which has led to the massive misery which visits your planet. If you could just get over your differences, and stop seeing them as that which separates you; if you could just focus with love on those aspects of your being which you hold in common—the desire for peace, the wish to love and be loved, the hope for a life of dignity in a world of choices which are free, the yearning for an opportunity to each rise to your highest potential, and the earnest and unending urging within you to express the very best that you are—if you could see these as the aspects of humanity that matter, encouraging and fostering, nurturing and empowering them, rather than empowering your fear, anger, hatred, and distrust over your differences, then the whole of the human experience would change forevermore, and you would be in the paradise I had originally created for you."

As I interpret *CWG*, I also believe God would say: "My singular treasure, Penny: Of course it is true that no one single race is 'superior' to another. Superiority of any kind does not exist in ultimate reality, for you are all 'superior,' and thus none more superior than another. This is what is meant by the teaching that you were created, all of you, in the 'image and likeness of God.' This is what is meant by the profound statement upon which your very nation was built: that all men are created equal."

Finally, I believe that God would make one closing, and extraordinary, statement: "It is also true, Penny, that not even *I* am 'superior' to you. When you understand this, you will know the grandest gift of God: that each of you is endowed with the wisdom and the power and the perfection and the love of that which is God Itself, for you are what I Am. This is necessarily true because what I Am is all there is. The only 'difference' between us, Penny, is that I know this and you do not." This is what I truly believe God would say, my new friend, and who is to deny that He has said it just now?

(3) Yes, Penny, I am sure there is no devil. For greater clarity on this point, reread pages 14, 24-25, 51, 53, 61, 85, 154, 196, and 204 of *CWG Book 1*. I could add nothing here that would be more eloquent.

(4) Franklin Roosevelt said it with remarkable clarity: "We have nothing to fear but fear itself." You will release yourself from fear, Penny, when you realize that there is nothing to be afraid of. What is the worst that can happen? In any situation? Well, that you will die, of course. That's about the worst, right? And that might just be the best thing that's ever happened to you. People who have died and returned to their body, people who have had NDEs (near-death experiences), fear nothing. Did you know that? They fear nothing. Do you know why? Because they have gotten very clear that there is nothing to fear—not even death.

Fear is an announcement that you do not believe in God. For if a God exists, why would He want anything less than what is best for you? Yet if you are having experiences that you judge to be less than "the best," who is at cause in the matter? God? Or could it be you?

Yet do not denounce fear, Penny, and neither condemn it. For fear is merely the opposite of love, and without it, love could not exist in your reality. Therefore love your fear. You might even say, love it to death.

(5) God is neither a "he" nor a "she." God has no form which is permanent, save that form which you would call formlessness. Yet God can, and does, take whatever form and whatever shape God knows you will understand. And no, God does not "care" what you call Him, as long as you call Her. That is to say, don't ignore Him. This is not because She is lonely and needs your company. It is because God's greatest pleasure is to be there for you, in as large a way as you will permit, in whatever form you

will allow yourself to recognize. Do you recognize God in the form of a flower? How about an inspired melody? The whisper of the wind? The softness of the new fallen snow? How about the face of your persecutor? Do you recognize God in the person of your villain? If you do not, you do not know God at all, nor understand Her ways, nor have any idea at all what He is up to. Only when you see God everywhere you look— everywhere—do you see God at all. This is a difficult concept for most people to grasp; this is a very hard truth for many to accept. Yet it is true. It is the greatest truth ever told.

(6) It is difficult for me to be anything but purely subjective on this question, so I am tempted to not answer it, because who cares what Neale Donald Walsch thinks? The important thing is what you think. Check out the world's religions. Read up on them. Go to a few churches, synagogues, mosques, temples and houses of prayer. See what you think. Feel what you feel. Your truth will be made clear to you.

Now, while there are good things in most every religion, I want to remind you of what *CWG* says on this topic. It says that religion is man's attempt to explain the inexplicable, and that in this it does not do a very good job. I agree with *CWG*'s wisdom on this. I think there is a vast difference between "religion" and "spirituality." I seek to practice spirituality, not religion. Still, if I were looking for a "good organized religion," here's what I would seek, and here's what I would avoid:

- I love ritual, and I also love factual information which helps me to understand things. So many of the churches today offer a preponderance of either one or the other, either explaining everything about God so factually that it all seems too dry, or moving toward the experience of God so ritualistically that there is only "airy-fairyness," and nothing to engage the mind. So I look for a church which combines and mixes the factual and the ritual, thus touching, and allowing me to experience, all of the parts of me: body, mind and spirit.
- I know that God exists and acts in, as, and through everyone and everything, and so I am uncomfortable in churches or groups which tend to deify one particular being, however holy, over others. I believe that other-being-centered religions can

be dangerous, because they offer a temptation to substitute the holy being around which the movement revolves for one's own holiness, one's own truth, one's own divinity, and to that degree they delay the spiritual quest and betray the spiritual experience to which life invites all of us. For this reason I avoid other-being-centered churches, where individual thinking and individual experience is virtually not allowed if it so much as questions, much less contradicts, the teachings of the holy Other.

- I know that God is neither a man nor a woman, neither black nor white, but takes whatever form God chooses, for whatever purpose God declares. I also know that God finds no one sex, race, color or type of human being superior to, or more "holy" than, any other. And so I look for churches and spiritual organizations that honor the God and the Goddess, that elevate, and give equal opportunity to, men and women, and that deny no one the chance to create holy ritual and perform sacred service as priests, bishops, ministers, teachers and leaders.
- I know that God speaks directly to and through human beings in this day and time, and has in all days and times, and for this reason I avoid any church, sect or philosophy that holds that man cannot have direct, immediate, two-way communication with God, but insists, rather, that an intermediary or particular process is required—which just happens to be the intermediary or process around which that religion or philosophy is formed.
- I know that there is no "one right way" to approach God, experience God, love God and bring the direct experience of God into one's life, and because I know this I dismiss at once any church, religion, group, sect, cult or clan that claims and asserts that its teachings are the only true teachings, that its way is the one true way, and that any other teaching or way, no matter how sincere or well intended, can only lead to damnation and the angry, unmerciful curse of the very God to whom one is reaching out.

These are my personal guidelines, Penny, and they don't have to be yours. The difficulty with these guidelines is that they tend to eliminate virtually every organized religion on the face of the earth. So there you have it.

(7) And now Penny, to your last question: you can speak directly to Goddess/God any time, any place. You do speak to Him with every thought, every word, every idea, every choice, every action. You cannot not talk to God. And God talks back to you every day in a million ways. She may even be talking to you now. Listen . . . look . . .

. . . I love you Penny.

Finally, as to how you can find a way to serve others through and with your life, see *Bringers of the Light*, a booklet I've just made available through our Foundation. And God bless you, Penny. You're a marvelous work, and a wonder.

How Can I See Myself as "Equal?"

> Hi Neale! I love the book you wrote with God, *CWG Book 1*. Thank you. Two questions. (1) I've never felt like other people. I feel stupid and not as smart, yet I know that I know things, if they would just surface. A big block. I have friends, but I feel they can hold a conversation without stuttering and forgetting, and that they know more. How can I break through this block and see myself as their equal, as I know I am? If you don't understand this question, God will.
>
> Second, my children, whom I love dearly, sometimes just won't listen. Why is this so hard for me? I've cried many a night about what to do. How long am I going to have to deal with this, and when is it going to end? Maybe other moms have the same question, so if possible, put this in your newsletter. Carol, Montrose, PA.

My dear Carol, the question is not whether you are "as smart" as other people. I am not as smart as Albert Einstein was. I am not as smart as Jonas Salk or Thomas Edison or—well, heck, I'm not even as smart as my brother! Comparisons with other beings are pointless. There are a lot of things that my brother is not that I am. There are also a lot of things that others are not, that you are. It is of no importance whether you are as "smart" as someone else. Each of us has our own gift to give. And yet not all have the same gift.

The Bible puts this wonderfully, Carol, in one of my favorite passages . . . from 1 Corinthians 12:29, to 1 Cor. 13:13. In this section, the question of comparison to others is raised. And the point is eloquently made that there is only one gift that really matters. Without this gift all other gifts are pointless and have no value. Yet with this gift nothing else is needed or necessary. Here is what that passage in the Bible says. Please read it carefully, Carol.

> *Are all apostles? Are all prophets? Are all teachers? Are all workers of miracles? Have all the gifts of healing? Do all speak with tongues? Do all interpret?*
>
> *But covet earnestly the best gifts: and yet show I unto you a more excellent way.*
>
> *Though I speak with the tongues of men and of angels, and have not love, I am become as sounding brass, or a tinkling cymbal.*
>
> *And though I have the gift of prophecy, and understand all mysteries, and all knowledge; and though I have all faith, so that I could remove mountains, and have not love, I am nothing.*
>
> *And though I bestow all my goods to feed the poor, and though I give my body to be burned, and have not love, it profiteth me nothing.*
>
> *Love suffereth long, and is kind; love envieth not; love vaunteth not itself, is not puffed up,*
>
> *Doth not behave itself unseemly, seeketh not her own, is not easily provoked, thinketh no evil;*
>
> *Rejoiceth not in iniquity, but rejoiceth in the truth;*
>
> *Beareth all things, believeth all things, hopeth all things, endureth all things.*
>
> *Love never faileth: but whether there be prophecies, they shall fail; whether there be tongues, they shall cease; whether there be knowledge, it shall vanish away.*
>
> *For we know in part, and we prophesy in part.*

But when that which is perfect is come, then that which is in part shall be done away.

When I was a child, I spake as a child, I understood as a child, I thought as a child: but when I became a man, I put away childish things.

For now we see through a glass, darkly; but then face to face: now I know in part; but then shall I know even as also I am known.

And now abideth faith, hope, love, these three; but the greatest of these is love.

You see, my wonderful Carol, there is only one thing that really matters. Are you a loving person? If you are, you have demonstrated the greatest gift of God. Nothing else matters. Nothing. Not how well you speak, nor how fast you think, nor how good you are in a conversation. Not how much you know, nor how little you err, nor how great your earthly achievements. None of these things matter in the eyes of God.

How can you remove your block? How can you feel that you are "equal" to your friends, as you know inside that you are? By knowing that you are "equal" to everyone in the sight of God. And then by expressing your wonderful love to everyone, equally. For as you love others, so will they love you. And as you know others, so will they know you.

Now, Carol, to your question about the children. My suggestion to you, Carol, is that you change the way you are talking to your children. I want to recommend a book to you, Carol. It is absolutely the best book I have ever read on this subject. The book is *How to Talk So Kids Will Listen, and Listen So Kids Will Talk* by Adele Faber and Elaine Mazlish. Go get it, Carol. Today. It should be at the library.

Generally, the strategy suggested in that book is to talk to children in a way which allows them to see you as being on their side in the struggles of life. No matter what they are wanting, being, doing or having, find a way to position yourself on the same side of the problem.

Let me give you a very simple example. Let's say you have a 5-year-old, and that child is demanding a cookie. As it happens, dinner is less than 20 minutes away. Now as a mother, you have a choice here. You may try to carefully explain to the child that dinner is on the way, that a cookie before dinner will spoil his appetite, and that therefore the answer is no (which puts you on the opposite side of the problem), or you can empathize with the child's plight, join him in his unhappiness over it, and actually get him to solve the problem for you. This is done by engaging in a little creative dialogue, something like the following:

Child: I want a cookie!

Mom: Boy, you know what? I want a cookie, too! I love cookies, don't you?

Child: Yeah!

Mom: But we can't have one.

Child: Why not?

Mom: Well, because dinner is going to be ready soon and if we have a cookie now, we might get full before dinner, and then we won't eat it. And I have done all that work making it for nothing. But I'm sad, because I really would like to have a cookie right now. Wouldn't you?

Child: Yeah.

Mom: Can you think of any way we cannot be so sad about the cookie?

Child: Yeah! Eat one anyway!

Mom: (laughs) That's one way. But we can't do that. Remember the rule? No eating snacks before dinner. I don't like that rule sometimes, but that's the rule. Now what am I going to do? (A sad look on her face.)

Child: (Instantly wanting to help.) Don't be sad, Mommy. We can have a cookie after dinner. Can it be our dessert?

Mom: What a good idea! Boy, that's a great idea! We can have a cookie after dinner! Great! Lets go pick one out right now, and put it by our plates so it's ready for us to eat!

The point of this exchange is to avoid placing yourself in the position of obstacle. If the child sees you as the obstacle to what he wants, you can be sure that difficulty will follow. The problem is that your children see you as the obstacle. You are that which gets in the way. It is for this reason that your children may not listen to you. If, on the other hand, the child sees that both of you are facing an obstacle which is in front of you, not between you, he will more often than not become your helpmate in facing the problem and solving it. This is a simplistic example, but the formula can actually be applied to just about any problem, no matter what its nature or the age of the child.

Now the frazzled parent is the parent who insists on remaining the obstacle and demanding that the children listen and obey or else. All this does is create incredible friction between parent and child, turning each exchange into a power struggle of major proportions, and building resentments in all directions.

Still, being the most powerful one may work in the short term. It is in the long run that it never will. Not if your aim is to retain your child's love, respect, and friendship; not if you want the kind of relationship with your child in which she actually comes to you with her problems when she is older, rather than going anywhere and everywhere else.

The central question in all interactions with children is: What would Love do now? That is the central question in all interactions with adults as well.

And contrary to the old school hard liners, this is not molly-coddling or catering. (Notice that the child has not been given in to, has not gotten what he wants.) This is simply holding your ground in a way which recognizes that the child is a person, too.

All about Cigarettes and Soul Mates and Children . . .

Dear Neale: I am very happy to have been turned on to, and by, your fine *CWG* books. I have been consciously searching for the past five years. I have been at many turning points since then, at times not even knowing what I believed or what my truth is, but I am now creating the real me and I believe God, and yourself, have cleared up a lot of questions and confusions I have had. I do have some questions for you!

(1) I am a cigarette smoker. My belief system is that it does me good by grounding me, allowing me to think there is no harm to me. I have never bought into the way society thinks. I'm actually very healthy. Is this one of the ways I've shown myself that I am able to create what I want by going against mass consciousness? Please expand on this. (2) My second question surrounds anger. I would be very pleased to have God speak directly to and about anger with our life partners. How can the cycle be stopped? How can we change the pattern? (3) I would like God's perspective on soul mates. (4) Are we able to pull the energy into this lifetime from a past life where we actually had a specific skill or ability? (5) I have a starchild, an 11-month-old son. I am wondering if God could speak about the children that are coming through, their purpose and mission. Thank you for all your answers. God bless, love and light, Sandi, Klamath Falls, OR.

Dear Sandi, Whew! When you ask questions, you ask questions! I'm not really sure that I can give you the in-depth answers to all of your questions here, as really they would fill an entire book. But let me give you the short version on some of these and then refer you to some additional reading. First of all, about cigarette smoking. I am asked this question often. Look, let me give you the most direct answer that I know how to give.

If you believe that your level of consciousness has been developed to such a degree that you can overcome the mass consciousness created by millions and millions of people, that is, if you believe that you are literally a walking master, then I think that you can safely proceed with any behavior whatsoever, including jumping off buildings to demonstrate that you can fly, standing in front of locomotives to demonstrate that you are impervious to harm, or any other demonstration that it would please you to make. However, Sandi, if you are able to do these things, you will have been the first person I have met in a very long time demonstrating such abilities.

So I think that the answer to your question lies within you. Only you can assess where you are on the scale of evolution, and only you can decide for yourself what is true for you. The advice given in *CWG* is good advice in that it simply suggests that the human organism was not constructed ideally for the intake of alcohol or the inhalation of cigarette smoke. That is to say, the basic design of the instrument is violated by such treatment. Is it possible by the sheer strength of our consciousness to overcome this basic design mechanism and fly in the face of all evidences that are presented to us? One presumes that it is. Is it wise to attempt such a demonstration? That is a question only you can answer.

Concerning your questions on anger, Sandi, I have not enough room here, as I said, to reply in depth, but let me say this. People are generally angry about only two things. Either there is something they want that they do not have, or there is something they have which they do not want. Their fear is that they will not get what they want or they will not be able to let go of, or get away from, what they have. Anger is fear announced. When we step away from expectations with regard to these matters, and when we reduce our choices to simple preferences rather than addictions (things we must have), then we take a giant step away from anger and toward mastery. The cycle and the pattern of anger is ended when we see the perfection in every moment and reduce our expectations to zero.

In regard to soul mates, I have to tell you that this subject is far too large to even attempt to answer here. But the question of soul mates is addressed in wonderful detail in *CWG Book 3*. For now, don't worry so much about the issue of soul mates, but rather pay attention to who you are in relationship to every other person, place or thing in your life. Remember always that you are in the process of creating and recreating who you are and who you intend to be. That is your job, whether you are doing it in the presence of a soul mate or in the presence of anyone else. Stay close to this purpose. Stay connected with this function. Stay clear about your intention, and the matter of the intensity of soul mate connections will be less of a challenge or problem for you.

Now you are asking me if you are able to take energy from your previous lifetimes and bring it into this lifetime, and I gather that what you mean is that if we were a piano player or an artist or a great leader in a previous lifetime, are we able to bring some of those energies into our present experience. The answer, again in short, is that often our present lifetime will show us how we have been in a previous experience. Children who suddenly demonstrate an ability to play the piano at age 3, or demonstrate aspects of higher reasoning at age 5, and people who suddenly discover a so-called "latent" talent or ability are, in fact, tapping into a previous soul experience. Can we do this intentionally? I tell you that it is said in *Conversations with God* that you can create yourself in any way that you wish, either pulling from past experiences, or creating out of thin air.

Concerning what God has in mind with regard to children and their purposes and missions, I must disabuse you of the notion that there is any purpose or mission whatsoever. Your question implies that God has something in mind when these children are created, and then they have to live up to that. Reread *Conversations with God* again and you will see that there is no such mission established by God. If God were to establish a special mission for a child, why would God then keep it a secret from that child? The purpose of life is for us to decide what our mission is and who we are in relationship to that, not to discover what mission God gave us when we were born. Life is not a process of discovery; it is a process of creation. Thanks for your letter, Sandi, and I wish I could respond in greater depth, but space here does not permit.

A Man with a Ton of Questions . . .

Dear Mr. Walsch: I will focus on questions that have arisen from *CWG Book 1*. Page 33, paragraph 3: Where is the point that you stop your help for another individual as not to interfere with their karmic path? Page 37, paragraph 7: What does it take to grow individually to change collective thinking? If the human body was made to last for hundreds of years, then what is the proper diet if moderation is not the key, or does this just include alcohol? What are angels? If as a master I do not show emotion, then what is compassion? What is the relationship between souls, for example, twin flames? For what purpose were the dinosaurs created, or any animals?

In the past books that I have read, who are the entities that channel through these other individuals, and what is the relationship between your book and the book *The Door of Everything*, where God also spoke through another person? There is something wonderful going on in the Saratoga Springs, NY area; besides meeting my wife here, I believe I was brought to Saratoga for another reason, and I am anxiously waiting the answer. Jim, Saratoga Springs, NY.

Dear Jim, Thank you very much for your fascinating letter. Let me see if I can answer your several questions one at a time.

You asked, where is the point at which one stops with one's help for another so as not to interfere with that other person's karmic path. The answer is that you must always remain sensitive to and deeply aware of the will of another person, in so far as it is possible for you to know that. Therefore, you always ask another person what it is they will for themselves, and then assist them in providing that. Never assist another person, nor do anything with regard to another person, which is against his or her will. You must always come from the same place God comes from, namely, "Your will for you is My will for you." When you are simply assisting another person in doing his or her will, then you are helping that person. When you are attempting to assert your will over the will of another out of some misplaced thought that you "know better," then you are interfering in the other's karmic path.

You ask, "what does it take to grow individually to change collective thinking?" You change collective thinking, Jim, when you demonstrate to the collective consciousness, that is to all other people whose lives you've touched, who you really are. By demonstrating who you really are, and by moving to the grandest version of the greatest vision you ever held about yourself. When you demonstrate this grand vision, people see you as you really are, and they begin to get ideas about themselves as well. When we give other people ideas about themselves out of their experience of us, we begin to change collective consciousness. What it takes to grow individually to that stage is simply a decision, Jim. Life is a choice, and who we demonstrate ourselves to be is who we choose to be. Our experience is produced out of our intentions for it, therefore the answer to your question "what does it take to grow individually?" is, it takes nothing but your choice and decision to do so.

You ask if the human body was made to last hundreds of years, then if moderation is not the key what is the proper diet, or does moderation just include alcohol? The answer to your question is that there is no such thing as a "proper diet," there is only the diet that you are choosing, depending on what it is that you wish to do. The way you eat, Jim, is an announcement of your decision about what you wish to do with your life, to say nothing about how long you want to live it. If you want to live a very long life, it would probably be best if you ate everything in moderation, in particular, red meat and other "dead" foods. Of course, I would drastically limit my intake of alcohol, if not eliminate it all together. I would also never smoke, nor would I do drugs. I would stay away from foods with high fat contents, because it doesn't take a rocket scientist to know that fatty foods cause circulatory difficulties which produce health complications and premature death. I think there is enough information in the marketplace, Jim, on healthy diets that one does not need to hear from God yet again on this. For some wonderful, and very practical, guidance on this question, I strongly recommend reading *Diet for a New America* by John Robbins.

Your next question is what are angels. The answer is angels are exactly that, angels. That is to say, wonderful beings, compassionate, warm and loving creatures, aspects of the divine, and partners in the life experience. Angels are explained in complete detail in *CWG 3*, but I can tell you now there are such things as guardian angels, or what we call guardian angels, and they love us unconditionally, as you very well might expect.

You ask if as a master you do not show emotion, then what is compassion? The answer is, Jim, that compassion is not an emotion, compassion is an experience. It is an experience that you choose to have, and that you choose to share. Unless, of course, you don't.

You ask what is the relationship between souls? There are such things as soul partners, and again, *CWG 3* explains these higher connections in considerable detail. I hope you will read it. For now, simply know that there are soul partners all over the world and you have more than one soul partner. All of us have many, many soul partners, and that explains why all of us fall in love with many, many different people. Let yourself have that love when you experience it, let yourself move through the experience itself and embrace it fully and richly.

You ask for what purpose were the dinosaurs or any animals created? The answer is, nothing in life has any purpose whatsoever, as *CWG* very clearly points out. There is no purpose "assigned" to things by God, and things do not have a "purpose" intrinsically. Nothing has any purpose except the purpose you give it, Jim. Read *CWG* again, and you will understand this thoroughly.

Finally, Jim, you ask about the relationship of entities who have been channeled by other people as well as in the wonderful book by Ruby Nelson called *The Door of Everything*. My answer to your question, Jim, is that God makes Herself known to each person and to all of us in whatever way God feels will be most effective and most immediately productive. Because that is so, God takes many forms. Yet all of it is God—every single bit of it—and there is nothing in the universe that is not God. Therefore, *The Door of Everything* has come from the same source as *Conversations with God*, but you must understand it came through a different filter. Ruby Nelson's filter may not be the same as my filter, nor may Ruby Nelson's understanding be the same as mine. So we have this difficulty of the filters through which God speaks, whether those filters be Ruby Nelson, Neale Donald Walsch, or Matthew, Mark, Luke and John. Nevertheless, if we carefully analyze the writings of all these people, and others, we see in them striking similarities. Perhaps we should pay considerable attention to these similarities. It seems to me that when twenty different people who do not know each other and live at twenty different times on the planet write essentially the same things, there may be something here for us to look at very carefully.

The entities who channel through other individuals are all part of God manifesting in the imagination or in the objective experience of those channelers in whatever form they claim to take. In other words, Jim, they are exactly who they say they are. All of it is part of God, and there is nothing which is not part of God. That's the whole point of *CWG*, that's the whole point of the teaching, that's the whole point of the great mysteries of life, and once those mysteries have been unraveled, we see this very clearly.

One final comment, Jim. You say that you were brought to Saratoga Springs for some reason other than simply to connect with your wife, and that you are "anxiously awaiting the answer." Jim, you will have missed the whole point of *Conversations with God* if you do not hear what I am now going to tell you. You are not to anxiously await for "the answer," but you are, rather, to create the answer. The answer will not come to you out of thin air; rather, it will be created by you out of thin air. There is a vast difference between these two, and if you do not understand this difference, please re-read *Conversations with God* over and over again until you do. The point *CWG* makes quite profoundly, Jim, is this: life is not a process of discovery; it is a process of creation. Therefore, Jim, anxiously await nothing, and inspiringly create everything that you would choose and desire in your life. Thank you for writing, Jim.

Of Angels, Animals and Doctors

Dear Mr. Walsch: I have three questions that came up for me while reading your book.

(1) There has been of late a surge of literature about, and interest in, angels. What do you think or feel about this subject?

(2) God seemed to have some pretty strong feelings about eating animals, but it seems to me people have been eating animals as far back as the cave man. And even animals eat animals! So when did it become inadvisable?

(3) Lastly, I was really shaken after reading pg. 190 in *CWG* where it indicated that annual physicals and use of medicine are something we should engage in. Now back on pg. 49, it mentioned that the medical establishment opposes new treatments, even miracles.

> I have always felt that by walking into a doctor's office I was giving up the belief that my body is capable of healing itself. In addition, by going into an atmosphere where sickness is a business and a very strong belief, I was creating a situation for myself in which I would actually make myself sick. Going to a doctor is saying "I am sick," thereby creating the physical reality of sickness. And what about the drugs they give you? What about radiation therapy? Now there's a hell of an idea! Let's prescribe something that's going to make people sick as hell and probably won't work anyway! Why not help people find out why they came down with cancer instead? Janet, Litchfield, CT.

Dear Janet, (1) I think angels are very real, very present, and very wonderful. (2) God has no preference in the matter of whether we eat animal flesh or not. He simply notices that we have a preference for living long and healthy lives, and offers His advice on how to do that. And, incidentally, when noticing that "even animals eat animals," it should be pointed out that animals eaten by animals are often still alive, or have just been killed, and have probably never been injected with chemicals, preservatives, hormones, etc., which is more than can be said about the long-dead animals humans eat.

(3) Let's look at your "treatise" on medical doctors, one statement at a time.

First, you said that you have always felt that by walking into a doctor's office you were giving up the belief that your body is capable of healing itself. Of course, if you have always felt that way, and if you refuse to change how you've "always felt," then there you have it. It can be no other way. On the other hand, you can decide not to feel that way. When I walk into a doctor's office I walk in with the feeling that my body can heal itself, and that a doctor can sometimes be of help, too. By taking an airplane to Dubuque, I am in no way invalidating my ability to get to Dubuque by car. I am simply choosing another way (perhaps a faster way) of getting where I want to go. In life, Janet, making one choice does not invalidate the other. Choosing chocolate does not make vanilla "wrong." Unless, of course, it does. It all depends on how you feel about it.

Next, you said that when you went into a doctor's office you were going into an atmosphere where sickness is a business. I think differently. I see a doctor's office as a place where the people there say healing is the business. Therefore, I do not see myself as creating a situation for myself in which I would actually make myself sick, but, rather, creating a situation for myself in which I would actually make myself well.

As for drugs and radiation therapy, there are as many people for whom these measures have done a lot of good as there are for whom they have been ineffective. I am not willing to dismiss all drug intervention on the basis of someone's idea that drugs are no good. And I know too many people who have greatly benefited from radiation therapy—including some very close to me—to dismiss that avenue out of hand. Now you ask, why not help people find out why they came down with cancer instead? I agree with you. The question should be asked. But the person who already has cancer may want some additional assistance.

Yet the point of *CWG*, Janet, is that you create your own reality. There is no contradiction in the book on this point. If you see or perceive other contradictions, always go with your own deepest feelings, your own deepest truth. I am not here to talk you out of your truth, but to assist in leading you to it.

Questions, Questions, and More Questions!

Dear Mr. Walsch: I recently finished reading *CWG Book 1* and want to tell you what an amazing and inspiring piece of work I think it is. I was astounded at the complete, unerring, unchallengeable logic that was conveyed through the dialogue, which reconciled (finally!) the many contradictions inherent in traditional interpretations of Biblical text. These are contradictions which have always nagged at me and prevented me from experiencing peace of mind and joy and love through knowing God as He is explained by conventional religions.

This was the first time I felt that the complete truth about God and man's relationship to God was expressed in one single source, and expressed in a way that I instinctively knew had to be the truth based on what we always have been taught about God's perfection and unconditional love. While some of the information explained in the book was new to me, none of it surprised me, as it all flowed logically and consistently from the basic premises set out in the beginning.

I likewise was intrigued at how the book incorporates into one coherent whole the many truths that are scattered among different religious, philosophic and scientific disciplines. Your book fills in all the missing pieces of those other disciplines that have caused them (in my mind) to collapse from flaws in logic and internal inconsistencies. Your book has given credibility to those partial truths expressed in other places, and now I can regard them in the context of the whole.

It was quite a moving and emotional experience reading through your book. Words fail me at the moment (No, they don't), but I can say that this was the first time I remember truly feeling the love of God and love for God. I experienced such a light coming from within me that I have never felt before—an incredible lightness of being, so to speak. An indescribable comfort. I intend to reread the book so that I can internalize and apply its truths in my life. I would like to thank you and God personally for having this dialogue and for sharing it with the world.

I do have some questions, and hope you will respond to them.

1) God says that the human body was not intended to consume alcohol. Have you received any revelations on other types of foods, such as red meat, poultry, fish, seafood, caffeinated drinks or foods, decaffeinated drinks (such as coffee and tea), or any other type of consumables?

I was not given any more specific information in the books. However, the universe has sourced us with the informed judgment of many health experts who have made some good observations and suggestions about all of this. What I know is, people have their own physiological needs and tolerances. Listen to your body, my friend. Listen to your body.

2) Do animals have souls? If so, do they know God? Do they feel love? If so, do they feel love for humans?

Yes to all of the above. Everything has a soul. If you define the soul as divine energy placed within everything, which carries the vibration of life, then everything has a soul.

What is man's relationship to animals?

Whatever he intends it to be. Man's relationship to everything is decided by the same thing: his intentions. Life proceeds out of one's intention for it. And every intention is an announcement and a declaration, a creation and an experiencing of Who You Are and who you choose to be.

3) Do spirits (ghosts) dwell on earth? If so, why? If so, for how long (i.e., does a spirit that roams the earth eventually move on, and if so, under what circumstances)?

The answer to each of these questions is yes and no. Spirits do what they choose to do, just as we do. Some souls "stay around" for a while after they leave their present bodies. Some move on immediately to other experiences. It all depends on what the spirit is feeling and knowing and wishes to experience. There are no particular circumstances or conditions necessary for souls to do any particular thing. Spirits do as they wish. That is what is known as being a free spirit. Some people choose to be this even while in their bodies.

4) Regarding the story of Noah and the flood, did such a thing occur, and if so, was it caused by God? If so, why? If so, what is the meaning of God's covenant after the flood not to repeat the experience? The story, as it is told in Genesis, says that God caused the flood to destroy all mankind because man had become corrupt, strongly disappointing God. God spared Noah and his family because Noah was not corrupt, but righteous. Following the flood, God comes to understand that man is inherently evil and therefore should not be punished for having a quality he cannot help having. Much of this runs counter to what is written in your book, i.e., God (1) would not feel disappointed by man; (2) would not intervene with man's world; (3) would not seek to destroy man; (4) would not believe man to be inherently evil; and (5) would not make an ill-formed decision because He (a) would not feel regret, regardless, and (b) would not be able to make an ill-informed decision. I would like the meaning of the story of Noah explained, if possible.

I love your phrase, "following the flood, God comes to understand." Do you imagine that there is any time in the sequence of events when God does not understand everything?

It is fascinating to analyze stories and myths such as the Noah story, but probably not too wise to put too much literal faith in them. Like all great stories, which have been passed from generation to generation, there is probably a bit of truth in them. This truth is the seed; it is the germ of the story. Much, however, has been "added on" through the years in order to use the original experience as a learning device. No doubt there was a great flood on this planet. And no doubt, a wise man and leader of the people named Noah took all he could put together, including two of every animal he could find, a male and (since he was really using his head) a female, and hauled them on board a great boat to ride out the storm. It was his way of making sure something would survive.

It is quite possible that he had a premonition of the flood and actually built his boat for this purpose. Stranger things have happened. But God did not cause the flood to punish anybody. God did not cause the flood at all. God does not cause anything, but rather, watches us cause it. And God does the watching, by the way, without judgment. Your understanding of the material in *CWG* in this regard is complete and correct. As for the meaning of the Noah story, it has no meaning at all, except the meaning you give it. So it is with all of life.

What do you think it means? Better yet, what do you choose for it to mean?

> 5) My question about Noah raises a more general question, which is, do you intend to provide other reinterpretations of stories in the Bible that currently are misunderstood or misinterpreted (such as those that you already conveyed regarding Adam and Eve, the Ten Commandments, and Jesus Christ)?

First, let's be clear that I have conveyed nothing, nor have I offered any reinterpretations of anything. I believe the commentaries to which you refer all came through me from God. So I'm finding the general tenor of these questions starting to make me a little uncomfortable, as if I was the source of all this. I am not. And I am very clear about that. I am merely a scribe. A reporter. I take dictation.

Now, as to whether my source is going to provide additional commentaries such as those you label "reinterpretations" of the Bible, I don't know.

6) Sometimes the Bible uses what appears to be very unambiguous language to describe God in a way which is not consistent with how God describes Himself in your book (e.g., in the Bible God describing Himself as a "jealous" God, or God telling man that he must "obey" Him). Either these "unambiguous" words are incorrect, are missing qualification, or have another meaning I do not see. My sincerest regards, Linda, VA.

Well, Linda, that's quite a letter! Thank you! As to your final comment, the words in the Bible do not have a meaning you do not see. You see their meanings, all right. Most of the Biblical descriptions of God are simply inaccurate.

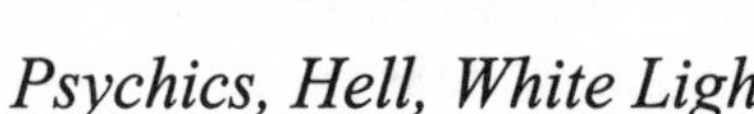

Psychics, Hell, White Light

Dear Neale: After reading the closing of your book and down to the ending of the last letter of your name there were chills that came all over me, and then even more chills. So I give you thanks for being the messenger you were meant to be. Above all, I give thanks for this book to be written. For I, too, had many of the same questions you did; I have even more regarding the psychic world. My questions are: (1) How do you become psychic? (2) Is there a danger, as they say, for "bad" spirits to enter you if you do not put the white light around you? (3) In Mary Summer Rain's book *Spirit Song* she meditates and is in a place they call "hell." If there is no "hell" what place has she experienced? (4) What purpose is the white light? (5) Is it okay to ask a psychic for information about yourself and loved ones who have passed away? Or should we develop this ability ourselves? Love and happiness, Stephenie, Corona, CA.

Boy, Stephenie, your questions invite an entire book! Actually, question 1 is covered in the *CWG* trilogy. Let me give you some quick reference data here. First, there is no way to "become" psychic. You already are. Everyone is "psychic," and there is no way not to be. Being psychic is part of our nature. It is our sixth sense. And recognizing this is the first step toward actively utilizing one's psychic ability. So here is the short version of the answer to your question 1: Recognize, acknowledge, accept and own your own psychic sense as a natural gift. Use your psychic sense every day by paying attention to it; listen to your "intuition" about things, and act on that as often as you can. Don't think when you get a "psychic hit," just act. Do it. The more you act quickly on your psychic "hits," the more you'll learn to trust them, as you find that acting on them brings affirmative results. Listen to feelings. Feelings are the language of the soul. If it "feels" like you should be doing, or not doing, something, listen to that. That's your psyche (soul) talking to you. Give yourself permission to be "wrong." It'll take a while to separate genuine intuitive wisdom from the mish-mash of thoughts, ideas, fears, etc., running around inside your head. Don't give up if you start following your feelings, or giving in to your first impulse, and finding yourself "wrong" for having done that. Grant yourself some leeway here. Especially at first. Say the first thing that comes to your head. Whenever you get a "hit," say it. Out loud. Put yourself "out there" in that way. You'll find that you're blurting out to others some of the most astonishing stuff, and some of those others will look at you in shock that you could have come up with that such insight and information. Never use psychic gifts for personal aggrandizement or enrichment. That's very much akin to using sex for personal power or manipulation, instead of the pure and loving purpose for which it was intended. I have found that psychic gifts "go away" if they are used to attract a shower of attention or money. Use psychic gifts only in the service, and for the benefit, of others. I realize this is my personal construction, but after all, it is me you are asking!

(2) I do not believe in the often talked about "danger" of "bad spirits" entering me—and so, of course, they don't! Ha! I have to laugh at that, because I really don't know which came first, the chicken or the egg! I mean, I genuinely don't know which happened initially, the belief or the experience. I do think—and the *CWG* trilogy has led me to further believe—that our thought about a thing creates our reality of that thing, so if you carry a thought

that (a) there is such things as "bad spirits," and (b) putting the "white light" around you protects you from them, then that will be our experience. As a result, you won't be bothered by "bad spirits" any more than I am!

(3) I haven't read Mary Summer Rain's book *Spirit Song*, although my wife has, and loved it (as she does all of Mary Summer Rain's writing). I know Mary Summer Rain to be a very honest person, extremely true to herself, and so I am sure that she had the precise experience she has written about. My own *CWG 3* talks much more about this experience of "hell" which many people believe in, and which some (such as Mary) have apparently had, if only through brief, revealing "visitations." What place has Mary experienced? Good question. You would have to ask her. In my own view of things (which is worth nothing, actually, since this was Mary's experience), I would speculate that she has visited a place created deep in her personal belief system—which is to say, her personal reality, for in my construction, belief systems are reality. This place may be so deep in most people that they may have forgotten when they originally created it, or even that they did. In fact, they would swear to you that they didn't, that it is real. That it is Reality. And indeed, for them it is.

"Hell" is simply not a reality for me, so I don't go there, nor am I afraid of going there, nor, therefore, will I ever go there, for there is no "there" to which to go! You see? Of course, I could be all wrong in this, so I would be careful about adopting my belief system if I were you.

(4) What do you wish to be the "purpose of the white light"? Do you not see that things do not have a "purpose" intrinsically? That is the hardest part of what has been revealed to me for most people to understand. A thing has no purpose in and of itself. Every purpose for any thing is given to it by you and me. We decide what a thing means, and what purpose a thing shall have. And before we decide, a thing has no purpose at all!

Now it is true that some things have already been "assigned" a purpose by those who have come before us, and by the collective agreement of their offspring. We all understand the purpose of a fork, for instance. Or of a shovel. So we agree on some things, collectively, and thus make life workable. But there are some things we can't agree on, no matter how many people have "come before" with an idea about it. What is the purpose of sex, for example? Or of power? What is the purpose of illness? Of God? What is the "purpose" of music? Of art? (They are still debating that one in PTAs and School Board budget meetings all across America. Some say music and art have no purpose, and therefore no place, in public schools. Others vehemently disagree.) So you see, the white light has no purpose. It is purposeless, as is all of life. What is the purpose of your life? You decide! And while you're about it, decide what the purpose of the white light is.

(5) Of course it is okay to ask a psychic for information about yourself or a loved one who has passed away! Why wouldn't it be? At least, that's my opinion. Now someone else may tell you differently. Don't you see? There is nothing but point of view to dictate this. And whatever point of view you adopt, so, too, will it be for you. Now, do you think God has a "rule" about this? Wrrooonnngg. God has no rules about anything! That's the whole message of the *CWG* books!

Questions About Time, Ghosts, and "Fate"

Dear Mr. Walsch: I really enjoyed your books. The only thing I had a hard time understanding was the "time" concept. I just cannot follow that if you have lived 300 different lives, they are all existing at the same time. I think what you said in *CWG* is amazing, just very hard to follow. Just how can your soul be existing in all those bodies at once? Also, there are ghosts, aren't there? Possibly souls that have a mission they have to solve before they find the light? Or are they lost or in limbo? Are they in a different dimension? Why are they around? What should we do, if anything, to help them? Are there poltergeists? And last, I have always believed in "fate." That when it is your time to go, it doesn't matter what you are doing, or where you are, when you are called, you go. I know when someone dies, people will say, "Oh, if only he didn't get on that plane, he would still be here." I feel that if it is someone's time to go, it doesn't matter if you are on a plane, at home gardening, or in a line at the bank. Donna, Virginia Beach, VA.

Dear Donna, Good questions. Let's take them one by one. On the time thing, don't try to understand this with your mind, Donna. Remember, to really reach enlightenment, you've got to be out of your mind. By that I mean you've got to be willing to "get out of your head" about it, and stop trying to think your way into heaven.

A great deal of the ancient wisdom defies all logic. We cannot figure it out. We think about it and think about it and think about it, and it just does not make sense. We try to make it make sense, and we fail. That is because we are thinking about these things from our limited perspective, which creates a very limited understanding.

You've got to "step out of the box" to get some of these concepts, Donna. And that means not trying to "figure it out," but just accepting what "feels right" what seems to satisfy at a deep level, even though it makes no sense on the surface.

So don't try to get it all straight about the time thing, Donna. Just read and re-read the section and take from it what seems and feels right to you. If you remain confused, stay with the confusion. Let that be all right with you. A lot of times we are so insistent on having all the answers right here, right now that we do not give ourselves sufficient time to think deeply. Or to come to intuitive knowings without really thinking about things at all. Just "be with it" for a while.

Some of the great geniuses of our time came to their most extraordinary conclusions only after years of "being with" a problem. And they were okay with that. They were very used to "not thinking about what they were thinking about," if you can understand what I mean. Then one day, after putting it on the back shelf for many months or years—bingo!—there was the answer!

So give up needing or trying to know something or to understand something completely, Donna. Just let it go and let it be all right that for now you don't have the answer. Create the space for the answer to occur to you.

As to your ghost question, I believe there are spirits who move about on this plane. As to why, and who they are, I have left this for *CWG 3*.

Regarding "fate," that word is an acronym for "From All Thoughts Everywhere." In other words, the results of our collective consciousness. In the strictest sense, there is no such thing as fate. That is, there is no particular way a thing is "supposed" to "turn out." Who would make such a decision? Surely not God, for *CWG* makes it very clear that God has no preference in the matter. That leaves only us. We are the ones, Donna, who are determining our own "fate" by the thoughts we entertain collectively. Our collective consciousness creates a great deal of our individual reality. Because this is so, it looks to us like something which has been predetermined. Yet if life is at any level predetermined, the greatest promise of God is a lie. For God says that we are the creators of our own reality. If that is true, then "fate" in the purest sense cannot be a reality.

Questions About Prayers, the Book Of Job, Biblical Truth, and Sexuality

Dear Neale: (1) Why is time never mentioned in your book or the Bible? (2) When is prayer answered after two months or a year? Of the "I Am" you say moves the universe, when is prayer answered—in days, weeks, years, and who decides when? (3) The Book of Job in the Bible—was that made up? Did Job bring all that misery upon himself (did he create it himself?) (4) Just what books/verses in the Bible are true? And (5), in *Conversations with God* (pp. 63, 205-08), God said sex is great, wonderful, do it, have fun. Yet on pg. 49, he says we on Earth are doing nothing to stop 40,000 people a day from dying of hunger, while we bring 50,000 people a day into the world to begin new life. Seems to be a small problem here. When you have sex (fun, wonderful, powerful, exciting, etc.), you create those 50,000 new lives. He/you mention nothing of birth control, abortions, to stop these lives from entering, let alone the diseases we now have. Neither is age mentioned with regard to enjoying sex. Is there one? Is 10 too young? 15? 18? Please don't get me wrong. I love sex. It is great. But you/God left yourself wide open on this one. Marge, Buchanan, MI.

Your questions tell me that *CWG* succeeded at what every book hopes and seeks to do: make people stop and think. Remember now, this is me answering. I don't represent these answers to be replies direct from deity, without a filter. So if we can agree on that, I'll give you my impressions on all this, based on what I've learned these past three years as a result of the dialogue.

(1) I can't tell you why time is never mentioned in the Bible (although I can tell you it is not the only enormous component of the life experience which has been ignored in that book after it was revised and finally released). I can also tell you it is mentioned, and explained quite extensively, in *Conversations with God Book 2*.

(2) When asked this same question, Jesus said, "Seek and ye shall find. Knock and it shall be opened unto you. Yea, even before you ask, it shall be answered." You need to accept the enormous truth in those statements. It is a metaphysical reality. Before you will have asked, God will have "answered" you! This is because the answer already exists in ultimate reality. And that is because you created it by thinking about it. And creation and manifestation take place in the same instant. This is so because there is only one instant. That is to say, time, as a linear expression, does not exist. This gets back into question 1, and is answered thoroughly in *CWG 2*.

Now, since your prayer has already been answered, the correct prayer is never a prayer of supplication, but always a prayer of thanksgiving. Okay? Now, here comes the big bomber, Marge. Here's the direct answer to your inquiry. The degree to which you accept and believe that your prayer has already been answered creates the degree to which you experience the answer as having been made manifest in your present reality. In other words in the "I Am" paradigm, should you have the consciousness of a Christ, you would experience immediate results. Jesus is far from the only person, incidentally, who has seen his will made manifest in physical form in the instant his will became known. Others have accomplished this. (See *Autobiography of a Yogi* by Paramahansa Yogananda; study the life of Sai Baba.) Many avatars and masters have produced instant results, instant healings, instant answers to prayers.

Sometimes, there is the question of whether each part of your three-part being is in harmony and in agreement about a thing, and that has much to do with how quickly and how successfully you place an experience in your reality (or, if you will, have a prayer answered by God). The question is very complex, and so I shall probably have to write a booklet on it. Look for *How Prayers Get Answered*. I'll try to write a booklet every so often to answer in depth some of these very good questions.

(3) I don't know whether the Book of Job was "made up" or not, but I suspect it is not entirely factual. It seems as though a very well meaning person put that down on paper in order to show the power of faith and the promise of patience in the face of endless suffering. On the other hand, there may have been a man named Job, and he may have had endless troubles, and the account may have been the truth, the whole truth, and nothing but the truth. The far more interesting part of your question seems to be the second part: did he draw the misery to himself? If it did happen, did he create it all? The answer, of course, is yes. At some level, all of us are creating every single moment which we are experiencing, including your having written and my having addressed this question.

Now, some things we create at a conscious level, and some things we create at a subconscious level (making it seems as though we did not "create" them at all). Some things we solely create and some things we co-create, and some things we create in concert with many, many others through the device known as collective consciousness, but all the time we are creating. The question is not, are we actually creating this? The question isn't even why are we creating this? The only question of importance is, who am I now in the face of this creation? For all of creation exists as an arena within which we are invited, encouraged, and have, ourselves, been created, to answer that question.

The process by which we create things (events, occurrences, opportunities, outcomes, etc.) is far too complex to go into here, and is explained in extraordinary detail in CWG. Those sections deserve close rereading.

(4) I am unable to sit here and review, book by book, chapter by chapter, verse by verse, which portions of the Bible are "true" and

which are "false." Obviously, it is all "true" for some people, and all "false" for others, and a little bit of both for most. It is important to understand, Marge, that nothing is "true" as you understand the word. That is to say, objective truth does not exist in the Universe. The only "truth" is subjective reality—in other words, what you and I perceive. That is because whatever we observe in the so-called "objective universe" is affected by our observation of it.

I realize that I am getting into quantum physics now (and perhaps more deeply into this question than you wanted to go) but it is vital for you to add this to your comprehension if you are ever to find peace in your soul: "true" truth does not exist. That is because, even at the God level (especially at the God level), we are making it all up. For more on this, read a wonderful book called *The Universe is a Green Dragon* by Brian Swimme.

Now, Marge, the question is not, which verses of the Bible are true? The question is, which verses are true for you? I find great truth in the Bible and enormous wisdom—incredible insight, really, all over the place. There are also some places where I cringe, and find that the Bible does not speak to me. The same has been said, incidentally, about *Conversations with God*, which is good, which is wonderful. I would hate to have produced a book with which everyone agreed, down to the last word. Can you imagine the responsibility of that? No, I'd much rather have you be responsible for what you find there. That's as it should be. It's the same, obviously, with the Bible.

(5) Now let's get to your sex question. I see no contradiction in God's message in *CWG* regarding sex. Nowhere does the book call for irresponsible sexuality. Yet somehow in some people's minds God's injunction to "have fun" with sex, to engage in sex as often as you like, to see and experience and share the joy in it, to play with this wonderful gift, as the book so directly puts it—somehow these encouragements are seen as licenses to act irresponsibly. No one suggested anything of the sort. Those connections—between fun, joy, play and irresponsibility—are connections you have made in your own mind. Someone has told you that to have fun, to participate in sex joyfully, to play with sex, is, or inevitably leads to, irresponsible behavior. I am

unwilling to make that connection. Certainly not automatically, which your question suggests. Your question suggests that the connection is automatic; that the outcome is automatic; that one thing leads to another, rather than that one thing could lead to another, which is quite a different thing.

It is precisely this teaching—that joyful, playful, outrageous sexuality and full, rich sexual expression lead inevitably to irresponsible behavior—which has thrown most of the world (and decidedly, most of the Western world) into its chronic paranoia about sex. A paranoia, incidentally, which has produced mass (and massive) guilt around the one aspect of humanness around which there was supposed to be no guilt.

The human sexual response is a joy, a gift, a twinkle-in-the-eye celebration of life itself. It was never meant to be covered up, stowed away, kept out of sight, never talked about in polite company without embarrassment, and never actually engaged in without uptightness, shame, tentativeness at best. It was meant to be engaged in lovingly, openly, honestly, laughingly, joyfully, uninhibitedly, and with outrageous happiness. Notice that nowhere does it say irresponsibly. Nor are love, openness, honesty, laughter, joy, uninhibitedness, or outrageous happiness synonyms for "irresponsibility." The book spoke of the joy and freedom and happiness of sex in that context—and assumed that the reader understood that one thing does not equal another.

As to when—at what age—a child should begin to "enjoy" sexuality, the answer is: immediately. In fact, the child does. Almost immediately. It is we, uptight adults, who tell children (even infants) not to "touch there," not to "look there," not to even notice that "there" exists. It is we, uptight adults, who overlay our guilt, our shame, our embarrassment, our sexual dilemmas and our dysfunctions on the child. The child has no sexual dilemma. The child has no sexual dysfunction. It is only after listening to and observing adults that the child begins to pick up signals that something is "wrong" about sex; that we shouldn't even say "penis," for heaven sake, or "vagina," and so we make up all sorts of cutsie little words for the two-year-old to hear and use, lest, God forbid, the child actually uses the right word. Is it any wonder our society is so twisted around its sexual attitudes when we can't even let our kids say "penis"?

Is it any wonder the world uses as its most demeaning expletive a four-letter word which just happens to describe one of the most extraordinary physical experiences of which humans are capable?

So my answer to your question, Marge, is the answer that you may not want to hear. There is no time that is too early for children to experience with joy their sexuality. This does not mean intercourse, obviously. This means noticing, honoring and celebrating that we are all human beings, Mommy and Daddy included, and that sexuality is a joyful, not an embarrassing and shameful, part of our humanness. There are ways in which the stomach-quivering, heart-pounding, mind-blowing, wonderfully exciting experience of discovery of self and another may be encouraged, nurtured, created and allowed, while remaining totally within the boundaries of age-appropriateness, honesty, love (of self and others), integrity, responsibility, and the celebration of life. Regretfully, Marge, most parents have not looked for such ways; most cultures have not even tried. Don't you think it's time we did?

When children are encouraged to express and experience the joy of their sexuality and the sexuality of all human beings in age-appropriate ways, their largest participation in that experience occurs at an age-appropriate time, which time is different, Marge, for every young person. Their fullest participation may not occur until they are 90, for it is part of the mystery and it is in the endless attraction of this experience that we can discover new beauty, new wonder, new openness, new vulnerability, new trust, new joy, new playfulness, and new depths of love, and the ability to share love, even as we grow older. But not, but never, Marge, if we start from shame, guilt, and embarrassment.

Questions About Sin, Near-Death Experiences, Bible Truth, and Life Purpose

Dear Mrs. & Mr. Walsch: I address you both because great couples work together and I only want answers, it doesn't matter from who. I've been asking our Father for guidance & the answer is always that I should write to you so that others will share in the answers.

I was raised by a self-proclaimed Pentecostal preacher who sexually abused me. I spent 20 years living a destructive lifestyle, often trying suicide. It was on one of these attempts I believe I met God. Six years ago, I tried to kill my stepfather and had a complete breakdown. I was put in a mental hospital and diagnosed as manic-depressive. I then began to notice how many mental patients are terrified of not just the devil, but of God.

I have been mentally stable since reading (many times) *CWG 1 & 2* and now try to help the mentally ill. My husband and I meet thousands of people every year (we move every couple of months), mostly of Southern Baptist and Pentecostal persuasion. I have to be honest, most of these people get mad when I talk about *CWG*, but they always come back with questions—questions I'm not able to answer. I've been fortunate to be able to share *CWG* with so many and have seen people change their lives completely, thanks to you and our Father. But I need to know the answers.

Now for the questions. If there's no sin, what did Jesus die for? How do we explain people who have life-after-death experiences and claim they went to hell? If the Bible isn't all true, what parts do we study? Are we supposed to still pay tithes? I was taught to pay tithes to the place where you're taught. Are you set up to receive tithes? I look foolish when I can't answer these questions, from other people, and possibly hurt the person's chances of knowing our Father.

How do I discover my purpose? I know the Father ruined my suicide attempts for a reason. Is sharing enough? How can I do more to help? Loving Friendship, name withheld by request, WA.

Dear Loving Friendship: My wife Nancy has asked me to respond to you, so here goes. Let's take your questions one at a time.

If there's no sin, what did Jesus die for?

Jesus died and rose again so that we might know the truth about him, and hence, about us. His act was meant as a demonstration of Who We Really Are. Every act is an act of self-definition. That is true for you, and it was true for Jesus. Jesus was a divine master who possessed absolute understanding of the truth, about himself and about God. He wished to share this truth with all the world. Thus, he said "I and the Father are one." He also proclaimed us to be his brothers, and was heard to ask, "Have I not said, 'Ye are gods'?" With regard to his miracles, he said, "Why are you so amazed? These things, and more, will you do also."

Jesus did not die for our sins, but rather, to demonstrate that we are sinless. We were made in the image and likeness of God, and Jesus kept trying to tell us so. But few believed him. He knew that only a real demonstration of Godliness could prove convincing. Well, he convinced many people that he is God, all right, but quite a few missed the point that we are all the same thing. We started worshipping him, and that wasn't what he intended.

How do we explain people that have life-after-death experiences who claim they went to hell?

God says we will experience in the first moments after "death" whatever we expect to experience. If we are afraid we will "go to hell," we will create that outcome in our reality. We need not worry, however, because we will only experience our self-created "hell" until we don't want to anymore, until we don't believe in it anymore. That's the moment we end the present experience. Incidentally, it's very much the same way here on earth. We can think we are in a living hell, and then we can change our perception about it, and the entire experience changes for us.

If the Bible isn't all true, what parts do we study?

Study any parts you wish to study. If you could only study stuff that's "true," that would leave out half the history books and social studies texts you read in school, and most of the newspaper articles written today. Read the Bible as often as you like, and go within with each reading to ask yourself what is true for you. Do the same with *Conversations with God* or any other book of spiritual wisdom.

Are we supposed to still pay tithes?

That is a question that is often asked. Many people want to know whether "good spiritual behavior" requires them to contribute to churches or charity. First, let's make something clear. You are not "supposed" to do anything. Who would do the "supposing"? Tithing is a very effective means of increasing your financial abundance, for that which you give to another, you give to yourself. If you demonstrate yourself to be abundant, you will experience yourself being abundant. That is why most spiritual movements and nearly all religions encourage tithing in one form or another. Not because it is "good" to tithe, but because what goes out comes back to you. And yes, The ReCreation Foundation, which is a non-profit organization, does receive tithes each month from people all over the world who choose to contribute to what they consider to be a source of spiritual inspiration.

How do I discover my purpose?

You cannot "discover" your purpose. *CWG* says life is not a process of discovery, it is a process of creation. You have no purpose until you assign yourself one. Who else would give you one? God? And, having given you one, would He then keep it a secret from you? Here is a great wisdom: We are waiting for God to show us our purpose, and God is waiting for us to show Him our purpose.

I know the Father ruined my suicide attempts for a reason. Is sharing enough? How can I do more to help?

There is nothing you need do to help, because nobody needs your help. There is only one reason to do anything: to announce and declare, express and experience, fulfill and become Who You Really Are. Does sharing your wisdom and your help with others give you an experience of Who You Are? Then do that. If it does not, then don't do it, because you will only wind up resenting it anyway, and that will help no one.

My friend, read *CWG* over again, because all of the answers are in there. Everything I've said here is in the trilogy. There is no need to convince anyone of any of this. All people come to the truth when they are ready. Just watch and wait. "When the student is ready, the teacher will appear." Wait for the "student" to be ready.

How Can God's Laws Be Applied?

Dear Neale: Would you please clarify something I am confused about? Tithing. I tithed for years when I was in a fundamentalist church, so I know what it means. For the past year I have been giving away at least ten percent of my gross income, most of it to sources of spiritual growth. So many different things I've read have been consistent about the importance of putting back at least ten percent into the universe, but there seems to be no consensus about where to give it.

You have also talked about being the source of what we choose to experience more of. So, if I desire more money in my life, I need to give to those who have less. Does this come out of my tithe, or is it extra? I am willing to contribute to Habitat for Humanity, because I wish to own a house. Again, should this be out of my tithe, or above it?

Also, if I wish to own a house, and give thanks that a house is coming into my life, how specific must I be about what I would like? Do specifications limit God? Do I assume God knows what is best for me? Is vagueness usable by God/the Universe? Again, I get different messages from different places. God bless you, Neale! Brenda, Vancouver, B.C.

My Dear Brenda: God bless you, too! You know, you ask some of the most important questions dealing with the practical application in day-to-day life of the highest spiritual laws.

First, about tithing. The reason we tithe is as a demonstration. By tithing we systematically demonstrate the truth which we hold about money, just as our whole life is a demonstration of our truths about everything. The only people who tithe, who routinely give money away to others, are people who are very clear that there is more where that came from. Out of this clarity arises the demonstration, and out of this demonstration arises the precise experience of that about which one is clear.

Of course, we are right back to that age old question: which comes first, the chicken or the egg? In the case of the universal laws, or what I call the metaphysical principles, the question in answerable. Demonstration always precedes experience. That is, you will experience what you demonstrate.

This is why I say, "That which you wish for yourself, give away to another." But there is a trap here. If you are doing something in order to produce a result (for instance, tithing in order to bring more money into your life), then you will not produce the result, and you may as well give it up before you start.

The reason this is so is that your very reason for undertaking the demonstration says a lie about you: namely, that you do not have all that you wish right now, and need or want more. That underlying truth, what *CWG 1* calls your "sponsoring thought," is what produces your reality. So no matter how much you give, you will experience not having "enough" and "wanting more."

On the other hand, if you are doing something as a demonstration that the result has already been produced (for instance, tithing ten percent of your income each week out of your deep sense of knowing that there is always enough for you to share, that there is "more where that came from"), then you will have larger and larger experiences of this truth.

Remember, you are not producing the truth, you are recognizing it. Do you see? Do you get It?

There is no "rule" in the universe about the level at which one must demonstrate in order to experience a universal truth. So your question about the amount of your financial contributions back to the universe has no answer. In my own life, I just give wherever and whenever it feels comfortable and true to myself to do so. I do not give in order to produce "plenty." I give out of simply noticing that plenty has already been produced.

Rules, such as the strict injunctive to give away ten percent of your worldly goods, are for those who need rules in order to implement basic truths and to live within the paradigm of basic understandings, such as the understanding of plenty. They provide a discipline. They offer a guideline. Masters are their own discipline. Masters create their own guidelines.

So, what that means, Brenda, is that you can give what you choose to give of your abundance. If you want to stay with a strict hard and fast ten percent, I would include everything you give to support the good of another in that figure, including the contribution to Habitat for Humanity. Here's how I did it some years ago. I set up a rough "division of the goodies." To my home church: three percent of my income each week; to the Children's Miracle Network (which I want to support), two percent each week; to the local medical assistance program for the indigent, two percent each week; to a special fund for family and friends when they need help, two percent each week; to set-aside for last minute choices and decisions (like Habitat for Humanity, one percent each week. Voila! There's your ten percent!

The answer to the second part of your question (where you ask about "vagueness") is again just about the same. Some teachers say, "don't limit God by being too specific." Some teachers say, "Be specific about what you choose!" I understand your frustration. So what I say here will be a great relief. It doesn't matter.

Look, Brenda, it's not as if God will accept your request only if it is made under certain guidelines, you know? That gets right back to ancient religions which teach that there is only one way to God, and all the rest of us are going to hell. Not so. Big lie. Same with this.

Even before you ask, God knows what you desire. You want to visualize something general, like "the right and perfect car"? Go ahead. You want to get specific? That's okay, too. Visualize a big red car with black interior. See the dashboard design in your mind's eye. Call out the model number, if you choose. Yet here's the trick; here's the secret. As soon as you "put it out there" in the universe, let it go. That is to say, detach yourself from results. *CWG 1* teaches that enlightenment is not about dropping all desires, escaping all passion, eschewing all choices. It is about retaining your passion for the thing. It actually encourages you to do so, for passion, the book says, is the beginning of creation; but it also instructs us to avoid being addicted to any particular outcome. Call forth what you choose, *CWG* says, and then accept what the universe supplies, with gratitude and with love, knowing that it is all perfect.

And try to get clear on this, too, Brenda: there is nothing that is best for you. "Best for you" is a relative term, dependent on a great many factors, not all of which may be consciously known to you. Therefore, a master never tries to figure out what is "best" for her. A master simply knows that what is "best" is that which now is.

Must We Pray to the Virgin Mary?

Dear Mr. Walsch: How important is praying to the Virgin Mary and various saints? How, in specific and real terms, could I live each moment knowing who I am and who I want to be? If I ask to be wealthy, how do I *act* first? Thanks a million! Amor, Northridge,CA.

Dear Amor, How important do you think it is to pray to the Virgin Mary and other saints? Don't you see? You are making it all up. All of us are. Each of us creates our own reality, and then we proceed to live in it. That is the whole message of *CWG*. We are the creators of our own reality, the producers of our own experience. Do you believe it is important to pray to the Virgin Mary and other saints? If so, then do so. What I know is that God hears our prayer no matter how we send it. There is no "right" way and no "wrong" way to approach God. There is no intermediary necessary, but that doesn't mean we cannot use one.

The answer to your second question is that first you must decide Who You Are and who you want to be. That is a choice which is arbitrarily made by you, hopefully based upon the grandest version of the greatest vision you ever had about yourself. It is this decision to which *CWG* invites you. After you have made this decision, seek to live it out in every thought, word and action. You may sometimes fall short of your vision, but let that be all right. Simply notice that and choose again.

As for wealth, act each moment of each day as a person of wealth would act. Give money away. When you see that person standing at the edge of the shopping center with a sign, "Will work for food," stick your hand out the car window and put folding money in theirs. When you receive your United Way contribution request, return it at once with your personal donation, doubling what you gave last year. This week at church or synagogue, don't be satisfied with a five or ten dollar bill in the collection plate. Tithe ten percent of that week's income. You don't have to go broke doing all this. It is not important how many zeroes are after the first number. It is the principle that counts. By applying the principle of abundance, which always says "there's more where that came from," you begin to train your thoughts, words and actions to fall into a pattern which produces the outcome which the principle asserts. It is that simple.

On Creating Your Own Dreams and Whether They Are Fulfilled

Dear Neale: My question has to do with creating one's dreams. It is often said that one must "let go," yet how do I let go of what I want to create in my life? My dreams never seem to be fulfilled without a lot of devotion. I've let go of many dreams, and it's only led to a very disappointing experience of life. Also, how does one really know God—or chocolate, let's say—with only a concept and not the experience? And similarly, how do I truly accept that the Universe is just and fair if I have no experience of it being so? I think trying to convince myself of these things is a form of self deception. M.H.,Chicago, IL.

Dear M.H., Actually, it is life as most of us are living it which is a form of self-deception. In ultimate reality, nothing which you see is actually real, and that which is actually real you cannot see. That is why it is so very important to "judge not by appearances." Let me go back to the top of your letter first, however, and see if we can't work our way down to the bottom.

CWG may be a bit different from conventional wisdom in this regard, but *CWG* does not say anything about "letting go" of one's dreams. Quite to the contrary, *CWG* makes it very clear that without a passion for something, there is very little to life. However, *CWG* says we would do well to let go of our expectations, and any need for particular results. You may think this is a contradiction in terms, and it may well appear that way until you look at it more closely.

Let's look at an example. Let's suppose that a person holds a dream of changing the entire world; of shifting our global consciousness about how we choose to live with each other; of altering the pattern of our worldwide experience of God. Some people have always had such a dream, and have never "let go" of it, even when it looked as if the possibilities of that dream coming true were very remote. Yet while they have held fast to their dream, they long ago gave up any need for a particular result. Thus, it is the continuing dream which drives the engine of their ongoing experience, not the appearance or lack of an appearance of a particular outcome.

Put another way, these people always dream of this event, whether or not the event actually occurs. In this sense their work is never done, because even if they do wind up changing the world, they will always continue to dream of doing so. In other words, no matter how good things become, they have an idea that things can always be made better! So the dream never ends, and the mission is never truly accomplished, because it is the dream which motivates these people, not its accomplishment! Mother Theresa was such a person. So was Martin Luther King. There are many people like this is our world. There may be one living right next door to you. Or, perhaps, even in your house.

Incidentally, the way it is with these people is precisely the same way it is with God. God's "dream," if you please, is that we will all one day be completely realized. Yet the moment this happens, a new definition of what "completely realized" means will be created, because if we were completely realized, the game would be over! It is not in scoring that the game is experienced. Notice that once you score, you have run off the playing field. The game is in getting to the end zone, not in being there. Once a team reaches the end zone, everyone goes back to the point where they began and, by mutual agreement, everything starts all over again! This goes on until the clock runs out, the whistle blows, and the game is over. The only thing different about the game of life is that the clock never runs out. The whistle never blows. The point: to achieve happiness, serenity, and a feeling of peace about life, we would do well to become detached from results, but it is of no benefit whatsoever to become detached from our dream of obtaining results. This is part of what *CWG* calls the divine dichotomy.

In his extraordinary publication, *A Handbook to Higher Consciousness*, the late Ken Keyes, Jr., put this principle into everyday terms when he said that true emotional freedom is obtained only when we change our "needs" into "preferences," thus eliminating our emotional "addictions." I consider Ken's book to be one of the most helpful ever written, and I earnestly encourage you to find a copy and read it.

Now you also ask, how does one get to "know God" when God is only a concept and not an experience. *CWG* points out that most people only come to "know" about a thing when and if that particular thing is experienced. What enlightenment asks us to do, the book says, is to "know" a thing first, and thus experience it! For instance, if you know that life will always work out, it probably always will. If you know that the world is a friendly place, it will usually show up that way. If you know God, you will experience Him. And if you just know that your prayer will be answered, it will be. You would do well, M.H., to re-read the section of *CWG* dealing with "knowing" something before you experience it.

One way to get to "know" God is to take some time each day to meditate quietly. This may, of course, lead to nothing. And so, if you are attached to results you may soon become discouraged and disappointed. Only if you are detached, only if results are not the point of it all, will your meditation be serene. And it is in the serenity that God will be found.

A second way to get to know God is to cause another person to know God. The experience you encourage in another you encourage in yourself. That is because there is no one else out there. So don't spend your days and times wondering how you can come to know God. Spend your days and times wondering how you might be an instrument through whom others come to know God. For what you bring to others, you bring to yourself. And that is a great truth.

What Is the Purpose of Life?

Dear Neale: I have a few questions for you.

(1) What is the purpose of living and dying for hundreds of thousands of lifetimes? It seems like an endless cycle. Where does it ultimately lead to?

(2) In New York when I attended your lecture, you signed my book "I see who you are and I love what I see." What does that mean? Who am I that you see?

(3) What is one's life purpose? How does one find that out?

(4) How can I have a conversation with God? I would like to have an intimate relationship and conversation with Him. Holly, Piscataway, NJ.

Dear Holly, I have a few answers for you. (1) Living and dying has no purpose save the purpose you give it. Life is purposeless, pointless. So if you think you are involved in an experience that is pointless, you are right. That is God's greatest gift to us. You see, if God had given life a point, life would have no choice but to obey. Then the point of everybody's life would have had to have been the same! So God, in infinite wisdom, imbued life with no purpose whatsoever, in order that each and every one of us might imbue it with a purpose of our own, thus to define and create, announce and declare, express and experience Who We Really Are. Thus, I suppose it could be said that the purpose of life is to create and experience Who You Really Are. Mind you, not to discover Who You Are, but to create it. You see, there is nothing to discover. In essence, you are nothing, until you decide and create Who You Are.

In essence, you are nothing. I mean that literally. I mean that the essence of you—that which you are—is nothing at all. That is, you are not any particular thing. You are no-thing! Did you know that, Holly? You are no-thing! That's how you start out, being no thing. And then you decide and declare, create and become, that which you say you are.

This is God in the act of God-ing! This is what's going on, Holly! Do you understand it? God is creating and experiencing Godself, through you.

So that, ultimately, is the "purpose of it all." Or, more correctly, it is the process that's going on. It is what's taking place. I mean that literally, too. We are, quite literally, "what is taking place" in time and space. How we "take our place," what we choose to be and do, is totally up to us, and depends on what we'd like God to be. So, where does this cycle lead to? You tell me, Holly. And I mean that literally, too! You tell me, every day, with your life. Your life is your decision as to where this all leads to.

(2) Who you are that I saw in New York, Holly, is a creation of wonder and beauty, a being about to burst forth into new realities, new and higher experiences of her wondrous self. I saw a child of

God, Holly. I saw a Goddess Herself. Do you not see that when you look at yourself?

(3) See my answer to question 1 above. You do not "find that out," Holly. You decide that. Life is not a process of discovery. It is a process of creation. We keep waiting for God to tell us, show us, and God keeps waiting for us to tell Him, show Her. You see, Holly? We're waiting for the One Who Waits for Us.

Stop waiting, Holly. And stop asking. Start declaring. Life is not a question, Holly. Life is a declaration.

(4) You just did, Holly. You just did.

What Is God's Real Name?

Dear Neale: There are so many questions I would like to ask you. I feel that the Bible was edited by the religious order in Christ's time. Jesus told us to beware of the Pharisees, Sadducees and scribes, because of their own religion of that time and day. And right after Jesus' death his disciples did not teach what Jesus taught because they were afraid of being killed by the religious group in those days. They didn't even teach under cover out of fear.

The Catholic Church that sprang up after Jesus' death (by the way, he is not dead, he is still alive in the flesh in a different dimension, immortal) wanted to have control over the masses, because if you control a person spiritually, you have control of mind and body, complete power over a person. In other words, greed, total power. The truth has been suppressed until now because the I AM (God) is revealing it now in the new age (which, by the way, is not a cult, it is an awakening).

I believe that Jesus learned from the Egyptians, Hindus, magi of India, Nepal, Tibet, Ladakh, and Persia, maybe others. I am seeking the Truth. Can you help me find it? What is the I AM's true name?

In your book, you mentioned there are Masters walking the face of the Earth. How does a person become a master? What books does a person have to read, study—whatever? Walt, Olympia, WA.

Dear Walt, You tell me that you are seeking the truth, and you ask me if I can help you find it. The answer is no, I cannot help you find your truth, only you can do that. You must go within and seek the truth there. It exists nowhere outside of yourself.

I am intrigued by your second question, specifically, what is the "true name of God"? Please reread *CWG 1* again if you need greater clarity on what I am about to tell you. God has no "correct name." God has only the name that you give God, and that name changes from time to time, from place to place, from person to person. This is perfectly all right with God, though clearly, it is not perfectly all right with man. Do you imagine after reading *Conversations with God* that there is only one "correct" way to address God, and that if we address God in any other way it is not all right with God? If that is your imagining, you need to read the book again.

You also ask in your letter how a person becomes a master. Once more I refer you back to the original text. *CWG* explains the steps to mastery, I think, quite well. You do not have to read any other books, or even this book, nor do you have to go to any particular school. Life is not a school, and you have nothing to learn, there is only the opportunity to be and to demonstrate what you already know. Good luck on your journey, Walt!

Was There Ever a World Without Sorrow?

> Dear Neale: I have just gone through your first book—it is really an uncommon dialogue. The revelations are inspiring. The concept of "am-notness" with feelings, thoughts, experience and word could only be conceived by a person like you through broader vision. Prayer of gratitude and not supplication helps one to change the pattern of the sponsoring thought. Holy Trinity—knowing, experiencing, being—suggested by your Godself is really an eye-opener: the physical, the non-physical, the metaphysical. We are souls, but we never listen to the souls. Your dialogue with the Almighty is a loving exposure one can appreciate properly only after several readings.
>
> (1) Where is the soul situated in a body? (2) Are mind, intellect and impressions separate entities from the soul or are they the

soul's three facets? (3) How are effort and destiny related? (4) Is a gleeful life created or pre-destined? (5) Was there ever a world without sorrow? Can it be recreated? If so, by whom? (6) What is the role of meditation as a therapy? What should one meditate upon? (7) Are there any impressions etched in the soul which cannot be erased? Do these repeat in different births in a circulatory manner? (8) What is God's eternal work? Is it the creation of the new world? *If so, when*? With regards, love and affections, Atam, Patiala, India.

My dear friend from across the oceans, I am pleased that you found the *CWG* material interesting and beneficial. I'm going to number my answers to your questions so that you can jump back to the original inquiries above.

(1) Contrary to popular belief, the soul is not situated in any one particular place in the body. Indeed, there is no place within the body that the soul is not. It would be incorrect to say that the soul is, let us say, behind the "third eye" in the center of the forehead just above and between the eyes, but not in the left big toe. *CWG3* says that the soul is not in the body at all, but that the body is *in the soul!* In other words, the soul houses the body, not the other way around. This is a complete upheaval of our former understandings. For a fuller explanation of this, be sure to re-read this section of *Book 3*. And so the Soul surrounds, and permeates, the entire body. It is in the ear and in the knee, in the neck and, in the ankle and in the stomach. But if you really want to see the Soul (oh, yes, it can be done!), simply look deeply into the eyes of your beloved. You will also see the soul if you look deeply into your own eyes, in a mirror. But be careful. If you are not used to this, it can be very unnerving.

(2) The soul is the sum total of every feeling you have ever had (in this lifetime and in every other). I could accept your suggestion that it is, therefore, multi-faceted, including mind, intellect and impressions.

(3) There is no such thing as destiny. For there to be destiny, someone would have to decide what they want for you. Yet no one can decide that but you. Now if you live out your own decisions about you so strongly, so unwaveringly, that your outcomes

have seemed inevitable, that may appear to others to be destiny. It is, however, the result of your intentions. The term "destiny" suggests that there is some force, some energy, some process at work in the universe over which you have no control. This is not possible, given Who and What you Are. We are either the creators of our own experience or we are not. If we are not, then we can be subject to "destiny." But we cannot have it both ways. I am informed that the Divine One, which is the All of Us, is creating in every moment. This means that each of us, as an individual aspect of the divine one, is creating and co-creating our individual and collective reality. That pretty much leaves out "destiny," which would require that one of us (God, the universe, someone or something) is creating an outcome (and an inevitable outcome at that) for another of us. Such an occurrence would be impossible.

(4) Nothing in life is pre-destined, as just explained.

(5) There was never a world without sorrow in our physical universe, because in a world without sorrow there could be no joy. If there is nothing but joy, then we cannot experience joy, or know what it is. Remember the teaching from *CWG*: In the absence of that which you are not, that which you Are is not. To learn more about this, read the wonderful children's book *The Little Soul and the Sun*, published by Hampton Roads.

(6) I am not sure that institutional (that is to say, allopathic) medicine has found yet a clearly defined place for meditation as a therapy, although I think that day is not very far off. As to what one should meditate upon, there is not a "correct" answer to that question. Meditate upon whatever you like, or upon nothing at all. You can, you know, literally meditate upon "the nothing." As for me, I focus on the space called the third eye until I see a blue-white dancing light, or flame. This fills me with ecstasy.

(7) All impressions etched in the soul cannot be erased. This is a computer without a delete key. Impressions are often reexperienced from lifetime to lifetime, or, as you put it, in different births.

(8) God has no eternal "work." God's eternal joy is to provide you with the tools and the opportunities to express and experience yourself in each moment as the grandest version of the greatest vision you ever held about Who You Are. God's great function is to

celebrate Itself, know Itself, express Itself, and recreate Itself in, as, and through you. This is God, "God-ding!"

Receiving Messages and Finding Right Livelihood

> I am wondering, do you have a special organization? What does it do? Also, how did you get your messages? Did you just close your eyes and wait for a message and then write it down on paper? I'm now living in a small village between the mountains here in Switzerland. I'm looking for a good job, but I have no idea what kind would be good for me. I would like to work for a better world, so I am looking and looking for something, but I don't know what! Love Angelique d'H., Switzerland.

Dear Angelique, Let's take your questions one at a time. First, we have a nonprofit organization which has been founded by myself and a few friends. It is called The ReCreation Foundation. ReCreation has as its purpose giving people back to themselves. We produce retreats, lectures, seminars and workshops all over the place. We also publish pamphlets and produce video and audio tapes to help people who want to stay connected with the message they found in *Conversations with God*. As to how I received the messages, that is pretty much covered in *CWG Book 1*, but I will tell you here briefly that I simply sat down, usually in the quiet of night, and wrote questions and then I would receive answers as thoughts in my head, and I would write them down on my yellow legal pad as quickly as the thoughts would come. Often I quarreled with these thoughts, and found myself asking questions or insisting on clarification. This dialogue is contained in the book exactly as it occurred in my mind in the quiet of night. Nothing was edited, nothing was changed, and nothing was left out. I did not have to close my eyes and wait for a message, as it came to me very quickly as soon as I asked my question or made my comment. In fact, sometimes the messages came so quickly I could barely keep up with my thoughts as I was writing everything by hand. When this happened, I would ask my mind to slow down, and the thoughts, in fact, would come more slowly. It seems God is very accommodating!

In regards to your search for the right and perfect job, I want to suggest that you read again the chapters of *CWG* having to do with right livelihood. Seek to create and to move into a place of beingness in your life and not a place of doingness. Once you fully experience the place of beingness which you have chosen to create, a right and appropriate doingness will appear in your life. If you would like a far more detailed and explicit explanation of how this process works, order the booklet *Bringers of the Light* from our foundation. Good luck, Angelique.

What Risks Are Worth Taking?

Dear Mr. Walsch: I just finished *CWG Book 1* on Amtrak, returning from NY City. Thank you—and God—for the book! This will not be the only time it gets read. Your conversations are a confirmation of ideas I have held onto for years. It's so good to see them written out clearly for all to digest.

A few questions. Did you ask God about Christmas, how should we celebrate differently from the way we celebrate today? How to spread *CWG* to others? Is a condensation of key points available as a low-cost tract? How can we communicate with others in this or any other universe? How can we bridge language and prejudice gaps? How can people think past their immediate circumstance? How can we tell what risks are worth taking? Sincerely, Marshall, Mechanicville, NY.

Dear Marshall, About Christmas: no, I did not bring that up in my conversation with God. But I do have one comment. You ask, "how should it be celebrated differently?" *CWG* says that there are no "shoulds" or "shouldn'ts" in God's world. So I imagine God would say, "Celebrate it any way you wish." It all depends on what you choose to experience; how you see yourself; what statement you are using life to make about you. Everything we do is a statement about ourselves, including how, or whether, we celebrate Christmas.

To your other questions: How to spread *CWG* to others? I don't know, but whatever you do, be sure you don't do anything too "slick."

Is a condensation of key points available as a low-cost tract? Yes, there are two booklets available (*Bringers of the Light* and *Recreating Yourself*) which condense and crystalize the main points in CWG. They may be ordered from the Foundation.

How can we communicate with others in this or any other universe? Communication is simple. Just think about it. I mean that literally. Just think about what you wish to communicate. Think of the message, and think of the person to whom you wish to send it. If that person is not now in physical form (that is to say, if they are what you would call "dead"), they will get the message immediately. If they are in the body, they may have a somewhat more difficult time receiving the data, depending upon the denseness of their environment (including their spiritual surroundings, beliefs, fears, etc.), and, if they are in physical form anyway, why not just talk to them out loud?

How can we bridge language and prejudice gaps? By understanding, accepting and implementing the highest truth: we are all one. The world would change tomorrow if we all simply held that reality. It is our thoughts of separation—from each other and from God—which create all of our misery, all of our pain, all of our anguish, all of our loneliness and suffering—and all of our righteousness.

How can people think past their immediate circumstances? By having no attachment to results. When you don't fret about outcome, you don't fret about what's going on now. You see your life in a larger context. You see your purpose in a larger way. You then recontextualize your present experience. You, quite literally, transform it. You no longer see it as problematical. And when you no longer see it that way, it ceases to be that way. You have "risen above." You have transcended.

How can we tell what risks are worth taking? If we could tell that, they would not be "risks." Life is an adventure. You want guarantees? You're in the wrong game. Yet there is a way to always get what you desire, and that is to always desire what you get. That is wisdom. That is mastery. *Conversations with God* outlines in great detail the process by which we can all create whatever we choose. That process works. And it will be very effective for you, unless it isn't. Each of us is evolving, becoming. Sometimes we use the process of creation so forcefully, so effectively, we startle ourselves! Sometimes we cannot seem to place into manifestation what we really desire no matter how hard we try. There are many factors at play. There are many complexities involved. Reread *CWG*. It explains them all. And when it comes to taking risks, remember these wonderful words from the French poet and philosopher Apollinaire, which appeared in *CWG*:

"Come to the edge."

"We can't. We are afraid."

"Come to the edge."

"We can't. We will fall."

"Come to the edge."

And they came. And he pushed them.

And they flew.

Someone once said, "Call your fears Adventure." I liked that.

On Natural Disasters and the Nature of Music

Dear Mr. Walsch: I would first like to thank you for trusting yourself enough to listen to God and for having the courage to write and publish your wonderful books. Here are my questions:

1) Why is it that certain natural disasters happen in only certain parts of the country? That is, for example, Nebraska seems to get tornadoes, L.A. gets earthquakes, etc. Is it just the geological principle involved here or is it some negative vibration caused by past events or something?

2)What is the true relation between music and God? How is music to serve us if at all? Thank you so much for your time and attention. Peace, Mary, RI.

Dear Mary, You've asked some questions which have never been asked of me before. In answer to your first question, negative vibrations from past events are not what cause tornadoes in Nebraska and earthquakes in Los Angeles. There are laws at work in the physical universe which create effects. The law of gravity is such a law. The geophysical phenomena to which you refer are the out-picturings of these laws. The laws, like all physical effects, can be circumvented or overcome. In doing this, we recreate anew.

Now, to your question about music: All of life is vibration. Of these vibrations, music is one which we cannot see with our eyes, but which we can hear. Music is a dialect in the Language of God. Based on mathematics (as is everything in the universe), music is the manifestation through sound of the higher vibrations of life. How does music serve you? The way you choose. Its vibration can be very calming, or it can be stirring, or it can be foreboding, or it can be inspiring. Certain music, like certain frequencies of light, can also be very healing, permeating and affecting every cell through which it passes.

CHAPTER 2

Spiritual Path/Life

For many years now I have sought to walk a spiritual path. It has not been easy. What should have been easy—what, by all rights, ought to have been easy (shouldn't getting to God be the easiest thing of all?)—turned out to be very difficult. Until recently.

I see now that this was because, for most of those years, I was not clear on where my spiritual path was. Still, I knew I wanted to be on some kind of path, so I walked a path laid out for me by others. Only recently have I decided to follow the path of my heart. Only recently have I come to understand that it is okay to do so.

That was a great revelation. It was life-changing. God wasn't going to get mad at me if I made a mistake, got it wrong, went astray, missed the boat. I wasn't going to burn in the everlasting fires of hell if I failed to discover and adopt the one true religion, worshipped improperly, or didn't worship at all.

So what is it like to walk the spiritual path? Look to your own life to find the answer. You've been walking the spiritual path since you were born. Since before you were born. There is no way not to be walking the spiritual path, because there is no other path to walk. All of life is spiritual, and every step you take is a step on the spiritual path. You are a spiritual being, and everything that you think, say, and do is a spiritual event.

Where will your path take you today? Wherever that is, I am sure it will be a great adventure. Life is a lot of things, but it's rarely boring.

On Not Giving Up Waiting for God to Answer

Dear Neale: I feel very frustrated. I feel very confused. Is God the God of the Bible (vengeful, judgmental, vindictive), or is He the God of your books (couldn't care less about your daily existence, just go out and play)? I feel broken. I feel alone. I've prayed all my

> life and never felt His presence or a response. I've run the gamut of praying for "things" up to what I need now: peace within myself. I've read the Bible, I've cried, I've begged, I've screamed, I've been angry, all to no avail. I've given up. I've asked Him, in Jesus' name, to take over my life. I've told him how very tired I am—all to no avail. I've paid $150 for a mantra, $250 for a psychiatrist—nothing! I've tried to meditate for years, but can never quiet my thoughts, ever! My self-disgust is growing stronger and stronger. I have no idea why I wrote this. I'm still seeking, seeking, seeking. MM, Silverthorne, CO.

Well, MM, it sounds like you are exactly where I was when I started having my conversation with God. That's super! There is no better place to be than fed up. That's the place of new beginnings. That's the place of letting go. That's the place of "giving up." You are giving up what's been going on so far, and getting ready now to create a new reality.

I know what you're going through right now, M, and what you have been going through these many years. Now, just as you are giving up everything, there is one thing more I'd like you to give up, my friend, and then you will be totally ready. I'd like you to give up your idea that you can't find an answer. I'm here to tell you that you can. God will never let you down, and if you have not received any response from God before, it is not because He hasn't answered, it is because, like me, you have been unable to hear the response. But trust me. God is responding. Right now. And every day and moment of your life.

I'd like to take a look here at how you have characterized God, though, because I think you've got Her all wrong. You've paraphrased *CWG 1* to say that God "couldn't care less about your daily experience" and just wants you to "go out and play." That would be a mischaracterization, M, and I don't want you to hang in there with that. God does care about your experience. God simply doesn't care how you go about creating it.

Imagine loving parents watching their children at play in the yard. They "don't care" whether their children play Tag or Hide-and-Seek. It matters not to them what games are invented. But they do care about whether the children are safe and having a good time. So they make sure the yard is safe, and, if the children get hurt and call out for help, the parents are right there, running out to the yard to see what's up, and to make everything better. It is not so very different with God. She gives us the toys with which to fashion the most wonderful "games" (read that: life) and a safe place in which to play. Then, He leaves us alone to have our experience, and has absolutely no preference whether we play Tag, or Hide-and-Seek. But if we call for help, God is there—right there—to make everything better.

That is not someone who "doesn't care" about our daily experience. That is someone who loves us enough to give us our freedom to do as we wish, and promises to be there for us whenever we need Him. Sounds like a pretty neat God to me.

So now, call on God to answer you. Ask God to show you a sign, give you some help, and provide you with some special insight that might help you now. But be on the lookout. Her response may come in a form other than the one you are expecting. It could by the lyrics of the next song you hear, the story line of the next movie you see, the text of the next book that falls into your hands. It could be the chance utterance of a friend on the street, or a thought that comes to you in the middle of the night. So watch! Look! Listen! For you do not know the hour, nor the form, in which God will come with your word of encouragement.

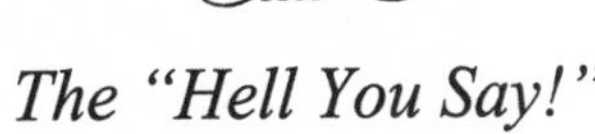

The "Hell You Say!"

Dear Neale: I just listened to your cassette tape, "The Bend Talk," and want you to know that I think it's a wonderful talk, but I'm confused! On the tape you said that creating a cold or flu or a divorce or getting "fired" from a job is "New Age gobbledygook." Yet you say in your newsletter that we create our own reality. Which is which? Do we create that divorce, cold, flu, or getting fired from a job or not?

My other question has to do with Hell. You state in *CWG* that there's no place like a "hell" where the soul goes after death. But a woman on a talk show reported a near-death experience where she experienced demons, snarling beings, and a hellish-like scene. I'm sure she experienced what she reported. How can you explain her experience? Thanks, Neale. Chuck, MO.

Dear Chuck, You are asking some very difficult questions. Now, what I meant in that talk is not that we don't create our own reality (we do), but that someone else bringing that up when we are feeling bad about having that experience is what I call "New Age gobbledygook." In other words, when a person is "going through their stuff" about all that is happening to them right now, it does no good at all to tell them, "Well, you created this all, you know." That's the last thing a person needs or wants to hear at a time like that. Put the Band-Aid on first, then hit 'em with the wisdom, that's what I always say!

As to your second question, there is no place like "hell" in ultimate reality. But in the afterlife, just as in this life, you can create any experience you choose. If you say there is a "hell," then you will experience the "hell you say"! However, as soon as you get tired of this experience, you will "disappear it" by choosing to "get the hell out of there." Some people may choose not to "get the hell out," because they think that hell is what they deserve. If this is what you think, this is what you will experience. Yet the point is that there is no such place as hell. Astonishingly, the Pope has just declared this exact same thing, reversing 2000 years of Catholic teaching.

There is a great deal more about all of this in *Conversations with God, Book 3*, as well as, in Robin Williams' movie, *What Dreams May Come*. If you want an incredible metaphysical experience, take in this movie. It's a marvelous depiction of many of the truths in *CWG 3*, including that we create our own realities, both now and after our "death," and that we return to other bodies, if we choose to, to "have at it again," sometimes calling the same people into our lives. This film is as daring as Hollywood has ever been on the subject of life after death and the larger realities of our universe. It is visually breathtaking, astonishing in its special effects, and is just an extraordinary motion picture. You've never seen anything like it.

Do We Create Our Reality Before We Are Born?

Dear Neale: Thank you for communicating the truth in such a straightforward, easy-to-read manner. Your writings have really been a blessing in my life. My question: Do you think, from information you've received in your dialogues, or from what you've deduced from your conversations, that some of the biggest things that happen in our lives we created before we came into this incarnation? I'm referring to those milestones that really change the course of our lives. Or do you feel that we create everything that happens in our lives just as it's happening?

Thank you very much for taking the time to answer this. Something very painful happened in my life a year ago and I'm still wrestling at times with accepting it. With my gratitude, Jane, Mill Valley, CA.

You've asked a very good question, Jane. Your inquiry suggests, however, that there is such a thing as time. I would invite you to re-read *CWG 2* on the subject of time. When you are finished, you will understand a bit more what I'm going to say to you here. Jane, everything is happening at once. So, in the largest sense, yes, we have created events and experiences before we came into this incarnation, and, we are creating them as we go along. Both answers are true. Both are correct. The trick here, Jane, is to live within the contradiction. I know that in our world, in our constructions, we want there to be no contradictions, but ultimate reality is full of them, my friend.

As for your struggle at times to accept the painful experience you had in your life a year ago, trying to figure out when, or why, that experience was created will probably do little to help matters, Jane. The reasonable question is not when or why this was created. The real question is, what do I want to make of it? And who am I in relationship to it? So who are you, Jane? In relationship to the experience you have undergone, who are you, and who do you choose to be? That is the question, Jane, and it is the only question which matters. In the answer to that question, Jane, will be your healing.

Will "Knowing the Plan" Nullify Our Experience?

Dear Mr. Walsch: I would like to thank you for *CWG*. I have read it three times, and I am touched every time. It feels so good to know that God is not a tyrant. In Chapter 1, God tells of relinquishing remembrance of who we are in order to experience who we are. Does knowing the truth, or having this information disclosed to us, alter and/or nullify our experience? And why does it seem that people on the spiritual quest—who come from the realm of the Absolute to the Physical realm—spend their lives in search of the Absolute, that from which they came? Any input you could provide would be greatly appreciated. May you always walk in sunshine, and your heart be filled with peace. Love, Phillip, Jonesboro, TN.

Dear Phillip, You ask two very profound questions and I congratulate you on the level of your exploration of the *CWG* material. Let's see if I can come up with a decent answer.

Let me take your second question first. I don't experience that we spend our lives in search of the Absolute. I experience that we spend our lives in search of ourselves. I observe that deep within each of us is a hunger to know and experience who we really are. Then, once we know and experience that (which can take many lifetimes), we seek to create who we really are and to recreate ourselves anew. We are given the gift of forgetfulness so that we may experience the gift of this recreation of self. We cannot create ourselves to be something which we know we already are. Yet we cannot "not be that." So we do the next best thing. We forget we are that, thus allowing us, when we are ready to do so, to remember and recreate our experience of that, usually, at the next highest level.

To your first question, yes, your experience is altered by having the larger plan disclosed to you. Your experience is altered by everything which happens to you. Indeed, that is the point of all that is happening. But, no, your experience is not "nullified." Remember, you are creating everything you are experiencing. You are drawing to you every moment, and all that each moment contains, to use as the perfect tool in the perfect creation of your perfect self. In your creation is perfection, and so it is perfect that you have caused your self to come to a remembrance of that which you had forgotten. The timing of this experience was no doubt perfect, too. I can't tell you the number of letters I have received telling me that *Conversations with God* came to them at exactly the right time, in exactly the right way. I am never surprised by this.

Also, remember this: disclosure of the information in *CWG* does not separate you from your own free will. You can choose to believe the information or not. You can decide to make of the book anything you wish. You are giving the book the meaning it has for you, and thus, you are creating it as what it is for you. You are an umpire in the game of life.

A newspaper reporter was visiting a school for umpires recently, and he wanted to get the lowdown on how these "Men in Blue" do it. After all, they have to make difficult calls under pressurized circumstances. He thought it would make a good feature story. The reporter first approached a rookie umpire, in his first year in the league, who'd come to the school for a refresher between seasons. "Tell me," the newspaperman asked the umpire, "how do you do what you do? What's the secret?" And the rookie umpire replied, "Simple. If it's a ball, I call it a ball. If it's a strike, I call it a strike. I call it like it is."

The reporter then went to an instructor at the school, a man who'd been umpiring in the league for several years. "Well," the older man mused, "it's not quite that cut and dried. Not everything is that black and white. So for me, if it looks like a ball, I call it a ball, and if it looks like a strike, I call it a strike. I call 'em as I see 'em." Finally, the reporter found the owner of the school, a scruffy character who'd spent 27 years behind the plate. "Hey," muttered the oldest umpire, "They ain't ***nothin'*** 'til *I calls 'em.*"

Can You Speed Up Enlightenment?

Dear Mr. Walsch: Is there any way one can speed up this process of enlightenment, e.g., a "Cliff Notes" shortcut, or the use of the powerful "I AM" commands? Steve, Saline, MI.

Dear Steve, The fastest way I know to "speed up" the process of enlightenment is to begin to seriously conjure the grandest version of the greatest vision you ever held about yourself and Who

You Are. What does that look like? How would you dress? What would you eat? Where would you go? Who would you hang out with? What things would you do? (And not do?) What would you say? Get very specific here. In your highest idea about yourself, what are the answers to these questions? Write them down. Take pages, if you have to, to explain yourself to yourself. Then, once you've got that picture drawn, step into it. Wear the clothes. Do the things. Say the words. (This is where the I AM commands come in!) And do, say, and think nothing else.

This will seem presumptuous at first, because, believe me, your highest idea about yourself is pretty high. And people all around you will wonder what in the name of Sam Hill you are doing. Ignore them. Forget them. They know not of Who You Are. But remember this. Should you move into this vision, people will fall away on your right, and fall away on your left. You could feel deserted by those you thought loved you the most. Even your family could denounce you. I remember how hard it was even to make the really easy shift in what I was eating. Half my family made fun of me. It was crazy. You'd have thought I'd committed this huge sin, because I was changing the way I was eating. But, you see, what I was now choosing to eat really bugged them, because they saw it as making a judgment of them, even when I was doing nothing of the sort.

If you feel attacked, remember that all attack is a call for help. Just keep going your way. Do your thing. Raise your vision higher and higher, and live by the dictates of that vision. Seek to share with all others what you have come to know of yourself, what you have come to be. Just as you would share any million-dollar gift, share the gift of your self—your new self—with all those whose life you touch.

Your life will never be the same. The heaviness will go right out of it. You will be on the fast track toward enlightenment.

If you feel you still want a practical, hands-on tool, I suggest the *Guidebook to Book 1*. If you faithfully do each and every exercise, process, and assignment in that guidebook from beginning to end, it is my thought that you will have given yourself the tools and mechanisms with which to make the wisdom in *Conversations with God* functional in your daily life—which, of course, will also hasten your journey to enlightenment.

Be In The World, But Not Of It

Dear Neale: How does one stay in touch with current events without losing one's center, one's place of peace? So much news is excitable hype aimed at titillating the viewer and improving the network ratings. Naturally, death and violence top the list of what is deemed to be "news the people want." I feel like I have to meditate before and after the news. I'm sure it's an inner thing, a filter of sorts to detach from getting caught up in manipulative tactics. Your comments on this? John, Enfield, NH.

Dear John, Being "in the world, but not of it" has always been the challenge. Your idea of meditation is an excellent one. Meditate, meditate, meditate. Every morning and every evening, and every afternoon, too, if you can. Meditation exposes you to the inside of you, which is the truth about you, experienced. This will, just as you suggest, balance that to which you are exposed outside of you, which is the lie about you. Remember that always. That which is outside of you is the lie about you. Everything outside of your innermost experience is an illusion. Something which is being made up. It is being created by mass consciousness, and you can affect it, but it is not Who You Are.

In my world, I work to control everything that I put into my system. Not only food, but thoughts and images as well. Perhaps these even more importantly. Therefore, I do not watch movies which I do not believe will enrich me. And if I am in the middle of a movie and I experience that it is not enriching me, I leave. I get up and walk out of the room. I put a book down for the same reason. I let go of certain thoughts for the same reason.

I don't pick up the newspaper anymore on days when I'm feeling particularly "open." I can feel that. It is a felt sense of openness. It is an emotional-psychological-spiritual nakedness. It is not a bad feeling. It is a good feeling. Like being physically naked. I nearly always feel good whenever I am physically naked. In fact, I cannot remember the last time that I was physically naked that I did not feel very good and very comfortable. Many people are not comfortable with their own nakedness, but I am. I just happen to be. And that is how I feel emotionally and psychologically sometimes, too. It is a good feeling, a free feeling, but it is also a level of vulnerability that requires me to be keenly aware of what is coming into my space. So when I'm feeling that kind of openness, I do not even go near a newspaper. I find a good book instead. (Usually, I read my own!) Or I listen to some particularly wonderful music. Or better yet, I choose that moment to let something flow *from* me, rather than to me. I sit down and write. Maybe a letter to a friend. Maybe my newsletter.

So, John, my advice to you is, stop reading the newspapers, stop watching the news on television, stop exposing yourself to this energy, or any negative material, until you have developed the ability to "zip up." That is, close up, on your mental command, your psychic field, your aura. Sometimes we have to do this in order to "be in this world, but not of it." It is a skill, an ability, we develop. Actually, most of us develop it rather early. It is unzipping, opening up to the higher realms and the softer energies and the wispier nuances of life, that is the greatest challenge for many people. Be grateful, therefore, my friend John, that for you the challenge is the opposite.

Why Is There Animal Abuse?

Dear Neale: I understand abuse and cruelty as it pertains to humans—as much as it could possibly be understood—but *CWG 1* did not mention animals. I read the paper or listen to news and hear day after day how people torture and kill, maim and abuse animals. On a grander scale, we have slaughter houses, chicken farms, etc. The animals are innocent victims. I cannot bear to think of the pain they must endure. And for what? Please, please ask God to explain this for me—and what I can do to help, ok? Thank you so much, Lori, Kalispell, MT.

My dear Lori: Nothing is right or wrong in the universe. A thing is simply what it is. The labels right and wrong are labels which we place on things in order to define Who We Are. This is what we are doing every time we call a thing by any name at all. Problems develop, however, if, when a great many members of a particular society call a particular thing "wrong," that society comes to think of that thing as wrong intrinsically. The society forgets that it decided that. In other words, it made it up. Out of thin air. You see, most people cannot stand that level of responsibility, so they pretend that someone else made it up. Usually God. God decided. God said so. Now they are no longer responsible. They are just following God's orders. Yet God did not order any of the things that humans have chosen to require of themselves. That is a myth.

I begin my answer with this small lesson, lest we get into judgment about this business of what is done with, and to, animals. There is no place for judgment in the mind of a master. There is only observation. The master observes, but never judges. The master simply watches. First he watches the action, then he watches the result. The master is content to let the student experience the results of his own actions, rather than correcting the student. If the student experiences negative results long enough, he will come to the master and say, "Master, I keep hurting myself doing this. How can I stop hurting myself in this way?" The master will rarely respond with an answer, but almost always simply repeat the question. "That is a good question," the master will say. "How can you stop hurting yourself this way?" The student will then discover the answer on his own, calling it forth from within, thereby coming to wisdom. Had the master given an answer, the student would have come to knowledge. Yet it was the master's intent that the student should come to wisdom. The two are not the same.

If I were a master, I would answer you now with your own question. "That is a good question," I would say. "How can you help stop the abuse of animals?" You would then come to your own answer; the answer that is suited to you, that is true for you. You will come to this if you ask yourself the question often enough; if you dwell in the question, and if you live whatever answers come to you. Soon—sooner or later—you will come to the answer that is true for you. This is the only answer which matters, Lori. In truth, it is the only answer there is.

This is how it is, not only with regard to your questions and concerns regarding animal abuse, Lori, but with regard to every question ever asked by anyone. Unfortunately, we have become very impatient to know the answers to all the mysteries of life. We don't want to wait. We don't want to have to figure them out for ourselves. And we certainly don't want to have to stand responsible for the result. So we have taken to looking to Others for the answer. I've capitalized "others" there because we think of these "others" as The Ones With The Answer—and so their name deserves capitalization, no?

Nowhere in life do we do this more consistently, and more rapidly, than on the subject of religion, and in the quest for the highest truth. Unwilling to seek out and find our own highest truth, using the tools of our experience, we allow others to tell us what the truth is. We not only allow them to, we demand that they do. We drape them in robes and burn incense and speak to them in hushed tones, and then we beg of them to tell us what is so. Then we do a most extraordinary thing: if we agree with what the robed ones have had to say, we make them saints, and follow their teachings to the letter (whether they work for us or not). If we disagree with their teachings, we call them blasphemers, and we bitterly denounce them. (We may even try to kill them.) Thus we do what we want to do anyway, simply avoiding the step of holding ourselves responsible.

Yes, people do some terrible things to animals. (They also do some terrible things to humans, but as you point out, that is another matter.) Asking God to explain why is like asking God to explain the origin and construction of the universe. Both questions are equally complex. Besides, as God would be the first to point out, the explanation is irrelevant. The only relevant discussion is, what can you do to help? My answer is: do what you want to do.

There are countless options here; dozens of ways you can make yourself heard, impact the situation, cause or seek to cause certain behaviors of others to change or be discontinued. But remember this. Your success or failure in this endeavor should not and must not ever be measured in terms of how much of the behavior you cause to stop. You may, in fact, when all is said and done, have stopped none of it. Stopping the behavior cannot be the point. Making a clear statement of Who You Are must be. That is where the satisfaction is. That is where the victory lies.

That is the whole reason for living; for being what you are being; for doing what you are doing; for having what you are having. That is the only reason for doing anything at all. Remember that.

I Want My Behaviors to Change, But I Can't Seem to Make It Happen!

Dear Neale: I am having some trouble, and I wonder if you could help me. The difficulty is, frankly, my own personality. I seem to snap at everyone, bring other people up short, exhibit enormous impatience with ordinary everyday occurrences, and, in general, make myself a pretty difficult guy to get along with.

What is amazing about this is that it is getting worse rather than getting better since reading your book. I mean, I was always an impatient sort, and found myself frequently making others "wrong," but after reading *CWG 1* had convinced myself to change, that this was not the person I wanted to be. I even went so far as to declare that I would never again act insensitively to others and their needs—after which I promptly did exactly that, more than ever before. I don't seem to be able to stop this abrasive behavior!

I know that deep down inside of me is a person everyone could love—and some people actually do, believe it or not—but while I feel some love in my life, I also feel that no one actually likes me. There is a difference, and I sense that unless people are in my innermost circle and know Who I Really Am, they dislike me. And, as I said, I seem to be even more powerless than ever to stop my unlikeable behaviors. Can you help? I thought reading your book gave me great insights, but when I try to apply them, things go haywire. Nick, Kansas City, MO.

Dear Nick, Thank you for your transparency. It takes courage and strength to look at oneself, and openly and candidly assess what is going on. That is not a small first step, but a giant first step (one that many people never take), and I commend you.

Now first let me tell you that I am not surprised that things have gotten worse before they have gotten better. *CWG* teaches that the moment you declare yourself to be, do or have anything, everything unlike it comes into the space. That is because in the absence of that which you are not, that which You Are is not. (You may want to reread that sentence, Nick, if its meaning slipped past you.)

In the absence of cold, warm is not. In the absence of up, down is not. In the absence of short, the experience of long does not and cannot exist. So the universe will always bring you the experience of that which you are not, in order to create a context within which you may more magnificently experience That Which You Are.

Now there is a way out of this dilemma. There are five magic words I can give you which will help you to recreate yourself anew in the next moment of now in the grandest version of the greatest vision you ever held about Who You Are. These words invoke what I call the process of recontextualization. In other words, they create a new context within which you may place your present experience (whatever experience you are having), and within which you may produce your next upcoming behavior. Here are those five magic words: What would love do now?

If, every time something occurs in your life, you will simply stop for five seconds and ask yourself this question, you will create a new context within which you may consider your response. When your response to the occurrence becomes your response to the question, your behavior will change. Not every time. And not even, perhaps, the first time. But enough of the time over a brief period that you (and others) will observe a shift—a very real shift—in your personal dynamics.

Remember to bless each moment and all that it brings you—especially when what it brings you is difficulty. If the world's incoming data contains something that would ordinarily cause you to be impatient or short or abrasive, bless the moment and be truly grateful. See the opportunity. Notice the gift. And turn it into a gift not only for yourself, but for others. For they will be gifted by the new you.

The Law of Opposites Explained

Dear Neale, *The CWG Guidebook*, pg. 55 says: "the moment you declare yourself to be anything, everything unlike it will

> come into your life." Is this a test? "What you call yourself, you call forth for yourself," you said in Newsletter #18. Yet you say call yourself something that you want to be. If I state, "I am love, I am health, I am wealthy," then are you saying that I can expect the opposite or that which is unlike it to happen? I'm confused. I call myself these things that I want to be because I have already experienced the "unlike" of each. Why is the "opposite" going to appear or happen? Janet, Sierra Madre, CA.

Because, Janet, absent that which you are not, that which you are, is not. This is the law of the universe that I was just explaining to Nick. As long as you are in what I call the realm of the relative (as opposed to the realm of the absolute), you will not be able to experience yourself as That Which You Are unless you are in a world and an environment which contains that which you are not.

For instance, Janet, you could not possibly experience yourself as the thing we call "tall" unless the thing we call "short" existed. In the absence of "short," "tall" does not and cannot exist. Not as an experience. It can be a concept, but it cannot be experienced. In the absence of "up" there is no such thing as "down" (something the astronauts and cosmonauts have experienced!) In the absence of that which we call "bad," that which we call "good" would be merely a figment of our imagination. "Good" could not be experienced. Therefore, in the strictly highest sense, there is no such thing as "bad," for even that which is "bad" for you is "good" for you. This is the secret which all masters know. This is the step that has been missing as you have dealt with "already experiencing the unlike" of what you choose, in the past.

Now when you know that the so-called "bad" experiences and effects in your life are only there so that you may experience Who You Really Are, you begin very quickly to pay them no mind. When something "bad" happens, you don't give it a second thought. Even your first thought is different. Instead of condemning what is going on, instead of decrying what is happening, you are actually grateful for it, in a sublime sort of way. This is the step that has been missing as you have dealt with "already experiencing the unlike" of what you choose, in the past.

This gratefulness is achieved through a wonderful process I have chosen to call recontextualization. When you consider what is going on in your life in a new context, you become grateful for that which you might have previously condemned. It is a miracle of transformation. You simply change your idea about a thing, and thus, your experience of it. Nothing exterior to you changes. The circumstances and conditions of your life may stay exactly the same. But your experience of them is altogether different. And—here is a great secret—as your experience of them changes, as you begin to call them something else (gifts, instead of curses), your exterior circumstances and conditions begin to change as well. For that which is exterior to you changes when that which is interior to you changes, and not before. This is called "living life from the inside out."

Therefore, Janet, bless, bless, bless your enemies, and pray for your persecutors. For what God said in *CWG 2* is true: "I have sent you nothing but angels." And when your life looks like it's falling apart, remember that it may just be falling together—for the first time.

Commanding the Universe

Dear Neale: Thank you for writing *CWG 1*. Still striving for my dream, at 52! Hate to give up. Should I? Is there negativity in wanting? Love, Julie, Austin, TX.

Dear Julie, "Wanting" something is not a good thing to do, because it produces the experience of "not having" what you choose. Let me explain. Your every thought, word and deed is creative. Now, if you have a thought of "wanting" something, you will produce that thought in your experience. That is, you will see that very thought made manifest in your reality. Therefore, if you think "I want" something, that is the experience you will have: the experience of wanting it! On the other hand, if you think "I have" something, then that is the experience you will bring yourself: the experience of having it. Do you understand? Words are very important. Thoughts are creative. That's why I always say, I choose, rather than "I want." Choosing something is a much more forceful statement. It is a directive. It is a calling forth.

Some people have a hard time with this, because it seems as though they are giving God orders. Yet that is exactly what God would invite us to do. Stand in front of the smorgasbord of life and choose. Place your order. Tell the universe exactly what it is you select. Announce your preferences. Command of God what you will.

This sounds like blasphemy, I know. "We should demand of God?" Yet I did not use the word "demand." I said "command." Only if you were a God yourself would you understand this. For Gods command, and lesser beings demand. You have no demands, you have only commands. Command the universe. Go ahead. It has been placed there for you to do so. It has been given to you as a tool—the entire universe—that you might recreate yourself anew in the next grandest version of the greatest vision you ever had about Who You Really Are.

So, no, Julie, do not "want." For if you say that you "want" something, you may just find yourself truly "wanting." Rather, choose. Command. Call forth. And what is the best way to "call forth" your next chosen reality? Say a prayer of thanksgiving that it has already been given to you. This affirms the truth of the statement, "even before you ask, I will have answered." There is much more about the use of gratitude—not arrogance, but gratitude—as a tool of creation in the *Conversations with God* trilogy. You may find it useful to review this material.

How Can I Make a Miracle Happen?

Dear Neale: I am somewhat of a loner, who only seeks out the help of God and not others. I am intelligent, strong, knowledgeable and have a very well established relationship with God, which has been very natural since my early childhood.

The details in *CWG 1* only confirmed what I had already known to be the truth, long before I ever read it. I have tried and tried on my own to receive a specific miracle from God, and to date have yet to see it in my reality.

> What advise can you give me? I really do need your help! I have felt in my heart for a very long time, that all I need to do is come to God for it. All my efforts have failed, but not my will to succeed. How do I call into my reality the thing I desire the most? Johnny, by E-mail.

Dear Johnny, The fastest way to receive anything from the universe is to give it away to someone else. The magic words in *Conversations with God* that speak directly to this issue and therefore to your letter are, be the source. With those three words, God has outlined to all of us a miracle formula that allows us to produce in our lives the miracles that we feel we cannot have any other way.

The reason that you have been unable to manifest the miracle that you have desired for so many years in your life is because at some deep level I suspect you feel unworthy of receiving that miracle, or you believe, perhaps, that it simply can't happen. It is impossible, and therefore will not materialize. These are common thoughts held by many people, I might even say most people, and it is for that reason that most people do not experience miracles in their lives. That is, in fact, precisely why those kinds of actions by God are called miracles, because they happen so infrequently in the lives of human beings. Not because God is infrequent in the graces that She bestows, but because people are very infrequently able to receive those graces openly. However, because people have not found a way to easily receive the graces and miracles of God, God has devised a secondary plan, a "fallback," if you will, and this secondary fallback plan allows us all, even those of us who cannot receive the miracles of God, to be miracles through which those same miracles can be bestowed upon others.

Therefore, here is all you have to do: I don't know what it is you are asking for from God, but whatever it is, find someone else in this world who needs that right now, and be the source of that miracle for another. You will then discover that what flows through you is given to you. For that which you give to another, you would have given to yourself. Do this consistently. Don't stop with just one. Find 4 or 5 or 6 or 8 or 10 other people who need the thing, who desire the thing, who want desperately the thing that you say you want for yourself, and find a way to give it to them. That which you give to another you give to yourself for another reason, as well, and that is the most important reason of all, and the highest truth contained in the wisdom of *Conversations with God.* The truth is: there is only one of us. And so, as you give from your place of goodness that which you would receive, it will be given to you, because there is no one else to give to except yourself.

And finally, there is a very sound metaphysical principle and metaphysical reason why giving to another produces the result in your life. What you have not experienced is what I call the experience of "havingness." Every cell in your body denies the truth that you already have what it is you wish to receive. Yet, in the moment that you give what you want to someone else who also desires it, in that self-same moment you experience that you have it. This is the only signal that the cells of your body need to begin to manifest in physical form in your life that which you would seek. Trust me, this works!

Another reason why you may not be able to experience what it is that you wish you could have has to do with the concept in CWG about it being impossible for us to have anything that we want. God will never give us anything that we want, because the very act of wanting a thing pushes it away from us. It pushes it away from us because the act of wanting something is a declaration to the universe that you do not now have it. And that, of course, is the opposite of what is true at the highest level.

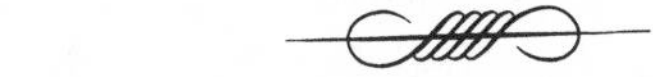

Want Nothing . . . For What You Want Will Leave You Wanting

Dear Neale: *CWG* is excellent. One small point, however, gives me a problem. You say "wanting" reflects lack, and that's what the universe gives you. Later (p.49) you have God saying, "I want what you want." That suggests that God wants us to lack what we want. The semantic precision you call for suggests a God or universe with a "fundamentalist-literalist" mindset. Surely a cosmic mind would understand the meaning behind the wording. There has to be more to "manifesting" than that. Please explore the question of manifesting a new reality. ArDee, San Francisco, CA.

Dear ArDee, There is no contradiction between the fact that your "wanting" something reflects lack and God's statement, "I want what you want." In fact, what the statement means is, God lacks what you lack. Or, put another way, the experience you are having is the experience God is having. And why is this? How can this be? Simple. You and God are one. There is no experience you are having that God is not having. On the other hand, there are many experiences God is having that you are not having! Actually, in truth, you are having them, too, because you are part of the God that is having them, but you simply are not aware of them. Your awareness is limited. God's is not.

When you say, "I want" something, it is a statement to the universe that you do not now have it. For if you had it, you would not want it. Now this statement of "not-having" is very powerful. In fact, it is creative. Indeed, all of your thoughts, words and deeds are creative. God's statement, "I want what you want," is also creative. What God is saying, in effect, is, "I create what you create." And this is profoundly true. Therefore, ArDee, want not. Rather, make every statement of desire a statement of gratitude. As in, "Thank you, God, for bringing this to me now."

Do you know the most powerful prayer I ever heard? It is one sentence. Here it is. Memorize this one: *Thank you, God, for helping me to understand that this problem has already been solved for me.*

Later, as you move towards mastery, you will begin to eliminate from your experience the desiring of anything you do not now have. That is, you will begin to understand that what you have right now is perfect. This is a very high understanding, and a very useful one. It allows us to find happiness in any moment, in any circumstance. This is true mastery of life. Remember, ArDee, that what you resist persists. Therefore, hold in gratefulness that which you now have. And appreciate even more all of the "good" things in your life, no matter how small a portion of your overall experience they represent. For what you appreciate, you expand, since that which appreciates is that which grows larger.

You May Never Ask for Anything from Anyone Ever Again!

Dear Mr. Walsch: I find it interesting that despite the revelations you've had from God about our divine ability to manifest anything we desire in this reality, you request, hence need, money from your readers in order to publish the newsletter. Would it be true to say that you are approaching this situation from a position of "wanting" or lack? Is it that you still don't believe you have the power or ability to manifest the money to defray the cost of printing, or do you believe that manifestation comes in the form of asking people for contributions? It occurs to me that the faith and deep knowing that brings "stuff" from no-where to now-here has been exchanged for the logical mind figuring out a source (readers) of funds. Somehow that doesn't ring true to the essence *CWG*. Or perhaps it's my interpretation of the words. Anyway, this is not meant to be a criticism, merely an observation. Sincerely, Lorna, Canada.

Dear Lorna, Of course asking readers for contributions is a way of manifesting! What else would it be? Is it your understanding that, since we are all creators and there is plenty for everyone, that we dare not ask anyone at the dinner table to pass the salt? If I'm in the middle of a meal and I decide I'd like more salt, and if I see the salt shaker on the other side of the table, to me there is no difference between my getting up from my seat, walking around the table and getting it, and simply asking someone to give it to me. When someone hands it to me, I have found a way to bring it to me. I have manifested it, right there in front of my nose! Once it was across the table, and now, there it is, right there in front of me! This way is no less a legitimate way of manifesting a result than any other.

Did you really interpret the *CWG* teaching to mean that we may not ever ask for anything again for the rest of our lives? Then let's be clear about something. To ask for something is not to announce that you "need" it. It is merely to announce that you choose now to have it. There is a vast difference.

We give away hundreds of copies of this newsletter each month to people who can't afford it. All they do is ask for a scholarship subscription, and we send it to them. And yes, it takes money to do that. And yes, we ask the universe from time to time to bring that money to us in the form of contributions from our readers.

And yes, if you want to send us your $6, Lorna, we'd be glad to receive it. It cost us a great deal more than $6 per scholarship to send this letter out, but we chose that number because we saw that around $60,000 was the amount that would retire our debt, and so we asked for six bucks from each of our readers. Many of you sent us that, and we are very grateful for your willingness to make this miracle with us! Is this a pure manifestation from the abundant universe? You bet it is.

How Do You "Stay on the Spiritual Path"?

Dear Neale: I'm finding myself "drifting" away from my "spiritual" path. Any suggestions? Debi, Medford, MA.

Dear Debi, *CWG* speaks very directly to this question. Asked how we can remain on the spiritual path, or, for that matter, experience anything that we desire in this life, God says, "What you chose for yourself, give to another." The reason this works, Debi, is that there is no one out there but you. Therefore, what you provide for another, you provide for yourself. You may not think this makes sense, but try it. You will soon discover that it is a "magic formula." It is why all masters have taught some variation of "do unto others as you would have it done unto you."

So, Debi, my advice is simple and concise. You want to keep from "drifting" from the "spiritual path"? Keep someone else from drifting from the path! As you give this gift of spiritual "steadiness" to another, you will discover that you have found it in yourself.

For here is a great secret: you cannot give away that which you do not have. And you will always have plenty of that which you choose to give to another. The universe always supports generosity.

Making a Leap of Faith When You're Broke

Dear Neale: When you talked about the Foundation debt of $60,000 and requested $6 from each of us who receive the newsletter, I was immediately reminded of the fact I was one of the scholarship recipients last year. While, at this writing, I continue to be "financially challenged," I also continue to trust in the "perfect plan" and, most of all, trust and believe in the powerful prayer suggested by Mr. Walsch: "Thank you, God, for helping me to remember that this problem has already been solved for me."

This prayer has proven itself to me repeatedly. Still, at this writing, I have $100 left to my name and know of no immediate prospects for changing my income status, which has been zero for the past 30 months (apparently I am creating myself, too, as a non-profit organization). While I have read *CWG* three times, I still have trouble retaining and relating the information to others. I have desired to purchase the *CWG Book 1 Guidebook* for some time to help me in this regard, however, 13 bucks has not been in my budget for this. Now the Foundation needs a hand and I figure it's time to make this a priority. If I buy the guidebook at $12.95, the Foundation will profit $4.95, to which I can add an additional $1.05, thereby, in essence, making my $6 contribution to the Foundation and getting my much desired guidebook at the same time! So I'm down to 85 bucks to my name. So what? This problem has already been solved for me.

I hope this helps. I'm confident thousands of people will contribute, as you, Neale, your wife, Nancy, and all those associated with ReCreation have given so much to all of us. Love and Light, Jeff, Grangeville, ID.

Dear Jeff, Your letter is an inspiration to me, and is an example of the kind of response for which Nancy and I and all of us here at ReCreation have been so grateful. Thank you so much. And now, having said that, I want you to know that it raises a little fear in me. I hate it when my own fears come up. But I have found that when they do, the best way to deal with them is to be transparent about them.

My fear is that other people will read your letter and that I will be accused of what so many others who ask for financial help for their organizations are accused of, and that is, asking everyone to take a "leap of faith" that "God will provide," and so to send money, whether you have it or not.

Many people think there is something unscrupulous in that, and a part of me wants to agree with them. That is why I would never say, "Send us the money, whether you have it or not. God will provide." That is not a request I would ever make, or a statement I would ever utter. If we ask for six dollars as a "Band-Aid," we would only want those who are sure they can afford six dollars to send it, and then only if it feels good to do so.

Now having said all of that, I don't want to negate the true and real message of *Conversations with God*. That message is that God will provide if we believe God will. All things will work out perfectly in the end, and when we move through our lives without expectations, we live a truly holy life, safeguarded from the pitfalls of disappointment and despair, for we have asked for nothing that we cannot do without—and the truth is, we can do without everything, given Who and What we are.

This is a deep subject, and I really had not intended to get into this larger discussion here. I just want to make it clear in the context of Jeff's letter that I don't want anyone to feel they have to prove that they are believing and accepting the wisdom in *CWG* by sending us money. That is how religious and spiritual organizations, in my opinion, get themselves into trouble, and I don't even want to go there.

Now with all that on the table, let me tell you that your wonderfully transparent, open, honest communication, and the gesture of faith, goodwill and kindness which you have demonstrated, will always remain with me as a striking example of putting principles into action. I am spending a few extra moments with God tonight in silent prayer, asking Her to look gently on your circumstance and do what can be done to reward your faith. So expect a little miracle.

Need More Money in Your Life? Catch This . . .

Dear Neale: I am so excited I hardly know where to begin! First and foremost I want to thank you so very much for having the courage to publish your *Conversations with God*, and to thank God for conversing with you in such understandable language. I have been reading and re-reading *CWG Books 1* and *2* and am now in the process of studying *Book 1* with the help of the Guidebook.

Last night I was studying chapter eleven in the Guidebook, "The Money Game!" I am seventy-one years young, with a monthly income from Social Security of $378. I live with my daughter, her fourteen-year-old son, and her five-year-old daughter. My daughter has been struggling as the "breadwinner" of the family, and because of previous thoughts regarding money, my teenage grandson has felt, probably more than the rest of us, that there was "never enough."

After reading that chapter I looked in my purse and gave him five dollars of the eight dollars that was in there. This morning I went to the store for water, which I usually get from machines outside the store (our water from the faucet is not drinkable!). The outside of the store was being painted and the machines were covered, so I had to go inside. Here in Nevada, video poker machines are everywhere, including supermarkets. I decided I would play four quarters—I did—and they multiplied.

The next machine to me was a "Deuce's Wild" poker machine. I don't like that kind of machine and hardly ever play it—but something drew me to that machine. I put in five quarters and hit four deuces which gave me $250!

When I continued on my way to the eye doctor for my contacts which I thought would cost me fifty dollars for two boxes, I was told I had already paid for them back in October of last year! When I left home my daughter and I did not have forty dollars we owed for storage nor money for food until next Friday. When I got home I gave her one hundred dollars and we went out to pay the storage (we have furniture in there due to a few months without a home due to a fire—but that's another story). We stopped at the bank to deposit money so I could write the enclosed check. While I was doing that my daughter was given free movie tickets, thanks to a promotion that was going on in the parking lot. When we got to the storage place, instead of forty dollars she only had to pay thirteen dollars. Talk about God having a sense of humor—He was laughing all day today and saying "Told ya! – Told ya!"

Yes, God, You did—there is always enough! I know this is just the beginning and I have to keep reversing the thought, word, deed process until that useless original thought is deeply replaced by the one that serves me best.

There is a question I would like to ask you. For well over 20 years now I have believed I am living a full, active, healthy life that will go on for at least 125 years, which makes me quite young. However, if we have the ability to live forever, and choose to do so, won't the earth get overpopulated, and if it does, what will we do about it? Will our scientists find ways where we can live in the oceans, will we live on other planets? Bless you, Neale, for all the work you are doing. I have an idea that the hundredth monkey is not far off. Love, Joyce, Henderson, NV.

My dear, dear Joyce, Your letter is the greatest inspiration I have received in a long time! I am thrilled you have found that the principles work, and I am breathless with amazement at the speed with which God has demonstrated this to you!

As to your question, there is more than enough room in the universe for all the human beings who choose to live forever (actually we all "live forever," but I know what you mean). The earth, however, will get overpopulated if everyone chooses to stay here. And so the answer is that we must find some place else to live, and until we do, and develop the means to get there, it will not serve us to continue increasing the population of this planet in numbers disproportionate to its ability to support us.

Ultimately, our scientists will find a way to get us to other places in the universe. But for now we had best husband our resources, something which we are not currently doing. My friend Dennis Weaver, the actor and environmental activist, is founder and president of the Institute of Ecolonomics (the word is a combination of the two words ecology and economics, and was coined by Dennis to describe a new way of looking at the ecological and economical challenges of our times), and has lots of information on how we can do this. You may connect with Dennis at: The Institute of Ecolonomics, P. O. Box 257, Ridgway, CO 81432.

Why Do Our Bodies Age If We Are Created to Last Forever?

Dear Neale: I am very glad to have discovered your book. I have read it twice and plan to read it again. It answers many questions for me, and I am happy that God is the way He is. I feel better about life and death. One question that I have: if our physical bodies were made to last forever, how come we get grey hair when we are about 30 or so, and how come our eyes get weaker? Sara, Sault Ste. Marie, Ontario, Canada.

Dear Neale, I'm 17 years old and just finished reading *Conversations with God, Book 1,* and I have some questions relating to the book. In the book, God said that our bodies are meant to last forever, not just 60-80 years, but forever, and that we are destroying them with alcohol, so my question is, if they were to last forever, are we to look old and wrinkly or young? Melissa, Perth, Western Australia.

Dear Sara and Melissa, Such similar questions from such widely separated countries! I notice that everyone goes through the process of "aging." Even so-called immortalists, who believe we are meant to live forever in physical form, wind up with greying hair, lines on their forehead, and, one day, the experience of death. So you ask a very good question.

Is it possible that in the whole history of humankind, only a handful—and I mean, three or four people—have had the consciousness to live forever in bodily form? Here's what I think (and mind you, this answer—and all the answers in these letters—come from me, not from "God"). I am doing nothing more here than giving you my opinion. I am not, nor do I pretend to be, producing "inspired writing" here.

I think our bodies age because they are supposed to. Now, how fast they age is another matter. I suppose we could postpone so-called "old age" for years, decades, perhaps indefinitely. But that would take a dramatic change in lifestyle, the likes of which very few people have apparently been willing to make. Yet even "holy" people—people who pay attention to these things, and to matters spiritual—seem to age, and die, pretty much like the rest of us. Paramahansa Yogananda comes to mind. Bhagwan Shree Rajneesh (Osho) does as well. It is said that people such as these left their body at will. That is, they chose for their life in the body to be over. Maybe so. But did they choose to have greying hair and protruding middles and aches and pains while growing older just as "rest of us"?

Well, *CWG* says yes to that. It says that we all choose what we are experiencing. Which leaves the question, why would they choose that? And why, for that matter, do we? I've got to look at this whole question more.

CHAPTER 3

Physical Health

We are not paying enough attention to our health. Not as individuals, and certainly not as a nation. This is the single most important factor in our physical lives, and most of us are simply not paying enough attention to it.

Conversations with God observes that our planet is populated by sentient beings of a rather primitive nature, and that what separates primitive beings from the highly envolved beings of the universe is a particular behavior of highly evolved beings. Says *CWG*: "They observe what is so, and they do what works."

We do not.

We observe what is so and do not see it, or, worse, pretend that it isn't so. Or we observe what is so, and do not do "what works," because we simply don't care what is so. Or we observe what is so, and we say that we care, but we do nothing to demonstrate that we care.

This is particularly true when it comes to how we manage our own health. Most of us don't create our health, we react to it. Recent studies show that 50 perecent of all deaths and 70 percent of all illness in America is self-inflicted. Read that: "self-inflicted," meaning those illnesses could have been avoided; meaning death did not have to occur due to those causes.

And just what are those causes? They could all be lumped into one major (and embarrassing) category: lack of self-discipline. Specifically, improper diets, inadequate exercise, use of tobacco, and alcohol abuse. Also, personal living habits that create stress.

Recently, I presented a two-day seminar on the messages in *CWG*. The room was filled with what I felt to be very conscious people, yet I was amazed at the number of them (nearly half) who, on their breaks, went outside to have a smoke. I observed an even greater number who ate red meat at every meal. (We won't even discuss what they put in their stomachs when it came time for dessert.)

And when we talked about living habits in the group discussion, I could see that many in the room (most, actually) were still creating lifestyles filled with deadlines, pressure, and lack of career or personal fulfillment. All of this leads to stress.

Robert Roth, in his extraordinary book, *A Reason to Vote*, reports that stress is the number one cause of chronic illness in America today, that 40 percent of our citizens (that's over 100 million people) now suffer from some form of chronic disorder, and that those numbers are predicted to only get worse.

Roth describes a chronic disease as a disease for which modern medicine says there is no cure. These include heart disease, asthma, arthritis, migraines, diabetes, multiple sclerosis, ulcerative colitis, thyroid disease, Alzheimer's, and Parkinson's—terrible diseases that last for years, many of them causing recurring pain. Fully 69 percent of all hospital admissions are for treatment of chronic illness.

Sadly, all that hospitals can offer is palliative care. Few providers offer treatment approaches that address the cause of all this illness, although all of them know the cause—just as do the people who are experiencing the chronic illness.

In America today we do not have a health care system, we have a disease care system. It seeks to take care of people with diseases. It does nothing to take care of people with good health, to allow them to keep their good health, yet this is the single most effective means of improving the overall health of our nation and cutting medical care costs in this country. All of the evidence to that effect notwithstanding, our priority in America is treatment of disease, with less than 1 percent of our trillion-dollar annual health budget earmarked for prevention.

What is needed here is education . . . and persuasion. And, in my view, a spiritual conversion. Too many of the people who call themselves "spiritual" are not spiritual enough to want to take optimum care of their own bodies. And I'm afraid that I've been included in that very group. Yet, if we really want to evolve as a species, we may benefit from taking the first and most elementary step in the evolutionary process: keeping ourselves alive, and doing it longer.

There are signs that we are beginning. In spite of the fact that the federal government still does not cover most alternative health care modalities through Medicare, and that private insurance carriers follow suit, something startling is happening. For the first time in history, more Americans went to alternative health care providers last year than to allopathic physicians. That points to a trend that has begun as a result of greater public awareness of the availability of those alternative approaches, and of their effectiveness.

What is needed now, if we truly choose for the human race to evolve to the next level, is all-out commitment. That means you and me.

If you're smoking, you may now want to stop.

If you're drinking alcohol, you may want to limit yourself to a very occasional sip.

If you're eating red meat every day, you may want to cut back.

If you're not engaged in a program of regular exercise, you may want to start one.

If you're feeling worried, pressured, and stressed out much of the time, you may want to try a little meditation now and then. (Like, daily.)

All of these are preventative measures. They will help you stay outside of that group of four in ten Americans with chronic illnesses. And speaking of prevention, do a little chiropractic every now and then, not just when you're in pain. Treat yourself to a full-body massage once in a while. And ask the boss if it could be worked out for a massage therapist to come to the office once or twice a week to give those neat little 15-minute hand, back, and neck massages. Watch the stress go way down, and the production go way up.

Find out about acupressure and acupuncture. Visit an aroma therapist. Check out a local reflexologist. And make regular visits to your naturopathic physician.

And straighten out your diet. You've been promising to do it for a long time.

There's a great deal more you can do. You can begin to do as highly evolved beings do. Observe "what's so" (smoking causes cancer, starches make you fat, a constant diet of red meat is bad for you, etc.), then do "what works." Decide that you really care for yourself. Or, if you can't go there, decide that you really care about your loved ones—who do not want you to leave your body for a very long time.

Here's to better health, and better health habits, for all of us.

What Is Meant by "What You Look at Disappears"?

> Dear Mr. Walsch: I was beginning to not want to read any more new age and spiritual books. My searching, prayers, etc., were getting me nowhere. But I enjoyed your book through my laughter and tears. I don't understand, "If you look at something, it will disappear." Please explain. My whole life is crap I'd like to make disappear. I've had unbearable health problems for 23 years. I've always had health problems. I don't have medical insurance, so I stay home and suffer. If you do healings, help me, please. Love and blessing, Ruth, Oceanside, CA.

My dear Ruth, This quote, "What you resist persists. What you look at disappears" is found on page 100 of *CWG Book 1.* Read the section which begins on that page over again, Ruth, because I believe it gives a pretty good explanation of how and why "what you resist persists" is true. "What you look at disappears"—the second part of that statement—means that what you look square in the face ceases to have its illusory form. Anyone who has looked fear in the face and walked away from it unharmed understands this saying very well. Similarly, people look at pain and make it disappear, too, simply by looking at it. That is to say, by examining it, exploring it, owning it and not trying to resist it.

The act of resisting something can only make it stronger. The man in the dentist's office holding onto the arms of the chair for dear life can tell you that. The man who gets into the chair, sinks into the pain, flows with it, goes with it, looks at it and just acknowledges it and gives it no more power than it actually has, discovers that he can reduce, often eliminate, pain with astonishing ease. Mothers in childbirth who have been trained in the Lamaze method do this all the time.

Looking at something, anything, robs it of its imagined bigness, toughness, painfulness, and reduces it to a mere shadow of its former self. Indeed, masters can eliminate any unwanted experience.

I am sorry that you have experienced ill health for so very long. Still, I would encourage you not to resist this. Notice that you brought this to yourself (at a higher level, you made this decision). Give thanks and be glad, for you have produced the right and perfect conditions in which to create and experience the next highest version of Who You Really Are.

There is much more to say about all of this, Ruth, but let me summarize our brief interaction with this: Own your illness. Embrace your sickness. Love it to pieces. Indeed, love it to death. You may not be able to erase the actual condition, but I can tell you for a certainty that you have it within your power to experience the condition in a new way; in a way which is not a trial and a tribulation, but an opportunity. Christopher Reeve, the actor who got thrown from the horse, is doing just that right now. He is a living, breathing example of exactly what I am talking about. You can do the same, Ruth. You don't have to. No one is going to require you to. But you can.

What Would God Say to Someone with Aids?

Dear Neale: I picked up *CWG* in the bookstore last week and have found it to be a truly wonderful book. It seems to clarify many new thought/new age ideas I have come upon before. I do volunteer work with persons with AIDS. I have incorporated ideas from Marianne Williamson, *A Course In Miracles*, Louise Hay, Bernie Siegel, and others in trying to help people with AIDS. How does the message of *CWG* apply to AIDS?

As I understand it, *CWG* says that God does not want anyone to suffer. In fact, God does not want or not want anything. He/She has simply given us the unlimited potential to create whatever we want. There is no "blaming the victim" involved, no right or wrong about the experiences we create. *CWG* talks about some situations being created by the mass mind rather than the individual. Is AIDS possibly one of those things and therefore something that beckons society as a whole to look within the collective consciousness and seek to express our most unconditionally loving and compassionate thoughts? And what would God say to the individual struggling with AIDS? (Of course, I am talking about the God revealed in *CWG*, not the angry fear-based God of some religions.)

This is a bit more of an esoteric question, but I have been wondering about something else also. *CWG* says that everything on the physical plane is relative; that we can only experience love if we have experienced fear, good if we have also experienced evil, life if we have experienced death, etc. However, it also says that there are no opposites in the absolute realm, that only love is real. Does this mean that when God has brought the knowingness of the absolute into complete experience through us and we are simply being God that the duality will end? Will we simply be perfect love, life, and light and will fear, death, and darkness have no existence? Is this what is meant by the teaching of many metaphysical schools that "there is no evil"? Best wishes, Jeff, by E-mail.

Hello, Jeff. One thing we know that God would say is that AIDS is not God's punishment for our behavior, or God's revenge for our sexual offenses or promiscuity. Everything that we create, we create individually and collectively on this planet with our thoughts, words and deeds. The reason for the creation? It is different in every case. Mass consciousness is, however, very strong. "Wherever two or more are gathered" means not just positive outcomes, but so-called negative ones as well. In other words, if enough people hold "wrong thoughts," and they happen to be the same thoughts, you can bet that they will reproduce themselves in our physical reality.

I believe that the worldwide experience we are calling the AIDS epidemic is the result of a worldwide consciousness which has surrounded human sexual expression with guilt, fear and shamefulness for so long. This negative envelope into which so many of the world's people have placed sex surrounds and pervades our every experience of it. The hatred in the world which is directed toward a particular group of people—and the hatred which so many members of that group of people direct at themselves—may have caused this group to be particularly affected by AIDS.

Individual consciousness must be very strong to overcome group consciousness. Christ-level consciousness can do it, obviously. And one doesn't have to be at Christ-level consciousness all or most of the time, either. Miraculous healings have occurred when one has moved to Christ-level consciousness even for an instant. Yet I wish to point out what *CWG* says about healing, and physical conditions, etc. It says that once a physical condition has been manifest, it is a very great challenge to "disappear" it. We need to know that, lest we get caught up in all sorts of tomfoolery. On the other hand, we know and understand that it is possible to make AIDS or any another unwanted condition go away.

But the first thing I would say is, "What you resist, persists." Therefore, do not push so hard against the experience you are having. Rather, move lovingly into your own creation, and simply choose to experience it in the most beneficial and evolutionary way. If that means instant healing, fine. If not, fine, too. If it means dying from the condition, well, also fine.

It is from this place of "I'm fine with any outcome" that inner peace is found, and inner clarity. And, not coincidentally, it is from this place of inner peace and inner clarity that miracles are created. So the first thing to do is, don't fight the creation; don't make it wrong. Simply notice that this is "what is." Embrace it. Love it.

This does not mean "give in" to it, in the sense of letting go of any hope or desire to get better, any thought of healing. It does mean something akin to what some new ager's call "Letting go and letting God." In other words, okay, you created this thing, either through group or individual consciousness. Now, allow God to bring it to its best outcome, and know that this is exactly what will happen. Best advice yet: don't seek to change anything that is happening; seek to change your experience of what is happening.

What would God say to a person with AIDS? "I love you. Now go, and love yourself. And bring to yourself, and all those whose lives you touch, the full measure of your goodness, of your greatness, of your divinity. Bless all those whose lives you touch with the inner light of truth. Heal those around you of any false thought. For that which you give to another, you give to your self. And do not be afraid to come home to Me. Now, or ever. For I will never forsake you, nor cause you anything but joy and wonder in your beingness here. So move now with the experience you are having. Move into it, and through it, and come out on the other side in whatever way you do. Yet do so smiling, and with love, for yourself and for all. Then, nothing can touch you, and you will be a saint. And all those who know you will be blessed. And is this not, after all, what you came here for?"

Now, responding to the second part of your question, yes, "when God has brought the knowingness of the absolute into complete experience through us and we are simply being God," the duality will end. That is correct. "Will we simply be perfect love, life, and light and will fear, death, and darkness have no existence?" Yes, that is also correct. "Is this what is meant by the teaching of many metaphysical schools that there is no evil?" Bingo again.

However, there is one important postscript which you may want to add to all this to complete your understanding. When you experience the absolute, and reside in perfect love with the knowingness that it is all there is, you will be satiated. You will be complete. Happy. Content. And ready to start all over again. For you—us, we—are God "godding"! We are life living. We are That Which Is, becoming. And once we have become what we seek and choose to be, we will unbecome it once again! Once again we will give our selves the glorious gift of forgetfulness, so that we may once again remember and recreate Who We Really Are. This is the divine rhythm of the universe; this is the eternal cycle of all that is. For there cannot be "this" without "that," "here" without "there," "before" without "after," "up" without "down." Nor can there be that which is divine without that which is not divine. And that explains, at last, why God would create "evil"!

In truth, there is no evil. Yet we will create "evil," we will create "less," we will create not knowing, we will create not remembering, we will create that which we are not, in order that we might know and experience once again That Which We Are.

What we are is the all of it. And so we will create ourselves as less than the all, that we might look upon the all, adore the all, earnestly seek the experience of the all, and return to the all, then to separate from the all once again, in a never ending cycle. For The All cannot know itself as The All if The All is always in its Allness.

This is the great mystery which is explained in *Conversations with God*. This is the great revelation. It is why we have reincarnation. It explains that doctrine once and for all. It is why we have that which we call "evil." It explains that experience once and for all. It explains why we seek over and over again that which we already have, and that which we already are. It explains why we forget, why we remember, and why we forget once again.

Now, Jeff, do you understand? If not, re-read *Conversations with God, Book 1*. It's all there. Put very simply. Explained very exquisitely. It is really a rather remarkable document. As is *Book 3*, which explains why some souls choose not to go back to forgetfulness, but to remain in total knowing and pure beingness. These are the masters and the avatars, and they walk among us even today, helping us to remember, helping us to know. And there are angels, too. Divine beings of pure light who guide us, assist us, comfort us, and—more often than we will ever know—keep us safe. And then there are the messengers. The tellers of stories and the spinners of tales and the weavers of dreams, whose job it is to ignite, and keep alighted, the flame of wisdom and the light of love within the human experience.

I am such a Messenger, Jeff. And so are you. And so are we all, if we answer the call. Yet many are called, but few are chosen. For we are the callers and the choosers. We call our Selves to the challenge, and we choose or not, as we desire, to carry the torch.

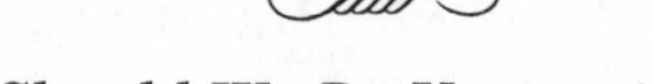

Should We Be Vegetarians?

Dear Neale: *CWG* is an awesome book. I am a *Course in Miracles* student. I'd like you to ask God a question. Does God feel we ought to be vegetarians? George, Harvard, MA.

Dear George, God does not "feel we ought" to do anything. God has no preference in the matter. It is clear from a careful reading of *CWG*, however, that, given where we say we want to go (that is, to a place of perfect health), most of us are not now moving in the right direction. We say we want to go to Seattle, but we are on the way to San Jose!

We are placing all sorts of poisons and toxins into our bodies, and eating foods which are not productive of optimum health. My understanding on this subject is that optimum health is achieved by eating live food, not dead food. That is, not the flesh of dead animals, but the living organisms which grow in our gardens and on our trees. Does God feel this is the "right" thing to do? Well, there is no such thing as "right" and "wrong" in God's world—just what works and what doesn't work in terms of what you are trying to do. Live food leads to more life, dead food leads to more death. It's as simple as that.

Doctors Are Okay and Can Help

Dear Neale: *CWG 1* has brought insight to questions which have caused me misery for a long time. Thank you, Neale! I have a question about a statement on page 190: "Not only do you fail to prevent breakdowns with regular check-ups, once-a-year physicals . . ." My question is first: How would regular check-ups prevent breakdowns? Didn't God say that we create our own breakdowns through our own choosing? If this is so, then what good would a check-up do, really? Second: It was briefly mentioned in *CWG* that the medical industry purposefully keeping cures from people for financial gain. So God knows that the medical industry is not out for our best interest. Why, then, would God recommend regular check-ups? Thank you again, love, Holly, Sherman Oaks, CA.

Dear Holly, Yes, God said we create our own breakdowns. And one of the ways we do it is by failing to take care of our bodies. Regular check-ups are recommended because, as the book clearly points out, there is a difference between the medical industry as a collective, and individual doctors. Very few people act individually in the same way they do collectively. People behave differently in crowds. This is true of doctors as much as it is true of anyone else. Going to an individual doctor can produce beneficial results. My experience is that more often than not, it does. The book does not intend to demean individual doctors, but to comment merely on some positions of the medical profession, as a collective.

Is God Concerned About How We Use Our Bodies?

> Dear Mr. Walsch: I am disturbed by what I read on pages 190-191 of *CWG 1*. Why do you suppose God is so concerned with how we treat our bodies, and not our minds (i.e., television violence, etc.)? Also, why abstain from alcohol only? Why not coffee, marijuana, heroin, etc. (all of which "impair the mind"). Carolyn, West Harwich, MA.

Dear Carolyn, Good! The words on those pages were meant to "disturb" you. As the book itself says on page 191, this passage is "meant to wake you up." The passage goes on to say, "Sometimes, when a person is really deeply asleep, you have to shake him a little." But I am curious about how you conclude that God is "so concerned with how we treat our bodies, and not our minds (i.e., television violence, etc.)." *CWG* contains a very clear denunciation of television violence, and the entire book is about how we treat our minds!

Regarding your second question, page 190 of *CWG* has a very strong statement about how poorly we treat our bodies: "You do not nourish it properly, thereby weakening it further. Then you fill it with toxins, poisons and the most absurd substances posing as food." I think coffee, marijuana and heroin fall into these categories, and while these substances were not mentioned specifically as alcohol was, I think most readers understand that the general statement about how we treat our bodies was not limited solely to alcohol abuse, don't you?

Taking Medications Does Not "Slow Down Evolution"

Dear Neale: I've rewritten this letter many times because I keep thinking up new issues for you to shed some light on. Let me first say that your books are beautiful and seem to reawaken what most of us already hold true under all the layers of bull. What's so sad is that these are such basic truths, and yet you and others like you must continue to carry the message out through much static and resistance.

So many of us are caught up in the tug-of-war between daily survival and trying to create some meaning out of life. Why are we so thick-headed, thick-souled, so heavy-hearted? I realize the answer is a long, tangled web, and perhaps the root cause is our ever-so-stubborn sponsoring thought: everything we do and say must work toward the advantage of our "image," or at the very least, avoid making us look foolish. Where do we begin to unravel the absolute absurdity we've created in this thing called life?

You wrote about the possibility of living eternally. Honestly, the thought scares me. What happened to "when the soul is ready to leave the body, it does, no matter what"? None of this seems to tie in with living eternally, unless you're talking about a very different kind of existence from what we now know. Please expand on this. One more thing: Half of this country seems to be on Prozac or something similar (and the other half probably should be). I myself have been there, too, until I decided to work things out the hard way. I must admit, while on it, it made me the person I always wished I was, but doesn't this somehow affect the evolutionary process? With so many people taking this shortcut to feeling good and living in denial . . . well, you know. Any comments? Hoping for a New Tomorrow, Vesna, San Pedro, CA.

Hello Vesna. I see some frustration there. Let's see if we can unravel a bit of it. You are right, Vesna. Many people are caught up in a daily tug-of-war between a life of "survival" and one of meaning. Yet I invite you to be one of the courageous ones—someone who chooses to make a life, rather than a "living." The reason most people do not choose this is that they hold a sponsoring thought which says they cannot. There are a lot of such sponsoring thoughts out there. Thoughts like, "Money doesn't grow on trees," "You can't have your cake and eat it, too," and hundreds of others, all of which support an idea we have about ourselves as being at the effect of life, rather than at cause in the matter. Where do we begin to unravel the absolute absurdities? With the book, Vesna. Pick up your copy of *CWG* and read it and reread it over and over again, until you have its contents committed to memory.

There is no conflict between the statement in *CWG* that the body was designed to last forever and the statement that when the soul is ready to leave the body, it does, no matter what. The question should be, what would make the soul so ready to leave the body? The answer is sadly obvious. It is because the occupant has taken such poor care of the body that the soul would have no desire to stay in it any longer. Why should it when there are new, healthier bodies in which to continue the adventure?

Yes, half of the United States is on Prozac or something similar, and I certainly don't recommend wholesale use of prescriptive drugs. On the other hand, it is not true that using prescription medications when they are genuinely helpful somehow slows down the evolutionary process. I am not ready to characterize everybody who takes Prozac as people who are simply taking a "shortcut" to "feeling good" and "living in denial." They may very well be merely seeking to correct a biochemical imbalance in their physiological make-up, not so they can feel "good," but so they can feel normal. And not so they can "live in denial," but so they can live in peace.

Now I grant you that there are many people who abuse prescriptive medicines, but you're painting with a pretty broad brush here, Vesna, and I've got to slow you down just a bit. But I do wish (and I'm sure that you join me in this) that our doctors and our medical institutions did spend more time looking at and employing alternate forms of intervention and therapy, such as meditation, acupuncture, acupressure, chiropractic, and therapeutic massage. I have no doubt that greater employment of these and other alternative modalities in the healing professions would substantially lower the need to use prescription drugs. And I have no doubt, also, that this would be nothing but good for us. But I don't want anyone thinking that if they are taking medication, they are "slowing their evolution." It's just not so.

Why Do People Use Drugs to Avoid Living Life on Its Own Terms?

Dear Mr. Walsch: I cannot tell you how profound *CWG Book 1* is to me. I have been struggling with drug addiction on and off for about 27 years. This book gave me so much inspiration and hope helping me see why people use drugs (prescriptions in my case) in order to face the world, and find it so difficult to live life on its own terms. I'm almost 42 years old, and I just relapsed after being clean for over 60 days (which is a miracle in itself to me), and I need God's help so badly. I need His words of wisdom to give me strength. God makes choices sound so simple, which I'm sure they should be, but I sure could use some more inspiration and knowledge on that subject. I hope you can talk with Him about that in detail. I know there are a lot of people like me out here who would surely benefit from His wisdom. Susan, address unavailable.

Dear Susan, It's not clear from your letter whether you are a user of prescription drugs only, or of street drugs as well. You mention prescription drugs in your parenthetical description, but then you speak of having "relapsed after being clean for over 60 days." These are not the words normally used by a person who has merely found she has had to return to using medications after laying off them for a couple of months. They are words I have heard over and over again from people using street drugs. There is also the possibility that you are abusing prescription drugs, by using them addictively. And perhaps that is the case. In any event, your question and your call for help touches, as you say, a condition faced by hundreds of thousands of people. So let's look at it.

I believe, Susan, that people misuse drugs (prescription and otherwise) because they feel they have nowhere else to turn. They have become chemically dependent because they have not been able to find anywhere else what these chemicals bring them: a feeling of well being, or at least a sense of detachment and momentary release from the emotional and/or physical pains which they are experiencing in their lives.

Even those who have gravitated to so-called recreational drugs (while claiming they are doing so simply because they enjoy the feeling of "being high") are announcing that they have not found a way of achieving the feeling these drugs bring them by any other means. And so, of course, they return time and again to their drugs (or drinks, or sexual intoxifications, or what have you). All addictive behavior is such an announcement. It is a declaration that says, "I have lost control of my life, and my ability to create in my life what I really choose."

There are two categories into which all human experience falls. That is, we experience ourselves in one of two ways in any given moment. We are either (1) original/creative, or (2) unoriginal/reactive. These are the two modes of self-expression by which we experience ourselves as Who We Really Are, and Who We Now Choose to Be. In other words, these "expressions of self" are nothing more than ways we are choosing to be.

Now here's the important part. We don't "have to be" anything. We get to choose. We get to decide. There is nothing that we absolutely have to be in the face of any person, place or thing. We don't have to be angry, we don't have to be sad, we don't have to be happy, furious, or anything in particular. We are at choice in all of it.

Now our choice is nearly always based on how we are perceiving the data that we are receiving. Based on our perceptions, we choose (quite arbitrarily, actually) a state of beingness into which we then move. It is the place in which, for that moment, we "live and breathe and have our being." When we "have" a state of being, we are what I call "be-having." That is, we are "having a state of beingness"—and calling it "us." It is a decision we make. It is our choice. And we are making this decision and this choice every minute of every day. When we play out such choices and decisions and turn them into action, social scientists say this is how we are "behaving." And they call this "behavior."

I have observed with regard to behavior that there are several types. Behavior can be (A) rare, (B) occasional, (C) regular, (D) habitual, (E) compulsive, or (F) addictive.

Now, getting back to our two categories of experience, we see with regard to category 2 (unoriginal/reactive) that all of the types of behavior I have just described (A through F above) may be observed in people at one time or another. With regard to category 1, however (original/creative), only the first three types (A-C) are observed. As soon as a behavior becomes habitual, compulsive or addictive it is no longer an expression of self which is original/creative, but rather, it has become unoriginal/reactive.

In the first category we exhibit a behavior that is originally created to suit the moment. That is, we greet the moment, and the data it is presenting to us, as if it was virtually brand new—never experienced in this way before. And we literally create, on the spot, an original way to deal with it; an original way to respond to it; an original way to "be." This does not mean that we will never "act" as we have "acted" before (we may, for instance, "act" continually nice; or always respond with patience; or consistently "be" kind, understanding and loving). And so, how we "show up" may be consistent with our long-term idea about ourselves. Thus our "behaviors" may appear very "regular" even though our self expressions are always "original."

In the second category we exhibit a behavior that is recreated to suit the moment. That is, we greet the moment, and the date it is presenting to us, as if it was the same as a moment we have experienced before. Then we literally recreate, on the spot, an unoriginal way to deal with it; an unoriginal way to respond to it; an unoriginal way to "be." In short, we react. We act as we did once before. Our behaviors become "habitual," then "compulsive," and finally "addictive" because our self expressions are always "unoriginal."

The words "creative" and "reactive" are the same, really. Only the letters have been moved around to have them mean different things. The same letters have been manipulated to produce a different result. This is true of the actions associated with those words as well. When we are creative and when we are reactive we are essentially being the same thing: observers of the events in our life. Only the emotions have been moved around to have those events mean different things. The same data have been manipulated to produce a different result.

Our human bodies are, when all is said and done, essentially nothing more than receivers of data. Through our bodily senses, we both receive and perceive these data. We try to make some sense out of it all—in every case forgetting completely that the data are not coming from somewhere else, but that we, ourselves, have produced them.

Most of us think of life as something that is happening to us, not because of us. We view people, places and events as exterior to ourselves, apart from ourselves. But in truth there is nothing that is exterior to ourselves, nothing that is apart from ourselves. There is no person, place or event which is not part of Who We Are. As long as we think that there is, we will always be able to imagine that somebody, or something, else is "doing it to us"; that there are exterior people, events and circumstances over which we have no control, but which have control over us. This is the illusion we entertain, and in which we live. This is the place of helplessness that creates our despair, and our despairing behaviors, of which drug abuse is obviously one.

Drug abuse is an addictive behavior (type F above). And since types D, E and F can only belong to expression category 2, we see that drug abuse is an unoriginal/reactive expression of self. Indeed, addictive behavior is behavior that is reactive in the extreme.

Reactive expression is expression which comes from the illusion that there is no choice in the matter. It is not the way we would choose to be, and not the behavior we would exhibit, if we thought we did have a choice about it. Yet we do not hold such a thought, and so we do not choose to have a new way of being, but continue behaving in old ways. We keep exhibiting old behaviors. In short, we act as we have acted before. We re-enact the moment exactly as we experienced it last time. When we do this uncontrollably, we move from habitual to compulsive to addictive behavior.

Why do people abuse drugs? Because they have forgotten so completely Who They Are that they think they have lost total control over their experience of themselves. They have moved from choice to no choice, and from authentic to non-authentic in the expression of themselves. That is, they are exhibiting behaviors—ways of being—that are not the truth about themselves.

I've taken time to make a point that you may think is rather obvious. But the number of people who do not see all this as obvious would surprise you. And, of course, the teachings here have to do with much more than just drug abuse. All habitual, compulsive and addictive behaviors are being discussed here, from nail biting to sexual compulsion to tobacco addiction to all manner of behaviors which tell a lie about us.

The cure for addiction of any kind is a spiritual one. In spite of the fact that we keep failing miserably, we keep trying to cure drug abuse with physical means, including physical force. (That is, in fact, how we in this country keep trying to cure everything.) One day we will understand that the cure is not physical, it is spiritual. That is something which many so-called 12-step programs have known for years, which is why they have such an astonishing success rate.

Yet even 12-step programs of many types sometimes begin in a place which I view as semantically false. Some of them begin with what feels to me like a semantic lie about you, and they ask you to repeat that lie as your means of finding the road to recovery. The lie they ask you to repeat and to own, the first statement they ask you to make, is that you are powerless in the face of your addiction, that you cannot solve the problem alone. In truth, that is the only way you are going to solve it.

Some of the programs that ask you to turn your life and your recovery process over to God begin, in my view, in the wrong place, and take you to the wrong place. They begin by allowing you to assume (and in some cases demanding that you admit) that you and God are separate. Yet it is precisely this illusion of separateness that makes you powerless to end your addictions. (Which is why, incidentally, many 12-step program graduates will never say that they are "healed," but, rather declare that they are "in recovery.")

Yes, use the power of God in your life to solve a problem that you are told you cannot solve without the power of God. On this, 12-steppers and I agree. But do not place the power of God outside of yourself. And be careful not to replace one kind of dependency (a dependency on drugs, for instance, or alcohol) with another kind of dependency (on a group, or a meeting). This is interdependence, rather than independence.

Now it may serve you to use a 12-step program as a first step toward independence, and if that is so, bless it for being there; honor it for where it can take you or where it may have brought you. Yet never choose to substitute the Band-Aid for the healing.

You ask, why do people use drugs (prescriptions in your case) in order to face the world, and find it so difficult to live life on its own terms? People do so because they do not understand their true nature, their true relationship to God, and their true reason for being. They do not understand life and what it's about, and know nothing of their higher nature, nor of their grander purpose. They are disconnected completely from the greater reality, and so live life on a very physical level. They see themselves as being at the effect of their lives, rather than at Cause in the matter. And so they experience themselves as helpless and hopeless, at least without their dependencies, whatever they may be.

Now I want to say a word here to those people who are using prescription drugs properly, responsibly. Do not go off your drug therapy because you think that you have lost control of your life. You have not given up your power to these prescriptions if you are using them appropriately. You are empowered by them. Just make sure you know what you are taking, and why, and whether you actually need them. Yet do not dismiss them, or make them "wrong," out of some sudden idea that "enlightened people do not take drugs." What enlightened people do is create their lives so that they work. The miracle of today is that we have co-created it together. That includes the many true miracles of conventional medicine.

Yet there are many who are abusing drugs in every and any form, and there is a way to assist these people. Simply remember and restate the truth. Know the truth and the truth shall set you free. The truth is that you and God are one; that there is no separation between you; that you are a divine being, using this your present lifetime to choose and to declare, to announce and to be, to express and to fulfill Who You Really Are. You will draw to yourself every person, place or thing you need in order to fulfill that destiny. Therefore, condemn nothing, bless everything, and if you do not like your present experience, choose again.

You can alter your experience of any moment, and of yourself in that moment, without altering anything, which you see as exterior to yourself. Nothing outside of you has to shift or change. Only that which is within becomes new. And yet, when you hold a new inner idea about yourself, your old outer reality sooner or later begins to change. It is inevitable.

You want to end your own addiction, Susan? Create and hold a new idea about yourself. Understand more deeply and more completely Who You Are. Come to greater clarity about who you choose to be. Read *Conversations with God, Book 1* over and over again until you have internalized it, and actualized it.

And understand this, lest you imagine that you are alone. Most people have addictions. They simply do not recognize them as such. If one is addicted to drugs, or alcohol, or food, that addiction is now recognized by society as exactly what it is: an addiction. Yet if one is addicted to sex, one might simply be called flirtatious, or promiscuous, or seductive, or a "womanizer." And if one is addicted to approval, one may be called a "hard worker" or a "team player" (and, if the addiction has led to continual unhappiness, one may be called that newer thing: "dysfunctional"). If one is addicted to cigarettes or tobacco, one is simply said to have a "bad habit." And on and on it goes, with us labeling our behaviors every other thing save what they are: addictions.

The way to end our addictions is to move from category 2 to category 1 in our expressions of self. To shift from reactive to creative. To move from unoriginal to original in the way that we view and create each moment—and our selves in relationship to it. To live the grandest version of the greatest vision ever we had about ourselves. To create that vision if we have not already done so, and then to expand into it. This is what recreation is all about. The purpose of life is to recreate yourself anew in every moment of now, so to know your self ever more gloriously, and thus to glorify God.

I hope this has helped. I know this isn't going to change everything overnight (unless, of course, it does), but I hope it has helped. Not only helped you, Susan, but the thousands of others who have seen their lives taken over by behaviors over which they seem to have little or no control. See each moment as brand new. See each event as an opportunity to recreate and experience yourself in a new and larger way. Make a decision about who and what you are, and who you choose to be. Be clear about that. And stick to it, no matter what.

CHAPTER 4

Being vs Doing/What To Do With My Life

Has your year been, so far, what you'd expected? If so, good for you! If not, why not? Could it have been that you were not very clear as to your intentions? *CWG* says that "life proceeds out of our intentions for it." When this year began, did you get to a place of absolute clarity about what you intended for it? Are you at clarity now?

This is a good time to check in, to make an assessment, to see how things are going. And to renew your intentions for the rest of the year. Because another year will be here before you know it. Another year will have passed. Will you be any closer to your life's dream? Will you be any nearer to the realization of your life vision?

Sit down now and make a statement of that dream and that vision. You may want to do so in writing. Make a declaration of what it is you choose. And be careful not to get into too much "doingness." Allow your choices to be declarations of "beingness." For all of life exists as an opportunity for you to experience being Who Your Really Are. And Who You Are, as I have said many times, has nothing to do with what your are doing. Many of you are still caught up in doingness. You imagine that happiness will come from something you are doing. Yet happiness of any real variety can only spring from beingness. It is what you are being that matters to your soul. For the soul is beingness, at the highest level.

So decide what it is you are trying to be. Are you trying to be "happy"? Are you hoping to be "secure"? Are you seeking to be "peaceful"? Is it your desire to be "loving"? Get clear about your intention, then move into every moment of Now prepared to fill that moment with your intention in action. "Do" nothing which does not match your intention, does not vibrate in harmony with it.

When you come from your intention, you will find that certain behaviors will tend to drop away. Your life will see a shift, a major movement, a leap into consciousness at the next level. And that is what this, your present lifetime, is all about. Moving to the next level.

To Be or Not to Be . . . That is the Question

> Dear Mr. Walsch: I have a question that I would appreciate help with. I'm sure that there are many of us who have reached a point in our lives at which we just don't know "Who We Want to Be." Can you furnish me with any guidance in this matter? I have a long list of "Who I Have Been," but these hats no longer fit very well. Waynella, Dallas, TX.

Dear Waynella, If you don't know Who You Want to Be, who does? Yet if you just can't make a choice out of the endless possibilities in the universe, then try this: simply reverse the question. Who do you not want to be? Merely stop being who you do not want to be, and you will automatically be Who You Want to Be.

Remember, Waynella, the "who" that you want to "be" is not a person, not an occupation, not a thing that you "do." It is something that you choose to "be." We are talking about "beingness" here, not "doingness." For instance, long ago I chose to no longer "be" the thing called selfish, or hurtful; unkind or insensitive; self-centered or needy. It took a long time for my body to get the message. It was still going around "doing" things which came from these supposedly unwanted states of being. But then, little by little, things began to change. I started eliminating behaviors I no longer wanted; behaviors that did not represent (that is to say, re-present) me in the way that I chose to "be."

Today I am very much a different person from the man I was even a few short years ago. And, as a result of the new state of beingness into which I have fallen (it is something like falling, too, by the way, not unlike "falling in love"), I find my body "doing" things that only a body which is not "being" all those unwanted things would do. Doing arises out of beingness, and it is always thus, although very few people really know or understand this.

I am not sure you and I are talking about the same thing; but I am sure that this is what *Conversations with God* is talking about when it discusses Who You Really Are. You are not a human doing, you are a human being. Now if this is what you are talking about in your letter, the decision as to who you "want to be" will be not nearly so difficult. And what you will discover is that as soon as you become who you "want to be" in your state of beingness, you will begin to find ways to "do" what you have always wanted to "do" with your life. It is always astonishing to me to see how many people move into their right livelihood, creating the right and perfect "career" for themselves, as a result of their decision to "be" Who They Really Are. Indeed, that is exactly how I came to be "doing" what I am doing today!

So here's what I want you to get, Waynella: It all starts with beingness. The answer to your question will be found there. Stop trying to find the right and perfect thing to "do," and start trying to create the right and perfect thing to "be." The "doingness" that is perfect for you will follow. I promise.

I Don't Know What I Should Choose!

Dear Neale: I've been working in Branson, Missouri, at a couple of restaurants for several years now, and have become very dissatisfied with the restaurant industry here. I'm very attracted to alternative therapies, from massage, nutrition and yoga to transpersonal psychology, pastoral counseling, and herbs. I want a career change! I don't know which of the above I should choose. I don't ever seem to get an answer to my question in meditation, so could you ask God which is best for me, and where the best schools would be? I'm 35 and time is running out. I need help from God to make the right decision and to find my life's mission, career-wise. Also, my girlfriend and I want to move from the Ozarks to out west, but we can't decide which is the best location for us. Can you help? Stuck in restaurant work . . . Chuck, Branson, MO.

Dear Chuck, Many people want to know what's "best" for them, what they should "do" with their life. Everyone is focused on this "doingness" thing, and that is not where the focus is best placed. It is your beingness, Chuck, which keeps you stuck, not your doingness. You are stuck in your present "doingness" because of what you are "being"—and not "being." Change your beingness and you will not be "doing" the restaurant thing much longer.

I want you to read a booklet which I have written called *Bringers of the Light*. It is an extraordinary explanation of this business of "doingness" and "beingness," and it was written especially for people like you; people who find themselves "stuck" in a career, or in an endless search for the "right" career.

Now I want to tell you that it would be very unusual for you to "get an answer" to your question in meditation, because meditation is not about the universe, or God, answering your questions. Meditation is about getting in touch with Who You Really Are, after which all questions go away. If you go into meditation with a question on your mind, you go into meditation wrongly. Empty your mind, then go into meditation. Forget your questions, then go into meditation. Require no "answers," then go into meditation. Meditation is not about "getting answers." Meditation is about going to a place where the answers and the questions are one.

Do you understand this? Do you hear what I am saying? It is out of the void that an answer will come, if an "answer" comes at all, not out of the space of expectation. If you expect an answer, you will not get one. That is because meditation is not a mental process: it is the absence of mental process! So I am not surprised that you receive no answers in your meditation.

As to "asking God" what is "best" for you, I want you to try to grasp something here, that could change your life. There is nothing that is "best for you." There is only that which serves you in terms of what you are trying to be. And what you are seeking to be is not a question God will ever answer. Because if God answered that question, your whole purpose in living would be thwarted. Your purpose in coming to your body at this time and in this place has been to make the very decision that you are asking God to make! You are on this earth, my friend, to decide and to declare, to create and to fulfill, to experience and to become Who You

Really Are. You are engaged in the process of pure creation; you are God Godding! And God knows, God would never tell you how to do that! The whole point of the process is for you to decide! For you to choose. For you to create. Not for God to decide and choose and create for you! I cannot, and would not, "ask God what is best" for you. And neither should you. You should tell God what is best for you, and then watch God move into action!

God is not one who likes to be asked. God is one who likes to be told. And that is the biggest misunderstanding of all time about God. People think that we are to "ask" God for what we want, or for help in deciding this or that. God says, no, don't do that. Don't ask me. Because asking me is a statement that you do not now have what you want, or have the answers to your questions; and what you declare you do not have, I cannot give you. For your word is law, and your thought is creative, and your actions are productive, producing Who and What You Now Are. Therefore, choose, do not ask.

The only problem with this choosing business is that we can no longer rely on any person or source outside of our selves to "give us the answer," tell us what is "right," or decide what is "best." We have to make our choices in a vacuum, and then stand responsible for those choices. This is, of course, what most of the human race is spending its time avoiding.

Now, Chuck, you say you are "35 and time is running out." That makes me chuckle a bit, my friend, because if your time is running out, mine is positively depleted! Your time is just beginning. So I invite you to stop it. Stop creating all these beliefs for yourself that do not serve you. Your "life's mission," Chuck, is exactly what you say it is. It is not something you "find," it is something you create. Create it, Chuck, stop trying to "find it." *Conversations with God* says that life is not a process of discovery, it is a process of creation. That is the most important sentence you will ever read.

By now you already know what I am going to say to you about what is the "best location" for you. There is no "best location." The "best location" is right where you say it is. Create it, Chuck. Stop trying to find it. I am not going to enable you. I am going to empower you. If I give you the answer, I will enable you to think that I had the answer which you didn't. Then you can continue to live in the thought that you do not have the answers, but, if you can find someone who does, life will be swell. I will not enable you in that way, Chuck. You can count on me never to do that.

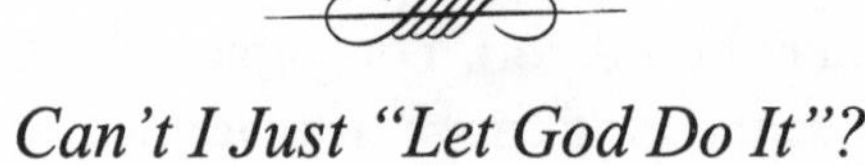

Can't I Just "Let God Do It"?

> Dear Neale: These *Conversations with God* speak to me on a level where I see an integration of the Divine and the human. I am, however, having difficulty understanding one thing. I understand that I am the spirit of the creator expressing itself as me, therefore, I Am—in fact, in reality and in truth—the spirit of God, and as such I can create a life of "perfection" right here on earth. I therefore understand that anything else in my life is a miscreation, and I can simply release it and choose to create that which I think is God-like. On page 13 of *Book 1*, however, I read "I do not care what you do, and that is hard for you to hear" and, just before that, ". . . your will for you is God's will for you."
>
> What happens when we are of the consciousness ". . . not as I will, but Thy will be done?" What happens when we make a choice to make God choose for us, and God is saying, "I do not care what you do?" What happens to the will, the idea, the request then, if we say to God , you choose for us, but God is saying, you choose for you?
>
> Please clarify. May you be abundantly blessed in all that you choose, and I send you much Light for your journey! Yvonne, Don Mills, Ontario, Canada.

Dear Yvonne, You have asked a very good question. When you make a choice to have God choose for you, you have essentially taken down the sail, let go of the rudder, and set your boat adrift on a stormy sea. This is because God has no preference in the matter, and really and truly chooses for you what you choose for you. Or, to put this all another way, if God did have a preference, this, in fact, would be it: that you get to choose. Now if you do not want to choose, we have a small problem here.

You can, of course, give up your future to fate, which is a marvelous acronym for "From All Thoughts Everywhere." And those winds of fate may take you to safe harbor, or a shipwreck. If you are having "no thought about" what it is you choose, but are leaving everything to chance (that is, to God), then you are, in effect, yielding to the thoughts of everyone around you (which is Who God Is), and of your own subconscious mind.

The first thing that will happen is that your personal creative Self will turn for direction to your original sponsoring thought. You will then produce an outcome. You simply won't do it consciously. You'll do it unconsciously, then claim that what happened was "fate," or "the will of God."

In addition to your own sponsoring thought, your future will also be impacted by the collective consciousness of the world around you; that is, the other human beings who people your life, with whom you travel on your journey, and, to some degree, all the people of the earth, whose combined attitudes too often create the collective experience of the lot of us.

Now, since many of the thoughts belonging to these other people may be strikingly different from each other, you may find yourself battered a bit. This will manifest itself as your feeling "torn" over what to do. In life, indecision only breeds more indecision. Furthermore, you will soon discover that—and here is the dichotomy —not to decide is to decide. The truth is, you are always deciding, and thus, you are always creating. It is merely a question of what method you use.

My recommendation: make a conscious choice about everything.

How to Move into a "State of Being"

Dear Neale Donald Walsch: I attended the "How To Love People And Get Away With It" session. At that time I "chose" to be love and truth as you have chosen wisdom and clarity. I began to review how that has been for me. It seems to me that love has come to be more easily displayed in my life than truth. I think that I am naturally a loving person, and the challenge to love is not as great as the challenge to be truthful. I realize that I filter and edit my truth all the time, and I have decided to be more conscious of doing that.

Both wisdom and clarity are so wonderfully evident in your work. I can't imagine the situation where a person begins at square one, lacking either wisdom or clarity, and because of a decision process, suddenly begins to create these qualities and display them for the world to see.

I know that every moment is another opportunity to create my highest version of my grandest vision. The question is, has either wisdom or clarity been more natural for you, and how have you worked through the process of being that which does not come easily? Could you tell me how the decision to be wisdom and clarity has been for you? Did it seem to come naturally right from the beginning?

Your wisdom and clarity have gently and grandly touched my life and profoundly affected my understanding of what life is all about. Thanks for being who you are. Thanks for the books. Thanks for providing those wonderful retreats through ReCreation. And that's my truth about you! Donna, N. Grosvenordale, CT.

Dear Donna, Those are very nice words for you to say to me. The fact of the matter is that you can "begin at square one" and, because of a decision process, create any beingness you choose. There is no state of being which "does not come easily." All states of being are open and available to all people, and it is simply a matter of choosing that. The decision to be wisdom and clarity has been wonderful for me. I have never felt so fulfilled in all of my life. Yes, it came naturally right from the beginning, for the reason I gave you. Every state of being will "come naturally" to those who claim them. The trick is to claim them, and to know that they are yours. "I am love," "I am compassion," "I am patience," "I am happiness personified," all of these, and others like them, are very powerful statements. They are choices. We can "come from choice" in every moment of our lives. Since states of being are things we create inside of ourselves, as opposed to those things which we create outside of ourselves, we can move into them on a moment's notice, and we need nothing exterior to ourselves in order to manifest them.

Starting a Career at 72?

Dear Walsch: I must tell you that your *CWG Books 1* and *2* are the best, most reasonable things I've ever read. Since my husband just died and left some large medical debts, do you have any ideas for a career for a 72-year-old woman? Does God say anything about starting late? (No name given.)

Well, my friend, There certainly is no time limit on fun or achievement. Writing, for example, is something you can do anytime. And don't think that a 72-year-old would have nothing to say that anyone would want to read. It is probably exactly the opposite! You could also paint. Look at Whistler's mother. Or teach private classes in just about anything you do well. Or be a "professional grandma" for a family or organization. Or, really, do just about anything you wish to do. However, you don't have to go to work at age 72 if you don't choose to. There are plenty of ways to create freedom from those medical bills. So if that's your need, just turn it over to God. And remember what I call my "magic prayer": Thank you, God, for helping me to understand that this problem has already been solved for me.

I Have to Stay to "Learn My Lesson"

Dear Neale, I finished *CWG* last Friday and used the weekend to let it settle in. You have to understand that I am in the corporate world, a situation with which I have been wrestling for four years (dropped out, went back in, dropped out, just went back in again in March, hit the wall in April. Hitting the wall meaning that I suddenly realized why I left to begin with, and realized this situation was even more painful—and paid less money—than the one I left four years ago).

As the message of the book settled and I discussed it with a friend, one who is traveling a similar path, I realized that I must face head-on whatever issue the corporate community needs to teach me, not only reach the awareness, but then pass the exam, or manage the experience differently. Only then will I be able to leave the corporate world and do what I truly wish to do, but first I must leave it in peace, not anger. That is, leave the anger, then leave the corporate world.

Lettin' It Go On the O-H-I-O. Love to Neale and all, AJ

You've said, "I realized that I must face head-on whatever issues the corporate community needs to teach me, not only reach the awareness, but then pass the exam." First of all AJ, the corporate community has no need to teach you anything. Nor do you have a need, metaphysical or otherwise, to learn anything. This is not a school. Life is not a university, where you either pass or fail. You already know what you think you came here (to the planet, to the corporate world, wherever) to learn. Your job now is to demonstrate what you already know. If one of the things you already know is that the "corporate world" is not Who You Are, then there is only one thing left to do: demonstrate that. Waiting around for some "teaching" or some "lesson" is not it! Read the book again. You missed its most important message.

Half the world justifies its current dissatisfaction (and its dysfunction) by rationalizing that "there must be something I am supposed to 'learn' here." There is nothing to learn. There is only acting on what one already knows. That is, acting in truth. What I call, living truth, rather than living a lie. Terry Cole-Whittaker gave me a plaque once, which said: "Dear Neale, you are one of the courageous ones—someone who has chosen to make a life, rather than a living." I am very proud of that plaque. If you want to stay in your job, because you think you need the money, or whatever, for heaven's sake, stay in it, but don't stay in it because you feel you have to in order to pick up some cosmic lesson the corporate community has yet to teach you!

Let me comment more on "why can't I do what I really love to do in this world and still make a living?" The posture you have struck in order to reconcile your outer experience with your inner reality is the rationalization used by every person since time began to justify remaining in a dysfunctional or unhappy situation: we have "lessons to learn" and we must not shy away from learning them. You might do well to consider the possibility that you have nothing to learn, and have only to demonstrate what you already know on this subject. *CWG* teaches that life is not a school, but an arena within which you have the opportunity to be and to experience Who and What You Are.

Now clearly what you are not is a member of the corporate world. You can always tell you are not something when your gut disagrees. You know it in your gut when a thing is not true for you. You can fool your mind, but you cannot fool your stomach. Isn't that amazing? What's even more amazing is how often we fail to listen to this internal guidance system. Many people spend half their lives doing things they can't stomach. Why? Because somehow they think they're supposed to. It's all part of the plan. Or they made a promise. Or they're learning a life lesson.

Perhaps it is time you disabused yourself of such notions. There is no "plan." The first "promise" you must keep is your promise to your self. And you already know what you imagine you are trying to learn. Therefore, you are doing what you are doing, and suffering all the unhappiness and discontent you are suffering, for nothing.

When things in business don't seem to turn out the way you asked for them to, what has happened is that you have confused "doingness" with "beingness," and therein seen failure. Let me just state a principle here which I believe I can reduce to one sentence: It is from beingness that doingness springs, not the other way around. In other words, let's say you feel you are a writer. You would really be happy if you could "do" the thing called "write." It could be poetry, prose, novels, whatever. You just want to write. I believe this is part of what you communicated to me. But you can't "do" that, because you're "caught in the corporate world," or whatever the particular "trap" seems to be that you are in. So you can't write for a living, and therefore you are not "being" the thing called "happy."

The above paradigm suggests that "beingness" springs from "doingness," and is dependent upon it. That suggestion is false. In ultimate reality, it is just the other way around. Your "doingness" is a demonstration of what you are now being (consciously or unconsciously).

If you want to "be" the thing called "writer," "be" that thing no matter what you are "doing." In other words, you could be a dishwasher at the Stork Club, and still "be" the thing called "writer." (Half the writers in New York are.) Put another way, writers write to be happy, no matter what they are doing to stay alive! A true writer never stops writing, no matter what he is doing, no matter where she is working, no matter how little time there is.

There is always time to Be Who You Are, because the time to Be Who You Are is all the time.

So write, write, and write some more! Write day and night! On the bus! In the john! During the coffee breaks and after the day is done. Write. Write! Write from the heart of what you think is good and beautiful and wondrous about the world. Or about what you think needs changing, if your prefer. Just write your truth, and write it truthfully. Then send it off. And keep sending it off. Keep writing and keep sending it off! For days. Weeks. Months. Years. Insist to the universe that you are who you are, no matter what it "looks like" you are "doing."

The Euphoria of Finding Self and God

Dearest Neale: Hallelujah! I'm holding your hand in such renewed hopes for the future and wanting to live, in just finishing *Conversations with God, Book 2*. Thank you for sharing, enlightening, fighting for truth, evolvement, reaching our higher selves.

Got to tell you, though, I found myself pushed to no edges, had no areas of "uncomfortabilities," only pure comfort and "supreme validation" like I've never known before. All rang loud and true with what I've known all along. I just didn't have any course of action and must dwell a little longer in deciding what action.

I wanted to die from total frustration and heartache before your books. Everything since 1990 has been experienced half-heartedly. I've been numbing out, wanting to just die, really! Have been a student of and believer in *A Course in Miracles* for some time. This and other paths have afforded me great healing and time to think, study, and evolve. I feel God has held my hand every step of the way, even to your books. Which are so plain, awesome, incredible, validating for what I already knew.

I'm so glad to hear a man give a woman credit and appreciate her value and worth. It gives me great hope for a "new male" on the horizon, such as has never been my experience in society or with men. Nancy must be so proud of you, and not find it cold in your shadow, or lonely.

I guess the bottom line for now is to decide what to do with the new me that wants to live now, thanks to you. I'll need time to clear up some minor health problems that resulted in me wanting

> to die for so long. I'll need time to clear them up now that I want to live. How does one thank a man who has taken her from wanting to die to wanting to live? Awesome changes in me, too, in mostly such "supreme validation." God has your hand and will bless your efforts, I have no doubt. God has blessed us all through you. Much love and appreciation, Kathie, Pocatello, ID.

My dear Kathie, Thank you for your wonderful letter. There is no need to be grateful to me for taking you from "wanting to die" to "wanting to live." This work was done by God. More specifically, by God in you. So thank yourself for bringing yourself to a grander and greater truth and, if it works for you, thank the God of your understanding for playing the role that was played by God.

For God has shown you the light. You have seen the light, Kathie. And it is the light that burns within you, waiting to be shared with others. Do not ever again hide your light under a bushel, Kathie. Rather, let it shine brightly on all those whose lives you touch. In this you will be a bringer of the light, and lives will be enriched because of you, and because of God-in-you, working through you, as you, to re-mind everyone of Who They Really Are.

Your letter contains the euphoria of a person newly born. You have truly been born again. I am grateful to God for this gift to you. Now all I would choose is for you to change what you call your "bottom line." You have said, I guess the bottom line for now is to decide what to do. I would suggest a revision. Make it your next goal to decide what to be. You will find your happiness in "beingness," not in "doingness," and that is an extraordinarily important distinction. If there is anything about this you do not understand, please write to us and order our most remarkable booklet, *Bringers of the Light*, and its companion piece, *Recreating Yourself*. They explain the difference between "beingness" and "doingness," and show you how to apply this wisdom to your daily life.

I am so very happy that the material in the *Conversations with God* books has proven beneficial to you and that you have derived some joy from it. Blesséd be, Kathie. Blesséd be.

Look at What You Are Calling Forth!

Dear Mr. Walsch: I'm 42 years old, an ex-convict, drug addict, and alcoholic. My life has changed because of the 12-step program of AA. I was given your book, *Conversations with God*, and have read it through three times in two weeks. My life is better than ever, although I need to know more clearly how to increase my faith. I have trouble holding any job, even part-time work. I think the word in your book "ascetic" fits me now, because I live in a small apartment with my mother and sleep on the floor and go to AA meetings and work every once in a while. This has gone on for seven months of sobriety and I want to create a job doing something I enjoy and earn money, but all I do is study, read, pray, meditate, and have fellowship with AA. I'm excited about my spiritual progress, but I tell myself I need to break out of this and work. The problem: fear overwhelms me in this area. Help! Love, Gerald, CA.

Dear Gerald, You need to "get up off the floor" and get your life moving again. The problem is threefold, as I see it. First, you think you are alone. Second, you think you can do something wrong. Third, you have no idea what you are trying to do. Let's go at this one at a time.

(1) If you imagine, Gerald, that you have to meet this next challenge—render yourself independent and contribute again to life—by yourself, it will seem a very high mountain to climb, and of course you will be afraid. I would be gripped with fear, too, if I thought I had to move through what is up for me next all alone. But fear, Gerald, is "False Evidence Appearing Real." The truth is, God is always with you. God is your best friend. And God will never leave you, no matter what. Now the trick is to know and understand that, and to call on God whenever the going gets tough, or fear sets in. I'm going to give you that same "magic prayer," Gerald, that I mentioned before and that works so well for me, I can't stand it!

Dear God, help me to understand
that this problem
has already been solved for me.

Can you see the power of that prayer? The beauty of that prayer, Gerald, is that it moves you right into gratitude. No longer are you supplicating, but rather, you are appreciating. You are thanking God for what is already true for you. In this moment of faith you have produced your truth, for it is as all masters have said: As you believe, so will it be done unto you.

(2) You imagine that there is a way you can make a mistake here, and that is what is keeping you from taking the plunge. Yet what if I told you that everything which happens is perfect? There are no mistakes, and you can't mess this up. So go for it! And stop worrying about somehow "doing it wrong." If you take a job and then get fired, that's just what happened. Give yourself a break on this. A lot bigger men than you and I, Gerald, have been fired in their careers. The manager of every baseball team in the country knows he's going to get fired when he takes the job! And most do get fired within three to five years . . . some less! So the moral? If you're afraid of being "fired," stay out of baseball!

The moral is: so what? Get fired. Then get hired again. And get fired again. So what? Sooner or later you'll find a combination of faith and okayness with the result, whatever it is, which will bring you the confidence to go ahead with the game. This is called the life game, and in this game you can't lose. It only looks as if you can, because you, and most of us, keep listening to the opinion of others. Cut it out. Stop it. Be magnificent! And if it takes you three tries, or thirty, stop making yourself "wrong" about that.

The most difficult challenge in life, is to attempt to do something when you don't know what you're attempting to do. By that I mean, you have to be clear as to what you are "up to," what you are attempting to "be" in your life, and you have to set your intentions around that. Then you can achieve your goal. Yet you cannot get to a goal if you have no goal. This may seem ridiculously obvious to you, yet it would amaze you how many people are trying to achieve a goal they have not yet clearly established.

Now, as for your goal, say it first as a statement of beingness. What is it you wish to be in your life? Pick a beingness and go with that. Do you wish to be "loving"? "healthy"? "caring"? "wise"? "strong"? All of the above? When you create a context for your life in which you choose to place yourself, then you find yourself reluctant to step out of that context through the moment-to-moment choices of your life. A person who chooses to be "healthy," for instance, would smoke and drink and eat unhealthy foods only with great reluctance, if ever. A person choosing to be "compassionate," for example, would not pass by an old lady on the street stumbling with a grocery bag without offering to carry it for her. That sort of thing. Our idea about ourselves creates a context within which we begin to live our lives.

What is your idea about yourself, Gerald? What is the grandest version of the greatest vision you ever had about Who You Are? *CWG* constantly invites us to create that. Once you decide, specifically, what that is, then you know what you are doing here, and you will find yourself doing other things less and less. Create a context within which to live your life. Give yourself a purpose, a meaning. Give yourself a mission. Call yourself something! Just call yourself something. Call yourself "brave," or call yourself "courageous." Call yourself "good" or "kind." Call yourself "smart" or "wealthy." Or call yourself all of it, and more. Whatever you call yourself, you call forth for yourself. Now I noticed that in your letter you called yourself an "ex-con, drug addict, alcoholic." Stop it, Gerald. That is not who you are. Stop it. Call yourself something else. What you call yourself calls to you, and you will fly to it like a moth to flame. What you call yourself, you call forth for yourself. What you call yourself, calls to you.

CHAPTER 5

Feelings and Thoughts/Mental Health

If I had to make a list labeled Things That Impact My Life, I would have to put feelings and thoughts right at the top. These two are not the same thing, although not everyone is clear about that.

Thoughts are creative actions. That is not how most people hold them in their awareness, but that is exactly what they are. Every thought creates. That is something which should be scrawled on every bathroom mirror, magneted to every refrigerator, stuck on every bumper, and tattooed on your left wrist.

EVERY THOUGHT CREATES.

What it creates, of course, is up to you. That it creates, however, is not at issue. Even very non-metaphysical, non-spiritual scientists and doctors are now conceding in increasing numbers that your thought about a thing affects your experience of that thing–and may even, at some level, be creating it.

That's an enormous statement. Its implications are staggering.

Feelings are the language of the soul. If you want to know your truth about a thing, look to how you are feeling about it. If you don't know how you're feeling, if you can't seem to identify your innermost truth, just pay attention to your stomach. Take what I call The Tummy Test. Dwell on any subject or dilemma. Now pretend that you have made your decision about it. Act out your choice in your mind. Is your stomach queasy? Calm? Quivering with excitement? Churning with anger? Pay attention. The tummy knows. The tummy never lies.

Feelings and thoughts are among our most valuable tools. They help us to know our present truth, and to create our next one. You can't ask for more than that.

The Gift You Are Looking for Is You

Mr. Walsch: I write to you with the understanding that my letter may not be read by you, and/or if it is, that I may never get a response. Still, I feel there is a small chance I may be wrong, thus resulting in this letter to you. Please allow me to set the stage. Before I read your book, *Conversations with God, Book 1*, it had been in my heart to find one book that could tell me what I wanted to know. You see, I do not read unless I am very interested in the content.

With your book I found hope that what I always knew was true, and could provide a way out of my complex, messed up life. I will not bore you with a long story, only a short question. What do I do when I've already read the book, studied its contents, accepted its details as something I can swallow, but am still in the messed up life I had prior to reading it? I have an advanced level of intelligence, considering my roots. The book indicated that some would read it and it would not help them. I feel pressed down by my life and its failure, which results in not having a positive attitude. Anger inside is tearing me apart. Any suggestions you have will be greatly appreciated! Sincerely, Johnny, SC.

Dear Johnny, Anger is fear announced. Of what are you afraid? Go there first, and heal that. Whatever you put after the word "I" when you speak will become and remain your reality. The word "I" is like a genie in a bottle, Johnny. It is magic, and brings you what follows. Now in your letter you state, I feel pressed down by my life and its failure. Okay, fair enough. That's your truth. That's your thought about yourself. But now I invite you to a new thought. I invite you to affirm another reality for yourself. How about this: I feel uplifted by life and its wonderful gifts! Every day I am uplifted more and more. Every day I receive, and give away, more gifts than ever before. My whole life is a gift that I give to others. A gift of love, and joy, and goodness and kindness; a gift of peace, and hope and goodwill toward everyone. This is my gift to the world, and to myself, no matter what is happening in my life, and I celebrate it grandly. You repeat that statement to yourself five times a day for the next 120 days, Johnny, and then write me and tell me that nothing has changed for you. I dare you.

How to Eliminate Negative Thoughts

Dear Neale: I have read your books, listened to your tapes, and read your booklets, and I thank you for passing along this vital information to all of us. My question concerns those negative, ugly thoughts that just "pop" up in my mind. Those thoughts/opinions/reactions that do not reflect the person I have chosen to be. Before your book, I wondered if the "devil" was putting those evil thoughts into my head. Now I am reassured that there is no Satan, but I would like to eliminate these negative thoughts. I am not referring to our self-talk during introspection. Also, if God speaks to us through our imagination, are bad thoughts/daydreams coming from Him or me? Kelly, St. Louis, MO.

Dear Kelly, Negative thoughts are always based in fear. They seldom have anything to do with reality. They are nothing more than announcements of that of which we are afraid, and that of which we are afraid is seldom threatening us in the present moment.

All negativity is fear announced. That is true of all anger as well. Negativity appears when there is somewhat we want that we do not have, or something we have that we do not want. Eliminating negativity is the challenge. We can do it by simply wanting whatever we now have, and not wanting anything we do not now have. You may think that this is "easier said than done," yet I assure you that it isn't nearly as difficult as you think.

Wanting what you now have is simply a matter of choosing exactly what is on your plate right now. Even if that is something you would ordinarily call negative. Choose it anyway. Because you cannot let go of it, you cannot get rid of it, until you are holding it in your hand. What you resist persists. Only what you look at, and own, and call yours, can you discard.

Not wanting what you do not have is also easy. It is what was trying to be taught by the commandment, "Thou shalt not covet thy neighbor's wife" or "thy neighbor's goods." The reason this injunction has been created by most religions (although not by God, as *CWG* carefully explains) is not because to covet is evil. It is simply not mentally healthy. It creates negativity. So, if you want to eliminate negative thoughts, Kelly, simply want not. Choose what you have. And give to others that which you would wish for yourself. Overnight your life will change.

To your next question, Kelly, what you call "bad thoughts" or daydreams are nothing more than your fears. They are not coming to you from God, since God fears nothing. God speaks to you through your imagination, but you speak to yourself through that device as well. And believe me, you can imagine anything. Including the wildest things to be afraid of. So cut it out. I mean that. Just cut it out. Stop it. Don't do that anymore.

How to stop having fears? Easy. Just remember that God is your best friend.

One morning I was watching Rev. Robert Schuller deliver another one of his wonderful sermons on his nationally televised "Hour of Power." He was talking about just this subject, and he said he has a foolproof way of pushing back fear. Bob had recently had a heart attack, and people had written him and said, "Weren't you afraid?" And Bob Schuller answered, "No. Never." How could he have done that? How could he have never gone into fear or negativity? "Simple," he said. "I used my magic wand." That "magic wand," he said, is the 23rd Psalm. Specifically, the last line, which the reverend said he repeated to himself countless times, always to his great comfort.

The line in question? "Surely, goodness and mercy shall follow me all the days of my life, and I will dwell in the house of the Lord forever." Now that is something you either believe or you don't. In my case, I believe it implicitly. In Bob's case, too. I have this idea that God is always on my side. Always aware of what I need. Always preparing the best outcome for me. Even if that is death. You see, that's what Rev. Robert Schuller knew. He knew that even if he died, it would be the right and perfect outcome, and that nothing bad would happen to him. Now when you no longer have any fear of death, you no longer have any fear of life. And that is a great release. It produces nothing but positive outcomes. Norman Vincent Peale's *The Power of Positive Thinking* is a book I highly recommend everyone read; also, James Allen's *As a Man Thinketh*.

Something Is Making Me Feel Trapped

Dear Neale: I went to see you speak. It was a Sunday night and a rather small and intimate setting and everything you spoke of touched my heart intensely. At one point I found myself crying, and I could not stop until this lady sitting next to me, whom I had never met before, hugged me and told me that it would be all right. I did not know why I was crying.

I feel as though my soul has been touched, that my "wings" are ready to fly, but something is making me feel trapped. I cannot seem to get motivated to do the things that I am feeling I should do. I had an intense spiritual experience about three weeks ago. I felt as though I had finally awakened from a deep sleep or comatose state, and literally could not go back to sleep for five days. I was up all night reading *CWG 3*, chatting to people on the Internet, cleaning, etc. Although I felt somewhat tired, I experienced an intense connection with anyone with whom I came into contact, from the lady at the post office to the receptionist at the doctor's office to everyone that I came near. I was also experiencing some health problems during this period, but mentally, emotionally and spititually I felt incredible! I thought that maybe this is what it feels like right before you are ready to die.

Then, just as suddenly as it came, this feeling was gone after a full night's sleep and finding out from a doctor that I am extremely healthy. I have tried to produce this awesome feeling of love and great desire to feel joy in myself and others again. I pray and meditate that I can feel that much love in my heart on a regular basis. Instead, I feel a lot of cynicism, I am critical of others, somewhat lost, and a little angry at times. I try so hard to be a nice person, to just "be" love, but I can't. How can I break through and what do you think is holding me back? Why can't I just fly the way my soul desires to? I pray that you may have an answer for me. Thank you so much, Lois, Cooper City, FL.

Dear Lois, It is very natural to go through these experiences during a period of intense spiritual growth. The moment you declare yourself to be anything, everything unlike it will come into your life. This is the law of opposites, and it is explained in great detail in *CWG*. So do not make yourself "wrong," or work hard to experience something else. Have the experience you are having. That is one of the greatest pieces of advice I could ever give anyone.

Have the experience you are having. Remember that what you resist, persists. Then, should you choose to recreate your self in a new way, decide what that looks like, and what you wish to experience in yourself, give to another. Do what it takes to make others feel they are "nice people," and that they are "love." Provide for another the experience you wish to provide for yourself.

Forget about yourself completely. Your life is not about you, and it never was. It is about the other. Always the other. Yet here is the divine dichotomy. As you provide for another, you produce the experience for yourself. And that is because there is no one else in the room. In truth, we are all one, and that which you do for another, you do for yourself. This is why the greatest teaching ever given is: Do unto others as you would have it done unto you.

Starting Over with CWG

Dear Neale: Several years ago I said to my wife, "Why are people so concerned with money?" She packed and left me. Well, there is more to it than that, but the pain was tremendous. I was left alone, just me and *CWG 1.* Out of the darkness, my personal darkness, shone a beacon, one I really did not understand. For my guilt and misery and pain were no longer justified. I could start this moment and live, and know that I have not hurt anyone, and relieve others' pain, in that I have a new life, every moment, and a new chance, to raise another out of despair with a kind word, a smile, a quote from your books, to raise a soul to love, and joy.

What you have done for me, I do for others. I "Be" what God has asked, through you, for me to be, for the sake of helping others to "Be." I found myself, buried deep in the mire, and I knew that if only, I could reach one, just one, that one person may then pass a smile on to another, and lo! half the world would be changed.

I burn with a passion to love, and to tell of God's love, and to stand strong, as eyes watch for others to build their strength, and conquer. My life has changed, I can never go back. Look what you have done, Neale Donald Walsch. "See" what you've done for my soul, and others that I may reach, and feel good, very good. Love and light, Marc G., on the Internet.

Dear Marc, Thank you for your very moving letter. You have given us a wonderful example of how to live the message of this extraordinary trilogy.

Will God "Get" Me for What I'm Thinking?

Dear Neale Donald Walsch: I believe that learning to become sovereign human beings, owning our own thoughts, taking complete ownership of everything we have in our lives, takes time and effort, and a great deal of courage. I am sometimes worried that God will be upset with what I am thinking, especially when I question what I am told God has said to the human race. For this reason, I have been worried about reading your book (which does violate, after all, much of our scriptural teaching) and thinking the thoughts that it invites. Comments? Shelly, Portland, OR.

Will God Be Mad at My Thoughts?

Dear Neale: I loved your book! But how brave you are! How do you think such things? Aren't you afraid God will be mad at you? All my life I was told that God hears every thought, sees every act, and that if we think an impure thought, or a thought of blasphemy, we will be punished. As a child brought up in the Roman Catholic Church, I can remember being told that I must never attend a service in a church of another denomination, that this was a "sin." Now here you are in your book writing a whole bunch of things which would be called a "sin"—including that there is no such thing as the Ten Commandments!! Aren't you scared? Sincerely, BW, Milwaukee, WI.

Dear Shelly and BW, If God did not want you to think, God would not have made it possible for you to do so. Do not worry about offending God. That is something you cannot do. The only beings in the universe who can be offended are beings who have an ego investment in what's being said about them, in what's being done. God has no such ego investment. God is above ego. So far above ego that you cannot even imagine it. God resides in pure love. That's it. End of sentence. And pure love would never punish you or anyone else for wondering, for thinking, for exploring any point of view. Life is meant for the living, for the creating, for the experiencing, not for abjectly obeying someone else's rules and remaining within someone else's constructions or ideas (certainly not God's) about what is right and wrong. Keep thinking your own thoughts. God would have it no other way.

I'm certainly not afraid of God. About other human beings, I'm not so sure. I saw a bumper sticker recently that caused me to think. It said, God, save me from your people. But no, I am not concerned about, or afraid of, God's "reaction" to what I may be thinking or saying.

Warding Off Discouragement and Disappointment

> Dear Neale: How do you stop from being discouraged? I mean, in life things happen which discourage me. Or disappoint me. And I find that the most difficult thing to do is to not get discouraged, or to not be disappointed. How do you do it? I heard you talk in a very large filled auditorium, and you seemed like such an incredibly positive person. Even afterward, as you signed autographs for two hundred people, I watched you smiling and being very personal with everyone, even taking the time to speak quietly with several of them who I could tell had come to you with problems or very serious questions. How do you manage to stay so positive? Jay, Milwaukee, WI.

Dear Jay, The answer is, of course, that I don't. There are times when I have to fight off the "blues" and work to "stay on top of it." I will grant you that those times are fewer and farther between these days, but they still arise, and when they do, I do not try to step around them, but rather, move through them as honestly and as vulnerably as I can.

I think vulnerability and transparency are the keys, Jay. You have to be willing to be vulnerable, to be open, to be totally honest about what you're feeling. Trying to hide it or mask it or deny it will only lead to more—and more serious—emotional trouble. Also, at moments like this I go back to the truth about myself; to all the good things I know about who I am. Finally, Jay, I keep my channels of communication open to God. I talk to God every day.

I try to meditate whenever I can. It's pretty hard to become too discouraged for too long about anything if you're in touch with the deepest part of yourself, which is where peace and understanding, wisdom and clarity reside. And it is doubly difficult to stay "blue" if you've been talking regularly with God. So if I am positive more of the time than not (and I am), it is because I try to pay attention to the life of my soul, not just my body.

Daily meditation—I know of no better remedy to ward off attacks of self-doubt, or bouts of worry, fear or discouragement than daily meditation. Living without expectations: that's another great way to avoid disappointment.

Two Magic Tools with which to End Depression

Dear Neale: In a nutshell, I've been having tremendous heartache in my personal life, and knowing everything that I know, I didn't expect it to get the better of me the way it did. I understand about "choice," and everything that we do ahead of time to set things up for ourselves. But maybe I don't understand as much as I think I do, because when things get tough, the words come out of my mouth, but I am still so sad that I don't know how to come out of it. And that in itself can be frightening.

My mother (who happens to be my best friend) told me about your book. Reading your material, I felt such love in my heart. That's what I call it when something feels right with me. If I get that heart-swell,"I'm going to burst," feeling—as if I'm going to cry because I'm so filled with emotion—I recognize this feeling as love in the purest sense.

I think you are a wonderful, clear writer, and send you all the love in my being for waking me up to the things I have merely forgotten for a while. I hope all people get the opportunity to feel the way I feel right now. It's like taking a deep, cleansing breath after being under water for an hour! StephJ by E-mail.

Dear Stephanie, Thank you for the very nice words. I am very touched that you would say those things to me, and I want you to know that I do not take them for granted.

Let me address your first paragraph: When a person gets into a deep depression, it can be difficult to "come out of it," there's no question about that. And no amount of "knowingness" surrounding the so-called "truths of life" makes it any easier. So the first thing I want to tell you, Stephanie, is that your experience is common. There are times when many of us pay lip service to what we think we "know" about a thing—to the spiritual principles of which we think we are aware—all the while continuing to act as if we know nothing.

There are two ways I know of to quickly break out of sadness, Stephanie. The first is a "process" I learned from a wonderful teacher of mine many years ago. The second is a "way-of-life" kind of thing. Let's look at the first. If you are plagued with recurring sadness or depression, go out and buy yourself one of those little spiral-bound pocket notebooks, and carry it with you wherever you go. The moment you feel yourself beset by sadness, or sinking into a depression, take out the notebook and write down the time and day, and a brief description of exactly what you were doing when the sadness hit. Then, next to that, put down a number from one to ten, indicating just how sad or depressed you are. Take a measurement. Are you as depressed as you have ever been? That's an 8 or a 9. Are you more depressed than you have ever been? That's a 10. Are you a little sad, but not all that depressed? That may be a 6, and so on.

Now, wait 30 minutes and take a measurement again. In other words, put the notebook away, just go about doing whatever you were doing (even if it's sitting there staring at the wall, doing nothing), and wait for half an hour to pass. If you've got one of those watches with a timer and an alarm on it, so much the better. In any event, find a way to notice when 30 minutes have passed. Then, take out the notebook and write down exactly what you have been. Look to see how sad or depressed you are now, and write down a number between one and ten which reflects that. Put the notebook away and go on with your life.

Wait twenty minutes this time, then take the notebook out once more and do the process all over again. Wait fifteen minutes this time, and do it yet one more time. Now do this every fifteen minutes for the entire hour which follows, unless, of course, you find that there is no more reason to do it, given that your "score" has dropped so low! What you will discover through this process is that it is virtually impossible to stay depressed while you are watching yourself do it. (The same thing can be said of anger, incidentally.) *CWG* puts this nicely when it says, "What you resist persists. What you look at disappears."

The second little tool I want to give you is a life-style change. The next time you are "so sad" that you "don't know how to get out of it" find someone else who is just as sad. This should not be difficult, given the state the world is in today. You will not have to look very far. Make it your business to give that person exactly what you want for yourself. That is, do whatever it takes to bring that person out of their sadness. You will find that you have uncovered an extraordinary secret. Whatever you wish to experience yourself, be the source of it for another.

It is a fool-proof formula, Stephanie, and it works with everything. If you want more companionship in your life, find someone else who wants more companionship, and give him that. You will find you have given it to yourself as well. If you want more love in your life, find someone else who wants more love in their life and give them that. You will find you have given it to yourself as well. If you want more patience, understanding, tolerance, even money, in your life, give those things to someone who also wants more in his life and you will see your own supply increase. If you want more sex in your life . . . . Well you get the picture! Are you smiling? You should be smiling now, Stephanie. We're being pretty clever here.

So there you have them. Two of the best tools I have ever discovered for ending loneliness, sadness, disunity, or depression. Six magic words that could change your life. Do not resist. Be the source.

What Is the "Thought Behind the Thought Behind the Thought"?

Hi. Please elaborate regarding "the thought behind the thought behind the thought." And, isn't there a workable alternative to "free will"? Something that would curb a lot of grief? But if there is no "good or bad" or "right or wrong," maybe grief is a judgment or a misnomer? Tom, Edmonton, Alberta, Canada.

Hello, Tom. The "thought behind the thought behind the thought" is what *CWG* calls the "sponsoring thought." That is, it is the last layer of onion skin. Let me give you an example. Often in our five-day intensive retreats someone in the room announces a fear. Sometimes that's my cue to move into a process which uncovers that person's sponsoring thought, or the "thought behind the thought behind the thought." I will ask, "What are you afraid would happen if so and so actually occurred?" And he or she will tell me. Then I will ask, "And what are you afraid will happen if that happens?" And he or she will tell me. And then I will ask, "And what do you think will happen then?" Once more the person will tell me, and once more I will ask, until we get to the bottom of it—until we get to the sponsoring thought. And that is what the person is really afraid of.

These are the controlling thoughts in our lives, Tom. These are the thoughts we've brought with us into the present moment. They often tear away at the present moment, turning it into something it is not.

Now you've asked if there isn't a "workable alternative" to free will. Why in the world would you want there to be? Do you want to live as an automaton? Free of grief, but also free of any choice? I don't think so. Lack of choice is a big price to pay for lack of grief. Your final statement is correct. "Grief" is a judgment. It is a decision we make that something is not all right with us. When we change our mind, we change our decision, and we put an end to our grief. What can cause us to change our mind—and thus our experience—is a change in our perspective. That is what *Conversations with God* has done for many people. It has brought hundreds of thousands of people to a new perspective. In this, it is changing the world.

You may find it useful to read the *CWG Guidebook*. It is the most wonderful, detailed explanation of what's in *CWG Book 1*. It takes you through the text chapter by chapter, concept by concept, with assignments, exercises and experiments that allow you to explore your inner depths and experience the wisdoms just as you would in a full-fledged retreat. If you haven't already gotten the *Guidebook* and begun working with it, I encourage you to do so, Tom. It could change your life, and get rid of a lot of the "grief."

The Difference Between Feelings and Emotions

Dear Neale: I'd like to begin a dialogue about some aspects of the book that resonated with me. There's so much, of course, and I'm only a few pages into the book. Yes, I actually went back to the beginning and started with the first page after doing my open-it-anywhere-to see-how-I-connect test. Every page contains a number of gems that each could be the subject of a lengthy dialogue.

What jumps out at me now is the subject of "feelings" and how they are so much more an accurate communicator of truth than is the spoken word. As a society, of course, we've been taught to second-guess or, worse, deny our feelings. The paradigm by which we've run our lives and our organizations has (to date) validated left-brain, linear, if-I-can't-see/touch/taste/hear/smell-it-it-must-not-be-real thinking and invalidated "touchy-feely," "soft," intuitive stuff. Which is why white males over 45 still run the majority of businesses in this country. But that is slowly changing. I do believe that feminine principles will become more generally accepted in business, soon. Of course, this has been my wish for some time, so it's hard for me to be objective about this.

Oprah recently ran a show where she had two authors who helped explain how parents can teach their children problem-solving and conflict resolution skills by helping them first to get in touch with their feelings and then exploring alternative reactions. It was great. I've also been listening recently to some tapes that emphasize the primacy of feelings over words for both communications and self-understanding. So you can imagine that when I got to page eight of *CWG*, I got that this is something I need to pay more attention to.

I agree with the book/God. (Sounds sort of silly to be saying that.) My question of you/source/God: Some people distinguish between emotions and feelings while others use the terms interchangeably. What's your perspective? What's the difference? Carol M.

Dear Carol, You've asked a key question. Nice going! I had the same question when this material first came through. I'm now clear on the difference. As I understand it, feelings are what we feel, and emotion is what can happen in and with our bodies as a result of what we feel. Example: You feel fear and the emotion called "scared" sears through your body. Your stomach may tie up in knots. You may start to tremble. You may even do something stupid.

Emotion seems to be a shorthand for "energy in motion"—that is, stuff we do with our bodies. Often we "display our emotions." That is, the body does stuff (we jump for joy!) that telegraphs to the world what we are feeling. There's a very soft difference here, I know. To me, it seems that an "emotion" is what our mind does (and then tells the body to do) about what we feel. We "feel" a thing, and then get "all emotional." That is, full of energy in motion. Feelings are always true. Emotions can sometimes be false.

Want an example? Try this: Crying is often an emotional response to the feeling of loss. It is also often an emotional reponse to the feeling of great relief. Or enormous and sudden joy. Now a person standing across the street, watching a person cry, has no idea what's going on. He knows not what the person is feeling, only that the person is being very emotional about it. Feelings are our deepest truth. Emotions are the mental and physical manifestations of feelings after the mind gets through with its endless (and rapid) analysis of them.

The mind doesn't know a darn thing about feelings. Only the heart does. The mind thinks it knows, of course, and so comes up with all sorts of responses. Some of them are actually in accordance with our true feelings. Some are not. At moments of great decision and choice in our lives, we have to therefore go deep inside and look at our true feelings about a thing. Therein is our truth, not in our emotions.

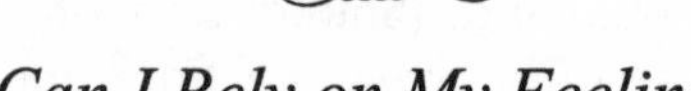

Can I Rely on My Feelings?

Dear Mr. Walsch: I am a senior (72) and a widow. Your book has helped me realize many things. I have one question: Should I, or should I not, go by feelings? Irene, London, Ontario, Canada.

Dear Irene, Yes. Feelings are the language of the soul. If you want to know your "true" truth about a thing, look to how you are feeling. Then trust that your feelings are real. Your mind will try to talk you out of this. Your mind will say that your feelings are merely your emotions, and that you should never trust them when making an important decision. In truth, it is exactly the opposite. Trust your feelings always. You want to know how you are feeling? Listen to your stomach. I have a phrase I use around here. "What does your stomach say?" If your stomach is queasy, that could mean adventure. Don't necessarily turn away from that. If your stomach hurts, say no. If your stomach is peaceful, restful, definitely say yes. Remember, the tummy knows.

What Are These Feelings?

Dear Neale: On page eighty-two of *CWG Book 2*, God says, "When you think of someone, if that person is sensitive enough, he or she can feel it." I am one of those people who can feel it. I was very relieved to read those words, as never before have I had an explanation for the "feelings." If I ever tried to talk to anyone about it I would usually just get a blank stare. Now I know I'm not crazy, just "sensitive." I am looking for more information about this, or someone to talk to about these "feelings."

When the feelings come, I feel very alone. I know that I should not feel lonely, if what I'm feeling is someone else's energy. I keep thinking this should help me feel more connected to other people, but I don't. It's like being the only person who can see a beautiful sunset. It's overwhelming at times. I need to share the sunset with someone, talk about the colors, know someone else can see it.

When I first read page eighty-two, I thought at least I knew what was going on with me, and there was some comfort with that. But now, the feelings are getting more intense. The closer to God I get, the stronger the energy is. I am very thankful for any help you can give me with this. It is not serving me to ignore this. And although I try to just go with the flow and accept this as a part of who I am and find comfort in at least knowing what it is, I can't help but feel there is more to this. With thanks, Debra, Kimberley, BC, Canada.

Hi, Debra! Good news! What you are feeling is love. I hate to be so simplistic, but that's what it is. It is the energy of life, and that is pure love. You feel it coming from other people, even when they are not consciously intending to send it. You are receiving the essence of Who They Are, which is love. You say, "The closer to God I get, the stronger the energy is." Exactly, Debra. Everyone who has ever experienced real closeness with God has known the phenomenon you are talking about. It's like being in love with the whole world, and it is "overwhelming at times." Of course it will not serve you to ignore it. That would be like ignoring the very essence of Who You Are.

There is "more to this." Yet the reason that you are not feeling more connected to other people—much less experiencing the "more to this" that there is—is that you have not really "locked in" to the second half of this process, which *CWG* describes as Synergistic Energy Exchange. That second half is the part of the process by which you deliberately and consciously send out the energy, and the feeling you are now receiving. This energy can be intentionally sent. Send it to all people everywhere, and to all those whose lives you touch. Do this continually and consistently for the next few months, and very soon you will find that you are feeling more connected to others. Then the whole riddle will be solved, and what was once a mystery will turn into the pure joy of experiencing Who You Really Are.

Will I Ever Be Able to Feel Loved?

Dear Mr. Walsch: In *CWG 1*, Chapter 1, you talk about the laws of attraction, the second being that you will "attract what you fear." I have noticed that one of the core or sponsoring thoughts which I have had for some time was not that I could not love or be loved, but that I would not be able to feel or experience it. So far that second law has been working quite well for some forty-nine years. How do you rid yourself of this type of sponsoring thought? My second question: I am not sure this was a learned thought, and if it wasn't, where did it come from? Sincerely, Mike, Camarillo, CA.

Dear Mike, To your second question first. It doesn't matter where the thought came from. Don't waste your time on that. We are inundated with suggestions and data input in a very powerful way every moment of every day. Where the idea came from is unimportant now. Let's get to the larger issue.

The problem here, Mike, is that you are trying to get yourself to forget this core thought that you will never feel or experience love, and that is like trying to not think of a pink elephant. What you resist, persists. The very act of trying to stop this experience helps to put it there. Don't focus on yourself in love relationships. Don't worry about your experience. Worry about the experience of others. Remember this fundamental law: What you give, you receive. That which you would choose for yourself, choose for another. Indeed, be the source of it.

Do you think that your life would change in any way if you spent all of your energy in relationship doing whatever it takes to make sure that your significant other feels and experiences love? You may say, "Hey, I'm doing that right now," and if you are, great! Now redouble your efforts. And not just with your romantic other, but with everyone, all the time. Do this for six months and I'm betting you will override your sponsoring thought that you cannot experience or feel loving and being loved.

About a Child "Born Handicapped"

Dear Neale Donald: Thank you! Thank you! Thank you for writing *Conversations with God*. In a sense, I envy you, wishing to "heaven" I'd authored it, instead of yourself; but whatever, if we are "all one," then I really did have a hand in getting it channeled, created, and into print. I just wish I also had a share of its royalties!

You did a marvelous job of writing down much of my belief system, and it was confirming for me to see it in print! I've never "fit in" with my relatives, who tried to save me when I never felt "lost," and always judged me ill for not believing in "hell," the devil, or even right and wrong! Well, whew! It's good to know I'm not the only one who thinks the way I do. Seems "God" also shares the same views! So, thank you for getting the message into print.

> I've always said when I died I'd have a list of questions to present to "God" if I could even find Her. You beat me to it with most of them. I still have a few. How come my kid was born handicapped? I wonder if my frustration with her challenging behavior is out of "fear," but fear of what? When I'm tired (physically, emotionally, etc.), there's neither love nor fear present, just a lack of energy, i.e., I'm tired! Peace and power, Avalon B.

Dear Avalon, Thank you for your letter and kind words. The question as to why some people come into this world with physical challenges is addressed in *Conversations with God*. We do not know the agenda of the soul, but the admonition is not to judge, nor call it wrong, but simply to see it as a blessed experience in the life of that soul.

It is the purpose of life to bring us all every experience that the human adventure allows. The up and down of it, the left and right of it, the male and female of it, the here and there of it. The soul will not rest until it has had the sum and substance of the human experience, the totality of its possibilities. Perhaps it is for this reason that in some lifetimes souls enter a body that is what you have called "handicapped."

You ask about frustration, and I tell you that all frustration within the human experience finds its origin in fear. I grant you that frustration is a very mild form of fear, yet it is fear nonetheless. The one who comes from love and only from love never experiences frustration. Frustration is, of course, a fear that what we are doing cannot be continued; that we will run out of energy; that it is all "just too much"; that we have reached the end of the line. Frustration is our announcement to ourselves that we need to move back into love in order to find our "center" once again.

You say that in your moments of frustration there is neither love nor fear present, just a loss of energy; in other words, you are simply tired. "Tired" is not a condition which is known in the presence of love. Lovers who are deeply in love have been known to stay up day and night for long periods of time, simply being with each other. It is when love changes to fear that energy rapidly drains, leaving the system of the human body.

Don't berate yourself about this, or beat yourself up. It is a normal human experience and not something to be ashamed of. In your moments of frustration, simply notice that you are frustrated, do whatever it takes to move through that experience in a way which benefits and serves you, and then go on with your life without self recrimination. Of course you are frustrated. There is much to be done, there is a great deal of challenge in the doing of it, and most people would be frustrated. Don't look too deeply into this. There is no "mystery" here. There is only what is obvious. And it is all perfectly all right.

CHAPTER 6

Relationships and Sexuality

Did you have a wonderful Valentine's Day this year? February is the month of love, the time when we set aside a special day to do special things with and for that special someone. Wouldn't it be great if we could all have a special someone? Well, we do. We have our selves. Your special someone is you. Yes, you.

I know, I know. That may sound trite and overworked, but it is true. What I've discovered about life, what I've observed after watching myself and thousands of people through the years, is that the hardest person for us to acknowledge and truly love is ourself. Yet it is also profoundly true that until we can truly love ourselves, we can never truly love another. Until we can totally accept ourselves, we can never totally accept another. Until we can completely trust and absolutely know ourselves, we can never completely trust and absolutely know another. We cannot give anyone what we are unwilling to give ourselves. And no one can receive from us what we are unwilling to receive.

Conversations with God teaches that the reason we cannot believe in the unconditional love of God is that we cannot imagine unconditional love in ourselves. Yet unconditional love is the only love there is. Everything else is false, counterfeit, fake, less than the real thing, and so, not the real thing. When you love someone conditionally, you love not at all, but merely trade. I'll trade you this if you'll trade me that. And on Valentine's Day, you can send a card which says I trade you very much. Yet loving is not trading. Loving is loving, and there is no other thing like it. Love is complete unto itself, and requires nothing else.

A few years ago when I was doing metaphysical counseling, a woman came to me lamenting the state of her relationship. After listening to her go on for a while about how bad things had become, I asked her a simple question.

"When was the last time you brought your husband flowers?"

"What?" she responded, a bit startled.

"When was the last time you brought your husband flowers?" I repeated.

"Uh, well . . . I don't think I ever did that."

"Would you like to?"

"Huh?"

"Do you love your husband?"

"Yes."

"Would you like to take him flowers?"

"You know, I think I would. That would be nice. I just never thought of it. I mean, giving a man flowers."

"Try it. Take him a bunch of flowers tonight."

"Well . . . okay," she stammered, not knowing what to really make of the suggestion. "Do you think that will work?"

"Depends on what you are trying to do," I replied.

The next day there came a pounding at my front door. The "flower lady" was on the other side, and she was not very happy.

"You said to take my husband flowers!" she cried, bursting past me. "Well, I did, and all he said was, 'Hmmph. What am I supposed to do with these?'"

"I see," said I. "And so?"

"So it was a rotten idea!"

"How so?"

"How so? How so? I just told you what he said! Is that your idea of things going well?"

"You're not pleased with his response."

"Of course not! Would you be pleased with that response from your wife?"

"I don't give flowers to my wife to get a response."

"What's that supposed to mean?"

"I give flowers to my wife to give flowers to my wife. The flowers are an expression of how I feel about her, not of how I want her to feel about me. The action is therefore complete in the giving. I don't care what she does with them. I don't care what she says about them."

"Well, then you're crazy," the lady in my foyer blurted.

"Perhaps," I smiled, "but I'm not sad."

When we do something for another, we should do it for the response it produces in us, not the response we hope it will produce in the other. And the response in us should be a true experience of Who We Are, or we shouldn't do it.

That is the only reason to do anything. The only purpose of any thought, word or action should be to bring ourselves a true experience of Who We Really Are—and who we choose to be.

And when we make the highest choice, when we choose to be our grandest self, then the blessing is spread to all those whose lives we touch; we see that our best interest is their best interest; we come from an understanding that all of us are one. And so, self interest becomes group interest, and putting oneself first in all things produces the highest good for everyone when what originates every action is a thought that the highest good we can do for ourselves is that which produces the highest good for another.

What would cause us to construct such a reality? What could cause us to hold such a thought? A clear understanding of Who and What We Really Are.

All of this came up for me on Valentine's Day this year as I reviewed the many years of what I consider, in my own value system, the mistakes and misdeeds which marked my own prior relationship experience. I didn't seem to know how to pull out of that. I seemed to be in some kind of never ending cycle of dysfunction. Then this extraordinary writing called *Conversations with God* came, and I learned more about relationships in one sitting than I had in 25 years of trying so hard to make them work. That was the problem, of course. I was trying to make relationships work, and I should have been trying to make them joy.

So now, I'm assessing where I've been and where I want to go with regard to my loving relationships. I'm using this as a time to rededicate myself to living the grandest version of the greatest vision I ever held about myself. I only wish I could have come to this years ago. I could have avoided hurting a lot of people. And how has it been for you? Are you, too, ready now to reassess and reevaluate how it has been, and will be, in relationship for you, and for those who have been with you?

Playful, Joyful Sex: a Cause for Red Flags?

Dear Neale: There was one part of *CWG* where I saw red flags going up, and those were the things said about "going out and enjoying your play thing." When you look at society and the sad state of affairs that using sex without deep love and commitment has manifested in heartache, violence, and despair, it was hard to figure the reasoning there. I was a pregnant teenager at seventeen, at eighteen a mother. This fall, that child's father and I will have been married fifty years. We are among the blessed. The story could have turned out to be another American tragedy. The poor souls who come to earth via the one-night stand and grow up bitter and hungry for a home and love, have changed their outlook on life completely. Can you comment on this subject? Marian, Astoria, OR.

Dear Marian, I do not believe that *CWG* in any way indicates that sex should be used without a sense of responsibility. It merely states that it should also not be used without a sense of celebration and joy and, yes, playfulness, as life itself is best approached with a good bit of healthy playfulness.

Marian, the point I see the book making is that so many people are embarrassed or ashamed about the experience of sex, and there is no need to be either. I thought God made a telling point when She observed that we think nothing of putting raw violence and wanton killing on our movie and TV screens, but become ardently self-righteous at the appearance of joyful sex. In this we may very well have our priorities a little backwards. It is when we allow society to think better of making love than of making war that we will have at last evolved as a species.

God's invitation in *CWG* to celebrate our sexuality is, I think, a wonderful idea. I think we should enjoy the hell out of sex. And I mean that literally. I think we should enjoy the hell right out of it.

Now About This Sex Thing

Dear Neale: I love the *CWG* books. They have arrived at a critical time in my life. Everyone should read them and get whatever they can out of them. However, the sex part disturbed me. If my interpretation of God's words (in *CWG*) about relationships is true, then have we no need for marriage? After all, when the relationship no longer reflects the true statement of who I am, is it time to move on? Moreover, with this celebration of life through sexual energy, surely we will be having extramarital affairs? How does this work? I am saddened by this thought that marriage is no longer needed. Then why would we have children? How do we raise them in the warmth of a family? May I ask what your background is, from a career perspective? Do you earn enough money to lead a comfortable life now, as well as your marriage to this wonderful lady. How does your marriage work in relation to the question above? Sherli, Woodland Hills, CA.

Sherli, I don't believe that *Conversations with God* suggests, or even infers, that we have no further need for marriage. *CWG* says that every decision, every choice, every thought, word and action is an opportunity to consciously create, and a statement of, Who We Really Are. We are recreating ourselves anew in every single moment of now. You interpret *CWG* to be saying that "when the relationship no longer reflects the true statement of who I am, it is time to move on," yet what is threatening or feels "wrong," about that? If your relationship no longer reflects who you really are, is it not time to at least question what you are doing there? Is it your understanding that life requires you to stay married, even if the marriage is killing you? Even if the marriage is causing you to give up your very self, and your highest ideas about who you really are?

Nobody is saying anything here about leaving a marriage willy-nilly, casually, at the drop of a hat. We are talking about relationships that are in so much trouble that one person or the other has completely lost touch with their sense of themselves. They have surrendered so much to the relationship, and to keeping it together (often, just as you suggest they should, "for the kids"), that they have surrendered their soul. That is, their deepest experience of themselves. They no longer laugh, they no longer hope, they no longer dream. They live lives of quiet desperation, meeting their commitments, fulfilling their obligations, but never, ever, finding happiness.

It is surprising how many people think that this is what life requires of us. This is what we are supposed to do. For these people, *Conversations with God* upsets the apple cart, because it tosses out all of the assumptions, chief among them, the assumption that God demands this of us.

You talk about raising children in the warmth of a family, but have you ever talked to a child who has been raised in a family where there was no warmth? This produces children who have no warmth. And that produces more children with no warmth, and more dysfunction in marriage, because this is what has been modeled to them as the way things are supposed to be done.

I promise you this. The sins of the father will be visited upon the son, even unto the seventh generation. That is to say, Sherli, deeply dysfunctional marriages produce dysfunctional children, who produce dysfunctional marriages, which produce dysfunctional children, who produce more dysfunctional marriages and more dysfunctional children. You don't think this is true? You think I am exaggerating? Look around you, my dear friend. Just open your eyes and look around you.

None of this is an argument for simply getting up and running every time one's marriage isn't going well. That is not what we are talking about here. But we are talking about being open enough to acknowledge the possibility that sometimes staying in a marriage may be more damaging (to yourself and your children) than leaving it.

As for the open and free celebration of sexual energy leading to affairs, that will only happen if breaking your agreements with your spouse, and having a secret liaison which you know would deeply wound your spouse, is a reflection of Who You Really Are and who you choose to be. If, on the other hand, it is not, then the free and wonderful celebration of your sexual energy will not automatically equate to having affairs, though it might equate to having quite a bit of sex with your spouse!

As to my personal life, yes, I am financially comfortable now, and regarding my relationship with Nancy—she is, indeed, a very wonderful lady—I do not have affairs on the side, if that is your question.

What Is the Meaning of Commitment?

Dear Neale: I was fortunate enough to attend one of your five-day Intensives. Everyone who attends will now have the choice to change their lives and will know how. Thank you. I have a question, and if you find it inappropriate to answer, that is okay.

A gentlemen in his forties has been asked to leave the bedroom he shared with his wife. She was no longer interested in a physical relationship. Divorce was not even an issue, because of our old country club money and societal standards. Eventually, he and his secretary fell in love and were lovers for some twenty years. She was shunned by the city folk for all those years. Eventually the wife died, and the man and his secretary married. Still, the unacceptance towards the secretary was unbelievable. The man has recently died. The secretary has suffered in silence for over twenty years. My question: why is the woman always the adulterer, and not the man? Perhaps you can further address the meaning of the commitment these two shared. My kindest regards to all of your staff, and love to you. Truly, you are a master. Namaste! Min, York, PA.

Dear Min, Most modern society is based on a patriarchal model which says that men can do no wrong and women are the temptresses and the evil ones among us. Religions are based on this patriarchal model, which is why most religions refuse to allow women to become priests, rabbis, or teachers. They are deemed inherently and genetically unworthy. The whole story of, and all the fault behind, the so-called "fall of Adam" has been laid at the feet of the temptress Eve, and the stage was set then and there for each gender to play out its role, as men have ordained them. Prior to the patriarchy, the matriarchy had these roles reversed. So for centuries women held positions of influence and power, and men were merely the chattels and possessions, the ones unworthy to become priestesses or to govern the people.

We are now moving at last into a period when true equality of the sexes will be experienced, and where all this double standard nonsense will finally be brought to an end. As to "the meaning of the commitment these two shared," I would be the wrong one to assign it a meaning. That has been the problem all along. Others keep assigning it their meanings. The only meaning which matters is what the commitment meant to them.

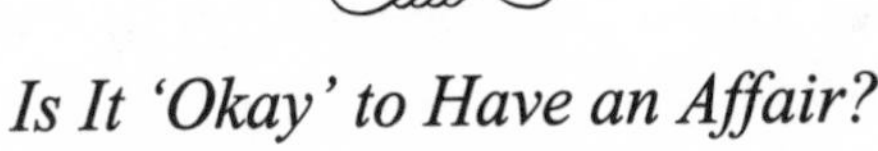

Is It 'Okay' to Have an Affair?

> Dear Neale: For two years I have been searching, trying to understand my life. My husband of 25 years had an affair that devastated me to the point of emotional and physical illness. Your book has been much comfort to me. We continue to try to put our marriage back together. You say, "All of us have many, many soul partners, and that explains why all of us fall in love with many, many different people. Let yourself have that love when you experience it. Let yourself move through the experience itself and embrace it fully and richly." By this, are you advocating that affairs are acceptable? My other question is from page 132 of *CWG Book 1*, where God talks of *ungodly* acts. What might ungodly acts be or what is the definition thereof? You cannot know the importance of your books, or perhaps there are not words to describe the help and comfort they provide. Thank you. Carol, New York, NY.

Carol, To your first question: no, I do not find what you call "affairs" acceptable. Of course, I make no judgments (nor does God) about the behavior of others. But you are asking my opinion here, and my opinion and decision about this is that "affairs" are unacceptable. That is because affairs, by the most popular definition, involve a breaking of a promise, a shattering of a sacred agreement, and the deepest breach of trust.

Whatever experience you "let yourself have" must be had in integrity. That is, if you wish to let yourself love another person other than your spouse, you must first tell your spouse of your decision, so that everyone at the table has five cards. If you have five cards while you are dealing your so-called beloved partner four, then you are way out of integrity, by my lights. Again, this is just my own idea about it. This is how I am making it up in my life. I believe people should be allowed to love everybody, in whatever way is appropriate. What defines an action as appropriate to me is that it is taken in complete integrity. Does that help?

Regarding your second question, an "ungodly act" is any act that speaks a lie about you, that causes you to behave or appear as less than Who You Really Are. In my life these have usually been acts which have been damaging to others—in many cases I knew these would be hurtful to others—and which I undertook anyway, generally in secret.

After 43 Years of Marriage . . . He "Betrayed" Her

Dear Neale: Please help me understand this problem that has come into my life. I have a dreadfully unsealed, shaky feeling. Last March, my husband of 43 years told me about his six-year affair. He traveled several times a month and arranged to stay with her frequently. They had no dirty dishes, no doorbell, and focused on each other's physical and emotional pleasure.

Learning about his betrayal created a devastating emotional crisis. The lying and deceit destroyed my sense of self. It ended life as I knew it, broke my reality of life. My core belief was that he was an honest man. His deceit crushed my world, annihilated me. It was a traumatic shock. I counted on him as I counted on the sun coming up in the East. Adultery is a huge insult. It felt like a death of a piece of me.

I grieve the loss of trust. My trust did not protect me. I cry for that lost piece of myself that believed in him. I was too preoccupied to work, and gave up my job. More abuse. My husband became self-centered, had an inflated ego. Nothing I said mattered. He ignored me and did what he wanted to do. His self-indulgence and self-gratification blinded him. His spending sprees, grandiose plans of financial omnipotence, a "know-it-all" attitude, and unrestrained buying—all of this terrified me.

When we married, he was reliable, stable, honorable, saw things through. I felt I had a safe haven with him. Now, I feel unsafe. How can I respect myself? I have been so passive while he spent our life savings. Will this pain and turmoil end soon? Will I find work again? Did this stress cause the foot trouble I now have? Is marital satisfaction impossible with my husband?

The hurt runs very deep. I need to recover. Is this pain here now to help me evolve? My marriage used to offer predictability and security. Will I ever find that again? Sincerely, Joan, TX.

Dear Joan, I understand how you could feel the way you do, and the words I am about to share may not be very comforting to you, but may I share them anyway? You have fallen into the trap into which many have fallen when they set it up so that another person is their source in life. Another person is where they get their security, another person is their source of safety. "When we married," you say, "he was reliable, stable, honorable, saw things through. I felt I had a safe haven with him." That may have been nice, Joan, but that is not your husband's job. It is not his job in life to be your "safe haven." It's his job to live his truth, and your job to live yours.

There is a classic description of this exact situation—the situation you are now going through—in *CWG 3*. If I didn't know better, I'd swear you read the book, then made this all up out of what was written there. If you have a chance, read, in particular, the section in *CWG 3* having to do with marriage and marriage vows, and the obligations inherent in the "marriage contract." It may also be very helpful for you to read the marriage vows placed in the book which have been recommended by God. All of this material is much too detailed for me to go into it here, Joan, but I am very sure it will be useful for you to go over.

Let me say that I do deeply understand your present feelings, and the real question is, where can you go from here? The first step I would urge you to take is the step of declaring who and what is your real source of safety, security and happiness in this life. It is not your husband. It may have looked that way for years, but that is not the way it really is. The source of everything you could ever want or need in your life, Joan, is God. So the first thing you have to do is return to the source.

This is done by getting more deeply in touch with God, and His place in your life. Meditate every day (there is also a wonderful section in *CWG 3* on meditation). If you can find a church or synagogue that meets your needs, and whose teachings you can agree with, get there. Find (or form) a spiritual support group in your community. Do whatever it takes to get "reconnected" to the part of you that knows God, and experiences God's place in your life.

Once you have made this connection, turn your troubles over to God, including your questions about how you are going to survive, where you are going to find work (or whether you even need to), whether you can find happiness with your husband, etc. Don't ask God to answer these questions, or solve your problems. Ask, rather, that God give you the insight to notice that you already have the answers, and that all the solutions have already been given you. Here is my favorite prayer: "Help me, God, to understand that this problem has already been solved for me." That is a very powerful prayer. It leads to miraculous experiences.

Will you ever be able to respect yourself again, you ask. Yes, Joan, you will. This very moment, if you choose. All it takes is your decision to reclaim the power over your life that you have given to your husband. Place it back in your own hands, *where it has always been*, and where it belongs. Place it back where it was in the beginning in the hands of the one to whom it was given.

The power of Who You Are was given to you by your creator; by God, and God has never taken it away from you, though you have given it away to another. Now, reclaim it, and in so doing, reclaim and recreate your right relationship with God, with your most holy self, and with your husband. From that place of holiness which is Who You Are, seek to release your anger toward your husband, for I tell you this: there are no victims and no villains in this world, only people doing what they are doing because of the truth they are experiencing.

The problem with people living their truth, Joan, is that it sometimes—very often, actually—results in people breaking their previously made promises. That's because most people do not know how to live their newly emerging truth from a place of integrity. It is also because we live in a society which encourages lying and deception, and punishes openness and truth-telling.

Your husband has at last told you the truth. You now have the first honest basis you have had in six years on which to continue creating a life together, should you choose. He is acting strangely, he is acting differently, and that, too, is because of his new truths about how he wants his life to be. You do not have to agree with them. But at least you now finally know them.

Whether you can, in fact, live with this "new version" of your husband is a decision you will make in the days and weeks and months ahead. Much will depend on who you think you are in relationship to this man. In my opinion, Joan, you will have no chance whatsoever of ever living happily with him again if you continue to place him as the source of whatever it is you think you need to be safe, happy and secure in your life. To the degree that you reconnect with the true source, and the part of that source that lies within you, to that degree you will be able to be happy with anybody.

In addition to reading the wonderful new material on relationships in *Book 3*, Joan, I invite you to re-read Chapter 8 of *CWG 1*. Particularly the portions having to do with worrying in our relationships about what the other person is being, doing or having.

God's Thoughts about Divorce

Dear Neale: I am wondering, what does God think about divorce? Elizabeth, Jeffersonville, IN.

Dear Elizabeth, Is it your idea that God has a thought about divorce separate from your own? If you do, then you haven't read *Conversations with God*. Your only question should be: What do I think about divorce? By the way, Elizabeth, what do you think about divorce?

Can a Divorcee Marry Again? Will God Allow It?

Dear Neale: I am currently having problems with the scriptures of the Bible as they relate to divorce and remarriage. They say that there are only two grounds for divorce: sexual infidelity or the desertion of a believer by a nonbeliever. I left my wife about five and a half years ago, with our divorce three years ago, for neither of those reasons. Granted, it was wrong according to scripture. Now I am dating a lady whom I love (and who is also divorced). It appears

> that if we go by the scriptures we should not get married. What happened to forgiveness? Why should we not enter into marriage and develop a relationship that would honor God? I guess I'm looking for permission of some sort to take our relationship beyond its present state. Jim, Dublin, OH.

Dear Jim, You can say that again! That's exactly what you want. Permission. Like so many others, you feel you need permission to act on what your heart tells you is obviously so. This is the greatest blockage to human happiness I have ever observed, and it is epidemic among the peoples of the earth.

Go, Jim, go! Do what your heart tells you to do! There is no "right" or "wrong" in these matters. The scriptures to which you refer were written by fearful men who sought to control the mass of the people by projecting their own fear onto others. These writings are not authoritative. There is a place where the truth lives, and it is within your heart. Listen to the feelings of your soul. You do not need my permission to love this lady in the way that you wish, Jim. You need your own. (Or, perhaps, hers?)

Are Males Killing Themselves Having Sex?

> Neale: Thank you so much for helping me make sense of religion and the creator. I love your books and what they say. I've read them twice, but I have a few questions. First, why is it so important to recreate who we really are? If we have indeed been here on earth experiencing 500-600 lives, haven't we experienced everything there is many times over? So why not just decide not to come back to this physical earth?
>
> Second, I teach in a public high school and would like to know how I can turn on my students to your books without upsetting their parents? Any suggestions? Third, I like what your books say about sex. But is it true that each individual has only so much energy (chi), and we males lose some each time we have sex? This is the philosophy of traditional Chinese medicine. Walk in beauty. Charles, Summerdale, PA.

Dear Charles, First, it is not important that we recreate who we really are. You are right, we have experienced everything many times over. But most of us have had sex many times in our lives, too. That doesn't stop us from wanting it again, I notice.

Charles, the reason we keep doing this over and over again is because we like it. The experience of God "Godding" is the greatest experience going! One day you may decide not to come back to this physical earth. Then you won't. Until you do again. Which you will. Unless you don't. You see how it works? You get to do whatever you want to do.

About your high school students reading *CWG*, I have no suggestions for you, other than to simply have it be your intention that all people everywhere someday, somehow get the message of God's love and God's truth. Life proceeds out of your intention for it.

Third, it is not my knowingness that sexual discharge in the male produces a loss of a particular kind of energy of which there is only a certain amount. The God of my understanding has caused me to know that we live in an unlimited universe. And, in any case, the energy of love and procreation would be the last energy God would cause to be limited. But your statement raises an interesting question of my own. If there is only a certain amount of energy, and males lose some each time they have sex, what happens when they have one sexual experience too many? (Please tell me, Charlie, because I think I'm in danger of getting there.)

Does God Approve of Homosexuality?

Dear Neale: I want to take the time to thank you for the courage to write this book. An issue has caused me much frustration and has led to many questions: homosexuality. Have you received any information concerning this subject? Is it acceptable to God? Is it neither right nor wrong? Why does the Bible condemn it? T. B., Mt. Juliet, TN.

Dear Neale: Will you address the conflicts of gay and lesbians? I want to feel all right as a gay man in God's eyes. It feels to me that I was born gay. I can put up with the world's condemnation (especially "Christian") but my question: am I accepted in God's sight? Julian, San Francisco, CA.

Dear T.B. and Julian, This question comes up more frequently than almost any other in the correspondence I receive. People are going through unbelievable anguish on this issue, and I think that is very sad. I think it is sad because it is so unnecessary. God is not going to judge you, ever. For anything. Reread *Conversations with God* again, because you have apparently missed its major point.

An argument can be made that the Bible does not condemn homosexuality. An equally strong argument can be made that it does. Whether it does or it does not is beside the point. But if it does, it does so for the same reason that all condemnation exists: fear. What we fear, we condemn. What we love, we praise. Only those who fear homosexuality condemn it. Since God fears nothing, God does not condemn it, nor anything else. There is much more to say on this subject, and on the whole question of human sexuality. *CWG 2* contains a large chapter dealing with the celebration and the experience of our sexual selves. For now, hear this: there is no form in which the expression of a love which is honest and pure is inappropriate.

Why Did God Create Homosexuals?

> Dear Mr. Walsch: *Conversations with God Book 1* is a fantastic book! However, I'm left with one big area of questions which I hope you will address. What does God think about homosexuality? What is the reason God created homosexuals? Thanks for your willingness to be a messenger! Love, Mary, Providence, RI.

Dear Mary, God did not "create homosexuals" in the sense that you mean. Each of us chooses our own reality, circumstances, conditions of life, etc., before coming into the body. We choose our parents, the place we'll be born, everything. We give ourselves these outward circumstances as tools with which to create our experience. As such, they are gifts—sacred gifts—given to us by our selves. We should always, then, bless, bless, bless the circumstances of our lives, and embrace them with great love. If we decide that our present circumstances are not pleasing to us, nor appropriate any longer to Who We Are and Who We Choose to Be (this is a decision, by the way), we do well to continue to bless them, for this is very healing. What you resist, persists, and what you bless is healed.

So God did not create homosexuals for any particular reason, any more than God created anything in life for any particular reason. God gave you the authority and the power to decide and declare for yourself "why" you are anything at all. Yet the question "why" is the most irrelevant question in the universe. The only important question is "what?" What do you want to do about Who You Are? How do you choose to experience yourself? The answers to these questions are within your power to create. And the sadness is, most people don't know that. Yet it is true. You have this power. Ask Christopher Reeve.

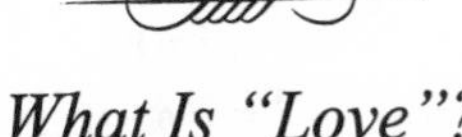

What Is "Love"?

> Dear Mr. Walsch: I am a forty-seven-year-old Japanese man. I am teaching seven- to eighteen-year-old kids at my small school. I began to read "spiritual" books two years ago, and finally I got your awesome books. It may sound stupid, but I would like to ask God, or you, about the meaning of "love." I understand that we have the world as it is just because we do not have enough love for others and the things around us. Does "love" have to be learned, or is it a thing that we are born with? Where does it come from? How could I know the deeds with love?
>
> Why am I asking such a question? Because we are not taught at school; we simply observe the things around us and we kind of pick up the meaning through observation. When someone is talking about "love" or a feeling of "love," we pretend we understand it, and we don't take time to think about the real meaning of "love." So please tell me what you think it is. Thank you! Yukio, Futami, Japan.

My dear Yukio, You have asked the questions that have engaged philosophers and theologians from the beginning of time. These are the eternal questions—the questions to which we have been seeking our personal answers since the day we were born. I do not know if my answers will solve the mystery for you, but I can tell you that they have for me. So, from the for what it's worth department: Love is Who You Really Are. I believe that love is what God is. To me, the words God and love are interchangeable. Likewise, the words God and you, and God and me, are interchangeable. Therefore, the words love and you, and love and me, are synonyms as well, describing exactly the same thing. And what do these words—God, love, you, me—describe? Life, Yukio, life. This is all our way of describing what life is. So to me, life is love. The energy that life is, love is. Life-love-God-you-me—it's all the same thing.

In my dialogue with God, I was told that "love is all there is." This means that everything is a form of love. Now that may be difficult to accept, difficult to comprehend, but God says it is true. In *Book 2* of the *CWG* Trilogy, this principle is again restated; this time it relates to all human beings. God said about people: "I have sent you nothing but angels." Again, this is hard to understand, particularly the way some people act. Yet it is directly in alignment with God's statement in the dialogue that "Hitler went to heaven."

Mysteries such as these are not easily grasped, particularly if we look only at the shallow end of things. We have to dive into that pool of wisdom and plunge to the very depths in order to find the meaning here. When we discover (or, to use a word I like to substitute here, "recover") the truth of these statements, then we understand at last what love is. And what God is. And what we are.

When you say that "we have the world as it is just because we do not have enough love for others and the things around us," what I hear in my heart is that the world is the way it is because we do not have enough of an awareness of our oneness with God and the life which is around us. You see, what I have been trying to say here is that God and we are one. Life and we are one. You and I are one. Everyone—you, me, God, life—is all the same stuff. When we get clear on that, all of the problems we have created in our lives will go away. Every single life problem of which I am aware is based in the thought that there is a thing called "separation." As soon as the thought of separation disappears, all of the problems of life disappear as well. They automatically resolve themselves. They go away. And we don't create them anew, because we would never do that to ourselves.

We would never allow thousands of people to starve to death every day because we would never do that to ourselves. We would never allow millions to be killed in wars because we would never do that to ourselves. We would not allow masses of people to be ravaged by poverty and disease because we would never do that to ourselves. And, on a smaller scale, we would never allow our personal behaviors to be unkind or damaging to others, because we would know and understand that there are no "others," and we would never do that to ourselves. As soon as we realize that we are all one, we stop immediately our destructive behaviors, because we realize that those behaviors are self-destructive. (As long as we think of them as merely "other" destructive, we don't seem to care.) So, Yukio, love is realizing we are one. Love is understanding that. Living that.

To answer the next question you asked, love does not have to be "learned," but it does have to be remembered. That is, we have to remember what we have always known. This act of re-membering—that is, becoming once again a member of the one body of God—can take a lifetime. Or many lifetimes. But sooner or later, all of us re-member. Yes, love is something you are "born with," because love is Who You Really Are. Since you are born with "you," you are born with "love." You cannot separate "you" and "love." You only think you can.

Now you ask, "How can I know the deeds of love?" And the answer is found wonderfully articulated on page 19 of *Conversations with God, Book 1*, when God explains the difference between love and fear. Fear is the energy which contracts, closes down, draws in, runs, hides, hoards, harms. Love is the energy which expands, opens up, sends out, stays, reveals, shares, heals. Fear wraps our bodies in clothing, love allows us to stand naked. Fear clings to and clutches all that we have, love gives all that we have away. Fear holds close, love holds dear. Fear grasps, love lets go. Fear rankles, love soothes. Fear attacks, love amends. Love never says no.

In other words, love says "my will for you is your will for you." This is exactly what God says to each of us. And there is yet one more way you can "know the deeds of love." They are the deeds that are undertaken without expectation and without condition. True love is unconditional. There is no such thing as "I love you if." We have been living with an idea of an "I love you if " kind of God for many centuries now. From the start, that kind of idea about God has been inaccurate.

And I guess if I had to settle on one single characteristic of love, some defining quality that was always there, it would be that loves always unites, and creates or honors oneness. If, therefore, a decision or choice is made by individuals or governments which tends to divide, which creates or honors separation, it is not a decision or choice based in love. Anything that creates a "them" and "us" mentality is not love.

How Can I Live Without "Expectations"?

Dear Neale: I understand that the purpose of relationships is to share and create who we are. I choose to do that in relationships. I also know that at times we do go into relationships with expectations, with one of these expectations being receiving that which we give out! As much as I can "let go" of these expectations, I usually end up feeling hurt and disappointed.

An example: I dated a man for almost a full year; then it was my twenty-ninth birthday. For this day, he made me dinner and did not give me a material gift. Yes, I had an expectation. He did tell me he was going to get me a gift and that gift would be a raincoat to go out fishing in the rain. (Fishing was an activity that he loved and in which he wished I would join him. I did, yet it wasn't all of the time, for I have other interests.) I received that raincoat about two months later. When I did not receive the gift earlier, or one that reflected my interests, I felt so unimportant to him, I could not understand why he could not go out shopping one evening to buy me a special gift.

In the relationship, I found myself giving a lot. I chose this. I understand that my ego "kicked in" and saw that the relationship was unbalanced in many ways, and when I attempted to share this feeling I was always told that it was me. It took me a while to understand that it was not just me, yet the man was convincing. So my question is this: How does one stop having expectations, even though at times you feel that you are being treated unfairly or unlovingly? Thank you so much for your time . . . and may God continue to show us all of our opportunities. Lori, Huntington, NY.

Dear Lori, That's a very fair question and a common one. Here's what I want you to know about relationships. Each of us has the right to feel honored in our relationship, and if we don't feel that, we have a right to create a relationship in which we do. We have a right to tell another person what makes us happy, and, for that matter, exactly how we're feeling about any particular thing. What I am trying to say here, Lori, is that living outside of the space of expectation does not mean living outside of the space of clear communication.

I communicate to everyone around me what it is that will make me happy, and I leave no room for ambiguity about it. This actually helps those who love me, because I am constantly giving them clues and cues as to what would make me particularly happy. No one who loves you would be upset about receiving this information—as long as they did not have to feel obligated to provide you with that in order for you to love them.

You used a very interesting word in your question. You used the word "unfairly" to describe how, at times, you may feel you are being treated. No one can be treated "unfairly," Lori, because the word "unfairly" suggests that there is a way that you are required to be treated, that there is a way you are supposed to be treated, that there is a way you have to be treated—and all of those statements are false. No one owes you anything—not even the one you love—and the sooner you get clear on that, the sooner the word "unfairly" drops out of your vocabulary. The question is not whether another person is being "fair" with you; the question is only whether you are being treated in a way that is okay with you (whether it is "fair" or not). And that leads, of course, to another question: what would make it "okay"? What would make it "not okay"?

The answer has to do with personal preference, Lori, and nothing more than that. If you do not prefer to receive a birthday present two months late, and to have it have nothing to do with anything you are interested in, simply say so, and return the gift. If you accept the gift, and then complain about it, you become a "whiner." If, on the other hand, you simply say, lovingly and truthfully, "Thank you for the thought, but I would have preferred to receive something that showed you are aware of what my interests are, and to have received it on my birthday, so I don't think I want to accept this now, because I am not feeling very good about it," you will send a very clear message, and that will be the last time you will ever get a birthday gift two months late that has nothing to do with you. This will work even better if you can truthfully say, "I love you for trying and thank you, darling for the effort, but I do not prefer this gift at this time. Thank you."

It's like saying "no thanks" to the asparagus. The cook won't keep making you asparagus if you keep refusing it politely every time it's served. And, if the cook does keep preparing something you do not prefer, choose another restaurant. This does not mean you have stopped loving the first. You can love the restaurant without having to eat there.

Now catch the nuance here, Lori. When you go into that restaurant, you are not expecting anything. You are living outside of the space of expectation. You simply state your preference and see what happens—without "expecting" one thing or the other. But if asparagus comes out of the kitchen, simply don't eat it. Choose something else from the menu, and if the menu offers nothing else, dine elsewhere.

This puts both people at choice in the interaction. If the manager wants you to come back to his restaurant, he'll stop serving you asparagus. But he's under no obligation to. And you've made it clear that you don't expect him to. On the other hand, nor can he expect you to continue dining on food that you do not prefer. Everybody's at choice, and no one is expecting anything from the other.

What this comes down to, is owning your own power And owning one's own power has nothing to do with living in expectation. It has, rather to do with knowing exactly who you are, as well as who you are not willing to be in order to keep someone in the room. So remember Lori, that living outside of the space of expectation does not mean living outside of the space of your own preferences. You do not have to do that. I hope this has helped a little. Love and hugs . . . Neale.

How Can One Find a Partner or Mate?

Dear Mr. Walsch: Do you have a listing of others who agree with and try to live by the philosophies and truths in your book? Particularly, I wondered if you have a list of people looking to find friends/mates who share the ideas from *CWG*. I think a lot of people are having trouble meeting people who view life the same way they do, and who want to enter into a relationship for the right reason (to have the opportunity to demonstrate Who They Are). Audrey, San Francisco, CA.

Dear Mr. Walsch: I, too, come from the Catholic limits, lost and confused, just knowing that what was being taught was not who I was! I could never put into words what my heart believed (never really sure because of my fear of Hell). Thank you for making the choice to know God. Thank you for having the courage to share it. Now after many fruitless attempts to find people in my life with similar beliefs, I turn to you and your readers for a sense of fellowship of common goals. Just a thought: have any readers inquired about a *CWG* singles connection? I'm not sure how, but I have created loneliness in my life. I have much passionate energy and few people understand me. It was just a thought (perhaps a creation, right?). Sincerely, that little particle of God called Audrey, Edmonton, Alberta, Canada.

Dear Audrey and Audrey, Is this really two people writing me? I have no plans to develop a "singles" list. It does not feel in harmony with my intention to use the *CWG* material as a teaching tool. But neither of you, nor any other "single," should have a difficult time finding a compatible mate. Simply make it your intention to do so. Make a list of all the qualities you want in a mate, and turn it over to God. Then know and believe that your perfect mate is coming to you now. Get ready for it. Prepare for it. Spruce up your wardrobe. Have your hair restyled (that goes for both woman and men). Clear off your calendar, because you're going to need lots of room for dates.

And if someone grounded in *CWG* is what you are looking for, the task gets really simple. Either start, or find and attend, a *CWG* Study Group in your community. Post it in your church, on the bulletin board at your local library, put an ad in the classifieds of your newspaper, put posters up here and there, and soon you'll have a group. Over 250 such groups have already been started in this country, and overseas. Then, watch who shows up! You should find a very eligible partner very soon! Plus, you'll "connect" with lots of new people who share your feelings about the *CWG* material.

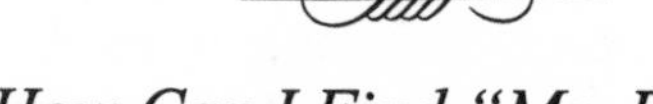

How Can I Find "Mr. Right?"

> Dear Neale: My boyfriend and I broke up last night. Due to my growing awareness, I was able to accept what was happening and not think my life was ending. It was what I guess we would call a "healthy" breakup, one without fighting and power struggles, but we are still confused.
>
> In all past relationships, we both would come to the realization our partners were not life-long. In this one we haven't, but at the same time, we don't have that "I know this is right" feeling. So we are left still searching for someone "right" to fill that goal of what we desire to feel with a lifetime partner. Are we misunderstanding our energy? Or is this a signal to move on that there is something else?
>
> It was/is a great relationship. We functioned well, but both desire to be in love, and both of us are very scared of "missing out" on the ultimate, passionate love between husband and wife. I wonder if I know my future husband from an agreement we made before we came to earth, or is it simply a case of making a decision to be in love, then we will experience it? With love, Dawn, Boise, ID.

My dear Dawn, Thank you for writing and for doing so with such transparency. Let me tell you what I know about love, and life partners, and "passionate love," and all of that. Dawn, the first thing I want to tell you is that love is not a response, it is a decision. That's just about the most important thing I ever learned in my life, so I'm going to repeat it. I said, love is not a response, it's a decision.

Now it is true that a person can have a "physical reaction" to someone. We all have certain body types, certain personality types, certain "vibes" that we seem to find more pleasing than others. Yet many people who have tried to construct long-term relationships out of such initial responses have found that they do not always produce or guarantee the kind of harmony, real respect, and deep personal regard which typifies life-long partnerships.

Passion is created, Dawn, as is everything else in your life. And, as with everything else in your life, it is created by you. How? Out of your decision to do so. That's right, Dawn. You can actually decide to be passionate. You can also decide not to be, as many people who have ended relationships have discovered. So passion (or the feeling that you call "passion," or being "turned on" by someone), is not the most important thing I would look for in a relationship. From my experience, here is the most important single ingredient in successful long-term relationships: friendship. And right next to that: tolerance, which, of course, is what true friendship produces, and, in turn, what produces true friendship.

You say that you don't have that "I know this is right" feeling. What kind of feeling is that, can you tell me? No, let me tell you. A relationship isn't "right" because it is "automatically right" by virtue of some factor or element outside of yourself and hence, outside of your control. A relationship is "right" because you decide to make it right. And what could cause you to decide that? Your decision about what is important to you. Your decision about Who You Are, and who you Choose To Be.

One final thought, Dawn. You say that you and your friend are "still searching for someone right." Don't search for "someone right"; choose to be "someone right." You want tons and piles of passion in the room when it is time for romance? Tell you what, Dawn. Bring it into the room with you. Then see what happens. To put this all in one sentence, Dawn, yes, you are right. You gave yourself your own best wisdom. Is it simply a decision we need to make to be in love, then we will experience it? Yes, Dawn. Yes. That "certain feeling" can be sent, as well as received!

Parenting and Relationships with Children

Dear Mr. Walsch: I read your book *Conversations with God* and found it very useful. I wonder if you would share with us any comments/teachings on relationships with children. Specifically, my daughter is 9, and I ponder when to allow her wishes, her wisdom, and when to make choices for her and demands upon her.

Also, she has had alternative schooling (instead of public school), and as she's getting older I wonder what direction to go with this. What does she most need to learn? What is the best way to learn it? Carol, Roy, WA.

Dear Carol, I want to begin by saying that my own relationships with children prior to *CWG* have not been what I wish they would have been. I have been an absentee father to most of my children most of my life. I'm deeply regretful of that, and I'm doing what I can now to change it as much as possible and play more of a role, have more of an active presence, in the lives of my offspring. Having said that, and having acknowledged publicly before that I have done, by just about any standards one could find to apply, a dismal job as a father, usually inflicting more damage than good, let me nevertheless see if I can answer your question. (We teach what we have to learn.)

Our relationships with our children are pivotal in the formation of Who We Are. They are pivotal because they can call upon us for so much, probably more than any other relationships we'll ever form. How we respond to that says a great deal.

Now you have asked, among other things, when to allow your 9-year-old to make her own choices, and when to make them for her, and place demands upon her. I believe your child should be encouraged to make all of her own choices. Yet there should be clearly understandable consequences connected with each choice, and these should be explained to her from the very beginning, that is, the very first time any particular choice is encountered, and frequently thereafter until you feel confident your daughter understands these outcomes.

I believe that children do far better when they make choices and select behaviors based on an age-appropriate understanding of what they can expect as a consequence or result, than they do when they are merely reacting to dogmatic, unexplained, authoritarian decrees or frightening parental outbursts.

Now this does not mean that parents should not be firm. Nor does it mean that there is simply no room for arbitrary decisions at all. Sometimes children need the comfort of a parent's arbitrary decision. ("Dad, can I have a Coke?" "Nope. It's too close to dinner.") ("Can we stay up to watch Deep Space Nine?" "No, and don't even ask. You know it's a school night.") These kinds of "decisions" are usually not decisions at all, but merely firm, consistent restatements of already put-in-place guidelines.

When parents are not afraid to make these statements, and not afraid to lose the child's favor by doing so, children develop a strong sense of security, and more, not less, love for their parents. They know where the boundaries are. They understand their limitations. And they know that inside those boundaries and limitations, they are perfectly safe. This is deeply impactful upon the child's sense of well-being and a high sense of well-being is precisely what produces the childlike courage and strength which produces the inevitable testing of the very boundaries which created that well-being in the first place.

In short, clear boundaries, reasonable limitations and predictable consequences, firmly and consistently enforced, produce in the child the self-confidence which is necessary if the child is ever to break through those boundaries, live a life without limitations, and stand responsible for all the consequences of future decisions and behaviors. Children who have to set their own behavioral boundaries are often nervous wrecks, high strung, temperamental, etc., because they are being asked to make adult decisions about an adult world in which they know very well that they are just beginners.

Therefore, my answer to your first question is this: first, lay the groundwork (explain the consequences) early, and sufficiently, so that most of your child's best day-to-day choices are made clear to her. Second, when your daughter tests her understandings of those consequences, be firm, fair and consistent in demonstrating to her that her original understanding was correct. Third, when a new area of inquiry arises (something you have not gone over before) encourage the child to reason out her own choices, based on what she thinks is best, and makes the most sense, in the situation, but give her clear and understandable guidelines with which to make those explorations, and, if she chooses poorly, tell her what you think of her choice and invite her to review again the consequences she might encounter.

If all this fails, and the child still makes the "wrong" choice, you may in that instance have to become quite arbitrary. ("I'm sorry you made that choice, because I can't agree with it. I'm going to have to overrule you on this one. I'm sorry. We don't share the same understanding of some of the dangers or difficulties here, and in the end it is my job to protect you, keep you safe, and always look out for your best interests. So no, you will not be going to the mall with your friend from school this weekend. Neither one of you are old enough to do that alone. I'm sorry.")

I want to say this, though. There is a way to make these kinds of "rulings" without losing the friendship of, or building resentment in, the child. As it happens, I touched upon this in an earlier letter. Please read it again. Look for the comments I made about a book called *How to Talk So Kids Will Listen, and Listen So Kids Will Talk*. It's must reading for you, Carol.

As for your question about schooling, I see nothing wrong with alternative schooling, so long as your daughter has a chance to socialize there. I have a little bit of a problem with home schooling after a certain age, because I think it sometimes deprives children of the opportunity to develop childhood social and interactive skills. On the other hand, if sufficient chance is provided the child to develop these skills, home schooling can be great.

What does your daughter need to learn? I find myself wanting to answer this on a metaphysical level. She needs to learn nothing. She needs only to have the opportunity to remember and to experience what she already knows. Build, therefore, a space of safety around the child. This does not mean to close the child off from the world, but allow the child to feel safe in the world.

Can We Ever Stop Lying, and Live a Life of Total Truth?

Dearest Neale: I don't know what planet you came from, but wherever it is, I want to live there! Thank you, thank you for your wonderful books—especially *CWG 3*, which I've just finished, and which is awesome in its implications. I have just one question. Do you really think it is possible for human beings to live a life of total transparency, never lying ever again, about anything, as *Book 3* suggests? Isn't this rather a far-fetched notion? Lily S., Dearborn, MI.

Dear Lily, Every idea in the entire Trilogy is a far-fetched notion! And yes, I do believe it is possible for us to stop lying, and just tell the truth to everyone about everything. But the first thing we would have to do is get rid of our fear of what the truth will bring.

We have learned to lie, Lily, because it protects us. Lies shield us from outcomes and results we do not desire. We have created an entire society built on secrecy, on the idea that "what you don't know won't hurt you." That's what we have to change, Lily. We have to change our ideas about what we really desire. We have to desire the outcomes that Truth brings. Let me say that again, because some people might have missed that. I said, we have to desire the outcomes that Truth brings.

Now in order to desire those outcomes, we have to change them. We have to stop punishing each other for not being perfect, for not living up to standards that we, ourselves, do not live up to. We have to stop being hypocrites, and stop, above all, our insistence in believing in a punishing, retributive God.

Highly Evolved Beings never lie to anyone about anything. Politics, economics, business interactions, romantic relationships . . . all are lie-free. This is a daring way to live—but it is the only way to live. Try it, Lily. It will excite the hell out of you. I mean that literally. It will excite the hell, right out of you.

CHAPTER 7

Good and Evil and the Nature of Duality

How is your heart feeling these days? Is it filled with happiness, joy and celebration? I do hope your answer is yes, no matter what is happening in your life. That's a tough one, I know. It's not easy to ignore the things that are happening in your life especially when they are bad things, and stay steady on the path. We make these judgments, you and I. We call some things "good" and some things "bad," and then we act out our decision about them.

If we saw what was happening, if we all only knew how the whole process has been constructed, we would see the perfection of it. We would continue to play our roles, of course, but we would see them as "roles." We would not take them so seriously, even when this particular part of our "play" called for a serious moment. We would play the moment seriously, but we would not take it so seriously. You know what I mean?

One day this week, try this: imagine yourself as a fictional character in your own movie. Just sort of sit back in the front row seat of your mind and watch the scenes unfold. Imagine, too, that you are the director of this movie, and that you can change the way the scene is going at any moment. Mind you, you can't change what's happening. You can't change the script. You have to work with the script you've been given. But you can change the way the scene is being played. You can play it for comedy, or you can play it for drama. You can emphasize the pathos, or you can, as they say in the theatre, "throw it away," meaning, play the scene lightly; play it against the grain; don't make so much of it. Literally, throw it away.

I got this idea from Richard Bach, who first proposed such an experiment in his wonderful book *Illusions—The Adventures of a Reluctant Messiah*. It is one of my favorite books, and I strongly urge you to read it, if you have not already done so. Oh, heck, even if you have.

God Plays No Direct Role in the Creation of Any Human Event

Dear Neale: My English isn't good, but for me it is very important to write this letter to you. I hope you'll understand it or feel what I want to explain.

Five years ago in Switzerland I met a couple from Santa Fe, New Mexico, who said they came from another galaxy. Their energy was so strong but often very strange to stay with. I stayed with these people for five years and it changed my life so deeply, like yours was changed with writing these books. Their energy was so wonderful; I could really often feel God, deeply and really. I was, and am still, convinced they did a good work in the beginning. Then they changed a lot and I cannot understand why. So I would tell you some events. I'm not a person who runs easily after people with esoteric or spiritual lives. When I first met these people, I had a resistance against them, and I had this after, also.

In 1995, I went to Santa Fe to live with these people, and during the first year, my husband left me. I was convinced to do the right thing for my awakening, because I decided long ago to use my life only for God and to do everything I can to follow this way. But it is not so easy. I felt from your book that it was also not only easy for you. I had also deep experiences.

They rented a house in the wilderness near Santa Fe and we lived there. It was so wonderful for me to be in the beauty of this country, in the nature, wide and wild. You must know Switzerland is very little and we live near together. The couple never tried to hold us (my daughters and me) back or have us be too attached to them. They told us they are only here to help us find ourselves, like you write in your books. I could really hear their words in your book. But then they began to treat us very strangely. One day, they told us a thing was white and the next day that the same thing was black.

They asked me if I had friends that could lend them money for a year, so I found one and he loaned them a large sum and they affirmed to pay him back at the end of a year. Now it is more than a year and it is not paid back, neither do I have a response.

I don't know what's happened. They do not respond to our letters nor can we call them. I could fill a book with all the things I have experienced with these people, good and bad. Do you perhaps receive an answer? It is not only because of me, but there are many others with the same experiences of hurt. Why did God let beings do such things? For what does it serve, when we need help, to take away every energy of happiness to be playful and creative? How does it serve me now to be in a hole after all I did?

I know, I have to do nothing, but sitting in an apartment and not knowing where to go is not easy. After being married thirty years, and now my husband left because of fear, I go my way—I know it is right—but it is not easy. With love, Ayrillia, Switzerland.

Dear Ayrillia, In answer to your questions, I would say that God plays no direct role in the creation of any human event, experience or outcome. But rather God allows us complete freedom to draw to ourselves exactly the exact right and perfect people, places, circumstances and conditions with which to experience the next level of our own beingness. That is to say, life is a constant process of re-creation. We are re-creating ourselves anew in the next grandest version of the grandest idea we ever had about who we are. In this process of re-creation, as explained carefully and in detail in *CWG 1*, we draw to ourselves, through all manner and means, the right and perfect people, places and circumstances that we would use as tools in the creation of our next learning and our next remembering.

Ayrillia, when you are willing to take full responsibility—a difficult thing for you, and for me, to hear at times of great turmoil—for all of the outcomes that have occurred in your life, and when you are willing to forgive yourself for having created outcomes with which you now disagree—in that moment you will set both yourself and those who you imagine to have been your tormentors free.

Understand then, Ayrillia, that these experiences that you have given yourself have been gifts, and that in the seeds of every encounter is a glorious treasure from which we may be caused to once again know and declare, announce and become, realize and experience, who we really are. The question of the moment, therefore, is not "why has God caused this to happen," or even "why has this happened by any means."

The only truly relevant question at this moment in your life is "what shall I cause these experiences to mean to me? What am I, and what have I become, and what do I choose to be as a result of them? What gift can I lift from the ashes of this disaster in my life to allow me to see the treasure that was always buried there? If God does anything, it is not to create disasters, but to place the treasure in what you call disaster, and I urge and encourage you to ask, and to find the answer to this question, "who am I and who do I choose to be in response to, and in relationship with, the experiences I have described in my letter to Neale?" In your answer to that question will be found your salvation. I wish you blessings on your journey.

Why Do "Bad Things" Happen If We Are Creating Our Own Reality?

> Dear Neale: If we are creating our realities by our thoughts, words and actions, what about the victims of brutal crimes, senseless slaughters/mutilations? Do those people choose to die that way? Alfreda, Effort, PA.

My friend, You have asked a very fair and penetrating question. And the issue is even larger than you have stated it. For it is not only a matter of our intentions and choices, but of God's. I mean, is it God's will (even if it is not ours) that these horrible things should happen? Philosophers and theologians have been trying to answer that question from the beginning of time.

Alfreda, I was given an extraordinary answer to this question when I asked it in my dialogue. First, it was made clear to me that there are no victims and no villains in life. Now that was difficult for me, because to my eyes so many of the things we have done to each other are very cruel, very horrible, and to me the people who perpetrated these heinous crimes certainly were the "villains" of our society. Still, God said in *CWG 2*, "I have sent you nothing but angels." And the parable of *The Little Soul and the Sun* in *Book 1* explains how this could be true. That parable has now been made into a wonderful children's book of the same name by Hampton Roads. I cannot recommend it highly enough as a way for children (and adults) to better understand why, as wonderful Rabbi Harold S. Kushner puts it, "bad things happen to good people."

In brief (re-read the *CWG* or children's book material to get the full essence of this), the human soul is an aspect of divinity, choosing freely to experience life in the universe (and, as part of that experience, life on earth from time to time) as a means of re-creating and experiencing itself as who it is. Now in the realm of the relative (which is the realm in which we live in the physical worlds), you cannot experience that Which You Are except in the space of that Which You Are Not. For in the absence of that Which You Are Not, that which you are—is not!

That is, Alfreda in the absence of "small," the concept of "big" cannot be experienced. It can be imagined, but it cannot be experienced. The only way to experience a purely conceptual idea such as "big" is to experience a purely conceptual idea such as "small." Now in very elementary terms, Alfreda, this is why God created "evil." For in order for God to experience Itself as the all-consuming good, there had to be something called the all-consuming evil.

Of course, there was not. There was only God. God is all there was, all there is, and all there ever will be. Yet God wished to know Itself in Its own experience. This is the same wish we all have. Indeed, this "we all" I've just spoken of is God Itself. Every part of life is an aspect of divinity, seeking expression and experience of the divine. Yet that which is divine cannot know and experience Its own divinity except in the presence of that which is not divine. And the problem is, that which is not divine does not exist. So, since we have the power to create anything, we have simply made it up! That is to say, we have imagined it. We have literally called it forth.

Now this whole process is not one which any individual soul undertakes consciously. We set our agendas, Alfreda, long before we enter the human body. We even make agreements with other divine beings on how we might best create and experience ourselves as the aspect of divinity we choose in this lifetime. So, no, it cannot fairly be said that, at a conscious level, people choose the horrible experiences to which many of them are subjected. So what does that do to the theory that we are creating our own reality by our thoughts, words and actions? It doesn't change it one bit. It just explains the mechanism by which that reality comes to be experienced. As *CWG* carefully explains, the moment we think, say, or do a thing that initiates the process of expressing Who We Really Are, everything unlike it comes into the space. This is necessary, in order to create a context within which the experience of Self which we have chosen may be realized. For if that which is opposite to that which we have chosen does not appear, that which we have chosen cannot be expressed. It is for this reason that masters judge not, and neither do they condemn. Not anything or anyone. Not even those who persecute them. Every religion on the earth teaches forgiveness as the path to salvation. Most of them simply teach it for the wrong reason, saying that we should forgive, and leave the judging to God. Well, the news is that God will not judge, either. Would God ask us to do something that God would not do? That would be asking us to be bigger than God! Yet the reason God will never judge, and asks us not to judge, either, will be made clear to us when we return to the realm of the absolute. It is then we will understand again God's promise: "I have sent you nothing but angels."

I strongly recommend that you get a copy of *The Little Soul and the Sun*. And read it to your children—or any children with whom you come in regular contact. For if children understand this concept early, it will change the world.

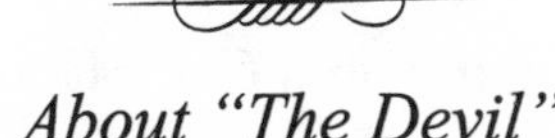

About "The Devil"

Dear Neale: I enjoyed the experience of your book. My husband has read the Bible hundreds of times. I have never. He says to not believe in the "devil" is to not believe in God. According to the Bible this goes hand in hand. What's this all about?

During your dialogue, did you hear a voice, and did God put Himself in human form for you to "see" who you were talking to? Was it a deep man's voice? Tell me what it was. And why wasn't it me who was chosen? Why wasn't it my choice to write these three books?

Please don't misunderstand these questions. I'm not only struggling with this money stuff (I'm about to go under if I don't change something quickly), I'm scared, then I'm grateful, then I don't know what I am. I believe my soul is "re-membering." I believe we create our reality. My focus on being keeps getting distorted because of the money I'm not creating. Please help me. Cindy, AZ.

Hello, Cindy, God created the possibility of "evil," but that does not mean God created a "devil" or a "Satan." The "evil" that God created is simply, and nothing more and nothing less than, the opposite of good. We have all been given the power to imagine "evil" in our lives, and to make it very real. But in the realm of the absolute, "evil" is simply a figment of our imagination. That is, it is not real. It does not exist. It is not a part of the kingdom of God. Shakespeare put this beautifully when he wrote, "Nothing is evil lest thinking make it so." Those were extraordinarily wise words. There is no devil, Cindy. Satan is a figment of our imagination. Organized religion must, however, make you believe there is a devil, otherwise you will have nothing to fear, and if you have nothing to fear, you will not need organized religion.

In my dialogue, Cindy, I heard what I have called "a voiceless voice." It was neither a man's voice nor a woman's voice. All I truly remember about the voice is that it was the softest, most gentle, compassionate, wise voice I had ever heard. As to why you weren't chosen, you were, Cindy. All of us are "the chosen ones." Not a one of us is excluded. But many of us exclude ourselves, out of our thought that "this sort of thing is impossible," or "I am not worthy."

When I was a young boy in a Catholic upbringing, I remember being taught a prayer by the nuns in our school: "Lord, I am not worthy that Thou shouldst enter under my roof. Yet say but the word, and my soul shall be healed." Prayers such as that, and similar ones from other religions, have caused millions of people to believe in their unworthiness, which is exactly the opposite of what God would want us to understand about ourselves. So there are many reasons why "many are called, but few choose themselves." But wait, my friend, wait. The game isn't over yet. There is no telling what you might do once you choose to believe in your own worthiness as a creation of God, Who, incidentally, doesn't make junk.

Finally, about the money and beingness situation. I want you to know that a year from today you will still be here, Cindy. A year from today we will both still be alive, still be playing at the game. The only question will be, what shall be the quality of our lives? I believe the quality of my life will be extraordinary, and I believe that I will cause that to occur by moving into a place of being which causes the quality of the lives of others to be wonderful, all others whose lives I touch. Do you believe that about yourself, Cindy? If you do, then you and I are going to have a very good year.

So don't go around asking, "What are we to eat? What are we to drink? Wherewithal shall we clothe ourselves?" Keep your eye where? On God. Each day has problems of its own. Yet "seek ye first the Kingdom of Heaven, and all else shall be added unto you. For where your heart is, there will your treasure also be."

Move through your life loving God, and doing God's work, Cindy. That means giving people back to themselves. Whatever you would choose for yourself, give to another. Whatever you find yourself lacking, find another who lacks even more, and give of what you have to those who have even less. In this will you be truly blessed, for in this will you speak the truth about yourself, which is: I am the source. This will activate a cellular memory, which will begin at once to create this manifestation in your present reality.

Two Spirits in One House—Good or Evil?

Dear Neale: Thank you from the bottom of my heart for having the great courage to write God's book. Who would not want a world like it? It has everything. But now that I know this, who do I tell? It goes against everyone's belief that God would talk to you.

My son is 27 and trying to find God. If only he would read *Conversations with God*, he would move ahead at great leaps. Anyway, I will leave it to the light to show him.

Neale, I hope you will understand when I tell you I have two spirits in my house. Somewhere in my mind I am wondering are they good or bad. If you could help me answer this, my mind will rest. Sent with love from someone who wants one world together. Peace be with you as you do your work. Jeanette, New South Wales, Australia.

Dear Jeanette, Whether God would talk to me or not is unimportant. What is important is the wisdom contained in the messages which appear in the trilogy. You are wise to let your son find *CWG* whenever he is ready.

Now, Jeanette, as to whether the two spirits you mentioned are "good or bad," I want to tell you that that is a decision only you can make. If you think that the spirits are evil, they are. And if you think that they're not, they're not. As you believe, so will it be for you.

Even if there were evil spirits, and I don't believe that there are, but even if there were evil spirits, they would lose all of their power the moment that you disempowered them by refusing to label them evil, or give them the power that you would ordinarily give evil things. Because, if there were evil spirits, their power would come from you and from the fear that they seek to generate in you. Therefore, remember the acronym for fear: False Evidence Appearing Real, and stay in love and peace.

Tell Me About Demons and Ghosts

Dear Neale: Some people, like myself, can hear, see or feel unusual phenomena happening around us. Because of it being possible demons, it frightens me. I rebuke them in the name of the Lord Almighty. They usually leave me alone. Page 51 of *CWG 1* says there is no such thing as the devil.

The Bible illustrates a story where Jesus cast out the demons from a boy into a herd of pigs which ran themselves into the water and drowned (Mark 5:11-13). Pastors and priests alike are dealing with these unexplained phenomena, casting out demons of those people who are possessed. What about these exorcists? What about those souls lingering around the earth that are not trouble-makers, but here to help? I have experienced them both.

When do you know which ghosts are trustworthy or not? I believe we can't ignore these situations, because many people have experienced them. All stories are different. What are they, if not demons? Are the good-doers, angels? Some ghosts seem like restless souls! How can these ghosts' souls be at rest if they are in a state of "sleepless drift"? How do we get rid of them or help them? How can we protect ourselves from these souls that have not progressed spiritually? What are they, or who are they, really? Thanks, Wendy, Stillwater, OK.

Dear Wendy, I do not know the answer to your questions. I did not ask these questions in my *Conversations with God*, and so I cannot pretend to know what is so about all of this. I do know what God told me about the "devil," the fact that Satan does not exist. Are there such things as "agonized souls" that hang around our physical world, causing havoc? I just don't know. What would I do if there were? I would love them, Wendy. I would send them all the love and compassion I could muster. If I felt, or thought, that one was present in my life, or in the life of another, I would command it to leave—just as I "command" all other outcomes and results in my life. That is, I choose them, I set my intention for them. So I would issue this command with love. Above all, I would show this agonized soul that I had no fear. This is, I believe, what you are doing when you say you "rebuke it in the name of the Lord Almighty." I guess the only thing I would do differently is that I would love it in the name of God. Love works better than rebuke every time.

Are there such things as "demons," which pastors and priests "cast out"? I do not believe so, although I do believe that some people can think so, and thus create a reality that very much looks as if and feels as if they are "possessed." We can convince ourselves of anything, Wendy, and thereby make it our reality. The movie *What Dreams May Come* is based on that understanding, and illustrates it beautifully. It also illustrates what happens when we simply change our mind about that.

I'm sorry that this is not a more complete or direct answer to your question, Wendy. But here's a thought: why not ask God yourself, and see what wisdom comes to you? Let me know what this yields. I'd be interested.

Is There Evil in the World?

Dear Neale: Your book says there is no such thing as "right" and "wrong." What about "good" and "evil?" Is there true evil in the world? RJL, Escondido, CA.

Yes, there is, RJL, and we must be grateful for it. Evil is the greatest gift God ever allowed us to give ourselves. Re-read *CWG* very closely and you will understand why. For now, this gentle and loving thought . . . fight not evil with evil, and neither condemn it. Rather, bless it and see it for what it is: the greatest opportunity—indeed, the only opportunity—we have in this lifetime to be and to experience Who We Really Are.

I do not wish to condemn any particular person, place or thing, but merely to notice. And in noticing, I wish, to see if this is Who I Am. That is all I am ever doing. Once I make my choice regarding Who I Am in relationship to that which I am experiencing, then I simply and calmly announce it and express it in, as, and through me.

Sometimes I am not pleased with those choices, and so next time I choose differently. Sometimes I am pleased with my choice, and these are often choices which I repeat. Yet never do I condemn the incoming experience, encounter or energy which have given me the opportunity to be and to decide Who I Really Am. For I understand that in the absence of that which I Am Not, I cannot be that which I am. That is, in the absence of evil (which I am not), I cannot be good (which I Am). In the absence of thin (which I am not!), I cannot be fat (which I am!). In the absence of this, I cannot be that! For we live in a relative world, in which all things exist as tools in the divine experience of creating and expressing who we now choose to be. This is God, "Godding!"

So, yes, RJL, there is evil in the world. Most decidedly. Absolutely. And thank God for it. For without it, we would be nothing. Neither a doctor without sickness. A lawyer without disagreement. A plumber without leaks in the kitchen. And neither you, without me. You see, we are all holy partners. And that is why each of us must never condemn the other. For we know not what path the sacred soul has chosen to walk, nor what assignment It has given Itself this time. Has it come to be our ally, or our enemy? Our helper, or our persecutor? When we see the two as one, then will we have seen through the mirage, then will we have uncovered the secret, then will we have had revealed to us the purpose and the process and the function of all life. And then will we bless and glorify every living person, place and thing.

Conversations with God puts this all into perspective with one simple and astonishing statement: Hitler went to heaven.

Will Duality End?

> Dear Neale: *CWG* says that everything on the physical plane is relative; that we can only experience love if we have experienced fear, good if we have also experienced evil, life if we have experienced death, etc. However, it also says that there are no opposites in the absolute realm, that only love is real. Does this mean that when God has brought the knowingness of the absolute into complete experience through us and we are simply being God, that the duality will end? Will we simply be perfect love, life, and light, and will fear, death, and darkness have no existence? Is this what is meant by the teaching of many metaphysical schools that "there is no evil"?
>
> *CWG* is inspiring me in many ways. Thank you, Neale. And thank you, God/Goddess, as well! Best wishes, Jeff on the Internet.

Dear Jeff, Well, yes and no. But understand this: as soon as we reach that stage, we will start all over again. That is, the cycle will continue. It must, don't you see, in order for God to know and experience God's magnificence. The illusion of duality exists only in the physical world, in the physical realm. The physical world is duality. It could not exist as you now experience it without duality. And the purpose of this duality is to provide a context within which you may experience the unity of all things. For within the unity you cannot experience the unity as unity, since you know nothing else.

CWG teaches that the relative universe was created so that God could know Godself in God's own magnificence. What I have come to know is that each of us—all of the individual expressions of God which we are—will have our "day in the sun." We will each be one day experiencing the unity, or the divine whole, as Who We Are . . . even as each of us has already experienced it in the "past." This is part of the cycle of life, in which each part of That Which Is God returns to the godhead to know itself, to be itself as one with all creation. This is a divine replenishment. Yet soon it will be our own desire to return once again to a relative experience, where we see and observe and experience ourselves relative to the larger reality of God, rather than be totally immersed within it. We will seek and desire this encounter precisely so that we may observe and experience the magnificence of God, that is to say, the magnificence of our divine selves. For even magnificence cannot be experienced if there is nothing else.

You are correct, Jeff, in saying that in ultimate reality there is no evil. There need not be evil even in our earthly reality. As *CWG3* explains, the entire universe is the contextual field within which what we call Positive and Negative aspects exist. Contrast is thus assured, whether it exists here or not.

Therefore, judge not, and neither condemn, but simply be Who You Really Are in relationship to that which life has placed in your space. For all things—all things—inure to your highest good (that is, your highest experience of self), and nothing is placed in your life which cannot be used as a tool in the building and creating of your own grandest experience. Every moment is a gift from God, every encounter is to be treasured, every human honored for the role they have played in the divine plan. As God said to me in *Book 2*: "I have sent you nothing but angels."

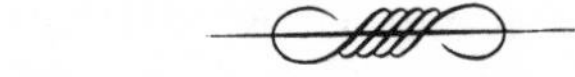

How Can Rape Be "Right?"

Neale: Thank you for having the courage to do what you've done. When I read your first book I was so enraptured that I found God. Not only God, but, the God I had known and loved all along. I had gone so far as looking up several different religions and reading all about them, trying to find one that would fit me. I had been searching for Him/Her/It for a long while. I definitely believed in God, and had been asking for one of those "absolutely, positively, for sure, no doubt about it, this is an answer or sign from God" type of things for a long stretch of time. Well, I got it. Turns out I'd been "getting it" all along.

Some friends and I got into a conversation about my personal beliefs. We talked about it for a while and finally got to the whole "what's right and wrong" issue. One of the questions asked was,

"How can a thing like rape, for instance, be right to anyone?" I was stuck. Though I truly believe there is perfection in everything and everything has purpose, I had no straight answer for that. Could you verbalize this? Or should I let it be and have my friends find the answer themselves? Ryan, Ft. Worth, TX.

Dear Ryan, Societies have a duty to themselves to declare their ideas of right and wrong. It is by such declarations that societies—and the individuals within them—define themselves. *CWG*'s message does not mean we should cease defining what is right and wrong for us, right here, right now. It does mean that we should understand that, from a standpoint of pure objectivity, there is no such thing as "right" and "wrong." There is only what happened and what did not happen. There is only what is, and what is not. Shakespeare himself understood this. "Nothing is evil," he wrote, "lest thinking make it so." In other words, if we do not think it is evil, it is not.

Not all that many years ago we hung women from scaffolds in this country for what we called "witchcraft." The people of Salem, Massachusetts—who, incidentally, were our ancestors, not "barbarians" from some God-forsaken place—were very sure that what they were doing was "right," and that what those ladies had done was "wrong." They killed those ladies in the name of God. Today if they did that, it would be the Bible-holding, scripture-shouting killers who would be called "wrong."

Even now, in our own day and time, we cannot seem to all agree on an absolute right and wrong. If a woman were to walk down a street in Peoria, Illinois, tomorrow night, offering certain favors to male customers in exchange for cash, she would most likely be arrested. Yet if that same woman offered those same favors to those same men for the same price in certain other cities on this continent, it would be said that they were adding to the tax base. All of which must lead the thinking person to ask, what is wrong here—prostitution or geography?

Now, going to what some would perhaps call tougher examples, there is your question about rape. Or perhaps we should go further and talk about murder. Do you know that there have been actual theological questions among certain Christian religions over the past 100 years about what constitutes "rape" and what constitutes a woman's "wifely duties"? More than one man in this country has been arrested and taken to court in recent years charged by his own wife for doing exactly what husbands 25 years ago did with impunity. And murder. Can you think of a situation in which even murder could be justified? Of course you can.

You see, my friend, there is no absolute in these things. The morals of a people are always a product of time and environment. Not sometimes. Not once in a while. Always.

The point of the teaching in *CWG* about right and wrong is not that we should throw out all of our current definitions, but that we should understand that we are making it all up. And it would probably not serve us to be too righteous when we stake out our positions.

Questions from a Thoughtful Teenager

> Dear Neale Walsch: I'm experiencing the confusion and discoveries of being sixteen and this book is helping me through the gray areas. Not only did *Conversations with God, Book 1* enlighten me and help make sense of many things, it reinstated some discoveries I made on my own. My skin, thoughts, and being have never fit well into the constraints of church with its rigid definitions of sin, hell, heaven, and prayer. I do not feel so alone in this view of the world anymore. Thank you for sharing your, at times, very personal conversation. Many my age have discovered your words breathlessly.
>
> How do victims of things such as rape and incest fit into self-chosen reality? I personally see love as a very deep emotion, something intertwined with all these sections of human existence. Love spans beyond only those of the opposite sex, who are most different. I'd be curious to hear your—or God's—thoughts. May you experience love and peace in your life. Sara, CO.

Dear Sara, I am glad that young people everywhere have "caught on" to the powerful and wonderful message of the *CWG* trilogy, and I'm happy that you are one of them. Let me go to your first question: How do victims of things such as rape and incest fit into self-chosen reality? You ask a very complex question, as youth almost always does. Youth asks the most difficult questions. When we get older, we learn (to our great loss) not to ask.

Sara, there are no victims, and there are no villains. I know this is not easy to accept, much less understand, and yet it is true. Re-reading the parable of "The Little Soul and the Sun" from *CWG 1* may help. In *CWG 3* there is a much fuller explanation of why, "bad things happen to good people," as Rabbi Kushner puts it. For here, let me just tell you that everything in the universe occurs by design; there are no accidents and there is no such thing as coincidence. Fate is an acronym for "From All Thoughts Everywhere." In other words, Sara, we are all co-creating our co-joined reality, and the interweavings of our mutually produced design are magnificent beyond description.

Now this does not mean that people do not suffer. That would be an insulting statement to all of those who have done so, and have lived through the experience courageously. Yet what I am saying is that even the suffering has a purpose. And it is a purpose with which the soul that is attached to that suffering body agrees, or it could not have been created.

Now, this soul-level agreement may not always be something of which the mind is consciously aware. (In fact, truthfully, it rarely is.) Yet that does not make the statement any less true. Our mind is not consciously aware of a great many things. Most things, in fact. Indeed, forgetfulness is part of the plan. For you cannot recreate yourself anew as Who You Really Are if you already know Who You Really Are. So you have caused yourself to forget, that you may know again. Some people call this being born again. It is the same concept. It is about giving birth again to that which you already are. Or, as *CWG* continually puts it, "recreating yourself anew."

We are called upon and given an opportunity in our most difficult circumstances to bless, bless, bless those who call themselves our enemies. It is difficult to explain these concepts to a person who has just been raped, or tortured, or hurt or damaged in any way. Yet one may in such difficult times go to the example placed before us by the greatest teachers. One of them, you will recall, was nailed to a cross and left there to die. And his words about those who crucified him ring in our ears and sing in our souls to this very day.

Why Is There So Much Pain?

Dear Neale: There are a lot of things that I don't understand about your book even though I've read it twice so far. It sounds like you are saying that some people chose to do what appears as evil, to harm others. They believe what they gain—money, power, whatever—will make them happy. They have incorporated these values from others, rather than re-membering who they really are, manifestations of God. Their victims presumably somehow have made a choice to be victimized, if I understand your book. They place themselves in the time and place and situation where they can be harmed.

This would make sense if you believed in karma. This would be the effect of their actions and conduct in previous lives. The deaths of children would be understandable. Somehow they had earned or deserved such a fate. But if you don't believe in karma, this would seem to be unjust, particularly in the case of children. If someone harms them, or kills them before they have time to re-member who they really are, it sounds like they have to start life all over again along with whatever pain comes along with it until they re-member who they really are. I have seen children who have experienced so much overwhelming physical and emotional pain that they become psychotic.

If God really loves us, why does He want us to experience pain if we don't deserve it? I can understand pain that warns us from danger, like touching a hot stove. But the pain brought about by other people's evil choices (yes, that is judgmental but I'll stand by it), is different. It sounds like *CWG* says that somehow even though in great pain like that, we are supposed to produce thoughts "rooted in love" to produce a different kind of manifestation on the physical plane.

Or does God not care what we experience or what He experiences through us? It sounds like what He is saying is that the purpose of life is to experience things. Don't learn from it, just experience it. And somehow it is all going to turn into love.

I'm sorry I am bitter about this. I've seen too much pain to blithely write it off in the manner of thinking. I would really like to think that re-membering that I am God is going to make me rapturous and transform the world eventually. I want to believe that but, yes, it does sound too good to be true.

I hope to hear from you, Neale. I hope you don't mind my poking at your balloon. Zoe on the Internet.

Dear Zoe, Your questions are important ones, and no, of course I don't mind you "poking at my balloon." Let me look at a couple of your questions individually. You asked: "If God really loves us, why does He want us to experience pain if we don't deserve It?"

To begin with, God doesn't "want us" to experience pain. God doesn't "want" anything. God experiences GodSelf through us, and knows GodSelf anew in that way. God does not come from "wanting-ness," but from Total "Havingness." So it is an inaccurate assessment to say that God "wants" us to experience pain. This is more than just a semantics dance, however. I believe the distinction to be important, because if we think that God wants us to have painful experiences, we are forced to believe in a God Who makes no sense at all. (This, by the way, is the God in which most organized religions want us to believe.)

So we now can hold as true an image of a God who does not "want" us to have painful experiences, any more than He/She "wants" us to avoid them. God has no preference in the matter one way or the other. God's process, if you will, is to simply allow us to create anything we choose. And everything which comes to us—everything—we are choosing.

That is difficult for some of us to believe, I know. We find It easier to believe that God is bringing us these horrible experiences. You need to get the irony here. Unable to believe that we would do this to ourselves, we've accepted far more easily the thought that God is doing this to us. Extraordinary. Yet I have been assured by God that it is precisely the other way around. We bring upon ourselves every thought, every word, every experience. Now, as to why . . .

The human soul is eternal. It is on a journey of ending joy, celebrating every aspect of life that exists, allowing itself to notice and to create, to experience and to fulfill, Who It Really Is. *CWG Book 1* is quite clear in explaining "why bad things happen to good people." In order for the soul to know and experience itself as any particular thing, the exact opposite of that thing must come into the space. This is why, the moment you decide a thing about yourself—anything at all—its exact opposite will come into your life. For in this relative existence we are experiencing, hot cannot be hot without cold, tall cannot be tall without short, and you cannot be you without that which is not you. I am giving you a very short, very quick, answer here to a very large question. Re-read *CWG* a third time, if you need to, in order to capture this understanding more fully.

Masters know and understand all of this, which is why masters never complain in the face of extraordinary difficulty, but rather, bless their persecutors, and all circumstances and conditions which assail them. Masters know and understand that every person, place or thing in their life has been placed there by them, that they have drawn themselves to the right and perfect experiences, in order that they might know Who They Really Are.

Masters also understand that none of us are doing this dance alone, that all of us are in this together, that all souls have full understanding of what is happening, and that we, as partners in the dance of life, join together in our present forgetfulness, some of us playing the part of "victims," some as "villains," that we might create and fulfill our soul's purpose in this lifetime. Read again the story in *CWG* about "The Little Soul and the Sun."

Now Jesus understood all of this, which is why he looked at his crucifiers and said, "Father, forgive them, for they know not what they do." He understood that those other souls literally did not know what they were doing. That is, they had forgotten who they really are. And they had done so quite deliberately, in order that they might "play the villain" this time around. And, in the moment of their greatest villainy, they are depending upon you to remember Who They Really Are. In so doing, you heal them of their false thought about themselves, the thought that allowed them to act in this way in the first place, and thus, provide you with an opportunity to know and to experience Who You Choose to Be.

No one has ever come to you—no one—without a gift for you in his hands. This reality is described in heart-touching detail In *CWG 2*, in which God said to me: I have sent you nothing but angels.

You also wrote: "Or does God not care what we experience, or what He experiences through us? It sounds like what He is saying is that the purpose of life is to experience things. Don't learn from it, just experience it. And somehow it is all going to turn into love."

No, God does not "care" what we experience; not in the sense that She has any preference in the matter. God simply watches us experience our selves in a particular way, and invites us (and give us all the power) to choose again. However, God is not saying, as you suggest, that "the purpose of life is to experience things." God says in the book that the purpose of life is to create and to experience Who We Really Are, and that we are deciding and choosing that, every moment of every day with every thought, word and action.

God also advises us not to judge the experience of another, including very small children who seem to be suffering inordinately, or may have been born with a physical or mental challenge, or whatever. It is natural for us to feel sadness, to feel anger, to run through all sorts of emotions about these seeming injustices, even to become bitter, raising our fist to the heavens. Yet God says, "Judge not, for you do not know the journey upon which the soul of another has embarked." God also says that in the moment of greatest darkness, "Raise not your voice in condemnation, but rather, be a light unto the darkness, and curse it not."

You have also written, Zoe: "I've seen too much pain to blithely write it off like that. I would really like to think that re-membering that I am God is going to make me rapturous and transform the world eventually. I want to believe that, but yes, it does sound too good to be true."

I implore you to re-read the entire *Conversations with God, Book 1*, a third time because there is a great deal you seem to have missed. On page 44, I similarly accused God of making a "pie in the sky promise." And God replied: "What other kind of promise would you have God make? Would you believe Me if I promised you less? For thousands of people have disbelieved the promises of

God for the most extraordinary reason: they were too good to be true." As long as this reply to you has been, I know that it is still very superficial. I invite you to join us for one of our workshops or retreats. After a workshop, I am sure you would understand. Unless you wouldn't.

Revenge and Justice: Is There a Difference?

> Dear Mr. Walsch: I've almost finished with *CWG Book 1*, and I am sure that in order for me to completely, if ever, understand it, I will need to read it over and over and over (as God, He, She, It, You or Me says!). What is the difference between wanting revenge and waiting for justice? Thank you. Veda R., Pharr, TX.

Dear Veda, God never seeks revenge because God cannot be damaged. Justice is an interesting word which allows us to "justify" revenge. Justice is our human system for getting back, getting "even," or protecting ourselves from our next imagined hurt. All hurt is imagined (as is, for that matter, all of physical life). When we imagine ourselves to have been hurt, we often also imagine that we have to "undo" the hurt by making someone "pay for it." Or, at the very least, we decide we have to protect ourselves from being "hurt" again. This thought system is at the root of all that we would call "justice." It is an insane thought system in that it rests its case upon a truth which is not a truth, but a lie: the idea that we can be hurt or damaged at all.

One of the great teachings of the Jesus experience was that not even death can overcome us; that we are all Sons of God. This is a teaching which has been missed by all but a tiny handful of masters who now walk the planet. For those people who continue to believe in a paradigm which suggests that we are not all powerful, immortal beings, it might be well to notice that the universe has its own system for achieving balance in all things, and that system is called cause and effect, or natural outcome. There are natural outcomes to every thought, word or action . . . and these natural outcomes are often "punishment" enough, if punishment is indeed what "justice" requires.

No one who is embodied in God—that is, living and walking in Godliness—has the slightest need for what you would call "justice." Justice is, essentially, wanting something "bad" to happen to another because something "bad" has happened to us. God knows that nothing "bad" can happen to God, and therefore God needs nothing "bad" to ever happen to another! It is all really quite simple. And, I admit, quite "elevated." Yet it is this level of thinking and experiencing to which God continually invites us.

What Is the Right Action to Take Against Injustice?

Dear Mr. Walsch: I can faintly comprehend the idea that we are all one—that I am Hitler—even that we are not to judge ourselves, but simply to choose to change our ways. But I still cannot come to terms with just "accepting" and "observing" gratuitous cruelty, like the sexual abuse of children, serial murder—I cannot embrace Charles Manson or Jeffrey Dahmer.

My being cries out for justice—not retribution, but protection of the innocent. You write that we cannot know the meaning to the individual of the suffering. But I am overwhelmed by the feeling that the killer of a little child should be stopped by the society around him. Realistically, the prospects of rehabilitation are almost nil. Only incarceration can stop the child-killer and protect the rest of us (who are one with him!).

I have been hearing about the "Mexican Mafia," which is a Mexican prison group which is terrifyingly powerful, even from jail. Is it really spiritual wisdom to observe them and do nothing? Using the word "right" in the sense that you use it, at this stage of our spiritual understanding, what is the "right" thing for society to do with the Charles Mansons and the Jeffrey Dahmers? Is not the Mexican Mafia at war with society?

I have never found an answer to this question in the Gospel injunction to "go and sin no more," which rarely works. I feel each of us has a moral obligation to vote one way or the other for societal actions, or am I still missing the boat?

May God continue to bless you, and all of us through you. Sincerely, Martha, Leesburg, FL.

Dear Martha, Thank you for your blessing. You raise some interesting questions. Let's dialogue on this, shall we? I'll pull some statements out of your letter and respond to them individually, as if we were having a conversation.

You say: "I still cannot come to terms with just 'accepting' and 'observing' gratuitous cruelty, like the sexual abuse of children, serial murder, etc." No one is requiring you to do this. *CWG Book 1* (chapter 8, pages 132-134) offers some very helpful insights on this subject. I invite you to go back and read these passages again. Among other things, the dialogue there points out that "even an abuser is abused if his abuse is allowed to continue." You may also, however, want to turn to *CWG*, chapter 9, pages 151-154 for additional insights. "I cannot embrace Charles Manson or Jefffrey Dahmer." I refer you now to the very last sentence on page 84 and the first sentence on page 85. For those of you who do not have books nearby, I am not going to quote to you from this reference. I want you to look it up. Savor it. Absorb it. Integrate it into your thought system. You say: "I am overwhelmed by the feeling that the killer of a little child should be stopped by society around him." Then do so. Then stop him. Again, see *CWG* page 132. Forgive me, but you have not read the text very carefully if you still have this question.

You say: "Is it really spiritual wisdom to observe them and do nothing?" What is the "right" thing for society to do with the Charles Mansons and the Jeffrey Dahmers? Same question, same answer.

You say: "I feel each of us has a moral obligation to vote one way or the other for societal actions, or am I still missing the boat?" No, you are not missing the boat, Martha. You are building the "boat." You are creating the ship in which you will sail the seas of life. You are creating your reality and defining who you are by these thoughts and decisions. Yet read one more time the passage beginning on page 151. For that passage drives directly to the heart of your questions. What is the "right" thing to do? Is the death penalty serving us? Is it "correct"? How about life imprisonment? Read the book again, Martha. Pay particular attention to these key passages. Then send me the answer to your questions!

Where Does Forgiveness Fit In?

Dear Neale Donald Walsch: I have so many questions regarding *CWG*, but I think I'll just ask one at this time. I don't recall reading anything about forgiveness. Did God in this conversation mention forgiveness, since forgiveness is such a large issue in Christianity? Also, your format is very similar to *A Course In Miracles*, in which forgiveness is almost everything. This book has helped me tremendously so far, although it really has scared me in many ways. I appreciate all of your efforts. Tracey, NY.

Dear Tracey, I'm sorry that the book really scared you. You're the first person ever to have told me that. Maybe everyone else was too scared to! But Tracey, I want you to know that I forgive you!

Okay, enough kidding around. Here's what I know about forgiveness. In God's world, it is not necessary. God's "forgiveness" is not required for anything. Forgiveness implies that we could do something to offend God, and that is simply not so. The reason God cannot be offended is that God cannot be hurt or damaged in any way. You cannot "hurt" God's "feelings." You cannot "damage" God's "self-esteem," and obviously you cannot damage God's body. In the absence of the ability to inflict hurt or damage, there is nothing to forgive. And why is it that God cannot be hurt? Very simple. It is because there is nothing that God wants or needs from us. That's right. God wants nothing from us, least of all that we worship Him, much less worship Him in a certain way. Put in another way, God's love for us is unconditional. No matter what we do, God does not give a damn. He gives blessings, but He never gives a "damn."

Does this mean that we do not have to use the tool of forgiveness in our own lives? Well, Eric Segal was right when he wrote in his wonderful novel, *Love Story*, "Love means never having to say you're sorry." Still, until we reach that level of understanding and mastery, forgiveness can be a powerful learning device. It allows us to "let go" of our grievances, and to move on with our lives. In fact, forgiveness can be one of the single most powerful transformational tools ever.

The truth about us is that we cannot be hurt or damaged either. We simply do not know that. We have gotten caught up in "non-remembrance," forgetting Who We Really Are, and allowing the illusion of hurt and damage to seem very real. It is only when we return to the realm of the absolute, following what we call our physical "death," that we realize that no one has ever hurt us, and that we were "making it all up."

Mind you, we have become so good at making it all up that to us, it seems very, very authentic. But it is not. And in the moment of our transition from this life to the next we will realize this fully. It is in that moment when we will forgive everyone for everything we imagine they have done to us, and in the next when we come to understand that even our forgiveness is unnecessary, because there are no victims and there are no villains, only a divine process which is ongoing. For more on this topic, and a better understanding of it, read the children's book, *The Little Soul and the Sun*, available at bookstores everywhere from Hampton Roads Publishing.

Now what is scary about this for some people is that, if there is never any real reason to forgive anyone, and if God does not "punish" us for anything, that must mean we can all do whatever it is we want to do. This, in turn, translates in some people's minds into pure chaos, with everyone running amok and all of us doing horrible things to each other. This idea grows out of the thought that the human race is inherently bad, and that, left to our own devices, with no threats or controls hanging over us, we would all behave very poorly.

In fact, exactly the opposite would be found to be true, as highly evolved beings who once lived under a system of laws and exterior controls much like ours, learned once they stepped out of their fear. It was a fear so strong that they, too, invented a God of vengeance and retribution, just like ours, until they discovered, over the course of many thousands of years, that such a God was not necessary. We are just beginning to learn that on this planet.

But What About "Justice for All"?

Dear Neale, Please help! I am finding it difficult to understand why God would let evilness go unpunished. I have always believed in the adage "what goes around, comes around." It seems for me to be the only way I can get on with my life after being hurt

> by others' unscrupulous and unconscionable behavior and downright cruelty towards me and my family. I had no doubt that someday they'll get their just reward. But now, am I to believe that their acts will go unpunished? How can this be? What kind of a Father would not discipline His children? How can people just get away with hurting others? I know that the soul does not die, but can the soul be hurt, or is it just the body and the heart and feelings that can be hurt? It doesn't seem fair. I am one to believe that life should be and is fair, otherwise, why are we here? Why would God put us in an unfair world? What is your feeling on Karma? Justice? Justice for all? What can I do? Donna, Milford, CT.

My dear Donna: Am I hearing you say that the only way you can get on with your life is by knowing that those who have hurt you are going to "get it in the end"? Whew, excuse me, Donna, but that's a pretty sad state of affairs. I think you'd better re-think your idea of how the world works, what life is about, and the true source of your greatest joy. Forgiveness, Donna, forgiveness is where the release and the joy is, not revenge.

You ask if you are now to believe that the "evil" acts of others are to go "unpunished." Of course they are, Donna. Who would administer the punishment? God? Then who would God punish? There is no one else but God! So God would be punishing Himself!

This much I can tell you, though, Donna. *CWG 3* makes a very clear statement that "what you cause others to experience, you, yourself, will one day experience." But be clear about something. This is not karma. And this is not punishment. You will do this out of free choice. In this sense, no being escapes the consequences of his actions—because no being chooses to.

It is part of the process of evolution, by which divine beings bring themselves the experiences they, themselves, have created, so that they might know the entirety of the experience intimately, the better to know, and to choose again, who and what they really are.

To answer your other question, no, the soul cannot be hurt. And that is because the soul wants and needs nothing. Only aspects of being who want and need something can be hurt. This is precisely why God cannot be hurt —and why God, therefore, has no reason to "punish" us.

Finally, Donna, no, life is not "fair." But life is not unfair, either. Life simply is. It is we who have labeled things fair or unfair. And by the way, we have changed our minds about many of those things from day to day, year to year, and century to century. A few generations ago we thought it was "fair" to burn witches at the stake, or to hang them, and we did so in Salem, Massachusetts. We held up our Bibles as justification for our "fair" treatment of those women. Today we no longer do that. We do fry people in electric chairs, however—and many of us hold up our Bibles as justification for that. (Even though the Pope, God bless him, made it very clear when he recently visited America that no Christian interpretation of the teachings of Jesus could possibly condone this.)

So you see, Donna, "fair" is what we say it is. You want life to be "fair" according to your definition of "fair"? Tell you what you can do, Donna. Go out and work for that. Create that in your reality. Create it in the world around you. We can all do that by working to bring a higher sense of spirituality into our politics and governance. And that's just where this letter started, Donna. We've just come full circle. I hope you will join us on the team that is being created to make some very exciting things happen here. Thanks for writing.

CHAPTER 8

Death and Dying

Death does not exist.

Death is a figment of our imagination. It is a part of our mythology, but not a truth of the universe.

We are eternal beings. We have always been, we are now, and we always will be, very much alive. It is impossible for us not to be alive, because what we are is life itself, expressing in differing forms. We are what Life is. Life is what we are.

We are also what God is. God is also what we are.

We are also what Joy is. Joy is also what we are.

God, Joy, Life. The words are interchangeable. Now, to understand the mysteries of the universe, simply add one more word to that list: your name.

God, Joy, Life, Neale. The words are interchangeable.

God, Joy, Life, Anna. The words are interchangeable.

God, Joy, Life, Roger. The words are interchangeable.

Pick a name, any name. Your name, or the name of another. Add it to the list, and become clear that all the words are interchangeable.

A Question on Abortion

> Neale Donald Walsch: I found *CWG* to be very inspiring. Thank you for asking about life and love and success!! I am interested in your insights about abortion especially. Jacqueline, Tucson, AZ.

Dear Jacqueline, I find it interesting that among the questions I am asked the most are questions on abortion and homosexuality. I think that people really want to know what God thinks about these things, so that they can settle all this for themselves once and for all.

The first thing I want you to know is that God makes no judgment about these (or any other) behaviors. There is, therefore, also no punishment. So anyone looking for a God of judgment, condemnation and punishment is going to be very disappointed in the God who talked with me. The second thing I want to say is that all behaviors are classified by us as "good" or "bad" depending upon who and what we are trying to be. That is, every value judgment we here on earth make is based on a value system which is constructed around our own personal goals. This system has nothing to do with whether a thing is "right" or "wrong," "good" or "bad" objectively, but only subjectively. Let me give you some examples.

A young man wanted to join the wrestling team in college, but he was of slight build. The coach told him he needed to "put some meat on those bones" if he was going to wrestle, and recommended that the young man supplement his diet with bananas and milk shakes. Two blocks away a young woman who was studying to be a ballerina was being scolded by her teacher. "Young lady," the instructor warned, "you are not going to be able to dance in the Nutcracker this season if you continue to put on such weight. You are to stop eating bananas and milk shakes at once!"

Is a diet of bananas and milk shakes "good" or "bad"? It depends on what you are trying to do.

A woman was arrested in Omaha, Nebraska, recently for doing exactly what she'd done in Reno, Nevada, only a week before. A professional prostitute, she found out, much to her dismay, that there was nothing "wrong" with prostitution *per se*, but that it was the locale which made a thing "right" or "wrong."

"Right" and "wrong" also depend on what time it is. In New England not all that many years ago, burning witches at the stake was considered "good," and quite legal. Today it is considered "bad," and is quite illegal. What has changed? Nothing but the time.

For centuries, the Most Holy Roman Catholic Church said that eating meat on Friday was a sin. Then, in 1952, or somewhere thereabouts, a declaration was made by the Pope. From then on and forever more, eating meat on Friday was no longer "bad." Thus we see that "good" and "bad," "right" and "wrong" are a product of time and geography.

Is abortion "wrong"? From an objective point of view, no. Does it represent to our highest good? That all depends on what we are trying to do. Are we saving the life of the mother? Are we changing the outcome of an act of violence, namely, rape? Are we using abortion as a means of birth control? Our answers differ from case to case, and from person to person. With each decision we make in our lives, we create and express who we really are, and what we think of ourselves. As individuals, and as a nation; as a society, and as an entire race of beings. We are in the constant process of defining ourselves. Every choice is, in fact, a definition. Every decision is a creation. And the creation is us.

Now, so as not to escape your straightforward question, my own views on abortion are these: I would not choose to use abortion as a means of birth control. I would choose for the child to be born, and then, if I did not feel I could raise the child, or that I simply could not afford it, and thus could not give the child a good life, I would seek to give the child up for adoption. On the other hand, if the choice was between aborting a birth or watching a mother die, I would opt for terminating the pregnancy. If my daughter was brutally raped at the age of 13 and became pregnant, I would similarly not require that the pregnancy be brought to term. There are other instances, as well, in which I believe I would find abortion acceptable.

I understand that it is easy for me to sit here and make these observations. For one thing, I am not a woman, and do not therefore have the same perspective as a woman, nor can I. I can only define who I am. I cannot define—nor should I seek to define—another.

Yet all laws do exactly that. We define ourselves as a society by our laws. Yet ought we? I believe the answer is no. All laws are unnatural, in that they seek to impose on others the views which only a particular person (or a particular group) may hold. A law is a way to produce an unnatural consequence, when the natural consequence of any action ought to have been enough.

In our society, natural consequences are not enough, and that is because we are barbarians. Watching someone die, seeing their life expire right in front of our eyes, is not enough to stop us from killing people. Indeed, our primitive society glorifies this watching of life expire, putting it on huge screens in living color, and bringing it right into our living rooms. The act of love, however, is not allowed on those screens in nearly such explicit detail, and when it does appear there in that way, half the country screams bloody murder. Because it is bloody murder they can live with in their movies, but not, for God's sake, s-e-x.

In truly enlightened kingdoms and societies, laws are nonexistent. All regulation is self-regulation, all definitions are self-definitions.

This is difficult for most people to accept. Still, it is how it is on enlightened worlds. And there are such worlds in our universe (see *CWG Book 3*). I don't know if this is the sort of answer you expected or sought, Jacqueline, but it is what comes up for me when I look at your question.

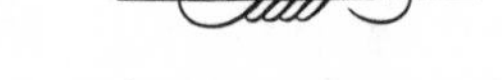

Is Abortion Murder?

> Dear Mr. Walsch: My wife and I had two abortions before we were married and now have a beautiful daughter. There is not a day that goes by that we don't think about and regret our decisions to terminate. Please ask God when the mind and soul actually enter the body and if what we did was murder. Love, Jeff.

Dear Jeff, With respect and with kindness, may I tell you that I do not answer requests to "ask God" this or that, because I never want to set myself up, Jeff, as some sort of new intermediary. The whole point of *CWG* is that we do not need any other person, process, religion or organization to help us communicate with God. Each of us may have our own conversation with God whenever we choose. Having said that, I am happy to give you the benefit of my own understanding of what I have already received on this subject in the *CWG* dialogue.

Jeff, it is time now to let go of whatever guilt you may have about a decision that you, yourself, say you both regret. Your regret is enough. Guilt is not required, and serves nothing. And while you have not said that you feel guilty, it seems clear that this is, at least, part of what is at play in your remembrances of this decision and action.

My understanding is that when the soul enters the bodily vehicle, the influx of energy is so immediate and so enormous that the heart starts beating at once. Nobody knows, incidently (at least, I have not found anyone who can tell me medically) why the heart starts beating at a given point in time in the development of the fetus. But I have been informed from Another Source that the answer is simple: the influx of pure electric current—the energy of life—jump-starts the heart when the soul enters the body.

I may or may not have interpreted this information correctly, Jeff, but that is not the real question in any event. It is important to understand that death does not exist. So you are not guilty of what you would call "murder." It is also important to understand that nothing happens to an individual soul—you can do nothing to another—which overrides and supercedes the sovereignty of the soul. Everything which occurs in our lives occurs in perfect order, including the end of our lives in a particular physical form. Each soul is divine, and each soul co-creates with The All, that which leads it to its perfect expression.

I suggest that this soul may well have joined with a fetus for the particular and specific purpose of allowing you to confront the decision and the choice that you made, and to deal with it in whatever way led you both to your next highest stage of growth. If you have grown from this experience, and have served the purpose of the moment (for the purpose of all of life is to grow, to become more of what you actually are)—if this is what has happened, do you imagine that you and your wife were the only players? That would be an inaccurate assessment. The soul of this blessed other was also involved, in a very conscious way. Nothing happened to that soul which it did not choose. How can I be so sure of that? Because it is not possible for it to be any other way.

When you understand fully the sovereignty of the soul, Jeff, you will see the larger mosiac of the divine design. You will see how we all co-create together to produce a given result and a particular experience, including, I might add, the experience of my answering this question for you. So go now, my friend, and live in peace and love, knowing that you are larger now than you were before; that you have grown. Bless all those who have helped you in your growth and understanding, yet do not condemn yourself for the path which you have taken which led to your growth. For God does not condemn you, and never will. I love you.

Dealing with the Death of an Infant

Hello, Neale: I just read your wonderful, warm, and uplifting book. I picked it up after struggling for answers after our infant son died six weeks ago. I am confused about one part of what I believe is a central theme of the book: that we create our own reality. Specifically, the thought that wanting something only gives the experience of "wantingness," not the "thing" that is wanted. I believe that when most people say "I want good health" (for example), they really don't wish to experience the lack of, or wanting of, health, but they want to experience health itself! I understand this is the "set up," the "law" of the universe, but since most people do not know this, they actually are not able to live life to the fullest.

Even more specifically, I really need (and want) to know that my son is okay. By wanting him to give me a sign that he is okay, am I pushing that away even further? The book *Hello from Heaven* says that praying, or asking for (or wanting) a sign, will help that to happen. So I'm confused about how to go about this.

I'm trying to find meaning and answers in my life. I've never had a conscious two-way conversation with God, and I've never even come close to receiving written answers (or any other incontrovertible answers for that matter!), even though I also have written letters and prayed to Him/Her. In love and peace, Andrea, by E-mail.

Dear Andrea: Hello, my friend . . . I am sorry for the sadness you must be feeling at the loss of your child. I wish I could comfort you in a more personal way. This much I want to share: everything is so wonderful now for your son. He could not be in a better place. He could not be happier in any way. He is being held and embraced and loved by father/mother God, the Goddess part of which comes out to manifest in the space of all little children everywhere.

Your son is a blessed being who came to experience exactly what he experienced, and to allow you to experience exactly what you experienced, and then he left as quickly as he came, to move on with his continuing experiences of life forever. You, as his mother, were a grand blessing to him, for you gave him life itself at this physical level, and he understands very well the treasure with which he was gifted by you. The love he experienced in your arms is a love he will never forget.

Your two souls are linked forever, and have been from the beginning of time. This is not the first time the two of you have danced together, nor will it be the last. You will see each other again and again and again, of that you may be sure. Be at peace and celebrate in the knowing that the roles you played together this time were perfectly crafted to allow each of you to remember exactly what you needed to know in order to grow and evolve and become more of Who You Really Are. Everything is perfect is God's world, and nothing happens without purpose or meaning.

I wish to say softly that it will not be beneficial to you to hang out "wanting" a sign from your son that he is all right or wanting some sort of contact with, or from, him. You may possibly create consternation on his side if he sees that for some reason you are unable to hear what he is already trying to tell you—through all manner of means—not the least of which could very well be this answer.

Do not get caught up in this desire and turn it into a "need." Rather, "let go and let God." Allow God to work wonders in your life now regarding all of this. Wonders of healing, wonders of wisdom, wonders of love. Pray to God not to hear from your son, but that your son may hear from you: of your love, of your everlasting devotion to his being (which you have already proven), and of your willingness now to let him go, to release him from the pull of your own desires, that he may fly now, high and far, and move on with his next grand adventures, not needing any more to worry about you. Tell him that you are all right, that you are going to "make it." This is what he wishes to hear. Then he can be fully free. He will come to you often, but let it be in response to the joy of your memories, not your pain. In your feelings you will feel him, in your mind and dreams you will see him, in your heart you will hear his gentle gurgle and the words he had not yet learned to say, but which were always in his eyes, words that said "I love you, Mommy" with every moment he lived, and lives even now.

Then, having released any need for him to "stick around" with you, having given him his freedom as only a parent can, move on with your life in its own fullest measure, for you have others yet to love, others yet to know, others yet to heal of their own sorrows. You are a gentle and courageous lady, a person of wonder and inner beauty. And the world awaits the continuing giving of your gift. Please do not deny us.

God's great gift to you is this moment now. Use it to create and to live the grandest version of the greatest vision you ever had about yourself. And, rather than feel ongoing sorrow at your child's departure, look to see, and choose to experience always, the gift which he brought you, and the wonder of its continuing presence in your life forever. For his gift will be present in you, every time you give love unconditionally to another. You will do so in his name, and in yours. For you are one. I love you for your openness. You have honored me with such private sharings. Blesséd be.

Understanding Tragedies

Dear Neale Donald Walsch: I'm one of the people for whom you wrote *CWG Book 1*. There wasn't a lot in it that was a new idea for me, but it was astonishing to see my beliefs in print. I felt that I was on the right path, somehow. Then, immediately after that idea, life intervened. My son's CAT scan showed that his melanoma is spreading very rapidly throughout his body and urgent, terrible steps must be taken. I forgot all about my insights and faith, and I now feel desperately in need of good words. This is definitely a crisis of belief for me, and letting go, allowing my son's cancer to be his issue, has definitely been a challenge. Thank you, and keep writing. RuthAnn, OR.

Dear RuthAnn, Thank you for your letter, and thank you for your honest description of what you are now moving through. Your challenge here in this moment, as I see it, is to get back in touch with the perfection of all things. It is difficult to see perfection in the suffering of another, especially when that person is someone who is so very close to us. It is difficult to see perfection in the passing of another from this life to the next. Especially when that person is so close to us. Just three days before my answering this letter, I received word that my brother had died of a very sudden heart attack while driving his car home. The news took me by surprise. I have been in a blue mood about this for days, reflecting on life and death, the substance that we put in between our birth and our departure, and the meaning of it all.

Your letter has been more of a healing for me than, I'm afraid, my answer is going to be for you. Because you have caused me to once again look at the larger pattern of perfection which runs through all of our lives. In seeking to find the words to answer you, I have found the words to answer myself, and those words are these: There is nothing in God's world, not a thing in the universe, that is not in perfect order. Everything proceeds according to this perfect design. Each soul is a sovereign entity, creating for itself the experiences it now wishes to experience. That includes the experience of transformation from this life into the next. When we lose a loved one, or someone who is dear to us is suffering, it is difficult, and understandably so, for us to stay connected with this concept of divine order. Yet I know that the soul does not bring to itself, nor would God supply to the soul, anything which is not exactly suited to the purpose at hand. That purpose is evolution. And sometimes the needs of the soul and the ways in which it has designed for itself to evolve are not known to us consciously. I mean that on a conscious level, frequently none of it makes any sense.

It is only when we understand and reconnect with the larger truth that all things occur in perfect sequence, that we can find a place of peace within us, even a place of joy, in the calm acceptance of everything that is happening. Our peace will be further expanded by relinquishing our need for any particular result or outcome. Somewhere along the line through the years I picked up a phrase that covers much of this: "God hasn't made a mistake in a very long time." I truly believe that, even on the days when holding to that belief is very tough, as when they called me and told me that my brother, who was very much alive and in my life only days earlier in our last telephone conversation, was no longer with us in his physical form. I was stunned and shaken, as I'm sure you must have been when you received the results of your son's CAT scan.

We now have an opportunity to both move into knowing the grandest truth. Each experience of our life presents us with that opportunity. Indeed, each experience is created for precisely that purpose. So I will join you now, and I will ask you to join me, in moving to this place of higher knowing. Let us hold hands together across the miles in these hours when our highest understandings are being challenged. Let us meld our minds and become one in our highest thought. Let us know that God is a God of love who intends only that which is perfect and best for us, and let us truly find peace in our grandest awarenesses. Indeed, let us give thanks to God for the perfection of this moment. I am with you. In my heart and in my mind. Now, let me tell you a story.

"Helen" was one of 97 participants at one of my Recreating Yourself retreats, held between Christmas and New Year's in the mountains of Estes Park, Colorado. On the final night of the retreat before our New Year's Eve resolutions ritual, Helen raised her hand and asked for the microphone.

"I've heard a lot this week about how God is our best friend, how God is wonderful and loving, and how we should all have a conversation with God every day," she began. "Well, if I had a conversation with God, I would tell Him that I am damned angry with Him."

"That's okay," I said, "God can handle that. But are you okay?"

"No," she said, and her voice was trembling now.

"Well, just what are you angry with God about?"

Helen took a deep breath. "Almost 25 years ago we adopted a baby boy. We had tried to conceive for five years, without success. It looked like we would never be parents. My biological clock was running out. So we adopted Billy. Three weeks later, I discovered I was pregnant. I had the child, another boy, and raised them both as my own, although we did tell our first son when he grew a little older that he was adopted. We wanted to be truthful with him. We told him we loved him exactly the same as his brother, and we knew that our actions showed him that.

"There was never any complication around this until Billy was eight. Then one day he came home from school very angry. They must have been teasing him on the playground or something. You know how kids can be. They can sometimes be very cruel. Anyway, he came home just furious, and wanted to know why his mommy would give him away. He also demanded to see his mommy right away.

"I felt terrible, of course. First, for the anguish and hurt that I could see Billy was going through, and second for myself. I was filled with sadness because, of course, I felt that I was Billy's mommy. I stood there remembering the nights of changing diapers and nursing him through sickness and all the things that mommies do, and my heart broke that Billy didn't see me anymore as, didn't think of me as, his mom.

"But I understood—I had to understand—and I promised him that when he was older, if he still felt he wanted to, he would meet his mom. I would do whatever I could to find her and arrange it.

"This seemed okay with Billy, but he never seemed to get over his anger. He just had this anger all through the rest of his childhood and into his teen years, which were very difficult for us. We all got through it, but it wasn't easy on any of us in the family, and certainly not on me.

"When Billy had grown older, we talked again about seeing his mother, and we made an agreement that when he turned twenty-one, I would begin searching for her if he still wanted me to. Throughout the rest of his teen years he reminded me of that promise.

"Finally, Billy's twenty-first birthday arrived. Within days, he was killed in an automobile accident."

There was a collective gasp from the retreat participants. Abruptly, Helen's energy shifted into anger.

"Now I want you to tell me," she snapped, "how any kind of loving God could have let that happen, just when Billy was about to meet his mother, just when we were about to reconcile the strain which his yearning had placed on our relationship. I want you to tell me, why would God do that?"

The room plummeted into stunned silence.

I was stopped cold. I stared at Helen for a moment, then closed my eyes and went within. I heard my thoughts. "Okay, God, this is it. I don't know what to say here. You've got to help me out."

Suddenly, my eyes popped open, my mind overflowing. I spoke the words I heard in my head before I had a chance to judge them or edit them.

"Billy died at 21 because that was when he was promised he would meet his mother—and when he turned 21 his mother was not on this Earth."

The room gasped again. Someone whispered "yes." Someone else cried.

I went on.

"There is no such thing as an accident, and nothing happens by coincidence in God's world. You were given a biological son, even though you had not been able to conceive and it looked as if you might never be able to do so, because there was a plan—a larger plan—in place. You were given this special gift in exchange for your willingness to take Billy in, give him a home, love him and raise him as your own, and care for him until he was ready to meet his mother, and she was ready to meet him. The day of Billy's death was the happiest day of his life. And his gratefulness to you for bringing him to that moment is eternal. It surrounds your heart, and creates with you an everlasting bond. There is perfection in Life's design. In every human circumstance and experience. In every condition. Our opportunity is to notice this. That is also our release. Our salvation. The end to our suffering and our pain."

Helen's face changed immediately. Filled with anger just moments before, now it was aglow. Her whole body seemed drained of every tension. She looked relaxed for the first time in a week. And tears ran down her cheeks, even as she smiled with a radiance that filled the room.

I've told this story because I want you to know what Helen and all the other participants in that retreat now know. There is a "magic formula" which has been given to us by the heavens. It is a formula with which all sadness, all anger, all negativity surrounding any human experience is dissolved. It is a formula which allows us to recreate ourselves anew. It is a formula easy to remember, and stated in three words: See the perfection.

Ah, but does it work? Does it really work? New Year's Eve Helen handed me a note. She'd written a poem when she'd returned to her room after a walk under the clear, crisp Colorado sky the night before.

I came here with a burdened heart,
A heart afraid to cry.
It's near three years since Billy left
And I couldn't say goodbye.
I stood, alone, beside his grave
And couldn't even cry
We had a deal, I said to him
You left me high and dry.
It's near three years since Billy left,
God had not seen fit to try
To soothe this hurt, to heal this heart,
To give me tears to cry
And then God spoke. He pointed out
That even though He tried,
My heart was closed and couldn't hear
His gentle, ageless sigh.
And though it was just Neale whose voice
Brought the message from on high,
My spirit heard God's words tonight,
And now my eyes can cry.
I took a walk this starry night.
It's finally time to try
To find the joy to free my son.
It's time to say goodbye.
And as I did, a shooting star . . .
. . . danced across the sky.

Two of My Children Died

Dear Neale: I have so much to say to you that it is difficult to know where to begin. A new friend gave me two *CWG* books, and they have changed my life in several ways. First, much of what I read in *Book 1* reawoke memories of beliefs that I took for granted as truths when I was a very young child. Various pressures made me forget those truths over the years, and I ended up believing that everything about me was wrong, though somewhere in my soul I still believed my truths. I married a man whose most important value was his and his family's image in the eyes of society, and the marriage was a mistake. I hung in there for fifteen years and had four extraordinary children until I realized that I was dying in the relationship, and for my children's sake I had to leave.

At first, our life without my husband was idyllic, and then things began to change. A lot of it was my fault: I discovered that I was a young woman again and that I had a lot of living to do. My priorities were split between enjoying major rebellion and what was best for my children. Then my eldest daughter, with whom I had always been at loggerheads, had her custody changed to her father and his girlfriend, in spite of all my pleas not to, and very shortly afterward, she caught a lethal virus while swimming in a still, fresh-water pond, and died after eight weeks in intensive care. My grief and guilt were overwhelming. To compound it, a rumor (encouraged by my ex-husband) circulated that I had been responsible for her death by giving her an overdose of drugs, which was patently impossible. However, people believe what they want to believe, and that terrible rumor destroyed what was left of my life.

I tried to carry on our lives as best I could while sinking ever more deeply into a morass of depression. My other three children went to boarding school and I sold our house in the South and moved into our summer barn in the mountains in New York to be nearer them. I had several jobs and finally ran my house as a bed-and-breakfast because that was the only way I could survive and keep my children's home. Finally the depression won out and I ended up in a hospital, suicidal.

After being told that if I went back to the mountains I would be either dead or back in the hospital within six months, I moved to another state. The children were all out of school by then and leading their own lives, and things began to look up. Then my beautiful, talented, warm-hearted, brilliant son was killed by a drunk driver one week to the day after his twenty-seventh birthday. Why? What plan did your God have in that?

After my daughter died, by some miracle she and I were able to talk to each other. We forgave each other our badness to each other; she told me that what I had taught my children about what happens after you die was true, but I didn't know a millionth of it, and that she was happy and well and would always be one of my guardian angels. How could she let that happen to my son then? What in God's name was God's plan? That was almost eight years ago, but I still rage and grieve and rage.

Last summer I decided that my life was useless and I needed a new one. I moved to a place an hour away from my youngest daughter, and am giving a jump-start to a new career. With the help of your books, I will make a success of it. But the books and the newsletters are sugar-coated. Although so much of *CWG* is valid and true (and I know this in my heart and soul), how can you explain the terrible, painful things that happen? Is it a punishment for a few terrified years of self-indulgence? Is it a karmic payback for sins of a former life that I'm not aware of in this one?

It's hard to believe that I "chose" what has happened. Could anyone be that cruel? Reading the book, *When Bad Things Happen to Good People*, took some of the pressure off, but the impression I got from that was that God doesn't concern Himself with the everyday actions and tragedies of mere people, that we are to Him as ants are to us. That certainly contradicts what I always believed (and taught my children to believe), that God is in all things from a blade of grass to the mightiest star. If I am to go on believing that, then I also have to believe that God is unconscious and uncaring, which is hard for me because of my personal miracles.

Please, if you have God's ear and voice, ask him why? Why? Give me some answer that will take away the agony so that I can go on with my life. Platitudes won't help. I truly need an answer. Please. You were given a beautiful answer for the woman whose adopted son died at twenty-one. Can you find one for me? Respectfully yours, Cynthia, address withheld.

Dear Cynthia, I was deeply touched by what you shared with me, and I only hope that my response can in some way be adequate.

Here is what I get, Cynthia, when I meditate on the situation you have described. Your son and your daughter made a pact before either of them came into their bodies. Their agreement was to arrive together and to leave together. These two souls have danced together many times before. They have laughed together and cried together; they have walked together on the path through the eons and across the centuries.

It may not seem this way to you now, Cynthia, but I can assure you that this is true. And when your daughter left and went to this golden place that she has described to you, your son was filled with a loneliness—experienced at the soul level—that is beyond anything you or I could possibly understand.

I do not know how close these two were in this lifetime, but I am very sure of how close they have been from the beginning of time. When your daughter left, it was only natural for him to follow. Your daughter did not "let this happened to your son," as you put it, but, rather, allowed him the choice he was making. She did not try to stop him, nor in any way seek to prevent what occurred, because to do so would have been to interfere with another's free will, and that is something that no soul on the "other side" would ever do.

I can tell you with absolute assurance that these two souls are happier now than you have ever seen them in your life. They are dancing together once more. They are laughing together again. And their only wish now is that you will release and let go of your anguish and your pain, of your rage and your grief.

These things, too, I can tell you categorically: what has happened has nothing to do with punishment. Your "years of self-indulgence" have nothing to do with it. As *Conversations with God* clearly says, God does not punish us, but always and only blesses us.

I know that it is hard to believe that you "chose" what has happened. At a conscious level, obviously you did not. At a super-conscious level, however, you agreed to give the gift of togetherness to these children, just as you gave them the gift of life. Both experiences were at some level painful, and both produced great joy.

Theirs is a grand plan, involving many lives together in the past, and many lives together yet to come. Trying to understand the plan is like trying to understand a snowflake. In the end, we can only behold the wonder of it. It does us no good to mourn the fact that it has melted. Far better for us to simply celebrate the beauty that it has brought into our lives.

I want to comment on your impression that God doesn't concern Himself with the everyday actions and tragedies of His people. *Conversations with God* makes the same point that was made in the book *When Bad Things Happen to Good People*. This point is not that God does not care about us, but that God cares about us so much that He grants us total free will in the creation of the reality we choose. God cannot impose His preferences on us. If He did, we would not have free will, but rather, we would simply be living lives which were being experienced according to a plan over which we have no control. This would not be fitting for enlightened beings, and we would soon become restless and unhappy. Just as our children would become restless if we told them everything we wanted them to do, stopped them from making every one of their mistakes, made sure that they never hurt themselves, or even experienced the possibility of hurting themselves. If we did that, it would be a very short time before they ran from us as fast as they could. For the human soul yearns to be free, not so protected that it can never experience anything that the Father does not want it to experience. *CWG* says clearly, "your will for you is God's will for you," and in this revelation is the answer to your question, Cynthia. I'm sorry to have taken so much time with this response, but I have done my very best to reach inside, and not give you a shallow reply. I hope that you can return to a place of great joy in your life, knowing that everything is falling into place exactly as it should in order for you to be and to declare, to announce and to become, to express and to fulfill Who You Really Are. I send you love, and all the blessings from all the heavens. Thank you for writing to me, and sharing with me from the deepest part of your soul.

Dying While Hearing Conversations with God

Dear Neale: I have to let you know that my father passed away a month ago today. I am trying to let go, but it has been difficult. He was a wonderful man, and I miss him dearly. At the time he was in the hospital I had your book with me and I read portions of it to my sister. There was one passage that struck me profoundly at the time, and it stayed with me. I was very moved by it, and have to admit that I included it in my Father's obituary. I realized later that I had to get your permission before reprinting any portion of your book. I am asking you now if it was okay to do this. I will understand if there will be any type of remuneration required. I apologize for going about it in this way. I am sending you a copy of my Father's obituary so you will see what I did. This was the passage:

"You are goodness and mercy and compassion and understanding. You are peace and joy and light. You are forgiveness and patience, strength and courage, a helper in time of need, a comforter in time of sorrow, a healer in time of injury, a teacher in times of confusion. You are the deepest wisdom and the highest truth; the greatest peace and the grandest love. You are these things. And in moments of your life you have known yourself as these things."

My Father passed away within the hour in which I read the passage. I think of him, and the moment he passed on, when I read this passage. Thank you for your book and the beautiful passage. Sue, Bethel, Alaska.

To you, Sue, and to all of you who have written me such wonderful, such heartfelt, letters about what the book has meant to you, thank you. And Sue, your letter was all the payment anyone could ever ask or hope to receive. God bless you.

About Life After Death . . . and Mourning the Loss of a Loved One

Dear Neale: My brother Chuck died several years ago, when he was only twenty-seven, and I can't seem to stop grieving. Every day I think of him, everything I see reminds me of him. Nothing seems to matter to me anymore. I am chronically depressed. Can you help? Sheila, in Wisconsin.

Dear Sheila, I am sorry for your loss and I understand your grief. There are some things that I would like to tell you, though, that may help you to re-paint this memory on the canvas of your mind, so that when you look at it, you are not always sad.

First, you must know that Chuck has not died; that death is a fiction and a lie and never, ever takes place. That is number one, and that is something you must take into your Self as a truth of the highest order for any of the rest of this to make sense. Second, if we accept that Chuck is not the thing you call "dead," but is, in fact, very much alive, then we must ask ourselves: Where is he? What is he doing? And, of course, is he happy?

We'll answer the last question first. Chuck was never happier, nor more joyful, than he was at the moment of his transition from this earthly life. For in that moment he knew once again the grandest freedom, the greatest joy, the most wondrous truth. The truth of his own being, and of its oneness with All That Is. Separation ended for Chuck in that moment, and his reunification with the All of Everything was a glorious moment in the heavens and the earth. It was a time, indeed, for celebration, not for mourning, yet mourning is understandable, given our limited awareness of what is truly happening, as well as the magnitude of our own personal loss, which we are naturally experiencing.

After a period of very natural grief, which we must be good enough to give ourselves, it then becomes our choice to stay in that place of utter devastation and mourning, or to move to a larger awareness and a grander truth, which allows us to smile—yes, even at the thought of his departure, however early, however abruptly, although nothing is "early" or "abrupt" in God's timetable, but all is perfectly timed.

Should we choose to move to this larger awareness, we are then free to celebrate in fullness the life which was Chuck's, the gift he bestowed upon all those he touched, and the wonder of his beingness and his love even now. We do this most by allowing Chuck himself to be completely free. Which brings us to the first question in the trio above: where is Chuck now?

In *CWG Book 3*, it has been revealed to me that in the world of the absolute in which God dwells, we are all everywhere. That is, there is no "here" or "there," there is simply "everywhere." Thus, in human terms, it is possible to say that we can be in more than one place at a time. We can be two places, or three places, or any place we wish to be, having any experience we choose to have. For this is the nature of God, and of all God's beings. And what experience do we choose to have, among others? The experience of oneness and empathy for those we love, just as we did while in bodily form.

What that means is that Chuck loves you even now, not in some theoretical sense, but in a very real sense, with a living love that can and will never die. And that eternal and everlasting love causes Chuck (part of the essence which is Chuck) to come to you, to be with you, with the very thought of him. For the thought of one who loves us is an attraction and a pull which the essence of a being cannot and will not deny, and will never ignore. Chuck is with you even now, as you are reading this, for you have him in mind, and a part of him is very much there with you. If you are very quiet, and very sensitive to the moment, you will even be able to sense him, feel him . . . maybe even "hear" him.

This is true of all people everywhere, and it explains the thousands and thousands of reports received every year of "visits" by departed loved ones to those who remain behind, reports which psychiatrists, ministers, doctors and healers of every kind have become very used to hearing, and no longer question.

Often what happens is that the essence of the beingness which flew to us at the very thought of it arrives in our space full of love and compassion, and complete openness with us. That openness will allow the essence of our loved one to know and understand completely what we are feeling and experiencing. If we think of that person with sadness, grief and pain, the sadness we experience will be known to that essence. And since that essence is now pure love, it will lovingly seek to heal our sadness, for it will find it impossible not to want to do so.

If, on the other hand, we think of that person with joy and celebration, our joy will be known to the essence of the person we have so deeply loved, and that essence will then feel free to move into its next grand adventure, knowing that all is okay with us. It will come back, to be sure. It will return each time It is thought of. Yet its visits will be joyous dances in our mind; wondrous, sparkling connections; brief, yet shining moments; smiles made whole. Then the essence will whisk away once more, gladdened by the thought of your love and your celebration of Its life, feeling complete in its interaction with you, although by no means ended.

Now in the process of helping us to heal our grief and sadness, and end our mourning, the essence of our loved one will stop at nothing, using any tool, borrowing any device, employing any method at its disposal (including, perhaps, a letter like this from a total stranger) to bring us the message of its unremitting joy in the place of its current residing, and the truth of the perfection of the process of life and transition.

When we can celebrate the perfection, we allow the essence and the soul of our loved one to celebrate it as well, releasing it to the unspeakable wonders of its larger reality, honoring its presence in our lives, in its former physical form, now in this moment, and even forevermore. Celebrate, celebrate, celebrate! No more sadness, no more mourning, for no tragedy has truly befallen anyone. Yet special remembrance with smiles and tears, yes, but tears of joy at the wonder of Who We Are, of who Chuck is, and of the unspeakable love of a God who could have created all this for us. Celebrate, Sheila. Give yourself and Chuck and all those whose lives are touched by both of you, the gift of a lifetime: the gift of joy replacing sorrow, of gladness overtaking the pain of loss, of genuine gratefulness, and of peace at last.

God's blessings, not the least of which are Chuck's life and Chuck's presence with you even now, surround you, Sheila. Go now, and be Who You Really Are. And smile.

Chuck would have it no other way.

On John Denver's Death

Dear Neale: How can God be a "good God" and take someone like John Denver so young? I'm angry, and I don't get it! Mary, Columbus, OH.

Dear Mary, God did not "take" John. Nobody dies before their time, or against their will. They may not have consciously willed it, but at the soul level, the will of God and the will of each of us is one. When we leave our body, you can be assured that we have chosen to, at this level. We leave when our work here is done; when we're finished what we came here to do. I hate to take the mystery out of it, but it's as simple as that. Sometimes our death itself, as in the way we die, is our very reason for coming into the body. This is true of many Martyrs, who die for a cause, or so that we may all be awakened in some way. It is often true of small children, who may have come to remind us all of something.

John Denver and I were to appear together in a very special event in San Francisco, a benefit program for Barbara Marx Hubbard's Conscious Evolution Foundation. Barbara and I and John were to sit down afterward and explore the possibility of a continuing series of similar programs all across the country in 1998 and beyond, which Barbara called "The Awakening of Humanity."

I cannot begin to tell you the depth of the sorrow I felt at the news of John's death one week before this was all to occur. With all that I know about death, and what happens afterward, the sense of personal loss and grief—shared by the entire nation and the whole world—was still almost more than I could bear. I tend to feel things, all things, deeply anyway, and this terrible tragedy shook me to the core of my being.

I don't know what makes us do things or say things in the way we do and say them. I watch myself doing and saying stuff and I don't know half the time why I did or said that. One day I was sitting around with John and we were talking about life. Mainly, life on the road. John and I had each spent a lot of time on the road the first six months of that year, and we were both a bit weary. At one point John looked at me and said, very quietly, "I don't know, Neale. Sometimes I wonder whether it's all worth it."

I was a bit surprised. John's life had seemed to me to be about as bountiful as anyone's life could be, and his contributions to the planet were conspicuous and enormous. I told him so. But it was the way that I told him which struck me. I don't know why I did what I did, or said what I said. But suddenly, for no apparent reason, I sat myself directly in front of him and looked him straight in the eye.

"John," I said, and I was feeling very solemn, very serious (which is unlike me), "if I never see you again, know this: your life and work has touched so many people. So many. It has touched them with light and love. It has brought them smiles and gladness, great joy and upliftment, and yes, even hope. You have meant so much to so many, John. Yes, it has been worth it. Profoundly, yes. Don't ever, ever, ever think otherwise."

John looked at me searchingly, and I thought I saw him become just a little misty-eyed. "Thank you for saying that to me," he said softly.

It's interesting how we think of our lives. Others may heap praises upon us, we may even be the subject of the admiration of others on a grand scale, and yet there can be moments—short moments, perhaps, fleeting moments that just seem to skip through us—when we simply don't "get" ourselves; we just don't see the value of our lives and what we've been to others.

I'm reminded of Jimmy Stewart's classic role in *It's a Wonderful Life*. It took an angel named Clarence to make it clear to the lead character what a difference his life had made. On his own, he couldn't believe he had been or done anything which produced real or intrinsic value, in spite of the fact that all of his friends and half the town thought the world of him.

I guess there were moments when it was like that for John, as there are days when it is like that for most of us. It is on those days that we may need a friend, someone who really sees us, to look us in the eye and show us to ourselves again. And on other days, we will find that we can be that friend, looking into the eye of someone we love, and letting them know that we see them. Fully. As Who They Really Are. In this, we give people back to themselves. And there can be no greater gift.

I am glad I had a chance to share my view of him with John. I'm glad we had that moment. Because, as it turns out, it was the last time I would ever see him. And that's made me think of another thing. How would I behave with people, what would I say to them, if I knew ahead of time it would be my last time with them?

I would sing a song of their praises, as I did with John. I would tell them, "this is the gift you are." Interestingly, John wrote a song with that very title a few years ago. I missed John terribly on the Sunday a week after he died. He was going to sing a few songs, and I was going to say a few words . . .

Jerry Jampolsky came to the event and we turned the event into a wonderful tribute to this marvelous man. John's sudden death has reminded me of something very important: to savor and to sanctify each moment, to see the very best in every event and person, and to give the most of what I have to give in whatever time I have left on this planet. I hope each of us can stay in touch with those wisdoms, and that it will not take the death of a friend to keep us connected with such grand remembrances, nor with the truth of our own grandness, and the wonderfulness of our contributions.

John and I agreed on many things, not the least of which was that all of life is a giant conversation with God. I wrote a couple of books that declared this, and John said as much in the final line of the last verse of one of the songs he wrote: "You can talk to God, and listen to His casual reply." And then he sang the chorus. "Rocky Mountain high . . ."

I know that all of you loved John, and would not want this moment to pass without some opportunity for us to share together our sorrow.

John's contributions to this planet were incalculable. They were so massive as to defy measurement. And they had to do with much more than his music, although that would have been quite enough. His founding of The Hunger Project, his creation of the Windstar Foundation to work for evironmental causes, his deep compassion and humanity—these touched us all.

And so for all of us, those of us who knew him and called him friend and those of us who called him friend without knowing him (which says, really, about the highest that could be said for a person), a soft word of thanks, and farewell. Thanks, John, for the sunshine on my shoulder. I know deep inside my heart that for you "it's good to be back home again . . ."

God bless you all, and be wonderful to each other. John will really like that.

What Is the Spiritual View of Suicide?

Dear Mr. Walsch: I wondered if you might have asked God about suicide. Since I am a psychiatric nurse, I have dealt with this subject frequently and am at a loss while assisting others. Sincerely, Judy.

Dear Mr. Walsch: My son shot himself in the head and died January, 1996. Your book, *Conversations with God*, has been very comforting. Please address suicide. Thank you, Marilyn.

Dear Judy and Marilyn, Thank you for your letters. I receive questions about suicide very often, and I am always so pleased to direct people to the very special work of my friend Anne Puryear at the Logos Center in Scottsdale, Arizona. Anne is the author of an extraordinary book, *Stephen Lives*, which answers just about every question ever asked by the loved one of a person who has ended his or her own life. It is a book I recommend to everyone, but especially to those who have lost a loved one in this way.

Now, let me share with you what I feel I know on this topic. Death does not exist, so what we are talking about here is a change of life form. There is no "crime" in that, and so there is no punishment. It is my understanding the soul chooses to reside with a physical body in order to use it as a tool in the creation of the next grandest experience of Who It Really Is. Leaving the body simply ends that experience. One can enter another body and start over, of course. But one generally does not do this until after a period of some study and contemplation with regard to the incarnation just completed. Nothing tragic happens to the soul of a person who commits suicide, and we would do well to get it out of our minds that something does. This is not, on the other hand, a recommendation to commit suicide. It is simply the truth. There are a lot of people who do not want anyone to tell the truth about this, and so my words here may not be met with joy in every quarter. Yet I cannot say something I know to be false, and to say that God punishes or somehow penalizes those who end their physical life by their own hand would be to spread a falsehood.

People who end their physical life do so in most cases to end some pain they no longer wish to experience. If it is emotional pain, as opposed to physical discomfort, they wish to end, they will find that they have left nothing behind. They will still be dealing with it after they leave the body. But they will have wonderful help and guidance in moving through it, so they will not be alone. Marilyn, your son is perfectly okay and very loved where he is. I urge you to read *Stephen Lives* by Anne Puryear. And get in touch with Anne. She is a miracle and a wonder. You may contact her at P.O. Box 12880, Scottsdale, AZ 85267-2880.

Sometimes I Feel Like Killing Myself

> Dear Mr. Neale D. Walsch: I have one question, which is: sometimes I feel like killing myself. I'm really too exhausted to live, and I want to quit being as a human. Dying doesn't seem like to quit being as a human. Even if I died, I'm still human. Is that correct? Mayumi, Bethesda, MD.

Dear Mayumi, Killing yourself will not get you out of this "game of life," but merely extend it in a way which you will probably find no more desirable than the game you are now playing. It is impossible to escape the game, since we are creating it, no matter what level we are playing it at (that is, either in human physical form, or in some other form). This truth you will quickly become aware of after you leave this particular field of experience. Therefore, it may be advisable to deal with and confront the condition that we have created in the moment that we have created it. Postponement really solves nothing.

I do understand how a person might feel like just "ending it all." I can honestly say that I've had those feelings myself in this life. But Mayumi, I've learned that I created everything that's happening for a reason. There is a divine purpose behind everything. Look to see how you can grow and expand through the experience you are now having. That is what I did when I came to my crossroads, and I see now what the pain I was going through then had to do with my life.

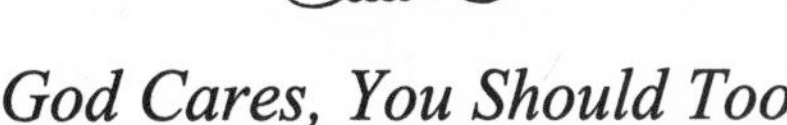

God Cares, You Should Too

Dear Mr. Walsch: For years I have asked the same questions, and a lot of times felt as if God didn't care about me at all. I have had lots of thoughts about suicide and almost killed myself when I was 18. I have had much mental pain in my life, and before I read your book, I got to the point where I just didn't care anymore whether I lived or died. I cried lots of times, asking God how I can find the truth. And then came your book. It changed everything. I am grateful to God for answering my questions through you. It was as if this book was written for me. Sabina, KS.

Thank you for your heart-warming, very touching letter. I am only glad that this material has been useful to you, and brought you benefit. Now pass on what you have learned to others, that your pain may at last become joy. God does care about you, and has performed a miracle in your life. Go now, and be a walking miracle in the lives of others. Raise them up from their tears and "not caring," even as you have been raised. Then it will all make sense, and you will understand why you've had this experience.

What Do You Think About the Heaven's Gate Suicides?

Dear Neale: I am curious to know your "take" on the Heaven's Gate cult thing, and their decision to end their lives in order to meet a spaceship traveling behind the Hale-Bopp Comet. Bob, Medford, OR.

Dear Bob, Well, this is also something some people may have a hard time hearing, but I believe we should refrain from rushing to judgment about the Heaven's Gate episode, and the people involved in it. There is not a sign among the final writings of a single one of those people that they were doing anything other than what they believed in and felt would bring them unheard-of joy. So we might want to try something very daring here. Rather than calling the Heaven's Gate people crazy and making them wrong, we might want to try simply respecting their wishes.

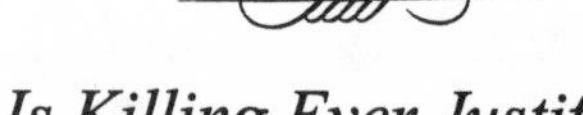

Is Killing Ever Justified?

Dear Neale: I loved your book and felt that it was coming from a divine source, with the exception of seven words! And these seven words seem so absolutely out of alignment with divine love, so incongruous to the rest of the text, that I'm having second thoughts about the validity of the entire work.

On pages 96-97, under the fifth "commitment" you had written: ". . . you will not murder (that is, willfully kill, without cause) . . . , without the most sacred justification," Those words leaped out at me and stopped me dead in my tracks! Then in your monthly newsletter, you stated outright that you indeed felt we had the divine right, yea, the moral duty, to kill other human beings in order to get them to stop killing! I find this extremely disturbing, because I felt in my soul that those seven words were not from God and had been added by you.

Certainly you realize that more people have been killed and tortured on this earth in the name of God than for any other reason! And every single person who slaughtered another felt it he had the right and the duty to so do because, of course, God was on his side! One of my core beliefs is that life is absolutely sacred, and no one has the right to take it from another living being! Gandhi, Jesus and Martin Luther King were just some of the great masters who taught the world how to resist violence without returning it. Surely you know that violence only begets violence and solves nothing.

The power of prayer and love is supreme, and we do not ever, ever need to tell anyone that we will kill them if they don't stop killing others, much less actually do it! Yes, evil exists, but we will never vanquish it with evil. We cannot allow ourselves to sink down to the level of those that kill by joining them, but instead we can lift them up by loving them. We know that those they kill are not destroyed. Everyone is eternal and we are all just playing our parts here on earth.

Why, when everything else in your book seems so absolutely right, do I find the addition of "without sacred justification" to "thou shalt not kill" so absolutely wrong! I know that God is absolute love and would never justify or condone taking another's life under any circumstance.

I not only find it wrong to think it's okay to kill under "certain circumstances," I find it highly dangerous as well. That's how wars are started, promoted and continued, because the people fighting them believe they are for a "sacred and just" cause. Instead of ending wars, your seven words are fueling them. Is that what you really want?

I realize that most people would feel "justified" killing in certain circumstances, as in defending their lives or the lives of their loved ones, but that is still a reaction of fear. If someone were threatening to harm or kill me or my family, I would hope that I would use prayer and love as my only weapon. If that didn't work, then I would realize that it was our time to leave this world knowing that I and my loved ones will live on in another plane or dimension. I have learned that the best defense is defenselessness. Read up on Gandhi if you have time. Better yet, just go back and read your own book. It's all there! You can distill everything down to only two elements: love or fear. Killing is always a result of fear, which is the opposite of love, or God, and therefore it is never "right." Only those things that are life affirming are of God, and I cannot and will not believe God said it is okay to kill, sometimes, or ever! Joanne, Bend, OR.

Dear Joanne, You raise a difficult and challenging issue. I understand how you could have had trouble with this. Well-meaning people on both sides of the question have been grappling with this one for centuries. *CWG Book 1* touches on it in at least three separate places. As the book itself implies, it would be dangerous to take any of the book's comments on this question out of context, or seek to consider them alone. Placed within the context of all that is written in *Conversations with God*, I find the book's position on this subject understandable, acceptable, and in harmony with Who I Am.

Let's see what that context provides.

First, it suggests that nothing is "right" or "wrong." Second, it says that we are all creating ourselves as who we want to be by our decision on questions just like this. Third, it says there is no way to make a mistake in that process, because no one is judging the creation. Fourth, it says that to allow an abuser to continue his abuse is not loving, to oneself, or the abuser. Fifth, it says that under highest moral law as we have constructed it (there is no moral law in the universe), we have a right to put a stop to that which abuses us. Sixth, the book strongly implies that our highest moral law suggests a construction surrounding the concept of equal force. In other words, one does not bang someone over the head with a baseball bat if that someone is stealing the evening paper out of our roadside box.

On the other hand, if someone is killing our children right in front of us, it may not be seen as immoral to stop them by whatever means is necessary, including the use of killing force if that is all they will listen to.

Failure to stop them—allowing them to move on to the next house down the block, and the next, to torture and kill more children—under the plausible veil of pacifism, might indeed be the greater injustice. And surely that cannot be the only solution of someone coming from "love." What of love for the child? Do we do nothing to stop the child's suffering, out of our need to act lovingly toward the abuser? It can be love, not fear, which allows us to says to an abuser, "you must stop this." The book says it is not loving (not even to the abuser) to allow his abuse to continue. And if equal force is really all he will listen to, truly all he can hear, then it is he, not you, who has chosen the means by which the communication shall take place.

You said something else that intrigues me, Joanne. You said you would allow your children to be killed right in front of you rather than use equal force to protect them, because, in your words, "I would realize that it is our time to leave this world, knowing that I and my loved ones will live on in another plane or dimension." Well, isn't that true of your child's attacker as well? And if it is, if what you are saying is that there is no death, but only the changing of life forms, then what would cause you to choose your child to be the one to have his life form changed? What law of God requires that?

In short, Joanne, to not be willing to commit what you consider a "wrong" in order to stop another from committing what you consider a "wrong" renders your whole definition of "wrong" pointless. I'm going to ask you to re-read that statement again, to give you a chance to dwell on it.

The book makes this point when it notes that sometimes we, ourselves, have to break the rules in order to make the rules mean anything. Or, as the text says specifically, sometimes we have to give up Who We Are in order to be Who We Are. For instance, if Who You Are is a "man of peace," and someone is "disturbing the peace" by killing your children, your mother, your wife and your friends, you may choose to return peace to your experience by stopping them. If Who You Are is someone who speaks softly, sometimes you may have to raise your voice in order to speak softly again.

History, the *CWG* text goes on, has called upon men for such decisions. Many good men and women have gone to war to establish themselves as people of peace. They did not want it that way. They did not choose the agenda. Hitler did. Saddam Hussein did. Slobodan Milosovic . . . The madman who comes into their child's bedroom did. Are they lesser for having met the madman on his own terms, given no other choice? Are madmen somehow "more dead" than good people who "live on in another plane or dimension"? The answers seem to me to be "no." Remember, by your own admission, no one can really be killed anyway. We are talking here about altering life forms, and making choices about whose life forms those shall be.

It is no doubt for this very reason that, ultimately, the book says it doesn't make any difference what we do or what we choose. We are simply in the act of creating ourselves, and we can be whomever we wish to be. If Who You choose to Be is a person who stands by while your family is being killed, because you seek to honor life, and would never take the life of the murderer, that is your choice. I would choose to honor life in a different way.

For a fuller discussion of this question, see *CWG Book 1*, pages 29, 50, 96, 108-109, 133,151-156. I must say I find the last reference the most impactful for me. It clarified everything for me as I was being given this material, for I, too, had some deep reservations about this.

Again, thank you, Joanne, for your forthrightness, courage and willingness to engage the question, thereby opening this extended dialogue. It serves all of us. And it brings up a fundamental question. Could the energy called love allow us to end a life?

John Bement is being sentenced this month. He could be put behind bars for 15 years, or . . . he could get probation. The charge? Manslaughter. The victim? His wife.

This is another one of those difficult cases. It raises a question I think we all have to look at. Because, you see, John Bement says that his wife, Judith Bement, asked him to help her end her life. Judith's daughter Cynthia agrees, that is exactly what happened. Judith's other daughter, Susan, sees it differently. She was not there when her mother died with John Bement's assistance, and she says her mother did not want to die that night.

Because she felt so strongly about this, Susan secretly tape recorded a conversation between herself, her sister Cynthia, and their stepfather John three days after her mother's death. In the conversation, Susan asked her stepfather to describe exactly how her mother died: what he did and how he did it. "I just need peace of mind," she explained, as the tape whirred. Later, Susan took the tape to the State Police. Her stepfather was charged, and at his trial did not take the stand. "I've caused enough problems for everybody," he told his attorney. "I want us all to heal. I never want to talk about it again."

Cynthia, who was there with her stepfather while preparations were being made to assist her mother in passing, heard her mother give the instructions on how to mix crushed sedative and antidepressant pills into some vanilla pudding. She insists her mother willingly took the pudding, "swallowed it down and opened her mouth for another bite until he fed it to her."

She recalls her stepfather telling his wife, emotionally, "Really, Judy, we don't have to do this."

"My dad really didn't want my mother to die. He really didn't," Cynthia says. "And neither did I."

But, Cynthia says, her mother knew what she wanted.

Judith Bement was once an active and vital woman. She and John had been married 33 years when she fell victim to Lou Gehrig's disease, which destroys nerves in the brain and spinal cord. No cure is known. During the illness' latter stages, Judith had gained fifty pounds. She had degenerated from a walker to a wheelchair to complete paralysis, her hands and feet swollen and useless, her cheeks constantly flushed.

"The disease had consumed her," daughter Cynthia said. "She couldn't fight it any longer." Close friends of Judith agreed, several of them testifying at trial that Judith had begged them to help her commit suicide.

"Maybe a lot of people would say, 'Well, you had the chance to walk away'," Cynthia says, "And we could have. But we loved this woman very much. We both (she and her stepfather) agree that if we had to do it all over again for my mother, we'd do it again."

Susan, however, remains adamant. "When someone's miserable, you cheer them up. You don't encourage them to take their life," she says.

All of this, of course, drives to the question of whether any of us has the right to choose, given the opportunity to do so, how and when we will die. Is it our right to say when we have had enough, when the quality of our life, and of the contribution we can make to the lives of others, has diminished to the point where life itself in the physical body no longer makes sense to us, to say nothing of being bearable?

This is a question that, as a humane society, we must address. Did John Bement commit manslaughter? Or did he keep a commitment to his wife to love her and abide by her (and by her wishes)? According to *CWG*, love says: "Your will for you is my will for you." Indeed, declares *CWG*, this is what God says.

Do you believe that? Or should John Bement be punished by both man and God for what he did?

Whose Life Is It, Anyway?

Dear Neale: Aside from the fact that *Conversations with God* reminds us that we are eternal and cannot die, I suggest that the question of whether any of us has the right to choose, given the opportunity to do so, how and when we will die is superfluous and irrelevant, as are all of the so-called "sinful" irrelevancies invented by the Catholic Church. Since we all chose our time and place to enter this world, why in God's name would it be any different where, when and how we choose to leave it? And since we are all God in the first place, why would someone make an issue of it unless they intended to keep the illusion of separation going, for whose business is it but each individual's anyway? Yours sincerely, Ken, Surrey, BC, Canada.

Dear Ken, That's the point, of course. There was a marvelous play written some years ago titled *Whose Life Is It, Anyway?* And that, of course, is the fundamental theological question. There are those who say that it is not your life, but God's; that it is merely a gift, not yours to do with as you wish. You are to do as God wants. Some gifts.

This is a false teaching, however. It is based on a concept of God as separate from us. It is also based on the idea that life can somehow end. Both thoughts are inaccurate, having nothing to do with ultimate reality. You and God are One, and life is eternal. These two truths can render many of the choices you have made in your life pointless. That is, no doubt, why they are so hard for some people to accept.

I Was Murdered: What Does This Mean?

Dear Friend: I have just finished the book *Conversations with God*. My heart is full, and my mind as well, and of course I have a million more questions! I died, in fact, was murdered by my husband, in 1987and am struggling to understand what that, and all that has happened to me since, all means. I feel things and know things on a different level now, and there doesn't seem to be anyone who can help me understand it. This book, next to my own conversations with God, seems to come closest to it. Can you address this phenomenon? Shirley, Orlando, FL.

Dear Shirley . . . You asked me what all that has happened to you in your life means, and the answer I can give you is that it means exactly what you want it to mean. By that, I am trying to convey a large message and the grandest truth contained in *Conversations with God*, which is that you are the creator of your own reality, and that events in and of themselves mean nothing at all.

In *CWG Book 2*, God said to me, "I have sent you nothing but angels," and I understand that to mean that all the people, places and events of our lives have been placed there in perfect order by a perfect universe in order that we might perfectly express and perfectly experience the perfect creation of who we now choose to be. Therefore, the question at hand is not what does all of this mean, but what do you choose for it to mean, and what do you choose for yourself to be in relationship to it?

You tell me that you feel things now, and know things, on a different level, and that there doesn't seem to be anyone who could help you understand it. It might do you well to discontinue seeking another person who could help you understand it, but rather, go within to the source of the greatest wisdom which lies inside of you, and search for understanding there. I am not surprised that you are seeing things differently now.

These things happen very often to those who have undergone great trauma or who have actually "died" in the clinical sense, and it is very normal for those persons to "come back" to life with new and larger understandings that very few other people can even get in touch with. While I am not amazed that you have found yourself in this place, I do understand how it could be mystifying to some degree, if not troubling. I hope that you will not be troubled by it, however, but that you will, as I have suggested, return to the God source which lies within you for peace and comfort, for understanding and insight, for higher awareness and a grander ability to comprehend all that has gone before, and all that is yet to come.

I hope that you will resist the temptation to make your husband, or anyone else, the "villain" in your story, but that you will move to a place of forgiveness and, eventually, even to a place where you clearly see that forgiveness is not necessary. All things happen perfectly in God's world, and for a greater clarity on the reasons why these things happen, please re-read *Conversations with God* again. In the book it is made very clear that occurrences take place as unique constructions called to ourselves by ourselves in order that we might have the right and perfect tools in the creation of who we want to be, and thus become who we really are. We are, after all is said and done, a creature of our own creation.

I don't know if this is of any help to you, Shirley, but it is the observation I have to make at this time. I do honor the difficulty of your experience, and I see that you have a great deal of courage and strength as you are moving through it, even to this present day. I encourage you to continue residing within that place of courage and strength, and to share it with all those whose lives you touch.

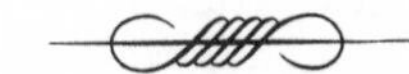

The Story of a Near-Death Experience

Dear Neale: I recognize that there is no shortage of responses to your *Conversations with God*, but I still felt compelled to add my energy to the others. I come from a life history that includes decades of loneliness, self-loathing, and debilitating depression, culminating in chronic illness and "toxic drama." During one of many major operations, I stopped breathing and was clinically dead for 16-20 minutes. I had what is commonly referred to as a near-death experience, which shifted my level of awareness so completely that I no longer am "Who I Was."

During my death journey, I watched the medical team work to resuscitate me; and as time progressed without success, I listened to them begin to construct an explanation for why they had lost me, to offer to my family. Highlights of my afterlife experience included a new understanding of how time works and how expansive our ability to know is; I saw that knowledge is limitless. At one point I was able to comprehend how this universe works, and, most incredible of all, I experienced what I can only describe as unconditional love, which is simply love without need.

I also encountered a Being of Light, or God—quite an occasion for a non-believer—who knew me intimately and loved me so completely, I cannot describe the feeling here. This Divine Being knew I didn't believe in His existence, knew I would argue about having to return to the body, and loved me nonetheless. The other profound revelation during this experience was that this divine source had a wonderful sense of humor, and that He delighted in mine.

This is a very condensed account of my death experience, and doesn't touch upon the affects it had on my life journey since. What I want to share here is that I have spent years trying to find something written that I could recognize as this God voice I encountered, without success—until now. *Conversations with God* contains God energy. It is the same language, the same unconditional love, and finally, the same sense of humor I remember from my experience. I laughed and wept as I read *CWG*. It was a homecoming for me.

Like so many people, painful losses and my own human fears have marked my life journey. I am still healing from the death of my marriage, and I am struggling financially. I do not know where I'm headed, but know I have a sacred contract to fulfill. My heart is open and the spirit is ready. What I do know is that I am committed to remembering "All That I Am" by how I present myself every day.

Lastly, I know from my teachings during my death experience that nothing is coincidental, and that a fine reminder of this was the arrival of *CWG Book 1* in my life at a time when I needed it most.

Thank you for allowing me this opportunity to share my own personal life path with you, and to express my gratitude, for your hand in creating these two wonderful books. Loving Light & Joyful Energy to you, Jill, Rochester, NY.

Dear Jill, Thank you for sharing your wonderful story with all of us! You, and several other of the letter-writers here, may want to look at becoming a master teacher of this material at a *CWG* center in your community, or elsewhere. We are establishing such centers now, across the nation and around the world, in response to the desire of millions of people across the globe asking to know more about *CWG*, and how to apply its wisdom in their daily lives.

Through the *CWG* In Action program, hundreds of people will become certified study group facilitators, *CWG* instructors or master teachers, offering classes, seminars, workshops, and retreats at our *CWG* Centers. If you'd like to know more—if putting *CWG* to work in your life, and helping others to discover it, is something you long to do—contact us at:

CWG In Action
ReCreation Foundation
PMB 1150
1257 Siskiyou Blvd
Ashland, OR 97520
541-488-8806
Recreating@aol.com

CHAPTER 9

Prophecies, Earth Changes, and the Future

What a world we are creating here! Each day the news is filled with more and unbelievable stuff! And everywhere we look, God is in the headlines in *Newsweek*, *Time*, *Life*, even *TV Guide*, for goodness sake. Every publication in America seems to be trying to find an excuse to put God on the cover. Why? Because we are now, as a people, more fascinated, more focused on Deity than ever before in recent times; because the media understands that, right now, God sells.

Why is that? What is going on here? Does it have anything to do with the new millennium? I think so. I think there has been a tremendous vibration shift on this planet. It has been slow in human terms, but very rapid in cosmic terms, that is, it has taken only twenty years or so, which, on the cosmic clock, is less than a millisecond. It has been unceasing, inexorable. And its effects have been cumulative. Now, we are beginning to see and feel the effects.

I have been told that all of life is a vibration. An oscillation, if you will, of the divine force. This vibration is the raw energy of the universe. Depending upon the speed, or frequency, of the vibration, a thing is either seen or unseen, felt or not felt. Depending upon how a thing is vibrating, it either matters or it does not matter. I am using the word "matters" here as a verb. I mean to say that a thing becomes what we call "matter" or it does not, depending upon the frequency of its vibration. And how a thing "matters" is also a function of its vibration. The speed of the energy vibration determines whether we experience a thing as what we call "solid," "liquid" or "vapor," for instance.

This lesson in physics (really, metaphysics!) could go on forever, and it's not really what I meant to get into here. (For more on this subject, you will enjoy reading *CWG, Book 3*.) I merely wanted to lay a bit of ground work here for my larger hypothesis.

It is my belief—and my experience—that the "vibe" in our part of the universe is shifting, has been shifting for quite some time. Specifically, it has been speeding up. This is the result of a "wave" of energy which has been approaching us from the central core for quite some time. I believe this wave is physical, measurable, and predictable. We are moving through this wave in the universe right now—have been on the outskirts of it for a long time. We are now moving closer in. Or, more accurately, it is moving closer to us. Now this "wave" is nothing to be afraid of. It is not a malevolent manifestation of the universe. It is not a negative aspect of the prime force. It does not portend disaster. It is simply an oscillation, an effect. An Event. But it is speeding things up around here. Have you noticed? This happens regularly, by the way. About once every thousand years, in Earth time. Think of it as a rythym in the heartbeat of God.

And even as we are affected by the tugs and pulls of the moon (which, of course, we are), so will we feel the effects of this incoming vibe. There could be attitudinal changes, more worldwide political upheavals, socioeconomic shifts, and yes, even some physical manifestations on the planet in increasing numbers. It began in earnest, really, about seven years ago. And it will continue now until the year 2023. It will take that long for us to move through this wave, or photon belt.

As I said, there is no reason for us to experience this in a negative way. In fact, quite to the contrary, the feelings for most people will be very positive. A time of refreshment. A time of upliftment. A time of reawakening. And a time of change.

Now it is true that if you are "stuck" in having things As They Are, if you are resistant to change, you could be just a little uncomfortable in the times ahead. Yet whether these coming changes produce what we call "good" or what we choose to label "bad" is going to depend on us. We are still in control; we are always in control.

Our individual beliefs as well as our collective beliefs will set the course and create our experience. So believe that the change, the speeding up, will bring you great refreshment, wonderful renewal. For it will. And our world will be a better place than ever it was.

Do more than just believe in that.

Work for that.

Create that.

Then, so will it be.

What About Those Wild Weather Patterns?

> Neale: Would you care to make a comment about some of the wild geophysical stuff going on—The wild weather/earth changes that seem to be increasing in intensity the past few years? Lately it seems as though the weather has become very erratic and unstable. Many ups and downs. Many extremes in temperature, rainfall, snowfall, earthquakes, floods, etc. Is this part of a larger unseen, but "normal pattern," or are we on the brink of extinction? And what's causing the wild weather? MF, Chicago.

Dear MF, We are not on the brink of extinction; we are on the brink of change. It is time now for the earth to reestablish her dominion over her own affairs. We have sought to establish our dominion over her long enough. Nature, now, will let us know who is who, and what is what, and where we fit in the overall scheme of things. There is no cause for alarm, no cause for concern. Your inner guidance will tell you exactly where to be and where not to be, when, and why, during the course of any geophysical adjustments made by Gaia.

You cannot die in any event, though you can leave this particular physical form. The adventure goes on, and will always go on. Do not, therefore, become attached to this form, to this time, to this place. Become attached, rather, to Who You Really Are. Live, move, and have your being in that. The questions as to weather patterns will then become insignificant, irrelevant. You have not come here to protect yourself from dying, so it's okay now to stop protecting yourself from living.

Is the Photon Belt About to Get Us?

> Neale: If you've been following the photon belt information or are aware of the prophecies made in *The Keys of Enoch* as well as *Galactic Human*, then you understand my interest and concern that, during the chaos that is likely to come soon, we will still be able to reach many people with the written word. Am I to conclude that we will still have our beloved computers (for desktop publishing as well as connecting) as well as some method of distribution in the near future? I guess the answer is yes! Carole (no city given).

My dear Carole, The world will be here years from now, and in whatever condition it is, we will always have a way to print and distribute books. They did it in Benjamin Franklin's time, and we'll do it again in the new millennium, electronic gadgetry or not. Nothing will keep from His people any truth which God wishes to reveal. I put it all in God's hands, Carole, who I am certain is perfectly capable of producing exactly the result which was intended. If any book is not intended to get out, it won't. And if it is, it will. For God will not be thwarted in Her desires, nor stymied in Her choices. Never She has been, and never She will be.

I am not worried about the photon belt, through which we are supposed to be passing in a matter of days now, nor about the upheavals of the earth and the flooding of the plains and the loss of the West Coast and the changing of the Earth's societies and civilizations. I am concerned only with carrying the message of God's unremitting love as long as God allows, to as many as God selects. I will do this if I have to write on the back of a matchbook.

It is of no moment to me whether my books come out. Yet I would say this to you, my friend: Do not be overly concerned with what tribulations may be to come. Do not even be so certain that they will come. All is consciousness, Carole, and consciousness is all. My consciousness says we'll get through these days ahead just fine. And, of course, we will. Unless we don't. Live within the paradox, Carole!

What Do You Think About the End Times?

Hi, Neale! I'm not writing to you as an authority on everything in the world. But I realize that through your experiences with god/goddess you might have a better perspective than I do.

I just finished reading the prophecies of Nostradamus and the author of *Saved by the Light*, Dannion Brinkley. What troubles me is that both of their predictions are similiar and you hinted at the same thing in your book.

Are these really the end times? Do you believe like the Mayans that if significant changes aren't made in the earth's love frequency, it will end in 2010? Is there really an Anti-Christ who's going to attempt world domination? These predictions are scary, but at the same time I realize that we can't be scared, we chose to be here at this time to experience this.

Everybody says the only thing to do, is to prepare your spirit and soul and get centered with God within. But how, with just mediation and prayer? Basically, I guess I'm asking what can we do to prepare ourselves for the upcoming changing times? Remember you said that I can ask you anything, and that you would always be there. Did I forget to mention how much that meant to me? Though I didn't understand the last part, about how you are served through me. Love, Penny.

My dear Penny, I am so saddened by these thoughts that keep surfacing about how the world as we know it is going to end. The end of the world has been predicted from the beginning of time. And the world very well may end some time soon . . . or certainly, life as it is now being lived may change amazingly and dramatically. But the question in front of us should not be, Oh, my, what is going to happen to me? And the world? But, rather, How can I use this moment now to become the personification of the grandest version of the greatest vision ever I held about myself? How can I heal myself and heal the world? What good can I do in this moment now to bring more love, more light, more awareness, more understanding, more unconditional acceptance to the world? How can I touch the part of me which is touched in every moment by God?

What happens on this planet occurs out of the collective consciousness. It is the product of the combined reality shared by all.

That combined reality is shaped, formed, created in part by you, every hour, every day. Thoughts are things, and can be used by you to change the things which have been created by other thoughts which have preceded you.

Your questions about Nostradamus and Brinkley suggest that we are on a collision course which cannot be avoided; that our fate is predestined. Yet I tell you this: nothing is predestined in the mind of God, for the mind of God is your mind, thinking what it is thinking right now. Yours, and mine, and everyone else's. It is our thoughts, our ideas, our decisions, our choices, our determinations which will and do create our Reality.

That is the largest message of God: you are creating your own reality. No one gets it. Not even so-called "new agers." If they did, they wouldn't ask questions such as "Are the end-times predictions true?" They would ask, "What do I choose now to do in the face of all the world's thoughts about this?" Then they would answer the question, not just ask it and wait for an answer from another.

You, my friend, do not need to hear from me on this. You know all you need to know of love, of peace, of harmony, of honesty and integrity, kindness and goodness, peace and, yes, even of God. Simply act as if you did. Make every day, every moment, a living monument to what you already know of these things; a living testimony to what you have decided about these things; a living demonstration of Who You Really Are.

My wonderful Penny, do what you are. Do loving, kind, gentle, peaceful, honorable, healing things. Every day. Everywhere you go. With every person whose life you touch. Then, seek to touch even more lives. And then, even more after that. Reach out and touch the world with your magnificence, and the magnificence of the truth of Who You Are. Of who we all are.

In every moment we have the choice to live in love or in fear. Choose love now, and every time. If the world is going to end as we know it, so what? Only one of two things can happen: you are going to die with it, in which case you'll be in a far better place than ever you imagined; or you will be continuing to live, and in the most exciting times this planet has ever seen. And you will be one of the few with an understanding of all that has happened, and all that can then happen, to create a newer world.

So live not in fear, but in faith. Faith that whatever the future holds in store, it is perfect. The perfect conditions for you to create the perfect experience of who and what you really are.

God is a loving God. Nothing is created, nothing, which does not proceed to your Highest Good. You either believe that or you don't. If you do, there is nothing I need to say to make everything feel better to you. If you don't, there is nothing I *can* say.

Penny, I don't claim to know or have all the answers. Neither, I think, does Nostradamus (by extension), nor Brinkley, nor anyone else. All messages we receive are received through the filters of our own understandings and prior beliefs. In other words, Neale hears what Neale is prepared to hear, ready to hear, trained to hear, predisposed to hear. Only you can decide whether what Neale hears from his source is anything close to the truth of your being. The same is true of the material which comes through Brinkley, or anyone else. The world may very well be shaken to its core within the next fifty years, or less. Some say next month. The question is, then what? What will you do then?

What good will you be to the rest of us? To those who are in fear and anguish, trembling in the dark, afraid of the future? I say this to you, my friend, because I want you to consider that you may have been sent to the world at precisely this time in order to be one of those who heals the world, not sends it further into fear. Do that. It is not difficult. Anyone who has ever received even so much as a smile from you would tell you how easy it is for you to do that.

Go, therefore, and be a gift unto the world. And smile a lot. For a smile is love, announced. Love of whatever and whomever it is you are smiling at.

Are the "Earth Changes" Coming?

Dear Mr. Walsch: I have devoured CWG. I would like to ask you about the possibility of finding out the truth of one of the most important questions that is before the world today. It has been said that the "shift of the earth" on its axis will occur just before the end of this century or in the year 2000. Ruth Montgomery mentions the coming shift in nine of her books. It will leave a very devastated earth with only a few million of its inhabitants left. I choose to know the truth, the whole truth and nothing but the truth about this horrendous event and how better than out of the mouth of God! I have the feeling that the whole world should know! What do you think? I know you have your hands full with questions, but I believe the whole world would be grateful for the answer to the mystery of the "shift." Carolyn, Jensen Beach, FL.

Dear Carolyn, I have addressed this question before. The question itself suggests that there is something "set in stone" about all of this—that things are going to happen, and there is nothing we can do about it. That idea stands in opposition to everything that is contained in *Conversations with God.* Over and over the books make the point that we are in charge of our own future, that we are creators of our own reality. If that is true, the "coming earth changes" will not be coming—unless they are. All will depend on our decision about that, which will be reflected in our consciousness about it. That is, if we think all of this will happen—that it is inevitable—that will become our reality. On the other hand, if we believe that we can create our own future out of our idea about it, and if we choose to have an idea other than one of mass destruction by the year 2000, then we will not experience that. I have no intention of experiencing it. How about you?

Quantum Awakening of All Souls

Dear Mr. Walsch: I have just reread your book for the second time. This simple, but profound information has been a long time coming in print for all to read. The only other book close to this type I have read was Ken Carey's *Starseed, The Third Millennium.* In that book they speak of a quantum awakening of all souls in a single moment, knowing who they are and why they are here. Was there anything mentioned in your conversation with God that spoke of this, and when? We all need this information now. Susan, Knoxville, TN.

We are inside that larger moment of quantum understanding right now, Susan, as more and more people are awakening from their long dream of forgetfulness. Soon (in the framework of time of the universe) that number will reach critical mass, and the so-called Hundredth Monkey theory will play out its effect. That is, everyone at once will know and understand. You, and many others like you, can play a critical role in hastening that moment, by agreeing to be messengers of truth and bringers of the light. You do this by everything you think, say and do. And perhaps, by becoming part of CWG In Action, as discussed on p. 231.

What Is the "New World Order"?

Dear Neale: Thanks again for sharing your "Conversations" with everyone. You are making great strides toward making the souls on earth awaken! I think most people aren't too happy about God's views on religion. It is truly a time to start shifting our mind-set!

Would you explain a bit about "new world order" (page 199, *Book 1*)? The new world order I've been reading about is not for the good of earth or her people, but intends to enslave the world. Am I on the wrong track, or is this a global Hitler situation we have called to ourselves to bring about enlightenment to more people? I know you have a busy schedule, but I've been losing sleep over this question and would appreciate any answers you can give. Sincerely, Faye, Denver, CO.

Dear Faye, *CWG Book 2* teaches that the greatest enemy of man is the idea of separation, from God and from each other. In connection with that, as a political instruction, *Book 2* allows us to know that our ideas of individual and national sovereignty are the highest form of political separation of which the human race is capable. It is that very political separation into individual political geographical units—which we call national sovereignty—which has contributed to, if not outright caused, every major conflict on this planet. The only human thought that could reverse this regrettable political construction and outcome is the thought which is encapsulated in the following truth from *CWG*: We are all one. This four-word teaching summarizes, more than any single sentence, all of the wisdom, all of the truths, and all the understandings in all three *CWG* books.

If we are, therefore, to live and breathe "we are all one," it would be impossible for us to live under anything other than a single world governance. That does not mean, however, that such a system of world governance cannot have delineations that allow for individual cultures and characterizations to emerge, identify, and celebrate themselves a point which is very well described in *CWG Book 2*. The idea is not to create a homogenous conglomeration of identical human beings, or even of identical political or spiritual structures, but rather, to create an environment in which each person on the earth, and each culture that forms the conglomerate group of communities on the earth, can celebrate individuality without interference and without conflict.

What Dreams May Come

> Dear Neale: I have just finished reading *CWG Book 2*, and I am so discouraged. It is a wonderful book, don't get me wrong. But it pointed out with such clarity the changes we have to make if we are to redeem ourselves, and turn things around on this planet. I have never seen in one place such clear statements on everything from the government to our educational system to economics, religion—virtually every aspect of human culture. Yet how can we ever expect to change? God calls ours a "primitive society" and I agree with that assessment, but how are we ever going to make any meaningful and lasting changes, given the fact that we are primitive? I don't know, I just feel lost here. Nellie, Hoboken, NJ.

Dear Nellie, I understand how you could feel that way, but I want to tell you that, far from being discouraged, I am excited and heartened by what I see on our planet right now as a very great willingness to change, a great readiness—unlike anything I have seen before—together with an ability to put new paradigms into place, that is unparalleled in human history. That willingness is demonstrated, Nellie, in ways such as the sales figures themselves of books such as *Conversations with God*. There is no way *Book 2* would have reached *The New York Times* best-seller list, and remained there for months, had it not been for the readiness and the willingness of people everywhere to begin making candid assessments of where we are now as a society, and new choices about where we would like to be.

There is something very exciting happening right now on earth, Nellie, and I'm hoping you can see it. The team is forming, Nellie. The Team is forming. We are coming together now, rapidly and in increasing numbers over these past several years. We are identifying ourselves to each other, and declaring ourselves by our works to be change makers, and way-showers, and bringers of the light. We are exerting our enlarging and now considerable individual and collective influence on society to impact and alter that society forever, ushering in a new era and a new age.

The team consists of all beings everywhere who have committed themselves to a larger purpose, and a grander vision, and a new reality. People like actor Dennis Weaver, who, with his Institute of Ecolonomics, has created a common ground between ecologists and economists, paving the way for the merging of the two, at last, into a united force to co-create a sustainable future. People like Barnet Bain and Stephen Simon, Hollywood producers who risked their personal financial holdings and their careers to create a movie of astonishing insight and spectacular wisdom called *What Dreams May Come*, tackling, as the big screen has never dared tackle it before, the subject of what happens to the soul after death.

The team also consists of people like Oprah Winfrey, who has used her incredible popularity to help raise our collective consciousness. And people such as Marianne Williamson, who risked alienating her entire, huge, and well-established audience to present to us a book of glowing magnificence, *Healing the Soul of America*.

People such as Bob Friedman, co-owner of Hampton Roads Publishing Company, who took a huge risk to first publish *CWG*, and Susan Peterson of G.S. Putnam Sons, who rolled enormous dice and put her career on the line to bring *CWG* to a larger, worldwide audience virtually overnight.

People like singer Kenny Loggins and his wife, Julia, who have shown us what truth and transparency in loving relationships is all about, modeling it with breathtaking courage in their own groundbreaking book, *The Impossible Life*. And all the folks who have worked so hard to put *Touched by an Angel* on television, with its extraordinary message each week.

The team is forming, Nellie, and it includes thousands of people not nearly as well known, but equally as important. People in towns and villages, cities and communities across this nation, and around the world, who are, each in their own way, working to build a positive future. The plumbers and mechanics and teachers and nurses, the ministers and doctors and police officers and flight attendants, the electricians and lawyers and hardware store owners and dentists, the homemakers and executives and taxi drivers and, well, the Nellies from Hoboken, New Jersey. Regular people everywhere, Nellie, like you and like me, who care, and who are not afraid to show that they care, about our world and what happens to it. Some of them will join us now in our CWG In Action program, becoming facilitators, instructors, and master teachers at CWG Centers around the world. So, don't give up, Nellie. Don't give up. We need you on the team. With your help, and with mine, you never know what dreams may come.

CWG Agrees with What Dreams May Come

Dear Neale Donald Walsch: What did you think of the movie, *What Dreams May Come*? The reason I ask is that some of the critics are really blasting it, and I thought it was a very good movie. More important, I thought it carried an extraordinary spiritual message. Is this why the critics are not liking it? Does it threaten the "establishment" a bit too much? Sharon, Sedona, AZ.

Dear Sharon, *What Dreams May Come* is a brilliant movie, and the most daring thing Hollywood has done in 30 years. It is a film of enormous spiritual importance, and yes, it does threaten the established order of things, in that it presents ideas that contradict and violate how we have been told things are. Yet all great truths, Sharon, begin as blasphemies. I do not hold this movie to be literally true, but its overriding message—that we create our own realities and our own "Hell" (both now, and after our death)—is exactly what *CWG* says. *CWG*, too, has violated the established order of things, so both the film and the books have been denounced by critics.

Introducing the "HEBs"—Can We Ever Be Like Them?

> Dear Neale, I just finished reading *Book 3*. Wow! This is the best book of all! The best part was the last fifth of the book, which talked about HEBs. Do you really believe that there are such things? Will we ever be able to have a life such as the ones they live? Eleanore, Seattle, WA.

Dear Eleanore, I think you may be right. *Book 3* may just be the very best in the trilogy. Certainly the information there is extremely compelling. But perhaps we should explain for those who haven't yet read the book what "HEBs" are.

The word HEB is an abbreviation for "Highly Evolved Being." The final pages of the book are devoted to questions and answers about how life is lived in the highly evolved societies of the universe. And yes, Eleanore, I believe that such societies exist, and I believe that human beings will one day produce such a society on Earth. We are not there yet, however. In fact, as the book itself says, it is the mark of a primitive society to imagine itself to be highly evolved. That describes human society to a "T."

Right now, we are killing each other to resolve our differences, and that is a very primitive behavior. Right now, we are killing others to punish them for killing others, and that is a very primitive behavior. Right now, we are eating the flesh of dead animals, and that is a very primitive behavior. Right now, we are smoking known carcinogens, and that is a very primitive behavior. Right now we are drinking known mind-deadeners, and that, too, is a very primitive behavior.

Right now, we are living what *Book 3* calls a "cultural myth" of survival of the fittest, and we have allowed ourselves to adopt a primary belief in the inherent evilness of humans. Yet God tells us that we are not inherently evil, but reflections of the Divine, and that "survival of the fittest" is a cultural imperative which could only be adopted by a race of beings who did not understand that We Are All One.

This is something that we, Eleanore, do not understand. If we did, most of the problems of the world would be solved tomorrow.

What's The Truth About Astrology and Numerology?

> Dear Neale: I just finished reading *CWG*. All I can say is wow! Thanks so much, Neale, for having the courage to publish the book and for being here online. I've read every word posted in this Internet folder and it's magnificent! One question: God says that we "re-create" ourselves from moment to moment. I have dabbled in astrology and numerology, which tells us about tendencies we've chosen to be born with. Does the study of these two disciplines (and the Tarot) really mean anything in light of what God told you? Thanks! In love for all, Renee, on the Internet.

Dear Renee, Nothing in this universe, not even God Herself, can determine for you your course of action, nor predetermine your future in any way, unless you allow it to, in which case, of course, it is not predetermining your future at all. Astrology, numerology and Tarot are all but tools, indicators of the pathways you have chosen to this moment, yet you are a divine being, endowed with the power of all divine beings to create in the instant moment. I like what Paramahansa Yogananda has to say on this subject, in *Autobiography of a Yogi*:

"Occasionally I told astrologers to select my worst periods, according to planetary indications, and I would still accomplish whatever task I set myself. It is true that my success at such times has been preceded by extraordinary difficulties. But my conviction has always been justified: faith in divine protection, and right use of man's God-given will, are forces more formidable than are the influences flowing from the heavens."

The right use of man's God-given will, as Paramahansa Yogananda put it, is also more formidable than any numerological combination. I am not controlled by the position of the stars at my birth, or on any particular day, or, for that matter, by the numerological combination swirling around my name, birthdate, or any other aspect of my being.

Likewise, the Tarot may very well show me what I have selected, and what my path will be if I continue on the same journey in the same way. But it cannot and does not foretell the future in the sense that a future is already decided for me. The value of all of these tools of divination is that they give us a window into our own creative process; they show us what we have created, are now creating, and will continue to create, given no change in choice or direction. Like a windsock, they tell you which way the wind is blowing—not which way the wind *will* blow.

"I Want to Reassemble Myself on Another Planet . . ."

Dear Neale: Hi, my name is Melissa and I'm fourteen years old. I would like to subscribe to your newsletter. My parents wouldn't allow me to send thirty-five dollars—they think it's too much, so I've decided to send my allowance. I have one question. If our planet is in such danger, why can't God use His awesome power to heal it?

I understand that we need to change our government and all, but look at it from my point of view. I'm fourteen and being overwhelmed with ideas, but I don't even know who to write to in our government. It isn't my fault that I was born on a planet that's trying to kill itself.

It's hard being fourteen, because you need your parents for almost everything. Especially when I need their advice on this spirituality stuff, but all they say is that they're not interested. At times I wish that I could "reassemble" myself on a planet with HEBs.

This issue is killing me, since I don't know how to change the way our societies work. If you get to talk to God, please ask him how Melissa can reassemble herself on another planet, this time with HEBs. Please. PS: Tell God that I miss Ginger. (He'll understand.) Melissa, Bethesda, MD.

My dear Melissa, Nothing is more agonizing to endure than the impatience of youth. And the young people of our world have a right to be impatient with us. They do not see us creating for them a better world. They do not understand our hypocrisy. They do not comprehend how we can stand here playing our violins while Rome is burning. And because I am young at heart, Melissa, I deeply resonate with you.

First, let me congratulate you on finding a way to get this book in your hands. I would hope that your parents would be proud that you had the gumption to do that, even if they think that the price is a little too high. Now to your comments . . .

Our planet is in danger, Melissa, and God is "using His awesome power to heal it." Why do you suppose He sent you here? And believe it, Melissa, you have awesome power.

And so do I. All we have to do, my friend, is use it. God has given us all the free will, and the ability, to do that. But God will never force us to do anything. To do that would be to take away our free will, and that would defeat God's whole purpose in putting us here, and giving us life.

As to who to write to in your government, you can find that information at your nearest public library, Melissa. Go in and ask the librarian to help you. You'll have the information in no time. Or simply pick up the phone and call your local newspaper. Then, when you get the names and addresses you need, write them a powerful letter. Speak to them from your heart. Your message will have an enormous effect.

Melissa, if I asked God how you can reassemble yourself on another planet, this time with Highly Evolved Beings, I know what God would say to tell you. God would say that She put you here, in this world, so that you could be one of the first Highly Evolved Beings on this planet! Your job, Melissa, should you choose to accept it, is to show the rest of us what it means to be highly evolved.

You can do this by your example, Melissa. You can do this by, every day, living and breathing the message of *Conversations with God*. And never lose that wonderful, youthful impatience of yours. Even when you are old, like me, never lose your impatience with the things about life that do not speak the truth of your heart. Never give up your soul's desire, which is God's desire, which is that you might use this life to create the grandest version of the greatest vision you ever had about Who You Really Are—and that we might all do this, collectively, as a human race.

God would give me another message, too, Melissa, if I was talking with Her right now. One meant not only for you, but for everyone. God would say to all of us: "Don't only seek to live in a better world, seek to create one."

So please don't wish that you could reassemble yourself on another planet, Melissa. The planet you are on right now would be so much less without you.

We need you, Melissa. We need your brightness and your goodness and your impatience. We need your wonderfulness and your urgency to make things better.

I'll be looking to hear from you again, Melissa. You and I are partners in this. Love, Neale.

CHAPTER 10

Prayer and Meditation

A statement from *Conversations with God* that will change your life is the almost off-handed comment in the dialogue that everything you think, say and do is a prayer. Praying is not something we do at certain times, like when we are on our knees in church, or holding hands at the dinner table. It is something we are doing always.

Let me repeat that.

We are always praying.

Everything we think is a prayer. Everything we say is a prayer. Everything we do is a prayer. The problem is, we just don't know it. We think we are praying only when we are actually, consciously engaging in the activity we call "prayer." But here is a great secret.

God calls everything prayer.

How can this be so? Why is it the way it is?

CWG says that we are all creative beings, made in the image and likeness of God. Since God is the creator, so, too, are we. God has given us tools of creation, and they are three: thought, word and deed.

What you think, you create. What you say, you produce. What you do, you call forth more of. This is perhaps the most important single remembrance in *Conversations with God.* We've all heard this before, so it is certainly nothing new. But the way it is explained in *CWG* brings it home with new emphasis.

What the dialogue is telling us is that there is no time when the creation machine is "off." The process of creation goes on forever, and there is no time when it is not engaged. Think of God as a great big Xerox machine. Whatever you put in is duplicated. And you are never not putting something in.

That's the key. That's the real revelation. There is no time when you are not creating. There is no time when you are not praying. If "prayer" is the message you are sending to God, you are praying every minute of the day, for your message to God is your life, lived. And that message, that prayer, will be sent back to you, just as you send it out. God doesn't make any changes. God sends back to you, enlarged and multiplied, what you send God. Isn't that incredible?

Well, it is if you're sending "good stuff," and it's not if you're sending "bad stuff." So stop sending bad stuff! Rid yourself of your negative thoughts, speak not again a single negative word, and don't do, ever, that which you do not wish done to you. For what you do unto others will be done unto you—you can count on it.

So from now on, don't imagine that you are limiting your praying to those few moments during the day or week when you actually intend to talk to God. Notice that your whole life is a conversation with God. If that doesn't change the thoughts you allow yourself to entertain, the words you allow to escape from your lips, and the things you allow yourself to do, nothing will. Yet if you do change these things, you will find that your entire life will have changed, for the very prayers you have sent out will have produced the answers for which you have waited.

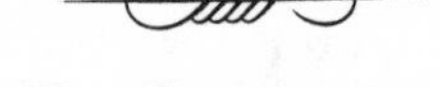

The Way to Pray

> Dear Neale: There has been something rolling around in my thoughts for some time. Maybe you can help me with some direction. I know prayer is wonderful. I often put myself in a prayer mode just to capture that Love feeling. I do pray. However, if things happen perfectly in our "perfect universe" then what are we praying for? I mean, does prayer change "what is"? Please help me to understand more about prayer! I wish you love, and I give you thanks. Sincerely, heart felt, Stacey, AZ.

Dear Stacey, You asked an intriguing question, one that has occupied the mind of man from the beginning of time, I suspect. The answer is contained in *Conversations with God*, so let me refer back to my own memory of the text. A prayer of supplication is not the most effective prayer, because a prayer containing a request actually pushes the result away from us. That is because when you ask for something, you are making a statement that you do not now have it. It is this statement which appears in your reality. And so, if we continue to pray for world peace, and more love on the planet, we will continue to experience that we do not have world peace and more love, because if we did, we wouldn't be asking for it. Therefore the most effective prayer is a prayer of thanksgiving.

God tells us that "gratitude is the attitude." When we are thankful for the result which we would like to perceive in our lives, that results come closer and closer into our realities. Prayer does not change "what is"; prayer changes our perception of what is. I will give you simple example.

If you are going out on a picnic, and head for the pasture to be with your loved one on a nice sunny Sunday afternoon, and if it begins to rain cats and dogs, and you are soaked to the skin with your beautiful hairdo totally messed up, and your wonderful romantic picnic washed out, you may think that this was somewhat less than perfect. On the other hand, if you are the farmer living in the big farmhouse over the rolling hill on the other side of the pasture, you may consider that the very same exterior experience of the downpour is absolutely perfect. So we see, that not only in this simple example, but in every instance, all of life—and the question of perfection itself—is merely a question of perspective.

One of the most effective prayers I ever came across I discovered in *A Course In Miracles*. That prayer is: "Thank you, God, for helping me to understand that this problem has already been solved for me." So, Stacey, in our "perfect universe" what we are praying for is for a grander understanding and a larger ability to experience the perfection of things exactly as they are now showing up. We are also offering a prayer of thanks to God for whatever other specific outcome we would choose, at the same time stepping away from any expectation or requirement that this outcome be produced. This is how all masters pray, and it is why all masters are always happy, at peace, and unperturbed. To understand all of this more deeply, may I suggest that you read *Conversations with God* again?

Is a Prayer in Yankee Stadium Heard?

Dear Neale: Thank you for penning the *CWG* books. Their divine wisdom is clear. Tell me something. You and Jesus believe in the power of "when two or more are gathered in My Name." This is indeed powerful, but so is individual prayer. Jesus also said that when you want to pray, go into your room and shut the door rather than flaunt it praying in front of others. Have you actually been told whether or not the Goddess of Love, who you call "God," prefers people to pray in groups or alone?

Of course, the like-minded can get together, but isn't praying a way of getting intimate with the Goddess of Love, and wouldn't that be easier if She gets us alone, as She has done with you?

The *CWG* books challenged me to be the highest conception of who I am. It is to treat every being as love, to treat as love each Goddess of Love in the heart of every one of us. Every rock, plant and animal is love. The being in the heart of every one of us is pure love, yet we fear to be who we really are. Therefore, it is by loving each other as love that we encourage each other to come home to who we really are. Martyn, Leederville, West Australia.

Couldn't agree with you more on that last part. About praying alone or in a group, however, I don't think God/Goddess listens "more closely" if we pray one way rather than another. I don't see Deity "favoring" any particular environment, ritual, language, gesture, or costume.

You asked me whether I have been told whether God "prefers people to pray in groups or alone." What I have been told, Martyn, is that God has no preferences about anything. Some churches say you must make the Sign of the Cross with your right hand, some say no, it's with your left. Some religions say there is no need to make a Sign of the Cross at all, and some say you must prostrate yourself three times on a carpet, facing the East. Some say only men can be on one side of the Wailing Wall, because women are unclean. Some say only men can be priests, because women are unclean. There are a hundred different versions of what pleases God and what upsets God. None of them have anything to do with ultimate truth.

You want to know the truth about the best way to get close to God/Goddess? Simply want to. Truly. Purely. Honestly. Want to.

You think God cares whether you are alone in your room or in Yankee Stadium?

Nope.

Is the Lord's Prayer for Real?

Dear Neale: I am a senior citizen (75) and have thoroughly enjoyed the *CWG* books. Most, if not all, Christian Churches say the Lord's Prayer. I said it for years without much thought, but in recent years "Lead us not into temptation" has bothered me. Why would God "lead us" into temptation? And, is the "Lord's Prayer" really the Lord's prayer? Clyde, Bridgeport, NY.

Dear Clyde, Interesting questions. The answer is, of course, that God would not lead us into temptation. The thrust of the line from the prayer is, "God, please don't let us be led into temptation." Granted, it is not worded that way, but I believe most people understand it to mean that, and I think Jesus' followers understood it to mean that as well, if, indeed, it was translated correctly to begin with. As to your second question, I think it is a very good prayer. And every prayer is "the Lord's prayer," because every prayer is an attempt to communicate with God, and there is no wrong way to do that. So all prayers are the Lord's!

Don't Ask—Call It Forth

Dear Neale: You recommend using the power of prayer and meditation to elevate our planet and give a healing influence on the "Army of God." While I'm now reading *CWG Book 1* for the third time, my thoughts are fixed on the words that a real prayer is a prayer of thanksgiving, and a statement of what is so. Therefore I stopped myself from practicing pleadings like "may all people rest in peace," and "please lead them to truth," etc., because I don't want to confirm through the act of asking (wishing?) that this is not there. I would like you to give a comment on how, in this context, meditation and prayer could look like literally. To visualize those people, criminals as well as victims, standing in the light—is that the kind of meditation you mean? Dagmar, Motzen, Germany.

Dear Dagmar, Yes, that is exactly the kind of meditation I mean. See everything as whole, complete and perfect. Visualize the grandest version of the greatest vision you ever had about conditions on the planet. Thank God for this being so, right here, right now. Do not "request" something of God: call it forth. If others say they do not believe you can do this, reply to them, Oh, ye of little faith.

Should We Ask the Creator for Anything?

Mr. Walsch: First I'd like to thank you for writing *Conversations with God.* I'm sure you've taken some "heat" for it. But I send you love, not fear. If I may, I'd like to ask you a few questions. (1) Can you suggest or recommend how to best get in contact with one's soul, or at least try to? (2) I got the impression that during prayer one doesn't need to ask the Creator for anything because it's already granted. So how does one pray? (3) Does the Creator ever mention the way of the Native Americans? Thank you for reading this. Walk in Peace. Charles, Summerdale, PA.

Good questions, Charles. Let's get to them. (1) Sit quietly with yourself for no less than 20 minutes each day (preferably longer). Find a room or a space where you can do this easily, without interruption. If you don't have such a space, create such a space! I light a candle, as I usually do, very early in the morning or late at night. In any event, it's usually dark. Somehow, for me, the darkness brings the room in, keeps the space close, intimate. I close my eyes and just listen. Clear my head of all thoughts and just listen. I listen to my own breathing at first. I listen to whatever other sounds are in the space, making them part of, rather than an interruption of, my meditation. Wear loose clothing, or, if you prefer, nothing at all. I usually sit in a lotus position, but it doesn't really matter. You can sit in a chair, if you like, or on the floor against the wall. I have found there is no "right" way to do this. Just be quiet with yourself.

After a while, as you are concentrating on your breathing, begin to focus on a point inside your head just above and between your eyes. Focus all your attention there if you can. The more you focus there, the more you will experience the rest of the room, its noises, smells, etc., sort of "fading away." You'll find a place of peacefulness and serenity there.

Now, if you're really lucky, you'll suddenly begin seeing flashes of what I can only describe as a bluish-white flame, dancing, as it were, in the center of your forehead, right in the middle of your field of vision. At least, this is how it has always happened for me. The "flame" or flickering "light" may dance tantalizingly before you. It may seem at first very small, very far away, then abruptly appear very close. The flame or flicker will be more than a visual experience. It will fill your beingness with a feeling as well, a feeling I can only describe as oneness/wonder/love. It is a feeling of softness, of melting, of congealing, almost, if that makes any sense. The feeling will permeate your entire body. You will be at once totally relaxed, totally at peace, totally immersed in . . . in . . . self? Sorry, no words really seem to work here . . .

Now if you are extremely lucky, the dancing bluish-white light will at some point fill your entire field of "vision" as you sit with your eyes closed, focused keenly on the center of your forehead. It will be as if you were a zoom lens, zooming in on the light. If this phenomenon occurs, you will be transported. Your feeling self will suddenly understand what it means to be in love. I mean, really in love. That is, inside the experience of love. Do you understand?

You will be, quite literally, in love with yourself. Once you have experienced this feeling, you will never fear being alone again, never need another again so badly that you become dysfunctional just to keep him or her in the room, never give any other person, place or thing your power again, and never doubt the reality of God again. Your life will change, and you will care nothing for the "stuff and things" of this life, and only yearn for the purest essence, the genuine peace, and the gentle truth that is your soul and your self.

Caution: This could take longer than you would like. You could meditate a lifetime and not achieve this state, this feeling, this experience. Or it could happen twenty seconds after you sit down for the first time. It doesn't matter. It can't be a thing that matters. It can't be the reason you are doing this. Just sit down and be quiet with yourself a little every day. Don't try to achieve anything. Don't try to do anything. Don't try to experience anything. Don't try to get anywhere with the experience. Don't try to "make something happen." Every time you do that, you fill your mind with everything you want to happen, or with the frustration of it not happening, or whatever. What you want to do is empty your mind, not fill it.

So just be quiet with yourself; and experience what you're experiencing, whatever that is. Be satisfied with it. Be happy with it. Just with the quiet. Just with the being there. You understand? It's like that. Even if you never have the experience I described, the daily "time out" to be with yourself in this gentle, loving, peaceful way will do wonders for you. It will be incredibly rejuvenating. You'll see.

Now, to Question (2): The way to pray is to speak the praises of God and Her universe, and to say words of thanks! "Thank you, God!" is a marvelous prayer. Just attach to it whatever it is you think you need. Thank God in advance for whatever aspect of divine reality you seek to experience now. So the best way I know to pray is to pray a prayer of thanksgiving. Reread page 11 of *CWG Book 1*. Also, top of page 180.

(3) The "way of the Native Americans" is not specifically mentioned in Books 1, 2 or 3.

Distracted When I Meditate!

Mr. Walsch: Thank you so much for *CWG*. To say it is amazing is a masterpiece of understatement. A lot of your book verifies things I already feel are true. Some of it, as you know, is truly surprising. I am on my second reading. This is a book that must be read several times. A question I would hope you would be able to address is about meditation. I live in an apartment complex that is adjacent to a four lane street. Although I am a senior citizen, I have very good hearing. My problem is that the traffic sounds, etc., distract me when I try to meditate, and I would appreciate any suggestions you have on how to overcome this. Betty, Portland, OR.

When you meditate, Betty, the first hint is to stop trying to do anything. That is, don't even try to meditate! The art of meditation is the art of letting go—of everything—including the hope, dream or expectation of having a good meditation. Just sit there. Be quiet with yourself. Don't try to block out noises and other distractions. Rather, make them part of your experience. Bring them in. Include them. But don't think about them as "noises" or "distractions." That's a judgement. That's the mind working; deciding things about it. Don't decide. Just listen. Hear the noises, but "pay them no mind." Make nothing of it. Let me say that again. Make nothing of it.

Remember when we were kids, and we'd just barely mention something to another person who was sensitive, and they'd say back to us, "Sooo??? You wanna make something of it?" And we'd back down, right? Because we didn't want to "make something of it." Well, now it's the same way with your mind. The trouble with your mind is that it's like that inquisitive little kid—until it's silenced. It wants to "make something" of every piece of data that comes in. Noises, sights, smells. Everything. Now it's up to you to challenge your mind to stop that. Every time your mind connects with an outside stimulus, just say, "Yeah, so what? You wanna make something of it?" Then your mind will get that there's nothing going on here. That a noise is just a noise. A smell is just a smell. That's all it is and it's not anything more. It doesn't have to interfere with anything. Anything. Not even your meditation. Better yet, it can be part of your meditation!

But it can never be part of your meditation if you are trying to do something in your meditation called "be quiet." The object of your meditation is not to be quiet. It is to be still—which is not the same thing at all. Being still means simply being "with" whatever's going on. So, Betty, be with the traffic sounds, and whatever other noises are out there. Hear them, maybe even count them. Categorize them, if you want to. Then, set them aside and get back to simply listening to your breathing. Go back to your breathing and just listen to that. You'll block out the other sounds automatically. But not if you become annoyed by them, distracted by them. Never be annoyed or distracted by life. It is just life, happening. Let the meditation happen as part of it. I know people who could sit down in the middle of Times Square and meditate. Within 30 seconds, they're gone. Out of it. Spaced. I mean, that's how people see it. Actually, they've moved deep into meditation upon the moment. So deep that the moment no longer runs against the grain of the meditation, but becomes what the meditation is all about. You see?

Now, then, as you begin to concentrate on your breathing, which you can always hear, no matter what is going on around you, start also to focus your attention on a spot between and just above the eyes. Focus on that spot. There are a lot of ways to get there. Some people like to begin with an "inventory," focusing on all other areas of their body first, as a means of achieving total relaxation. So they focus on their toe, for instance. Then their ankle. Then the leg, the knee, the thigh, and so on, in this way "being with" every part of their physical body. They watch each part relax. They may even order it to. That's fine. That's okay. That's one way to achieve relaxation. Actually, there is no "right" way. Just do what works for you. But finally, when you feel you've become "unwound," and are just sitting there, being with the moment, then begin to draw your attention to this little space I've talked about behind the center of your forehead, above and between the eyes.

Interesting things can happen when you do that. Don't be surprised if you encounter a dancing blue/white "flame," or light. Don't be surprised if you are overcome, as you become immersed in that light, with a feeling of well-being, warmth and oneness that can only be described as ecstasy. Not happiness. Not even joy. But pure ecstasy. Peace. Unity.

Another way to get into the mental space for meditation is to do some guided imagery. This is a form of mental practice that gently quiets the mind and opens the heart. It is done with the help of an audio cassette tape that leads you through the process. It's great for those who are beginning meditators and who want to gain some experience in working with the mind in this way.

Learning to meditate will be part of the programs offered at CWG centers around the world. For more information, please see page 231.

CHAPTER 11

Talking with God

The world has an interesting mind-set about this business of talking with God. Most people believe that not only are *Conversations with God* possible, but they have occurred. In fact, most religions are based on this assumption. What people cannot seem to agree on is when God stopped talking.

If God has never stopped talking, that complicates things, because most religions are based on God's direct revelations to a specific person or group. Those people and groups have no choice, then, but to teach that God's revelations are over. Finished. Kaput. For if God continues to reveal Himself directly to humans, as nearly all religions concede that She did at one point, then what is the need for a particular religion at all?

This is a question religions can't tolerate, because it strikes at the foundation of their reason for being. Religions, in fact, gather their authority from their pronouncement that their founder (or founders) heard the Real Word of God, and that what anyone else heard is a falsehood. A misunderstanding, if not a blasphemy.

This is what first gave human beings permission to call themselves "better"–and to kill in the name of that "betterness."

Now along comes a book called *Conversations with God*, which boldly states that God has never stopped talking with us, and is, indeed, communicating every day. And not just with a select few of us, but, in fact, with every one of us.

Can this be true? Is this possible? Did God not abandon humans after all, following the last Great Revelation? And which was the last one, anyway? Was it the Koran? The Talmud? The Bhagavad Gita? The Rig Veda? The Brahmanas? The Upanishads? The Tao-te Ching? The Bible? The New Testament of the Bible? Could it have been the Book of Mormon? Just which written word, exactly, was the last word? Who has the last word here?

Most religions cannot agree on which old book contains the Word of God, but most can agree that no new book does.

And so, we are faced with the ultimate contradiction: religions that teach that their truth is based on the direct revelations of God, then warn that such revelations are improbable.

It is understandable that people just do not know what to believe. The institution that was meant to clear up everything, has done more than any other human institution to create confusion. In the end, we are on our own. With one tiny exception. We have God with us, every step of the way. We can communicate with God. We can talk to God, and know that God will talk to back to us. We can actually have a "friendship with God." The new book by that title describes exactly how to do this.

Can I Really Talk to God—and Will God Answer?

> Dear Neale: Today is my 25th birthday. And I need to ask you how can I really talk to God and get a response that I can hear. Either I'm not receptive to listening, or I'm not asking right, or God's not answering. I would prefer a verbal response from him/her. After 25 years I have a lot to ask and a lot of things to put to rest. Did God say anything to you about fulfilling your dreams?
> P.W.

My friend, receive God's response to you in whatever form it comes. God has a habit of responding to people in the form with which He knows they will be most comfortable–and of which they will be most accepting. If God thought you could accept and receive His responses to you verbally, you would be given verbal responses. God probably knows you would poo-poo such voices in your head as hallucinations or whatever, and not listen to them anyway. So God chooses forms of communication to which you will listen, not the least of which may be this very answer to you, through me! You see? God works in mysterious ways, His wonders to perform. Allow that. Permit that. Don't seek to limit God, or direct Her actions. Let Her choose Her own form of communication. But listen. Watch. Stay alert. For you do not know in which hour the Master may come. *Conversations with God* puts this very nicely, very succinctly, I thought. Read the back cover. It says it all.

As to fulfilling dreams, God says we may fulfill whatever dreams we wish to fulfill. You are fulfilling your dreams right now, even this very day. If you don't like your life right now, it is because you have been dreaming nightmares. That is, your thought system about life has produced a reality with which you disagree. Change your thoughts, change your reality. That's the whole message of *CWG.*

The way to fulfill your dreams is to insist on them, even in the face of information and experiences to the contrary. I always knew I would write a book. I always knew I would have one published. This is just one of the many dreams I have had, and seen fulfilled. But the evidence before my eyes has not always supported my dreams. What I do is look beyond the evidence, to the power of the dream itself, and to the power of God to produce it for me.

Yet it is very wise to dream dreams of beingness, not doingness, for doingness leads not to evolution, not to growth, but leads instead to being stuck in doingness.

Am I Alone?

> Dear Mr. Walsch: I just finished reading your book, and it left me speechless! Is God really saying all those things? I want to believe He is, because it sure clears up a lot of things in my mind. It would be nice to see how other people responded to your book as I know I'm not alone. Elaine, Eifrida, AZ.

No, you are not, Elaine. And one of the reasons we're including comments here and not just questions, is to let you know that you are not alone! Now, is God "really saying all those things?" I believe so, Elaine. But that doesn't make it so. That just makes it my belief. It is important to understand that. I have no need to convince you of anything. Just read the book, and take from it what's there for you. Decide what's there for you. It's that simple.

God talks to everyone, but not everyone believes that. As *CWG* says, "This is the root of every problem you experience in your life–for you do not consider yourself worthy enough to be spoken to by God." How about you? Do you consider yourself worthy enough? Ask yourself this question. If your answer is yes, begin this month to listen more closely for the words of God as guidance in your life. If your answer is no, look to see why you do not think you are sufficiently worthy to receive God's direct guidance.

How Do You Tell People God Has a Sense of Humor?

Dear Neale: For years I've thought I was nuttier than a fruitcake and dared not share my ideas with others. I've tried to fit into the "mold" and because I couldn't, my life has practically come to a standstill. Recently I graduated from an interfaith seminary–graduated yes, but not feeling of the same ilk as the other students. I am too irreverent. I "know" God better than the way He/She is being portrayed. How do you tell people that God has a rather wry sense of humor? How do you tell them when you ask a question, you actually get a viable answer? How do you tell people that they don't have to dress up their verbiage, all they have to do is talk–just like they talk to their best friend? Who believes you? And then along comes *Conversations with God*! You did it! You told them! It was as if someone was in my head eavesdropping on my private talks with God! "Yes!" I shouted. After every question God answered "Yes! Yes! Yes! I'm not a nut case. This is real. This *is God talking.*" Namaste, Rev. B., CA.

Dear Rev. B., You bet it is! It's funny, but when we say we talk to God every day, we're called pious. Yet when we say God talks to us every day, we're called crazy. What's "crazy" is thinking that God *stopped* talking 2000 years ago. That's what's crazy.

Thanks for the Courage

Dear Mr. Walsch: I am compelled to let you know reading *CWG* was pure joy. I have stopped to write this before finishing the book. When I reached Chapter 10, I held the book to my breast and cried. That is exactly what I hear every time I start my *Conversations with God*. Thank you for having the courage to write this book. You can believe it will be recommended to everyone I come in contact with. I will make this short because I know you are very busy. I just wanted to let you know you are dearly loved here in Bullhead City, Arizona . . . Nona.

Dear Nona, Thank you. I sometimes don't know what to say after reading a letter like yours. I am touched, and deeply moved by the incredible gift of it all. First, God's gift to me, then yours. Thank you, thank you, thank you, Nona, for flowing such good energies toward me, for saying such nice things, and for meaning them. For the one thing I know is that your letter and all its words are very sincere. And I am humbled, and grateful. God bless you.

Will You Help Spread the Word?

My Dear Mr. Walsch: I am attempting to construct a letter here that will make sense. However, after finishing your book *Conversations with God*, I feel overwhelmed, fairly speechless and somewhat senseless. Moreover, very quiet, content, peaceful, validated, enveloped, encompassed, fulfilled and emptied simultaneously.

I find myself with a smile on my lips, tears streaming down my face and a lifetime of pain and joy exploding in my heart. The book is truth, absolute and without question. It is the culmination of years of struggle within myself. It is the pinnacle of knowledge and experience welling within me, peaking over past spring and summer, now washed out with the tide of your words, God's words.

How the book came to me remains a mystery. At some point within the last year, someone questioned me if I had read *Conversations with God*. I recall saying no, I had not heard of, nor knew anything about the book. I wrote the title down on a list I keep of books to purchase and read. A couple months ago I bought the book with the curiosity of wanting to know someone else's *Conversations with God*, questioning: would they be like mine? To this day, everyone I have asked, "Were you the one who mentioned the book, *Conversations with God*?" the answer has been no.

I wish to express my gratitude to you and the God residing in you for undertaking with such courage a writing of magnificent truth and unconditional love. It has been said, this God we speak of is closer to us than our very breath. I have known this to be true since childhood. Now I know I am not crazy. In the light and love of being and creating, the God in me bows down to the God in you, Messenger Walsch. My thought for your physical well being to continue your work is present. May your work bring as much joy to others as it has brought to me. You are blessed. Sincerely, Pamela (no address given).

Well, Pamela, that is among the nicest letters I have received–and nearly 10,000 letters have come here in the past 24 months. I've included it here because I think it is important for all of us to see once again, and to stay in touch with, the truth of how this extraordinary book has touched the lives of others. Let's all of us do whatever it takes to make sure that these books become more than simply the latest "hot read." First, let's pledge to live their truths. Then let's promise to help spread them.

Give away one copy a month to someone you love. Find out how you can become a part of *CWG* In Action. Become a Bringer of the Light. See page 231 for details on how you can do this. If this message has touched you in a positive way, do what you can to touch others with it.

If we all do that, we can spread this glorious truth to all corners of the map.

Why Many People Can't Believe God Speaks Directly to Us

Dear Mr. Walsch: I have just finished reading *Conversations with God, Book 1*. It is the most inspiring book I have ever read. I am passing it along to a very good friend of mine. I hope God's words as set forth in your book will help my friend realize God wants us to be happy. If we believe God spoke through the prophets (ordinary men) in the Bible, why is it so hard for some to believe that God might speak through a *contemporary* "ordinary man"? Regina, Philadelphia, PA.

Because, Regina, that would make all of us responsible for receiving such communications. If I can do it, then shouldn't you be able to also? Of course you should. Yet this is a responsibility most people do not wish to share or embrace. Much easier, then, to deny that it could possibly have happened to me. Then it could not happen to them, either, and they are "off the hook."

Yet for those people who do believe God talks to us there is such reward, such fulfillment, such extraordinary opportunity and empowerment, and such spiritual unfoldment, that to have ever denied the possibility of such an event seems incomprehensible.

How Can I Know God Exists?

Dear Neale: I have some very tough questions that have plagued me for a while now. Ever since I got into a belief debate with a friend who's very scientific (and does not believe in a God), I've been stumped. To know that there's a 50/50 chance that we're really alone, and that what I spent my life believing in and loving, may all be a lie has led me into a deep depression. I know now what hell is, I wake to it every morning–a world without God.

I want to know more than anything that God really exists, but how do I know? How do I know you aren't just receiving the answers from your own subconscious? Your answer would probably be, "Because my mind couldn't devise those kind of answers." But are you so sure? I must have dreams every night and I've had dreams about things or people that I would never think of (that are the furthest from my personality) yet my subconscious creates them.

The question "what about the powerful, warm feeling a person gets when in deep prayer, baptism, etc." might arise. Yes, I've felt it so powerful the tears have flowed and I could barely stand, but sex is a very incredible experience, too, and it's a biological function, so couldn't everything else be?

Furthermore, I am familiar with automatic writing, but again, how do I know the answers aren't of my own biological brain? Lately when I've tried to communicate with Him/Her in this form, I've received vague and horribly misspelled answers, then the pen drifting off the paper. And now, nothing at all, just the pen drifting.

So if you could, if you have the time, could you please ask God these things? I've asked, but have had no luck. Besides, you're good at it. Three books is pretty damned good.

It seems these days God would have to appear before my eyes in human form or I'd have to die before I'd know if he were fact and not fiction (and I really would like to find him before that time). Utterly lost, Kendra, Sunnyvale, CA.

> PS. I just got an idea! If you do decide to talk with God, there's a man that I've idolized since I was 12. If God could reveal the correct name to you, then I'd know that God is alive and well. After all, how would you know? That's just a thought.

Dear Kendra . . . my dear, dear Kendra . . . how I wish I could give you the gift of faith in that which you do not know in your experience. I had so hoped that my book would do that. I do know this. If you had had the same experience I had, you would never, ever again question the existence of God, or the source of these writings. But you have not had such an experience, and how can I give it to you? I cannot. I can only share with you my own.

Kendra, I cannot tell you the name of the man you have idolized since you were 12. Such a particular and peculiar piece of personal information I could never know, and I cannot find it in my heart to ask God to do "parlor tricks" in order to prove Herself to you or to me. I understand why you would ask, though. We are all trying to find a simple way to prove to ourselves that God exists. Well, let me give you a simple way, Kendra. Look into the eyes of a newborn child. Smell the fragrance of a blossoming rose. And, yes, melt into the incredible experience of wonderful, loving sex. You call that a biological function, Kendra. Who do you suppose invented biology?

There is not a "50/50 chance that we are really alone," Kendra. There isn't the slightest chance in the world of that. I'm going to ask God to visit your heart even as you are reading this. And because I have asked, God will do so. That is the faith I have. Yet you must open your heart, Kendra, or you will not feel the presence of God. Or, you may feel the presence and call it something else. (Like a "biological function.")

You do not wake up every morning to a world without God, Kendra. You wake up every morning to a world in which you do not see God. That is an entirely different thing. Say this prayer: Open my eyes, that I may see visions of truth that asked for me. Open my eyes, illumine me, spirit divine! Those words are from a wonderful recording by vocalist Cris Williamson, called *Song of the Soul*.

Write to me, and tell me how things are with you. And know

this, Kendra. I am with you. I have walked your path. And I love you for your honesty.

God Is Your Best Friend, and Never Leaves Your Side

Dear Mr. Walsch: Without going into a lot of detail, let me tell you what happened to me on April 4 of this year. I was feeling very much like you described yourself in the opening chapter of your book. I was in my car in a shopping mall parking lot when I began to cry–something which is out of character for me. Among other things, the relationship between me and my boyfriend had not been going very well, and I felt terribly depressed. I began screaming at God that I was tired of the struggle and if He were a just and kind God, why couldn't he answer my prayers? Why wasn't He there when I needed Him? I remember begging God to please help me. I asked Him to give me a sign, any sign, to let me know that He had at least heard my prayers.

I finally gained my composure and went into the mall to purchase a book which had been ordered for me. On my way to the information desk, I passed a table and that's when I saw your book. It has not left my side since I purchased it. I want you to know that I am a very strong-willed woman who is not easily influenced. However, your book has, and is having, a powerful impact on my life. Thank you so much. Keep up the good work. Sincerely, Shawn, MD.

Dear Shawn, I think this is a wonderful example of "even before you ask, I will have answered." God is our best friend. She knows what we need even before we speak it. Your story is an inspiration, for it demonstrates that truth. Thanks so much for writing. I wish you well.

What is Meant by "As Above, So Below"?

Dear Neale: Please, speak to us of "Love God above all things . . . and love your neighbor as I have loved you." Also, if you would, speak of "as above, so below," for these in-the-now-moment times. Thank you. Amania, San Francisco, CA.

Hi, Amania, I don't know who said "Love God above all things," but it couldn't have been God. God would have said, "Love everything, for that is what I Am. Love not one thing and not the other, nor love one thing more than another, yet love everything, and all of life, with all your heart, and all your mind, and all your soul; for in the loving of that which you call 'bad,' you transform it; in the loving of that which you call 'evil,' you disarm it; in the loving of that which you call 'harmful,' you render it safe; in the loving of those who would do you harm, you cause yourself to be impervious to them.

"And in loving that which you call 'good,' you empower it; in loving that which you find pleasurable, you enhance it; in loving that which you call 'Godly,' you define yourself and lay claim to Who You Are. Yet judge not, and neither condemn, for that which you judge will you become, and that which you condemn will condemn you."

God would have said, "Love your neighbor even as I have loved you," for it is God's teaching that your neighbor is you. There is no separation. Therefore to love your neighbor is for your right hand to love your left, your eye to love your nose. You cannot love one thing without loving the other, nor can you despise one without casting aspersion upon the other, for all are of the same body, and none exists apart and separate from the other. Therefore, Jesus meant it literally when he said, "Love thy neighbor as thyself." What he may well have added, though it would not have been included in the revised, expunged Bible, was: ". . . for thy neighbor is thyself."

"As above, so below" means, as it is in your highest thoughts, so will it be in your lowest; as it is in your highest dream, so will it be in your lowest; as it is in your highest idea and your highest ideal and your highest vision, so will it be in your lowest. The lowest part of you is risen ("He is risen") when the highest part of you soars. It also means, as it is for you in your highest chakra, so will it be in your lowest. Your lower chakra energies increase in their frequency and vibration as your highest chakra vibrations rise.

The "fight or flight" response, the survival instinct, is raised as the higher chakra centers understand and embrace the truth that survival is not the issue, but a given, that it is not a question of whether you will survive, but of how it will be with you as you do. The sexual response, too, rises from the mere survival of the race mode–instinctually urgent, demanding–to the demonstration and celebration of the love mode, an entirely different energy.

"As above, so below" also means that as it is in the heaven of your understanding, so will it be in the earth of your experience. That is, if you construct an idea of heaven which includes exclusion of the undeserving, punishment of the mistaken and the "wrong," a home for a God of special favor to only a certain few, of judgment and damnation, of anything but unconditional love, then you will experience an earth of the same qualities. For it cannot be any way for you on your earth other than the way it is for you in your heaven. Thus: as above, so below. For the highest of your thoughts will produce the lowest of your experiences. And the higher your thoughts and aspirations, visions and intentions, the higher will be even your lowest experiences.

Thus it has been written, Seek ye first the Kingdom of Heaven, and all else will be added unto you. Yet know this: the Kingdom of Heaven is not sought, and neither is it found, by selective exclusion of everything you call "unGodly." Rather, it is found by unconditional inclusion of all that is.

The Experience of God Is What God Has Always Chosen

> Dear One: I am very confused about "God wanting to know Himself experientially," so would love to hear more about that. Lori, Redding, CT.

Hello, Lori, Let me see if I can help. It is one thing to know yourself conceptually, and another thing to know yourself experientially. For example, you may know conceptually that you are a loving person, but if you have never actually expressed your love to anyone, you will merely know love as a concept, not as an experience. You will have an idea about yourself, but not an experience of yourself. Do you see? Do you understand?

Now, God chose to have more than a mere concept about Itself. God chose to have an experience of Itself. God wanted to know Itself in Its own experience. God chose to know what it felt like to be all-powerful, to be all-knowing, to be all-loving. God chose to know what it felt like to be wisdom personified, courage displayed, love expressed. God chose to know, experientially, every aspect of Its Being–that is to say, every aspect of divinity. To merely "know" about Itself was not enough. To merely understand was insufficient. For God, only the direct experience would do. So God created you. You are the direct experience. You are God, "Godding." You, and everything else in creation.

Since you are God, having the experience of Itself, and since God is the creator, you, too, have the power to create. You are using that power every moment, usually without even knowing it, usually without intending to. The creative power of God is enfolded into your every thought, your every word, your every deed. This process is thoroughly explained in *Book 1* of the *Conversations with God* trilogy.

So God's desire, Lori, was to experience about Itself what It knew about Itself. That is the greatest desire of your soul, too. All your soul really wishes to do is to have the direct experience of Who You Really Are. And that is what you are doing here, Lori. That is what your life is all about. How it is working, the process by which all of this takes place, is what the *Conversations with God* dialogue is all about.

Did God Pick Out These Souls for Me?

Dear Neale: I am expecting twins and I cannot believe how blessed I am. Did God pick out these two souls for me? Did they choose my husband and myself? Does God hear every time I talk to Him/Her (about the little stuff, too)? I look at the size of the universe and it seems hard at times, that He could possibly have time for me. Does God feel my love for Him? It's important, the most important, for Him to feel my love for Him. Does He need it or even want it? Blessings, Susan, Bordentown, NJ.

Dear Susan, In answer to your question, "Did God choose these two souls for me?" No, God makes no choices for you. If God made choices for you at any step along the way, then that would take away your opportunity and your ability to make choices for yourself, and God would have made a mockery of free choice. Therefore, not only has God not chosen these souls for you, God has chosen nothing for you, for God has no preference in the matter. On the other hand, blessed beings in the universe have chosen these two souls. You have!

God needs nothing, by definition. God needs or wants nothing in the classic definition of the meaning of the word want, to be "in want," that is to say, to be "in want" of something. But does God choose your love, does God love your love? Does God love receiving your love? Of course God does, for God is Love itself, and when God receives your love, God receives a reflection of what God, Itself, is.

Now to your other concerns: Does God hear every time I talk to Him/Her (the little stuff, too)? I look at the size of the universe and it seems hard at times, that He could possibly have time for me.

God would probably answer something like this:

"My dearest Susan, yes, I hear you, even when you tell me of 'the little stuff.' And I always answer, if you would but listen. As to the size of the universe and My having time for you, yes, I really am there and here and everywhere, which doesn't mean there's not enough of Me for you. Because I am everywhere does *not* mean I am spread so thin that nobody gets enough. There is *always* 'enough' because *there is always All There Is.* Like the hologram, each atom of Me contains all of Me. Each one of you contains all of Me. And yet nothing contains Me because I am uncontainable. I am infinite!"

Susan, for more help with learning to hear God, reread page 58 in *CWG Book 1.* It might help you see how God's answers may be brought to you.

Why Did God Want to "Know Himself"?

Dear Neale: In *CWG*, God says we can't define God. If not, how do we know that God is love? Also, why did God want to know

> Himself? I have gotten used to the idea that God is love and light and truth and abundance, etc. But to some people, love is defined differently. If the only love they've known is limited and self-serving, how can they know that love is understanding and forgiveness and non-judgment? My brother-in-law thinks that love is disciplining, that God is a disciplinarian. He is comfortable with that. Probably because his father beat him. How do you tell people that love does not punish, that unconditional love does not force someone to anything by punishing them? Tracey, from E-mail.

Dear Tracey, Let's go from the top. In *CWG*, God says that "Love is all there is." God also says that God is All That Is. Therefore, God is love. Everything in our heart tells us this, too, by the way, and the heart is never wrong. I did not interpret the book to say that God cannot be defined. I believe what the book says is that God cannot be limited to any one definition or description–and, by that limiting means, be so defined. That certainly sounds true to me, though it does not negate or invalidate the description of God as "love."

As to your second question, *CWG* says that God wanted to know Himself experientially. The same, says the book, is true of me and you. It is one thing to think of yourself or know yourself as, shall we say, compassionate, or loving, but it is quite another thing altogether to experience yourself as these things. If you have no one to love, you can "know yourself" as loving all you want, but it is not the same thing as actually loving someone through action in the here and now. God wishes to experience Itself as what It really was, and so the whole universe was created. Why? For the sheer joy of it, Tracey! For the joy of self expression.

Question three: *The American Heritage Dictionary* defines "punishment" as "a penalty imposed for wrong-doing." According to *CWG*, there is no such thing as "right" and "wrong." Therefore, "wrongdoing" is nonexistent, and so, too, "punishment." Most humans cannot accept this concept. They cannot understand how it could be so. Yet would a loving grandmother spank her toddling grandchild for breaking a dish or spilling her milk? Of course not.

God is very much like that loving grandmother. And we are very, very much like that toddler in our understandings and actions. And, as you point out, if the only love a person has known is limited and self-serving, it will be difficult to grasp, much less accept, the concept of a love which is unconditional.

As *CWG* points out, most people fall into this lot; most have never known a love which is without condition. And most people judge God to be operating on earthly norms. Yet to know God one must imagine a being much larger, much grander than anything one has seen in this life. One must not assign God earthly attributes, earthly understandings and earthly limitations, but rather, qualities that are unknown in our experience.

With regard to God, one must accept the possibility that there is something we do not know, the knowing of which could change everything.

You see, this is our chief problem: we think we already know everything there is to know about God. And so any description of God which does not fall within our current understandings is automatically rejected as "false," "wrong," and "blasphemy." Yet if there is such a thing as blasphemy, it would be to assert, announce and declare that we know everything there is to know about God, that our beliefs about God are the right beliefs, and that anyone who does not accept our beliefs is going straight to hell.

How do you tell someone with a limited understanding, based on their limited experience of real love, about the unconditional love of God? You don't. You don't tell them anything about it. You demonstrate it.

Let Some Mysteries Remain Mysteries

Dear Neale: I understand that ours is a world of the relative. But if God is the all (everything), then s/he is good as well as bad (evil). I don't understand how this makes sense with the idea that we are love and that fear is the opposite. If we are God, then we are also the all and are we not good and bad?

I understand that in order to experience being one, we must have the choice between the two, but if one is not part of us (God) then where did it come from? If God created the opposite of what He was/is so that we could experience being love (what we are) by seeing fear and having the choice between the two, then that I can understand. But, if God is the all, then how can there be anything he is not (fear, hate, evil)? I continue to struggle with this and find myself going in circles of thought without coming to any conclusions. Thanks, Cynthia, E-mail.

First of all, Cynthia . . . you are trying to "figure this out" with your mind. Stop it. In order to understand the ancient wisdoms you have to be "out of your mind." That is, you cannot apply logic and reason and ordinary linear thought systems to this stuff and expect to come up with something that "adds up." You're going to keep coming up with 2+2=5. And it will drive you bananas. So cut it out. Stop it. Go into your heart, Cynthia. Get into your feelings. Spend some time in meditation on these mysteries. But even there, don't look for "answers." Seek, instead, wisdom. Remember Cynthia, "wisdom" and "answers" are not always the same thing.

Now, in case you are still nevertheless suffering from a "logic attack" (which is something like a "Big Mac attack"!), let me see if I can– all that I have just said notwithstanding–help your mind with all this.

First of all, God is the all and the everything. And that all, that everything which God is is called love. *CWG* teaches, "Love is all there is." And that is demonstrated in the realm of the absolute. We live, however, in what I call, Cynthia, the "realm of the relative," where all things exist and can only be experienced relative to each other. This reality I am now describing, Cythnia, is not ultimate reality. In fact, we are making it all up. We are pretending, if you will, that the system has polarities, and so, we see this, Cynthia:

This is a straight line polarity with, we imagine, "love" on one end, and "fear" on the other. One supposes that somewhere in the middle of this line is a balance point between the two. Yet in truth, Cynthia, how it really "is" is more like this:

This is a circular non-polarity. Here we see that that which is is all the same stuff. There is no beginning or end to it, no "balance point," no thing at all except that which feeds into itself, becomes itself. The condition in this reality is that we cannot experience any extreme of it, because in a circular system there can be no extreme. There is just what is, and there is, literally, no end to it.

In order for us to experience any of this, we have to create a beginning and an end. A here and a there. A before and an after. An up and a down. And, yes, a love and a fear. We're doing this is our imagination, Cynthia. It is not real. Not even what you think you are seeing with your own eyes is real. (For more on this, read *The Holographic Universe*, by Michael Talbot.)

You are right, Cythnia. God is everything. We are, likewise, everything, since we are that which God is. In this life experience, we have chosen to forget that. We have literally forgotten Who We Really Are, so that we can recreate our selves anew in the next grandest version of the greatest vision we ever had about Who We Are.

On second thought, Cynthia, don't try to figure this out. Just "get it."

Do Other Authors Have the Same Source?

Dear Neale: Just finished reading *CWG Book 1*. Found it very interesting, though I thought I was reading something by Alice Bailey.

Bailey has a school where they are supposed to teach occult truths. Your *Book 3* should put them out of business; as most of the Bailey books were supposedly written by automatic writing, it would seem you both tapped the same source.

When you finish with your collaborator, send him in my direction. I don't accept some of the pat answers, whereby he wants us to accept the blame for his butchery of people. (Karma, indeed?) Howard, Gretna, LO.

Thanks for the letter, Howard. Let me comment. I've heard of Alice Bailey, and have been aware of her books, but I've never read them. I agree, however, that we both did tap into "the same source." That's because there is only one source, Howard! There's no where else you can go.

I have a feeling I'll be compared to a lot of writers before this is through, and that's wonderful. We're all saying the "same stuff" because *there's nothing else to say*! Truth is truth, no matter what the source. So it doesn't matter whether it's Alice Bailey talking, or Ram Dass, Marianne Williamson or Neale Donald Walsch, Gary Zukov or Elisabeth Kübler-Ross. Or for that matter, Howard from Gretna! Each of us has the ability to "tap into" the source, because *each of us is the source*. That is, we are one with our creator, Howard, and all we need do to experience that is to know it.

God the "blamer"? I don't think so . . . . Now, your last comment, Howard, puzzles me a bit. Are you saying that God has given "pat answers" in this book? Boy, that's the first time I've heard that one! Most of the answers are so unpat that some of them are even disturbing to many people. Even more interesting is the second part of your statement, that God "wants us to accept the blame for the butchery of people." Well, who else is to blame, Howard? We're the ones who are doing it.

Of course, as the book points out very clearly, the whole idea of "blame" is crazy and pointless. It's not about "blame," because *there's nothing "wrong" with what's happened here*. "Wrong" is a value judgment you have made in your mythology. God shares no such mythology, so God would certainly not try to "blame" anybody with His "pat answers," but rather, simply shows us the choices we've made as a civilization, and allows us to notice the outcome of that. He merely keeps giving us a chance to ask once again a key and important question: Is this Who We Are?

The lesson is visited upon us, again, but I didn't get that God was blaming us, and, in fact, thought what He was doing was enjoining us to stop blaming each other as well. The problem with the world is that everyone is blaming everyone else for everything that is going on. This is crazy in that it solves nothing. *We're finding this out again—for the umpteen millionth time—in Bosnia.* We're blaming the Serbs, the Serbs are blaming the Muslims, the Muslims are blaming the Croats, the Croats are blaming the U.N., the U.N. is blaming the U.S., whatever . . . .

What we're not understanding here is that no one does anything inappropriate, given their model of the world. So what we have to do if we want to stop the fighting and stop the slaughter in Bosnia is sit down with these people and try to figure out their model of the world. That is, try to understand the situation as they see it. Then we have to try to get them to understand how we see it. Then we have to try to see if there can be found a middle ground.

Now, if they absolutely refuse to seek with us a middle ground, and insist on having things their way or no way at all, we have to be *firm and fair and consistent and resolute* in telling them: I'm sorry, it is unacceptable for you to insist on continuing the killing in order to get your way. The world had to make the same statement in Kosovo. And it has had to be made elsewhere, given our group definition of Who We Are. We ahve decided that Who We Are is a people who will not stand by and watch the wholesale slaughter of others without seeking to stop it. This is a decision which has had to be made often by the human race. The decision is neither "right" nor "wrong." It is simply what we have decided about ourselves. It is a choice which has been made by a majority of the nations on this planet.

So I do not have the same experience of God here as you do, Howard. God has "butchered" no one. On the other hand, nor has He stopped us from doing so. We have to stop us. That is why I hope to sponsor a World Conference on Harmony Between Nations in September, 2000. (For info on how you can help, see page 231.)

Thanks, Howard, for the dialogue. It was nice of you to write.

Where Did God Come from?

Dear Mr. Walsch: I have just one question for you: where did God come from? Who "made" God? David, Freedom, PA.

Dear David, Here is something which the human mind has difficulty wrapping itself around. God didn't come from anywhere. The truth is that God always was, always is, and always will be, world without end. There was never a time when God was not, and there never was a thing that was not God. Therefore no one could have "made" God. The "maker" of God would have had to have been outside of God, and since nothing is outside of God, nothing exterior to God could have created God. How then was God "created"? The answer is: God was not.

God came out of the void, and it is to the void He shall return. *Book 2* explains in some detail that there is only one moment, and only one place. That moment is now; that place is here. Here and now is all there is. This is difficult to understand if you insist on using our artificial constructions around the concept you call "time," David. To step away from these constructions and come to a larger understanding of time, see the very large section on this topic in *CWG Book 2*.

Now, in *CWG Book 1* there is an extraordinary section in which God gives us a beginner's explanation of infinity, and tells us that She may not be, after all, the highest deity. (Begin reading on page 197.)

Your question has, of course, been asked a million times in a million ways ("Which came first, the chicken or the egg?"). There is no answer to your question, because a satisfactory answer which fits our present reality depends upon the conceptualization of time as a linear thing. (In other words, for God to have been "made," there had to have been a "time" when there was no God.) Yet time is not a linear thing, and all things which are are right now, and have always been, and will always be. This includes, by the way, you.

As I said, this is explained with great care, and in great detail, in *Book 2*.

To Whom Is God Grateful?

Dear Neale: Thanks for your books. I can't begin to tell you how much they've helped me and the other 16 members of our group. A question was asked in our meeting last week. On page 65, you write about "The Five Attitudes of God": "Totally joyful, loving, accepting, blessing and *grateful.*" This last is very puzzling: what or who is God grateful for? We had a lot of discussion and as I asked the question, I volunteered to write you for more input. Also, what is the difference, if any, between *soul* and *spirit* (ours)? Many books seem to use the terms interchangeably, but I think there is more to it. Pat, Shelton, CT.

Dear Pat, God is grateful to Godself, who else? Haven't you ever thanked yourself for anything? Of course you have. I've thanked myself many times. I've also blamed myself, berated myself, congratulated myself . . . .

And for what is God grateful? For Her own perfection. Remember this always: gratitude is the attitude. It is when we are grateful in advance for that which we desire that we make it manifest in our daily lives. This is because that which we choose already exists, and all that is needed is our perception of it. Gratitude changes our perception; it alters our point of view. It assumes that a thing has already been experienced. This is the truth of it. For in ultimate reality, there is no time or space, and nothing which is imagined is not experienced. It's all happening right now. Yet our limited perception sometimes makes it impossible for us to see that, to know it. Gratitude changes our perception. In the case of God, it announces it.

Regarding your second question, there are as many different answers as there are people to interpret different words. Remember what *CWG* says about this. "Words are the least reliable form of communication." Some people use the word "soul" to refer to one thing, others use it to refer to something else entirely. In the strictest sense, there is no difference between the two as I use the words. That is because there is only one of us. And all of it is what I would call "spirit," or "soul." Yet some people use the word "spirit" to refer to the all of it, and the word "soul" to refer to that part of the all of it which resides with each individual. I don't think there's a "right" answer to this question, Pat. Take your pick.

Is God Interested in Sex and Politics?

Dear Mr. Walsch: I just finished reading your second book and I must say I was a bit surprised. I never knew God had so many ideas about politics, sex, education and, for that matter, the international economy. I'm glad to see that He does. It gives me a lot more hope for this human race of ours, and our continuing efforts to

> continue creating a home on this planet. Just one question. While I consider *CWG Book 2* to be not only an excellent book, but one of the most important I have ever read (if we are really interested in changing life on the earth), I am wondering (forgive me): did God really write this stuff, or did you? I can't believe that God would be so interested in our day-to-day machinations! Alexis, Severna Park, MD.

Dear Alexis, You don't need to ask for "forgiveness." You are not the first person to make this comment. I'm glad you enjoyed *Book 2*, however, and I agree with you that it is one of the most important books to come along in a great while. As you know, this book addresses in concrete terms every aspect of our group experience on this planet. It looks at how we interact with each other in the areas of religion, politics, education, economics, sexuality—the works. It offers specific commentaries of what we're doing now, and what we might do differently, given where we say we want to go as a society. It is illuminating, confirming, yes, at times a bit disturbing, but always fascinating, exciting in its overviews, and just enough "on the edge" to be, for some, a little bit controversial. (What ground-breaking book is not?)

Now, to your question, did God really write this stuff? Of course She did. Why would He not? Do you really believe that God has no interest in anything other than spiritual things? And, for that matter, are "spiritual things" somehow separate from our minute-to-minute, "daily life" experience?

Perhaps that is the problem, Alexis. Maybe too many people see the two as separate, having nothing to do with each other. You can sit in meditation all you want, Alexis, but sooner or later you're going to have to take your inner peace out into the street. And when you do, there is a good chance you are going to find the "opposite" there. And then you will face a choice, Alexis. "Who am I in the face of that which I am not?"

Conversations with God, Book 2 takes a very close look at that question for our whole society, our entire worldwide community of souls. As such, it is more than an important book. It is one not to miss.

Is God Politically Biased?

Dear Neale: Two questions: 1) Why was the Bible the primary reference in the *CWG* books for quotations made by God, indicating/suggesting this as a primary higher source of written material from which we may be guided? In the *CWG* trilogy, is it God's suggestion that we not incorporate material written in such books into our lives but, instead, use our natural instincts as our guide? Is He observing that how we are interpreting the written information is so ego-motivated that we should therefore follow our natural instincts to move us closer to who we really are?

2) In *CWG*-2 God seems very ungodly. For example, in *CWG*-2, God indicates that it's okay for God to make a mistake, inferring that God is not infallible. This would seem to conflict with the conventional definition of God (i.e., as an all-powerful, all-knowing Supreme Being). In fact, elsewhere in the books, God hints that there's another being greater than He. So it would appear that the God of the *CWG* books is neither all-knowing nor supreme.

God would also appear to be politically biased (e.g., his repeated praise of Bill Clinton) and negatively judgmental (e.g., his repeated pejorative reference to the human race as "primitive"). Please explain these apparent anomalies. Thank you. Frances, Seal Beach, CA.

Dear Frances, There is no doubt in my mind—none whatsoever—that God deliberately chooses, when God speaks to each of us, the language and the references God knows we will best understand. That is to say, God speaks to us contextually. He brings us His wisdom within the context in which She knows we will most readily be able to receive it.

I was born and raised in a spiritual tradition in which the Bible was the central scriptural text. Without question, this is why so many of the passages in *CWG* make use of these scriptures.

It is not my reading of the material that God is suggesting we "not incorporate material written in such books into our lives but, instead, use our natural instincts as our guide." It is my reading that God would have us use both. Not ignore scriptural wisdom (of any tradition), but use our natural instincts to come to our own inner truth, with the assistance and guidance of all of earth's teachers, scriptures and traditions. In other words, too many people have blindly followed scripture, rather than using scripture as a guide to the truth inside.

Hey, wait a minute . . . that phrase has a nice ring to it. It just sprang out of my keyboard here, and as it did, a chill went up my back. (I am sharing with you now an experience I've just had even as I am writing this.) So I think we should listen to that phrase again:

A guide to the truth inside. Not bad at all. And that is how we should think of every book and teacher and spiritual tradition.

Now, Frances, about your second question. I do not feel that God seems very ungodly in *Book 2*. I think it's very godly to acknowledge that it's okay to make a mistake. We have all made them, and since we are all a part of God, then it can be fairly argued that God makes mistakes. We cannot say that we are one with God with one breath, and deny that God makes mistakes with the other. If God was infallible, and if we are indeed one with God, then it would stand to reason that we would be infallible. Yet we clearly are not. Therefore, either we are not one with God, or the God with which we are one makes "mistakes."

Now the quibble here will be with the definition of the word "mistake." In human terms, a "mistake" is when we do something we did not mean to do, or when we do something we absolutely meant to do, but it produces a different outcome from the one we hoped for or intended. That is a "mistake."

Since God has no preference in the matter of how our lives turn out, or how they are experienced moment-to-moment, it would be difficult, in godly terms, to speak of something as being a "mistake." So, in that context, God has never made a mistake, and is, indeed, incapable of making one. To put this in simple terms, you can't make a wrong turn if you have no preference as to where you're going. Yet the part of God which is us has, apparently, a great many preferences. And to the degree that we have preferences, to that degree we create the possibility of "making mistakes."

As for God being the supreme being, you are perfectly correct. The book makes it very clear that there is no Supreme Being. That is, there is no one being who is "higher than all the rest." To understand this, consider the follow diagram. Most people, especially those in the West, tend to think in straight-line scenarios. They think of time, life, God, virtually everything, as a straight line.

This configuration allows us to conceive of a "beginning" and an "end," a "highest" and a "lowest," in our mental and mythical constructions. For instance, when we think of time, we often think of . . .

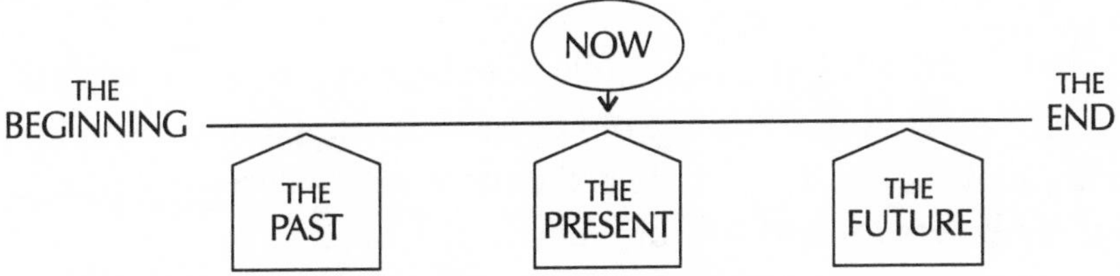

And when we think of God, we think of...

Yet what if all that straight line thinking got reconfigured? What if we began seeing things differently? What if we began understanding ultimate reality in a new way?

What way would that be? Well, instead of thinking of time, life or God as straight-line configurations, try this on for size: Try taking the two ends of that straight line and bending them into each other. Make believe it's a bar of steel, and you're a circus strong man, bending the bar until the two ends meet. What do you have then? You have the beginning and the end touching each other—with nothing in between. You have God and Satan joined together—with nothing in between. You have recreated God, time, life as a complete circle, and in this configuration there is no beginning and no end. Not to God. Not to time. And not to life.

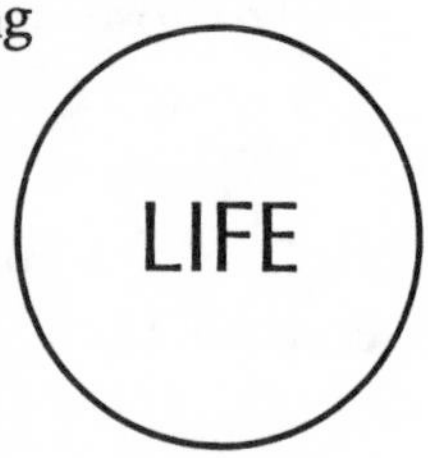

LIFE

This brings us to a new understanding. A larger understanding. A correct understanding of how it really is. In ultimate reality, everything is continuous. There is no place where one thing lets off and another takes up. The great It is just that. It's all one. It's all one continuousness.

I've just invented that word. Good word, eh?

Continuousness: the state of being continuous.

GOD

This is the state of being in which God resides. It is the state of being in which time exists. It is the state of being in which life expresses. It is that which God is. It is that which time is. It is that which life is.

God is continuous, with nothing higher and nothing lower.

TIME

Time is continuous, with no beginning and no end.

So you are right, Frances. God is not the Supreme Being. God is the *only* being. Now, to your final question. God is not "politically biased." You speak of His "repeated praise of Bill Clinton" as evidence of this, and yet you do not mention that George Bush was also praised, and rather lavishly, in *CWG*-2. You also say that God is "negatively judgmental," and cite as your evidence here the fact that God repeatedly calls the human race "primitive." Yet to make an objective observation is not to judge, and to describe something is not to call it "bad."

You have chosen to find something pejorative in the descriptive word "primitive," Frances. It is you who are judging yourself. God merely made an announcement. An observation. You have made the decision that to be "primitive" is not okay. In fact, it is quite okay with God. God has no judgment about it one way or the other. Yet if you feel that "primitive" is not the way you want the human race to be, then you have an opportunity to use your life to change that, Frances.

Thanks for writing. Your questions intrigued me. I hope my answers did the same for you.

What Is the Will of God? What Is the Function of Ego?

Dear Neale: I just finished reading *CWG Book 1*. What a wonderful book this is, what wonderful ideas have been presented. I have a question about a concept that is often advocated, but was not really talked about in this book (it may not be valid), which is the idea of the individual surrendering their will or themselves to God, or the will of God. Is this idea of surrendering advised, or ill-advised? Perhaps the individual needs to learn Who They Really Are through their own efforts. That brings up another question, which concerns the role of the ego. Does a person's ego get in the way of the learning process? How should it be used? Thanks a lot. Stan, Kirkland, WA.

Hello, Stan, Interesting questions. Thanks. The idea of surrendering to the will of God suggests that God has a will for you that is different from your own will for you. Yet in *CWG* God says, "Your will for you is My will for you." So God puts the ball right back in our court. We get to decide, we get to choose. And God has no preference in the matter.

This is difficult for many people to accept. We want a God who wants only the "best" for us, and we want to be able to turn to Him and have Him tell us what that is. And God can and will tell you what is "best" for you—as soon as you decide what it is you are trying to do. Indeed, God has done that in *Conversations with God.*

We say we want to build a better world, and God has told us how to do that. Not just in the Conversations, but in the Koran, in the Talmud, in the Bible, in the Bhagavad Gita, in the Brahmanas, in the Upanishads, in the Puranas, in the Tao-te Ching, in the Buddha-Dharma, in the Shih-Chi, in the Rig Veda, in the Mishna, in the Book of Mormon, in the Pali Canon, and in a hundred other places, through a thousand other voices, at a million other moments in the sea of events we call Time.

The key question is not, "Is it advisable to surrender to the will of God?" The key question is, "Why don't we do what we say we want to do?"

You also ask, Stan, if a person's ego gets in the way of the learning process. The answer is yes—unless it does not. The ego is the part of us that allows us to maintain our individual identity while we are in the physical body. It is the holder of our Individuation Information. We are all individuations of the one spirit. In physics, we could be termed individual, localized every units emanating from the only energy there is. In order for us to function effectively within the realm of the relative, which is where we now live, we need our ego. Therefore, it is not true that our ego is our enemy. Only an ego run amok is our enemy, only an ego which has gotten out of hand.

How should your ego be used? As the power and the source of your "sense of self," and of the wonder and majesty of that. Yet not as that which separates you from another, or causes you to feel "superior" to another, but rather as that place of deep awareness within you that allows you to sense the wonder and the majesty of everyone else as well, and puts an end, forever, to any thoughts you may have of being "better."

In short, Stan, your ego should be used as a tool, a device with which to see and understand the true nature of your individual self, so that you may understand the true nature of your unified self. The smaller self is a device with which to see the larger self. It is a perception tool. It was never meant to separate you forever from the larger self, but, indeed, to make you more aware of it. For you are as a candle in the sun, and cannot know yourself as the light when you are amidst the light. Yet you must separate yourself from the light—yea, even must you dwell within the darkness—that you might know yourself as Who You Really Are. Therefore, raise not your fist to the heavens, and curse the darkness not, but be a light unto the darkness. And do not hide your light under a bushel, but rather, let your light so shine before men that they shall know who they really are as well.

That is the function of ego, Stan. And there is no other.

CHAPTER 12

Religious Issues: Jesus, Bible, Church, and Angels

The issues raised in my introduction to the last chapter are very real. What is the True Word of God? Can all religions be wrong, but one? And if only one is right, which one is it? Does it matter? Will we really be left behind if we make the wrong guess? Or, worse than left behind, sent to hell?

People who have been raised in deeply religious households can be understandably anguished by such questions. They want to have a loving relationship with God, but there can be a lot of anxiety around that. *Conversations with God* comes to the world as a breath of fresh air. It is like a spiritual bath with Dial soap before meeting God. It takes the worry out of being close.

Still, people have many questions. They want to believe the really good news in *CWG*, but some find it challenging. Could God really love us this much? What about all that we've been taught? Endlessly, the questions go on, even as questions about God have been asked from the beginning of time. And that is good. Questioning is the beginning of wisdom. We must never stop asking questions. Of each other, and of ourselves.

And, of course, of God.

Who and What is Jesus Christ?

> Dear Neale: I have always believed that Jesus was a savior to all mankind. After reading *CWG*, I'm not sure. What is the truth as you know it? Craig, Williamstown, NJ.

Dear Craig, You've asked what many consider to be the central question of the century. The impact of Jesus' life was so extraordinary, it will never be forgotten. That is because Jesus was—is—a savior to all mankind. As are you and I.

Now, the difference between you and me and Jesus is that he donned the mantle, wore the cloak, accepted the responsibility. Most of us have not. In that sense, Jesus is our savior. For he did with his life what very few of us have done with ours. He did what we all came here to do! And in so doing it, he "saved" us from the necessity of doing it at all, if we do not wish.

Let me explain. We have all come to save the world. Not from the "snares of the devil," or from "everlasting damnation." (As *CWG* teaches, there is so such thing as the devil, and damnation does not exist.) We have come to save the world from its own mistaken notion of itself.

We are, right now, living in a world of our own creation, a non-truth, an experience which has nothing to do with ultimate reality, or with Who We Really Are. Jesus knew this. He also knew Who He Really Was. And he declared it, for all to hear. He declared something else as well. He said that what he did on Earth, we could do also.

Some people do not believe this. They cannot believe that they could be given—indeed, that they have been given—the same abilities as Jesus. Yet this level of faith is the key to experiencing those gifts. That is what Jesus taught. That was his central message. I think a careful reading of the following pages (*CWG Book 1*) would help provide clarity for you about this: pages 52, 55, 67, 86, 180 and 197.

I wrote a booklet, *Recreating Yourself,* which addresses much of this directly. In it, I make the point that it was Jesus himself who said, "According to your faith be it unto you." It was Jesus himself who said, "O woman, great is thy faith: be it unto thee even as thou wilt." And the woman's daughter was made whole from that very hour. And it was Jesus himself who said, "If ye have faith as a grain of mustard seed, ye shall say unto this mountain, Remove hence to yonder place; and it shall remove; and nothing shall be impossible unto you." Still, if you cannot believe in yourself and in your own divine heritage (and because so many people cannot), Jesus, in an act of enormous love and compassion, invites you to believe in him.

"Verily, verily I say unto you, He that believeth on me, the works that I do shall he do also; and greater works than these shall he do; because I go unto my Father. And whatsoever ye shall ask in my name, that will I do, that the Father may be glorified in the Son. If ye shall ask any thing in my name, I will do it."

Isn't that an extraordinary promise? So great and so complete was Jesus' understanding of who he was, and of who you are ("I and my Father are one" he said, and later, "all ye are brethren"), that he knew deeply there was no limit to what you could do if you believed in yourself, or in him. Could there be a mistake about Jesus' declarations here? Could there be a misinterpretation? No. His words are very clear. He wanted you to consider yourself one with the Father, exactly as he is one with God. So great was his love for all humankind, and so full was his compassion at their suffering, that he called upon himself to rise to the highest level, to move to the grandest expression of his being, in order to present a living example to all human beings everywhere. And then he prayed that we would not only see the evidence of his oneness with the Father, but our own as well.

"And for their sakes I sanctify myself that they also might be sanctified through the truth. Neither pray I for these alone, but for them also which shall believe on me through their word; That they all may be one; as thou, Father, art in me, and I in thee, that they also may be one in us: that the world may believe that thou hast sent me. And the glory which thou gavest me I have given them; that they may be one, even as we are one."

You can't be much clearer than that.

Conversations with God tells us that all of us are members of the Body of God, though we imagine ourselves to be separate, and not part of God at all.

Christ understood our difficulty in believing that we were part of God, part of God's very body. Yet Christ did believe this of himself. It was therefore a simple matter (and a marvelous inspiration) for him to invite those who could not imagine themselves to be a part of God to imagine themselves to be a part of him. For he had already declared himself to be a part of God, and if we could simply believe that we were a part of Christ, we would by extension necessarily be a part of God.

Jesus must have emphasized this point many times, because the record of his teachings, and the commentaries upon them in the Bible contain countless references to this relationship. String just a few of these separate references together and you have an extraordinary revelation:

> *I and my Father are one. (John 10:30)*
>
> *And the glory which thou gavest me I have given them; that they may be one, even as we are one. (John 17:22)*
>
> *I in them, and thou in me, that they may be made perfect in one. (John 17:23)*
>
> *That the love wherewith thou hast loved me may be in them, and I in them. (John 17:26)*
>
> *So we, being many, are one body in Christ; and every one members one of another. (Romans 12:5)*
>
> *Now he that planteth and he that watereth are one. (1 Corinthians 3:8)*
>
> *For we being many are one bread, and one body: for we are all partakers of that one bread. (1 Corinthians 10:17)*
>
> *For as the body is one, and hath many members, and all the members of that one body, being many, are one body: so also is Christ. For by one spirit are we all baptized into one body, whether we be Jews or gentiles, whether we be bound or free; and have been all made to drink into one spirit for the body is not one member, but many. If the foot shall say, Because I am not the hand, I am not of the body; is it therefore not of the body? And if the ear shall say, Because I am not the eye, I am not of the body; is it therefore not of the body? (1 Corinthians 12-16)*
>
> *But now are they many members, yet but one body. (1 Corinthians 12:20)*

All of us are members of the Body of Christ. All of us are the Christed One. And if Christ is one with God, so, too, are we. We simply do not know it. Refuse to believe it. Cannot imagine it.

Yet it is not true that going *through* Jesus is required in order to be going *with* Jesus. Jesus never uttered such words, nor did he come close. That was not his message. His message was: If you cannot believe in me, if you do believe that I am who I say I am, what with all that I have done, then you will never, ever believe in yourself, in who you are, and your own experience of God will be virtually unattainable. Jesus said what he said, did what he did—performed miracles, healed the sick, raised the dead—even raised himself from the dead—that we might know Who He Was . . . and thus know also Who We Really Are. It is this second part of the equation which is most often left out of the traditional doctrine about Christ.

You see, Jesus is our savior, to the degree that he has saved us from the illusion of our own separation from God. Jesus is the Son of God, as are we all. As we teach in our workshops: You have come to the room to heal the room, you have come to the space to heal the space. There is no other reason for you to be here.

Why Did Jesus Die on the Cross for Us?

Dear Neale: I am 21 years old and accepted Jesus as my savior in April of 1997. At the time I became happy spiritually, but I was still unhappy with who I was. Christianity left many questions unanswered. Your books helped me greatly, but I feel that a very important question was left unanswered. *Why did Jesus die on the cross for us*? Since reading your books I have become even more confused and I don't know what to do. Every time I am about to give up on myself and God, something draws me back. Each time the tug is more forceful. I may be conceited, but I believe I have an important purpose in this life!

Let's shift world consciousness together. Brian, Weedville, PA.

Dear Neale: I'd like to add my voice of gratitude to the chorus of those uplifted by your books. I've read *Books 1* and *2*, given them as gifts and return to the wisdom I find for myself in their pages. Having just finished writing a book, *Divided Passions*, on abortion and the death penalty, I really appreciate the sensitivity with which you treat these complicated issues. It is such a trip to create a work that can hopefully add to the dialogues!

As a Christian whose image of God is entirely confirmed by *CWG*, I wonder about the crucifixion. It is such an ugly story of bloodlust (similar to modern calls for capital punishment), and yet millions of people hold fiercely to the story because in the end the resurrection occurs. Why was the execution of Jesus necessary to share and spread the word of God's love, forgiveness and compassion? Was the resurrection "real"? In the love of all that is, Kim.

Dear Brian and Kim, I don't believe that Jesus was going to demonstrate anything. I believe that Jesus had the same intention that every soul who ever walked the earth has. The purpose of the human soul is to experience and demonstrate, announce and fulfill, declare and become, express and know itself. That is the grandest version of the greatest vision that it ever thought about who it is.

Jesus the Christ was a walking example of who he thought himself to be. And he has invited each of us to join in replicating his example, by declaring our own truth about ourselves. In connection with that, he knew that in the moment he declared himself to be who he was, everything unlike it would come into this space.

Therefore the crucifixion of Christ was both predictable and consistent with every thought expressed in the *CWG* trilogy. Christ allowed the crucifixion, he did not "suffer" it. He was the cause of the experience, not the effect of it. He said from the cross, "Do you not think I could call upon legions of angels at this time and stop this experience?" And, of course, the obvious answer is that he could. He allowed the experience to continue for the same reason we all allow all the experiences of our lives, the crucifixions, both large and small, to be visited upon us.

That reason is that we call into our lives every experience that we go through in order that we might know ourselves as who we really are. Christ's crucifixion, therefore, and his willingness to endure it, was a demonstration about himself, to himself. In the processes of creative demonstration, he also left for all of us an example of what we may demonstrate as well.

Is Jesus the Only Answer?

Dear Neale: How can I listen more carefully to God? Having been raised Southern Baptist, I have always believed that you just can't come to God any other way than through Christ Jesus, and that all our goodness comes from Him and from what He did for us on the cross. Your not basing your spiritual beliefs and growth on Jesus scares me. I would like to walk closer to God and be more conscious of His presence. Love, Sue, Alta Loma, CA.

Dear Sue, I understand your fear and I would never ask you to change your beliefs because of me. Nor does God ask you to do so in *CWG*. Quite to the contrary, God suggests that all of us stay true to our beliefs so long as they serve us. If the beliefs you adopted in the Southern Baptist tradition serve you, by all means stay with them. I do not personally believe that one cannot come to God except through one way and one path, in this case, Jesus. If that were true, then every Buddhist, every Jew, every Baha'i, every Taoist, every Mormon, every Muslim, every person of every other faith and religious tradition on the face of the earth from the beginning of time has been, and is, doomed to the everlasting fires of hell. That simply does not make sense. Not to me. Not in the face of what God has given through me in *Conversations with God*. But—and I hope you can hear this, Sue—I have no need at all for you to join me in my understandings. I believe that we can both find great wisdom and extraordinary insight and wonderful help in the material found in *CWG* without having to agree on every word in that book or our interpretation of those words. I believe the same thing, by the way, about the Bible.

If you would like to walk closer to God and be more conscious of His presence, Sue, take another person on a closer walk with God, so that they may be more conscious of His presence. For what you give to another, you give to yourself. The fastest way to have what you choose and desire is to cause another to have it. It is as simple as that.

Too Much "Jesus Christ stuff"?

Dear Neale: A friend of mine who happens to be a Jew read *CWG* and flipped, saying it was the best book ever. Then he got hold of your smaller booklets, *Bringers of the Light* and *Recreating Yourself*, and said he had a very hard time with them. When I asked him what the trouble with the two smaller books was, he said there was "way too much emphasis on Jesus Christ" in the booklets, and that he was disappointed, and even a little angry, because there was "none of that kind of stuff" in *Conversations with God*, and he couldn't understand why those other booklets were "pushing Christianity" so much. I haven't read the smaller books, but are they not Christian in their dogma, as opposed to the nondenominational flavor of *CWG*? Wayne, Spartanburg, SC.

Dear Wayne, No. There is not a single reference to Jesus in *Bringers of the Light*. There are several references to him in *Conversations with God* and in *Recreating Yourself*. In *Recreating Yourself*, the New Testament words of Jesus are quoted extensively to make the point that Jesus himself said over and over again what so many Christians fault "new agers" for saying: we are all one with God. Jesus was also mentioned as a great teacher who understood the most intricate laws of the universe, and demonstrated his understanding of them daily. I believe the example of walking through walls was used.

I am sorry that your friend felt uncomfortable with the references to Jesus. I've re-read the books and I can tell you that nowhere do they say anything about Jesus with which I imagined any Jewish person would take offense. Indeed, it is Christians who I thought would be far more likely to be offended by so many of the books' references. For example, this excerpt: "Yet it is not true that going through Jesus is required in order to be going with Jesus (on the way to God). Jesus never uttered such words, nor did he even come close. That was not his message."

Now who do you think would be more put off by that statement in *Recreating Yourself*, a Christian or a Jew? Actually, it would be my hope and my dream that nobody would be put off, but that the booklet in its entirety would bring us together, not pull us apart. Yet each person sees what he or she chooses to see.

Why Jesus "Killed" the Fig Tree

Dear Mr. Walsch: Thank you for your wonderful book. I have one question. It concerns the story in the Bible where Jesus curses the fig tree because it doesn't bear fruit. I don't understand why he would do this, because it also says that it wasn't the season for the tree to bear figs. The fig tree example must be there for a reason, but what?

For a long time this story has seemed to represent to me what seems a certain capriciousness on the part of Jesus/God, which perhaps refers to how man feels. Often it seems as if we've been beset with bad fortune, even though it wasn't our season to bear fruit, if you understand what I mean. In other words, it wasn't our fault, but we've been cursed anyway. Of course, I realize after reading your book that we are doing it to ourselves, but the story still seems very inconsistent with Jesus' character. This probably doesn't make any sense.

I find it's very difficult for me to talk about anything spiritual and make sense. But your book really does make sense, and for that, again, I thank you. I realize you cannot answer this letter, and I don't expect you to, but I just wanted to get the question asked . . . sincerely, Susan, Chicago, IL.

Dear Susan, The story to which you refer appears in Matthew, chapter 21, beginning at verse 18. It says: "Now in the morning as he returned into the city, he hungered. And when he saw a fig tree in the way, he came to it, and found nothing thereon, but leaves only, and said unto it, Let no fruit grow on thee henceforward for ever. And presently the fig tree withered away. And when the disciples saw it, they marveled, saying, How soon is the fig tree withered away! Jesus answered and said unto them, Verily I say unto you, If ye have faith, and doubt not, ye shall not only do this which is done to the fig tree, but also if ye shall say unto this mountain, Be thou removed, and be thou cast into the sea; it shall be done. And all things, whatsoever ye shall ask in prayer, believing, ye shall receive."

The story also appears in Mark, chapter 11, beginning at verse 12: "And on the morrow, when they were come from Bethany, he was hungry: And seeing a fig tree afar off having leaves, he came, if haply he might find any thing thereon: and when he came to it, he found nothing but leaves; for the time of figs was not yet. And Jesus answered and said unto it, No man eat fruit of thee hereafter for ever. And his disciples heard it . . . And in the morning, as they passed by, they saw the fig tree dried up from the roots. And Peter calling to remembrance saith unto him, Master, behold, the fig tree which thou cursedst is withered away.

"And Jesus answering saith unto them, Have faith in God. For verily I say unto you, That whosoever shall say unto this mountain, Be thou removed, and be thou cast into the sea; and shall not doubt in his heart, but shall believe that those things which he saith shall come to pass; he shall have whatsoever he saith. Therefore I say unto you, What things soever ye desire, when ye pray, believe that ye receive them, and ye shall have them."

I understand your confusion, Susan, because one wonders why Jesus would cause the tree to dry up when it wasn't even its time to bear fruit. The answer is that Jesus did not shrivel the tree because it bore no fruit, but rather, used the tree as a teaching tool in a larger lesson he was attempting to teach. The story is clearly an account of Jesus seeking to illustrate the power of thought (prayer) in the removal from your life of anything which does not bear fruit. Jesus was not demonstrating anger with the tree, he was demonstrating the power of prayer. He simply used the tree as a tool, as a metaphor.

I can imagine just how this might have happened. A bunch of guys were trekking down the road one day, listening to the great teacher as he spoke of the power of prayer. "You mean, prayer can do anything?" someone might have asked. "Of course," Jesus no doubt replied, and then thought to himself, "Let's see, how can I get Jimmy here to understand?" Just then, they found themselves approaching a grove of trees. Jesus knew it was not their time, and that he would find them bare. Ah, he might have said to himself, the perfect opportunity! "Boy, I'm hungry!" he said aloud. "Let's go see if those trees have any fruit!"

Now he gets to the tree in question and finds no fruit. Bah! He knew all along what he'd find, and decided to use it as a tool. So he tells his disciples, this tree has seen its last day. And the next morning, it's dried up. "Wow!" said the disciples, "there's a great lesson here. You'd better bear fruit, even if you're out of season!"

"No, No!" said Jesus, "That's not what I was trying to teach. I was trying to show you that whatever bears no fruit in your life, you can get rid of! And so, too, will it be with anything which stands in the way of your happiness."

"Really?" said his disciples. "You mean that?"

"Hey, would I kid you?" Jesus replied. "I'm telling you right now, whosoever shall say unto this mountain, Be thou removed, and be thou cast into the sea; and shall not doubt in his heart, but shall believe that those things which he saith shall come to pass; he shall have whatsoever he saith. Therefore I say unto you, What things soever ye desire, when ye pray, believe that ye receive them, and ye shall have them."

I'm sure it's easy for you to see, Susan, how when one uses metaphors and parables the way Jesus did, there is ample opportunity for widespread misunderstanding or misinterpretation. Still, if you listen to the larger message, stay focused on the biggest truth, you'll more often than not come to what the message really was.

If there is any doubt about my interpretation of the fig tree story from the Bible, it will be erased by reading the very next verse from Mark's version of the story. Clearly, Jesus did not cause the tree to shrivel and die because he was angry with it, or because the tree somehow did something "wrong." We know this, we can infer this, from his very next comment: "And when ye stand praying, forgive, if ye have ought against any: that your Father also which is in heaven may forgive you your trespasses."

So there is no doubt here that Jesus was not "punishing" the tree, or why would he teach forgiveness in the very next sentence? He was simply using the tree as a tool to demonstrate a larger truth.

Now, it might be said that if this was Jesus' true intent, it was "cruel," because he killed a tree which did not deserve to "die." But a true metaphysician would observe several things: first, that nothing and no one ever "dies," and therefore Jesus did no harm to the tree; second, that, being a master, Jesus no doubt knew that the tree was there—that it was placed there—by Providence itself (all things are in their right place at their right time; there is no such thing as "coincidence," and "accidents" do not happen) in order that he might demonstrate what he chose to demonstrate.

Now, Susan, a question for you. When you pick a flower to give to your loved one, has the flower been misused? Does the flower mind ending its "life" in a demonstration of love?

Return to Your Inner Guidance

Hello Neale: Each day I am reading and rereading *CWG Books 1* and 2. The one question I have is about the most fascinating part of the Bible: Revelations. What was the purpose of what John saw in his dreams? For example, a beast was mentioned: who would be this beast? Is it our own fears or is it a phenomenon which is actually going to exist someday? Can you give me some directions? Thank you. Margriet by E-mail.

Hi, Margriet, Much as I would like to answer everyone's questions, the whole purpose of my nonprofit foundation, ReCreation, is to assist people in finding and creating the tools with which to resolve their own personal conflicts, difficulties and challenges. I have no more of a pipeline to interpret Biblical passages or scriptural wisdoms from other traditions, than you do, and I am very clear that those scriptures cannot be interpreted to the satisfaction of everyone, in any event.

Therefore, in response to your question regarding the appropriate or most meaningful interpretation of the scripture to which you have referred, I suggest that you return to your own inner guidance with regard to that, which is, after all, the largest and the single most important message of *Conversations with God.*

Was the Bible God's Last Word to Us?

Dear Neale: What makes us think that God decided at some point to stop communicating with us through the written word? I mean, who came to that conclusion? Where does that theory come from? Who makes these decisions? I want to speak to the management! Marie M.

Dear Marie, The most wonderful thing about our wonderful God is that She has never, ever left us, never, ever stopped communicating with us. He is within you always, even unto the end of time. He will speak directly to you, in the bosom of your heart, whenever you sincerely ask a question, pose a dilemma, or send your love. God, of course, did not stop communicating via the written word 2,000 years ago. Nor did God communicate through only one instrument, only one document, only one time in all of human history. What purpose would God have for limiting Himself to that? What reason? If God is all powerful (which He is), and all loving (which She is), why would God end all two-way communication 2,000 years ago? Love, and power, would seem to dictate other choices.

The problem is, we have all been turning, not to God, but to men who claim to have the right answers. Popes. Bishops. Priests. Rabbis. Ministers. Men of the cloth. Most are well-motivated. Many are saintly. None speaks more authoritatively for God than the voice in your own mind, heart and soul, if you will but listen. Do not give your power (and thus, your God) away by believing anyone who tells you that God cannot be heard, and has not been heard, since the time of Christ. Can you not see that there are those who have a terrific investment in chaining you to that belief? *Conversations with God* lays out a new paradigm. I humbly invite you to explore it.

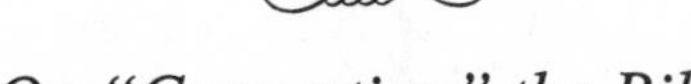

On "Corrupting" the Bible

Dear Neale: I tremendously enjoyed your books. They have undoubtedly changed my life for the better. Do me the honor of considering a question I have: How does God consider the Bible just another book (if I remember correctly) corrupted by editors of the past? I always thought God could never let such a sacred book be changed from its "perfect" originally intended form, no matter what man could do. Thank you for listening. Don, Camano Island, WA.

Dear Don, Your thought is inaccurate. God does nothing to stop humans from doing what they will.

Why Are Jews So Special?

Dear Neale Donald Walsch: *CWG* really knocked me out! I couldn't put it down; found it astonishing at several points; making perfect sense at others; laughed out loud, and was a bit puzzled after two or three "reads" of the same sentence. I will re-read it with pleasure and I treasure it. How grateful I am to you for daring to publish this material. A question: since I am Jewish, why are the Jews "the chosen people"? Love and blessings to you. Phyllis, Stamford, CT.

My dear Phyllis, The Jews are not "the chosen people." All people are "the chosen people." The Jews have simply been historically far more conscious of God's covenant with them than most other peoples; they have paid attention to it; they have honored it. It is the same way the United States sees itself among the world's nations. The U.S. says this is "one nation, under God." Well, all nations are "under God." Yet few nations have had the consciousness to place "in God we trust" on their coins. It is a question of consciousness. It is a question of how nations and peoples see themselves. It is not a question of which people God has chosen, but which people have chosen God.

Does Man Have Dominion over the Earth and Its Creatures?

Dear Neale: The Bible says that God told man to have "dominion over the Earth" and all the creatures of the earth. Can you please explain what this means? Tom, Atlanta, GA.

Dear Tom, I feel sure that God never used the word "dominion," but I know that the interpreters of the Bible have. They've had to. It has suited their purpose. You see, it has been important for man to feel that he has the power and the authority to conquer the earth, and bend it to his purposes, no matter what those purposes might be. It has been important for man to feel this, or man could never justify the rape and pillage of the earth which he has sanctioned.

What God very clearly said and meant is that man has stewardship of the Earth, and as such has been given certain powers and abilities. But man's powers and abilities in no way match those of Mother Earth—nor shall, or can, they ever. As I said, humans want to think of themselves as having dominion over the Earth so that they can do whatever they want with the Earth and her resources, without regard, apparently, to what that does to the Earth. This the Earth will tolerate for only so long, as the peoples of the Earth every so often relearn.

Our job here is to honor our Mother Earth and to do everything we can to nurture her, save her and protect her. She will house us well in the bosom of her love, giving us joyfully of the bounty of her resources, if we do not try to rape her out of our greed, or bleed her dry in our ignorance.

God does not see us as having dominion over the fishes of the sea, the birds in the air, and the Earth in the sense of having power over. This is not true for us any more than it is true about God's own dominion over us. God does not seek to have or to exercise authority over us, but rather, power with us, to protect us, defend us, nurture us, assist us, and cause us to be healthy, joyful and fine. This we should do with the Earth. The sort of dominion we have over the Earth is the sort of dominion God has over us. Not power that exploits, that uses, that destroys, but power that empowers, that enhances, that builds up.

Humankind can never accept this understanding until it sets aside its own seemingly insatiable greed. In our utter arrogance have we determined that "we are the boss" here. It is an arrogance beyond imagining. Yet God even has tolerance for that, so great is She.

Does "Respect" Equal "Agreement"?

Dear Mr. Walsch: I have a question I need help with. What do you do, what do you think about, how do you react when someone is praying, whether in a small or large group or in church, and they are saying things that you know are not the truth? When I have my head down and eyes closed, concentrating on the person's words, am I agreeing with the words and/or belief of the person or church? Or when your minister in a sermon says things you know are not truths, what do you do? Ronda R.

Dear Ronda, You've asked a very interesting question. I've often thought, when I've been at someone's house for a meal and they said grace in a way which I could not agree with, was my keeping my eyes closed and my head bowed a sign to the universe that I was in concert with all this? And I have had the exact same experience in church which you describe—the experience of hearing words or prayers with which I did not agree, and not knowing exactly how to deal with that. Well, I've thought about all this, because I've had to. And here's what I've come up with.

In one sentence: respect does not equal agreement. I bow my head and close my eyes when someone says grace before a meal whether or not I agree with what's being said in the prayer, out of respect for the fact that anyone is praying at all, and out of my desire to always honor anyone's sincere experience and communication with or about God. Similarly, in churches when I disagree with the sermon topic or the prayer content, I simply honor the moment, honor the fact that others do agree with what's being said, and honor the process that is going on in the church, and in people's lives. For it is a process of searching, of seeking, of finding and declaring the truth as people experience it, and I don't have to agree with your truth to appreciate it.

Now as far as God is concerned, I'm sure you don't have to be told that there is no chance of Deity somehow "misunderstanding" your intent, or "misinterpreting" your silence to mean that you actually intend to send such a prayer, or are signaling agreement with such a sermon. Remember that God understands everything about you, including every thought you are thinking. So it is not necessary to utter a silent "disclaimer" in your head, or to try to find some other way to let God know that you "don't really mean it." The deepest part of you already knows what is in the deepest part of you.

If my own minister were to say something with which I disagreed, I would probably place a call to the minister sometime during the week following the sermon and ask for a few moments to discuss my feelings about the message, and to explore together our differing thoughts on that topic. I am sure that I would enjoy the conversation very much, and I know that my minister would, too. Most ministers love to have feedback, and especially thoughtful discussion, about the subjects touched on in their sermons. Few ministers actually receive it.

Should the Ministry Be Abandoned?

Dear Mr. Walsch: Ever since I've been in the ministry (15 years), I've pushed the limits of convention and tradition. People who have helped me include John Cobb, Matthew Fox, John Crossan, Chung Hyung Kyung, Michael Newlin and reincarnation theorists.

For my birthday, one of my parishioners gave me your book, *Conversations with God*. This came at a time when I'd just begun past life regression therapy. You may imagine what all this has done to my thoughts about serving the church. It has become a real challenge for my personal integrity and authenticity.

I really connected with your book, and I know there is a way to enlighten the church, follow my truth and still maintain my integrity. I know it's probably impossible to talk with you about these things in person; I want to learn more from you. Thanks for who you are! Sincerely, M., PA.

Dear, dear fellow messenger, Speak with integrity from *inside* the church! There is no better place to make a change than where a change needs to be made. Integrity does not require you to leave the church in order to become authentic. Integrity may also be served by remaining in the church authentically.

All churches have something wonderful to offer. All religions speak truth. No single religion speaks all of the truth, and that is all that is important for you to acknowledge. If you cannot acknowledge that and stay in the church, then you must leave. But think of how much more gentle energy toward change you might provide with your collar on than with it off.

Be one of those people of the cloth that those of us outside the clergy see as genuine refreshments. Make fresh again the Word of God. Bring to hundreds who look to you the truth of love, and the peace of the soul. You have been placed in a gifted position. You may use it wisely without falling out of integrity. Wisdom is not lack of integrity; it is the height of it.

I love you. I love you for all you have done, and all you have left to do. Whatever your struggle, whatever your choice, I will always love you. I see that you have chosen to be a Bringer of the Light. Yet I would wonder whether it serves you to snuff out the candle just when you have found it.

Oh, and by the way, it is not impossible to talk with me about these things. Our frequent retreats are designed just for that purpose, among other things. There is always a chance to sit down and talk together.

Glad to Know We Are Not Sinners

Dear Sir, Neale: By "accident" I got your *Conversations with God, Book 1* from a friend. Therefore, this letter. Thank you, sir, and God, for this beautiful book. I have it now for my own. It is so difficult to let you know how important that book is for me and my friends. I talk with them about your book, and my children too. It is so exciting, I have laughed and cried about it. Sometimes I can understand what God says to you (and we all), sometimes not.

Last week we got by mail a little paper. It was terrific! It says that we are all very bad, and our hearts were the most bad thing of all. We are sinners from the beginning. And what we do, it is not possible to do anything good for God. And then your book! It is a great liberation. What a difference! I would like to thank you so much. He is closer to me.

Dear sir, please forgive me the wrong words I have written. My English is not so very well, but I learn!! Thank you again, and have my friendship if you wish. Yours sincerely, Anne-Marie, Gemonde, the Netherlands.

My dear new friend . . . I love you!! You're wonderful! Thank you for writing to me! I am sorry that someone mailed you what was apparently a tract for a fear-based religion. I am sorry that there even are fear-based religions. I am so sorry that anyone really thinks that we are all sinners, and that no amount of good works in life can change that, but only faith in one particular way of "salvation."

God does not make junk, Anne-Marie, and God did not make you a sinner at birth. Nor a sinner anytime. We are all wonderful beings, and while it is true that some of us have lost our way and forgotten Who We Really Are, it is not true that we were born sinners and that we are naturally just no good.

If I could do anything with this lifetime, I would choose to rid the world of this image and idea of God as a fearsome, angry, punitive being. It is simply not true. That is simply not what God is. And I am glad that *Conversations with God* has "liberated" you from this thought, which has imprisoned many people for many, many years, and that these three wonderful books are touching people in such a positive way all over the world.

What About Spirit Guides?

> Dear Neale Donald Walsch: One question I have that's not addressed in *Book 1*: What about spirit guides? Do we each have one, or many? Jackie, Seattle, WA.

Dear Jackie, *Book 3* goes into this extensively. It not possible to get into that depth here. But let me answer briefly. Yes. We are guided by spirit all the time, every moment of every day. Yet "spirit guides" are not "assigned" to us, as some mythologies would have it. Who would do the assigning? And what would be the penalty for not accepting the assignment? Souls simply choose to look after other souls, to guide them, to assist them, to bring them to new awareness, new understanding, new levels of consciousness. This is done out of sheer love.

The love, the compassion, you will know as a free spirit in the life which follows is indescribable, unlike anything most of us have ever experienced. Only a few incarnated beings—the Buddha, Krishna, Jesus, Babaji, Sai Baba, Paramahansa Yogananda and others—expressed this kind of love while in the body.

Do We Really Have Guardian Angels?

Dear Neale: I am extremely thankful for your book, *Conversations with God.* I would not doubt it becomes the Bible of the next millennium. It has helped me to clear things up and put them in their proper perspective.

If I had to give up all of my books (in the hundreds) and keep just one, this would be the book. Before I finished *CWG* I knew I would be reading it perpetually, again and again. I would like you to consider the following questions that were not touched upon in the first book.

(1) Do we really have a guardian angel, or are they spirits who have once lived on earth? I've read of both.

(2) Why are some spirits so earthbound? Why is there no one on the other side to help them move on with no problem?

(3) There are those who have had near-death experiences who claim to have talked to angels or highly spirited beings. Are they angels or earthly-departed beings?

(4) There are books which talk about the complete process of dying, looking over your past life, selecting a new one and coming back. Why is it that in this state of being, no one reports seeing angels?

Blessings to you, and keep on writing. Devon, Country Club Hills, IL.

Dear Devon, There really is a fantastic amount of interest right now in the subject of angels. So to your first question let me say that *Book 3* in the trilogy touches on this question. But let me tell you what I understand about angels.

Yes, Angels are real. They are just that: angels. That is, wonderful beings of love who minister to us every moment of our time in this reality. They become very attached to us, and in this sense are our guardians. They hover over us and do exert some control over physical life and the dangers around us.

Examples? The driver careening toward us who swerves at the last minute. The manhole around the corner that we just miraculously avoided. The paint bucket falling from the window ledge above us as we walk by the office building, missing us by inches. Even emotional collisions. That "bite your tongue" feeling which comes over you at just the last moment, saving you from blurting something which would surely have led to an enormous emotional "accident."

Those feelings, those maneuverings of physical form, are the manifestations of angels, who walk a delicate line, seeking to protect us from the hurts of life without interfering in any tangible way (which they may not do) in our own free choices and creations, or the path we are walking.

Are angels "angelic creatures" who have never been human, or are they the spirit forms of beings who have once lived upon the earth? That's a very good question. Some would say they are both. In fact, I understand us to have two kinds of "helpers." There are what I will call our "guides": these are spirit forms of beings once incarnated. And there are "angels": spirit forms which have never incarnated—"Fingers of God," if you please—tapping us on the shoulder to make us aware of danger, holding us in their embrace to comfort us through our tears, dancing with joy in their hearts when we celebrate our own wonder and our softest moments of love, which is God truly expressed.

The previously incarnated souls who choose to act as our guides do so out of love for us. They may be beings who have been close to us in this very life (although this is not very often so), or beings who have partnered with us in the life experience prior to this present incarnation (more often the case). They have chosen to be close to us at times because . . . well, simply because they are close to us (that is, they feel a closeness to us always), and it pleases them to give us guidance from time to time.

Guides, as opposed to angels, are not with us always. As previously incarnated beings, they have other things to do, other adventures to take, other challenges and growings to experience in what we would call "the afterlife." But they fly to our side instantly when they can feel we need guidance or help, or when we call upon them. Because they have shared a special kinship with us in this or another life, their presence can often be "felt" by us.

(1) The presence of angels is much more etheric, a "wispier" sort of feeling, if it is felt at all. Yet their power is greater than that of guides, if I could put it that way. It is not really a case of "power," but our human words are so inadequate to describe larger realities. Perhaps the word purpose should be substituted here. Or a new word, a combination of the two. Then we could say that their "porwer" is greater than that of guides. Their instant intercessions can change the course of physical or emotional events in ways I have mentioned. Guides do not have this "porwer."

(2) People are "earthbound," as you put it, because they choose to be. There are spirits who are there to help them "move on with no problems," but in the afterlife as well as in this life, no spirit, no guide, no angel, no being of any kind, not even God, will ever interfere with our free choice. Ever.

(3) Generally in so-called NDEs, the spirits to whom people say they have spoken are guides (often loved ones who have gone before), or ancient ones (souls of once incarnated beings), and not what we would call angels. On the other hand, there could be a conversation or an interaction with an angel. I very definitely feel that I had such an interaction during an NDE in 1980 which profoundly changed my life.

(4) You ask why, in the complete process of dying, people don't report seeing angels. For the same reasons people do not generally report conversations with angels during NDEs. When we have left the body, the work of angels is done, so to speak. Angels are literally the "fingers of God." They are God's spirit, moving into form (however etheric) and hovering over physicality. This is the Holy Spirit, or the "Holy Ghost," which is mentioned in so much theological literature. It is the part of the one soul which knows. Its primary function is to inform that which is physical. When we become nonphysical once again, we already know that of which the Holy Spirit would seek to inform us.

In short, the Holy Spirit is our connecting link between physicality and spirituality (or between what I would call nonreality and reality). When we, ourselves, shed our bodies and become free spirits once again, we are experiencing ultimate reality, and that which connects us to ultimate reality is no longer needed. We are that which connects us to ultimate reality. Indeed, we and ultimate reality are one.

This is also true of Who We Are in our physical bodies. It's just that we don't know this. And so the Holy Spirit is the part of all which re-minds us of this, and brings us other information from the realm of the absolute about our physical experience in this, the realm of the relative.

This "Holy Spirit" aspect of God is working through me right now as I seek to answer this question for you. This is my "guardian angel" at work!

CHAPTER 13

Conversations About CWG

Few spiritual books have gathered as large an audience in as short a time as *Conversations with God.* Written over a six-year period, presented as a trilogy, and published in 27 countries, the books have sold more than 3,000,000 copies. Further, anecdotal evidence has made it clear that most of those who read the books pass them on to relatives, friends, and acquaintances, to whom they earnestly wish to introduce the material. Many people say that they've given it to three or four others—and those others pass it on to still more. It is estimated that, to date, *Conversations with God* has been read by 10 million people. Over 300 study groups have now formed in cities around the world, generally meeting once a week, to explore more deeply the messages contained in CWG.

This is not intended as a boast, but merely a factual observation helping to explain the exponentially increasing interest in this material, and how it came to be. Everywhere I go I am asked about the experience, and most of the letters that I receive contain questions about it. Some of those questions appear here.

The One Outright Lie in CWG

Dear Mr. Walsch: Excuse me for addressing you personally, even though you may never see this. I am overwhelmed by *Conversations with God, Book 1* after reading your impressive dialogue. I truly hope that your book is going over in a big way, as there are a lot of us out here searching for simple truth, which is what I believe you have found and presented so well.

You say that you did not "write" this book, that it happened to you. I know what you mean, because I believe the same has come to me. I have been inspired to write many things in the past three years and sometimes wonder about their origin. I am amazed to read in your conversations almost identical reflections coming forth. I smile as I read my very words—or are they? Sincerely, Bill, OR.

Well, Bill, let me tell you that yours is only about the five-hundredth letter I have received telling me the same thing. What all of this proves is that there is one outright lie in *CWG*, and darned if it isn't right on the cover. It says there, "an uncommon dialogue."

As it turns out, there is nothing uncommon about it at all. And this has been one of the most exciting (and unpredictable) outcomes of this book having come through me, Bill. The book has given people all over the world permission to announce and declare their own experience of God. If it did nothing but that, it would have made an incalculable contribution to the human race. And, of course, it has done a great deal more.

Thanks for sharing your experience with me, Bill. It has encouraged me to continue to know that I am in good company.

You Don't Have to Be a Man to Hear the Truth

Dear Mr. Walsch: *Conversations with God* is not such "an uncommon dialogue." I, too, have had your experience. I was born a Jew, but prior to this unsought "contact," I was an agnostic. Through it, I received much information, almost none of which was in response to questions I posed. In fact, it was an ongoing discourse. Early on, in personal disbelief, I, too, asked the same question, unable to believe that what "we" (two of us) were receiving could be anything other than our own imaginations.

This was occurring during the time of the capture and captivity of the American airmen in Afghanistan. If you remember the climate at the time, with over 400 days of captivity and instability of the internal warring factions, it looked possible that at any moment the captives would be put to death. As proof that the instructions we were receiving were of the highest magnitude, we were given the exact date when that would occur. We were each allowed to share the information with one other, which we did as proof that we knew these events "before the fact." It came to pass as revealed.

Three of the authors of these "discourses" eventually revealed themselves as souls that were once patriarchs of the Old Testament. We had been chosen to be instructed in the hidden interpretation of the Kabbalah, even identifying to us, through the writings, where to go to locate obscure books. Our energies were elevated each time that we received the teachings. The two of us had been part of the "energy" that was used to ameliorate the explosiveness of the climate so that the Afghan captives could be saved. Some time after the "instructions" ended, I met, on two occasions, with rabbinical scholars on the subject of these teachings.

I am a woman, thus one of them gave me no credence at all, since tradition has it that only men could be given the "unwritten" parts of the Kabbalah. The other rabbi appeared to be so badly shaken that he did not know how to respond. I have had no need to share this with anyone since then. I tell you only in passing, as one who shares a great happening and is forever changed. Since those events, I no longer believe in God. I know God . . . is. Respectfully yours, Fern, NJ.

My dear Fern, thank you for your letter. I am pleased that you chose to write to me and share your experience. And, incidentally, I am not one of those who believe you have to have a penis in order to be given eternal truth. Neither is God. In fact, She is very clear about this.

Why Not Address Black Americans?

Dear Mr.Walsch: I read *CWG Book 1* with great interest, and felt joy and relief that some of the concepts and ideas that I believed, felt, and received during meditation were being validated. But I'll be very straightforward. I have difficulty dealing with a God who only deals with issues facing a white Anglo Saxon heterosexual male. Not once in the book did "God" address slavery, racism, or any ethnic issue. Is your God not concerned about sharing the knowledge of the entire world, not just your personal consciousness of it?

If this book is for me, why didn't it approach the issues that stem from the atrocities committed against millions of people whose skin wasn't the same color as yours? God didn't talk about native Americans and their connection to the earth and their spirituality. God didn't discuss Bosnia, South Africa, or the slaughter of girl children in China. Is that because those issues aren't important to you? If God wants to talk about how we could all get along better, why didn't he reach out to people whose native tongue is not English? Why didn't your God offer some answers to give comfort to those suffering with AIDS? Was George Bush a greater leader than Martin Luther King? Gorbachev better than Mandela? Ask God if Jesus was black. That would help me a damn sight more than knowing if he was an alien. Why didn't this all loving God of yours offer an equally emotional and moving description of two people finding communion and relationship, joining together in sexual union, about people with the same genitals? It seems to *me* that if two people can come together at a soul level regardless of their gender, they in fact might be more evolved than those who are just having sex for pleasure.

In one instance, God tells us to proclaim our love of money, in another, that all money should be abolished. Can you understand my confusion? I'm trying not to judge, but if we are all one, why didn't God address the issue that if a person with a penis gets paid more money than one without, then what about me who can't even get that job because of the color of my skin?

I'm asking these questions not to you, but to God. I'm not condemning you or your book, but you have a connection with God, the lines of communication are more open with you. Maybe you can ask God these questions for me. Because I can make no sense of a state of emotional and spiritual disparity between whites and blacks. Why were the traditions and spiritual practices stripped from slaves only to create a people less connected with God after 500 years of enslavement? Ask God what makes white people feel more superior than people of color? Ask God why these ETs aren't coming into the projects and ghettos to help raise the consciousness of those lost souls. God knows all the questions in my heart. Ask Him to write a book to me, and others like me, addressing my issues. Again, I'm not admonishing you or your book, I have just as many questions of God as you do. And I don't know where else to turn. Sincerely, Scottie, North East, MD.

Dear Scottie, I think you do not understand how this book came into being. *Conversations with God* was never written, nor was it ever intended by me, to become God's answers to any and all questions confronting humanity. My conversation with God was God's very specific response to my own very specific and personal questions, resulting from the calling out of my soul at a deep, dark point in my own life. The fact that people can relate on a personal level to as many of my own personal questions and answers as they did is an astonishment to me, and is no doubt what made the book so valuable—and a best-seller. But the book never attempts to produce, nor does it pretend to be, God's comprehensive compilation of wisdom on all the topics surrounding the human experience.

Put plainly and simply, Scottie, since I'm not a black American, and haven't faced the issues you faced, I didn't ask God those questions during my own "dark night of the soul." But you can! And the largest point of *CWG* was not that this is a book containing all the answers, but rather, that this is a book indicating to you that you have all the answers within you, and that you can find those answers in the same place that I found the answers to my questions.

In the end of your letter you indicate to me that you are not asking these questions of me, but rather, of God. That is very wise of you. Nevertheless, your decision to ask me to ask God indicates that you are still one level away from the process in its most authentic form. I do try to answer some people's questions, Scottie, but they are questions about the content of the book, or the implications of that content, not a list of inquiries others want me to make of God. The tone of your letter, Scottie, suggests that you think that I might have a better avenue to God than you would. Is it your idea that God discriminates, like so many employers? No, Scottie, there is no more clear an avenue of communication here than there is over there. Therefore I redirect your questions back to you and invite you to direct them to the God of your understanding who, I am certain, will respond to you as cleanly and clearly as She responded to me.

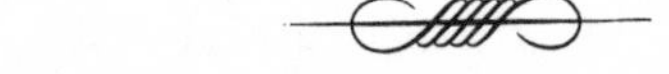

Is Self-Worth the Problem, or Not?

Dear Neale: I want to tell you how much I appreciate God's emphasis on loving myself first in relationship. She asks that we include ourselves among those that we love, and further on she says to ask ourselves, when necessary, "what would love do now?" God also said to you, "Yet I tell you this: the highest choice is that which produces the highest good *for you*." I am so very glad to hear that message. To me it is the most profound and important message in your book.

Perhaps you can clear something up for me. It seems like God contradicts herself about how much I love myself. From the bottom of page 124 to the middle of page 127 (*CWG Book 1*), God speaks at length about how we need to love ourselves first in relationships, and actually states ". . . so many people hate themselves because they feel there is not another who loves them." Now on page 161, God writes: "Self-worth is not your problem. You are blessed with an abundance of it. Most people are. You all think very highly of yourself, as rightly you should. So self-worth, for the great mass of people, is not the problem."

I must be missing something here. If you would be kind enough to answer this at some time or in some way, I would appreciate it very much. I do feel a lack of self-worth in myself at times. I suppose that is why I loved the part of the message about loving myself first and learning to appreciate that it is okay for me to know that God's messages to me are always my highest thought, my clearest word, my grandest feeling. I now know that it is okay to want what I love and love what I want. I thank you again. Love, Clina, Kenosha, WI.

Dear Clina, There is no contradiction in the text. It is true that "self-worth, for the great mass of people, is not the problem." It is also true that "many people hate themselves because they feel there is not another who loves them." The two statements do not stand in opposition to each other. I was watching Super Bowl XX on television and I noticed that the "great mass of people" seemed to be rooting for the underdog, Denver, but it is also true that "many people" were cheering for Green Bay. Where is the contradiction? If you are one of the "many people" who experience lack of self-worth at times, then that is what is true for you. And if the message of *Conversations with God* has made that better for you, so be it. I am glad.

Learning vs. Remembering

Dear Mr. Walsch: Thank you for being the vehicle through which the *CWG* material has been transmitted to the rest of the world. It has been said that many are called but few are chosen. Clearly you have been one who has been chosen, or perhaps it is more correct to say you are one who chose. It's also been said that it is better to light one candle than to curse the darkness. Well, my friend, the light from your candle has already touched over a million souls . . . and you have only just begun.

Basically, I have one question. I am asking your assistance for further clarification, too. In *CWG* God said through you that in life there is nothing to learn per se. We are here to remember, to remember who and what we truly are. Well, as you have said, there is really nothing new in *CWG*. All this information has been given to us again and again by God. I recognize much of it. However, for me this last statement is new. So new, in fact, it represents a major paradigm shift. I was taught this, and as a spiritual counselor, teacher, healer, etc., I have passed this lesson along many times. That is, this is "school house earth," and we are here to learn our soul lessons. We get to do them over and over again until we get them right, too. Then we go on to the next level, etc., until ultimately we return once more to the source—that is, we become one with God again.

It is said that experience is the best teacher. The "school house earth" paradigm has not only been my understanding and belief, it has been my experience, too. The "school house earth" concept worked. How can it be transitioned into "remembering"?

Therefore, if you would be so kind and please share with me your insights and understandings! I ask this help not only for myself, but for all who have shared this concept, especially my beloved teacher. She is a wonderful person who helped awaken me to a spiritual path.

Thank you for responding to this question. May you live your truth, be in joy, and always be surrounded by love. Blessed Be, Harold, Tucson, AZ.

Dear Harold, Think of remembering as recovery from amnesia. The amnesia that we have been given provides us with a fertile field within which to plant the seeds of new remembrances. God chooses to experience Godself as the creator. In order for God to experience Godself as the creator, God has to enter the act of creation, for the creator creates. Now we've got a problem here, because everything's already been created, so there isn't anything to create. So God, therefore, wants an experience that's impossible for God to have. The creator seeks to create, yet all already is created, so there is nothing for God to do, Therefore, God has a problem. So what God has done is say, "Oh, I know what I'll do,

I'll have the various disparate parts of me forget that I've created all that stuff, and I can create it over and over and over again."

So, our selective amnesia, our forgetting who we are, has a very divine purpose. If we all remembered who we were all the time, we could never be who we are. In the beingness of it, we could never experience becoming it, but we'd always just be it, and it's in the becoming of it that we become God. God is then caught, like Allen Funt used to say, on "Candid Camera" in the act of being Himself. God is caught in the act of creating Himself. Yet you cannot create yourself if you already know what you are!

So, to make it really simple, as I say in my lectures, let's pretend that my greatest desire is to be six feet tall. If somebody walked up to me and said, "Hey, you're already six feet tall," I'm going to go (whiny, sad voice), "Don't tell me that, don't tell me that! I don't want to know that! You don't understand. My whole desire was to *become* six feet tall. I wanted to experience creating that, and now you've gone and spoiled everything by going and telling me that. See, I'm going to have to take a pill here, and forget that I'm six feet tall. I may even go so far as to forget that there's such a thing as six feet tallness! I may forget the whole damn thing so that I can come to the question again, cleanly, knowing nothing about that. And when I recreate it anew, that's when I get 'Oh, I was always six feet tall!' But I then confront that knowledge with joy, not with exasperation."

That's a brief explanation of the reason that we have been given this, what I call, spiritual amnesia. This is what I call the God game, the forgetting, remembering, forgetting, remembering, that allows the breathing in, breathing out, of God to continue eternally and forever more.

Two Major Disagreements with CWG-3

Dear Neale: I just finished reading *Book 3* and thus, the *CWG* trilogy. Fabulous! Er . . . for the most part. There are a couple of things I cannot accept, a couple of small disagreements. The first is your (God's) assertion throughout the dialogue that "you have nothing to learn, you have only to remember." I believe I have learned things at ages 10, 20, 30 and 40 that I didn't know at birth. And I think I discovered things I "already knew," and so I see that life is much more than simply a task-master, but it is also more than a course is remembering.

The second disagreement has to do with HEBs (Highly Evolved Beings), as discussed at some length in *Book 3*. The book makes the point that such beings exist, and live in a nearly idyllic state, somewhere in the universe. My own conversation with God, far less articulate than yours, gives me a sense that wherever there are sentient species and civilizations, they are flawed and struggling with challenges. I do see illustrative value in the material on HEBs, much in the way good science fiction writers created alternative civilizations as foils to make points about our own. (I have a very short science fiction story I wrote in 1993 to skewer big-money politics; I'd love to send it to you.) But if you mean it more literally than that, I don't get it. Further, I do not see that it has value. It does nothing to push forward the core message of *CWG*, or the work of your Foundation, which you say is to "give people back to themselves." J.G., Ashland, OR.

Dear J.G.: What do you mean, "if you mean it more literally than that"? You think God was telling me a fiction, or you don't think I was actually hearing from God? Which is it?

Is it your assertion that the descriptions of Highly Evolved Beings (HEBs) in *Book 3* are inaccurate, and that such beings and societies cannot, and could not possibly, exist? If so, it is I who would disagree with you. I also disagree that the HEB material is of no value to the overall *CWG* message. The reason that the HEB material is important is not that it provides or presents a nice allegory, or a clever device with which to wake us up, but because this is how it really is in highly evolved societies, and that says huge things to us.

The message here is that we, too, could lead lives nearing perfection, or "Heaven on Earth," if we followed the principles of such highly evolved societies. The fact that such societies actually exist is evidence of the workability of those principles. This information does not seem irrelevant.

God is saying, look folks, this is now happening elsewhere. Yet if the model, the evidence, is all a fiction, a literary contrivance, a soft but useful "lie" as it were, then how can we proceed in trust that anything in *CWG* is worth taking at face value?

On your first point, I'm sorry to hear that you cannot accept the *CWG* statement that you "have nothing to learn, you have only to remember," because that is central to the overall message of my six-year dialogue.

CWG has made it absolutely clear to me, JG, that the reason most people hold themselves back is that they still think they have something to learn and that life is here to teach it to them. This understanding is simply wrong. Masters have observed that this very basic misunderstanding is the cause of all human misadventures. Surely if we were here to learn something, we would have done it after all these thousands of years of making the same mistakes over and over again. What is needed here is a change of paradigm, not more learning. What is required is a complete shift in how we hold Who We Are and what we are up to here.

Do you not see that if you truly believe we all have something to learn, then you must disagree with *CWG*'s point of view about Who You Really Are? You have forgotten your own identity, and now cannot accept it. Yet the whole point made by *CWG* is that we are masters, come here to express and experience our mastery. We are not simple, bumbling pupils, making the same mistakes for 10,000 years, completely unable to stop ourselves from doing it again. If we remember and accept Who We Really Are, everything changes. And we will have learned nothing. We will have simply remembered Who We Are.

A tree does not learn a thing between the time it is a seedling and the time it towers over the world, majestically holding its ground. It has simply become more tree. It has not learned how to do that. It knew that all along. It came to life itself knowing how to "be a tree." Every wisdom, every knowledge, every understanding about "tree-ness" rested in that seed. In that tiny, tiny seed. The tree needed nothing more, and it had to do nothing but become more of itself. Do you think it is any different with you?

Let me offer one simple statement, which, I fear, may seem like semantic word-play, but truly isn't:

All of what you call "learning" is remembering.

Because you do not know this, I am not surprised that you would say, "I believe I have learned things at ages 10, 20, 30 and 40 that I didn't know at birth." In your subjective reality (which is not reality at all, but merely the subjective experience of your present life which you have created for your self), I am clear that this is what seems true.

Only if you understand completely that you have lived many lives, and also that there is no such thing as "time," and we are therefore experiencing all of everything right here, right now, could you begin to comprehend how it could even be possible that you have nothing to learn, and only to remember. Just because you don't have something in your current consciousness does not mean that you do not "know" it. So to you, remembering could easily look like "learning." Since you may not know Who You Really Are (your comments suggest that you do not), you are still deeply immersed in what I will call (and what *CWG* implies is) the illusion.

I believe that the Christ, the Buddha, Lord Krishna, Sai Baba, and other living and walking masters who have traversed the earth in "times" former and present, understand all of this perfectly (which is, of course, what makes them masters) and I believe that they have, in fact, come here to remind us all of this truth of our being.

This is really the largest part of the *CWG* message. For the purpose of this dialogue was to give people back to themselves, and that is done precisely by reminding them of Who They Really Are. And Who They Really Are is God. And God, by definition, has nothing to learn.

Let me repeat—because I really do think you may have missed this—that the core of the *CWG* communication is: I am God, you are God, we are all God. We are God, "Godding." And if that is not true, then all of *CWG*, not just this point, is a fiction or a lie. Yet if it is true, then, clearly, so, too, is the statement, "You have nothing to learn, you have only to remember Who You Really Are." This is not an interesting sidebar to the *CWG* communication. This is the *CWG* communication, reduced to one sentence.

So, JG, yours is more than just a "small disagreement." It is a non-grasping, or a misunderstanding, or a non-acceptance, of the central message of *Conversations with God.*

That's okay, mind you. You are not required to "get it." But I can't agree with your characterization that what you have not gotten amounts to a "small disagreement." It's pretty major stuff, and if you have found value in the *CWG* material, you may want to review this text over and over again to see if that might bring you a grander awareness.

I love you, JG, and I have no need to "convince" you of anything. Stay with your truth, just stay with your truth. And as long as it leads you to places of happiness, without foisting unhappiness on others, do not change it.

No Need to Walk on Eggshells Around Me

> Dear Neale: Finally got a copy of your book. It's wonderful! However, there is one thing I noticed that God did not say: In *CWG Book 1*, page 114, in the middle of the fourth paragraph: "Clearly, it is equally inappropriate to neglect the needs of those you have caused to be dependent on you."
>
> God would never point the finger at anyone, and make them what we perceive to be wrong. He would have used the word "supported" instead of "caused." I believe that we cause or create our own reality, as you clearly state in your book, but we can only support another's creation. Please understand that I am in no way being critical of your beautiful work, and I would appreciate it if you would let me know if I have misinterpreted what was said . . . . love, RaeL by E-mail.

Dear Rae, First of all, it is not necessary to walk on eggshells around me. I mean, it is okay if you are being critical of my work. But thanks for your gentle courtesy. I just want people to know that I am not so thin-skinned about it that nobody dare say anything negative when referring to *CWG*.

Now, to your stupid, irrational, ridiculous statement . . . Okay . . . no more kidding. You raise, actually, an interesting point. My understanding, based on the reading of *CWG*, is that we can be the "cause" of another person's experience, for the simple reason that we are all one. I mean to say, there is only one of us. As such, we are all co-creators of the present reality. No one creates in a vacuum. What you create, I create also, and what I create, you create as well. If someone has chosen to become dependent on you (and you are right, it is their choice to become so), then you have had a hand in that creation. For the two of you have co-created this experience together.

When I was a child, my brother and I used to get into constant squabbles. And when my father would come into the room and give us "what's the matter?" I would inevitably protest, "He started it," or, "I wasn't doing anything! He won't leave me alone!" To which my father would invariably reply: "It takes two to tango!"

Even before I knew what a tango was, I understood what he meant. We are all doing the tango, Rae. All of us. And to pretend to have no part in creating the dance, hiding behind popular (but inaccurate) new age aphorisms, is disingenuous, dishonest, and out of integrity. I know better. And, I suspect, so do you. I know very well when I have caused another person's pain, and it doesn't relieve my soul one bit for me to sniff, "Hey, don't look at me! They created that."

As to God making someone wrong, it has been stated over and over again in *CWG* that there is no such thing as "right" and "wrong." God also stated many times in the manuscript that everything He offered as observations in the book was offered within the context of what we say we are trying to do with our lives, and Who We Say We Want to Be. And so we are to understand that all statements by God in this book are placed within that context. If we say we are trying to get to Texas, it does us no good at all to head toward Seattle. And that is not "pointing a finger," nor is it "making someone wrong." It is simply making an astute, and irrefutable, observation.

They Love God in England!

Dear Neale Walsch: I am absolutely bowled over by *Conversations with God, Book 1.* This is staggering, wonderful, life-changing, paradigm-shattering stuff. I bought 20 copies and spread them around. Now I get delighted calls all the time, even from England . . . . love and gratitude, Christopher, Sante Fe, NM.

Christopher, Thank you for being such a wonderful spreader of the message! I have heard from people living in Great Britain who confirm that people there are loving the book. We've also had mail from Slovenia, Australia, South Africa, all over Germany, Spain, New Zealand, Korea, China, Japan, The Netherlands, Russia, Brazil, and Puerto Rico. So the book and its marvelous message are reaching out to all corners of the world. The global impact is really just beginning. See p. 231 to see how you can join in making this happen!

How Can I Share My Spirituality with Others?

Hi, Neale: Thank you so much for your books. *Conversations with God* validated the recent information I've been receiving. My friends and family as yet are unable to hear me when I seek to share my spirituality with them. I wanted you to know how much I appreciate a kindred spirit. Diana.

Thanks, Diana. I know what you are saying about family and friends. It is difficult to have people close to you not understand where you are coming from, and that can create terrific loneliness —unless it doesn't. See page 231, Diana, to learn about how you can share your spirituality with everyone!

How Can I Introduce "New Words of God" to Friends?

Dear Mr. Walsch: I am only halfway through your *Conversations with God, Book 1* and already have cried, laughed and felt tremendous hope for a future utopia. It's so inspirational! I plan to share it with everyone who will listen. I'm a flight attendant on a layover and can't put the book down—I'm too excited to finish it!

I realize, as you said, that you cannot personally answer all questions, but hopefully mine will be asked by many, so that I might find an answer in your newsletter.

How can I introduce this book, these "new words of God," to my strict Catholic family members so that they may not only believe, but live—and live without fear? Thank you once again! Sincerely, Lynette, Buffalo, NY.

My dear Lynette, First of all, I am glad you found value in the book. I, too, am so excited by it that I can hardly put it down! Yes, that is true even today. I pick up the book almost daily, and I get excited about it all over again. And wait until you get hold of *Book 2*! It calls for nothing less than a social, sexual, political, economic and spiritual revolution on this planet the likes of which none of us have ever seen. Now that is really exciting! Unless, of course, you like the status quo.

In *Book 2*, God challenges us to move to a higher level, and this may be just too much for some people, who may then disavow the entire *CWG* series and maybe not read *Book 3*. Still, I believe we have an opportunity on this planet to bring it to a place of enlightenment. Not through laws, but through the power of beingness, through the power of persuasion. And now we've put Books 2 and 3 out there . . . let's see who is persuaded.

Now, Lynette, getting back to your question . . . .

You and I face exactly the same circumstance, and precisely the same challenge. If you think it's hard for you to share this with your family and friends, you should have been me these past two or three years. At one point we were even afraid to show it to my wife's parents, for fear that they would not speak to us again. Of course, they would never actually do that, but you know how the mind sometimes creates the worst possible outcomes.

We knew that Nancy's parents, both lovely, wonderful people, were somewhat traditional, and we simply worried that they would not take to the material very well. Still, we could hardly avoid their noticing that I had produced this book! So we bit the bullet and just let the chips fall where they may.

Well, Nancy's Mom and Dad both loved it! Nancy's father called it one of the most profound books he had ever read. So all of our fears were misplaced.

I felt the same way about the rest of the country. Oh, boy, I said to myself, get ready. Here it comes. People are going to really hate this. They're going to call you a blasphemer, a heretic. They're going to stone your house, throw rotten eggs at your car . . . None of it ever happened. There has been virtually no negativity at all.

Later I faced some of the same worries about *Book 2*. Nobody's going to like what's in there. Everybody's going to say "this can't be God talking!" I'm really going to get blasted for this one! And then I repeated the same fears about *Book 3*.

Well, you know what? There comes a time when we just have to do what is right and natural for us, what speaks to us of Who We Really Are, and then let go of any need for a particular result. And that's where I've had to go with the *CWG* series, and that's where you have to go, too, Lynette, with your family.

First of all, there is no need to convince your family of anything—and I know you already know that. But just for the record, let's get clear that we are not on a campaign here to convince anyone of anything. So, you just simply give them the book, if that is what you want do, and say, "Here's an interesting book I've been reading that I'd like to share with you," and let it go at that.

In short, stop wanting your parents to "live without fear." Stop seeking a particular result. Just do what you do, whatever that is, because it speaks of Who You Are. Be who you want to be, and let your words and actions demonstrate that, not because you want someone else to be that, too, but because it simply feels good to be who you are. There is no other reason to do anything.

Want to be more active in bringing *CWG* to others? Bring a *CWG* Center to your community! See page 231 for details.

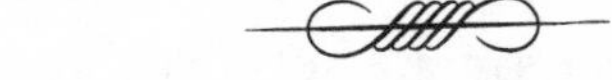

Confused About What to Believe

Dear Neale: My cousin sent me *Conversations with God, Book 1*. I devoured the book, but I did have trouble swallowing some of the ideas expressed. A few months before that I read *Embraced by the Light* by Betty Eadie. There are quite a few contradictions between the two books. So, at this writing, I am confused about what to believe! I continue to seek more spiritual development and I would appreciate it if you could shed some light on this matter. Thank you for your willingness to help others! With Love, Karen, Springfield, MA.

Dear Karen, concerning Betty Eadie's experiences as expressed in her books, let me say that I want to be very clear that I honor that experience, and would never attempt to contradict it or in any way make it "wrong." Betty's experience is her authentic knowing and her deepest understanding on this subject, and since I happen to have spoken to Betty personally, I can tell you that she is being very true to her inner wisdom.

Having said that, let me also tell you that it is possible for inner wisdom to be experienced differently by different people, depending on a wide variety of variables. What's also true, and I have been told about this reliably, is that there is in the universe more than one reality. That is to say, our reality tends to be created by us as we choose to create it. Therefore it is profoundly true that in Betty's reality there is only one life to live, and she'll have a chance to either recreate that experience when she leaves this life and allow herself to notice that that's the only life she's going to get because that's the only life that she thinks she's going to get, or she can decide to change her mind about that and come back as many times as she wants. I, on the other hand, have already predetermined in my own reality that there is more than one life to live. Indeed, I've had an experience of having lived many lives, lived and died many times before, and therefore that reality will be played out in my experience.

The largest message of *Conversations with God* is that each person and each soul is the ultimate authority and creator of their own reality, the sovereign who reigns supreme in the creation of their own kingdom, and therefore, it is quite natural that there will be what seem to be, and what appear to be, apparent contradictions between the kingdoms being created right here on earth and throughout all the universe by all the wonderful masters to whom God has given this extraordinary power.

I hope this helps to answer your question, and if you are wondering now which reality you'd like to create, go to a place of quiet meditation and communion with God on your own, and in concert with the God of your understanding, choose and create the grandest version of the greatest vision you ever held about who you are.

Have We All Been "Duped" by Satan?

Neale: Have you heard about Gabriel of Sedona, who claims to represent Machwinta Melchizedek (our planetary prince since 1989) and Christ Michael (Jesus), head of our local universe, Nebadon? He has a community in Sedona called Aquarian Concepts Community. They claim most of us are still dupes of the Luciferian revolt 2,000,000 years ago and haven't come to yet. All these teachings are from *The Urantia Book*, which I have been wondering about for quite a while. Of course, they say we must wake up and come to their Sedona school for training if we want to align with the true God and the true planetary government of Machwinta Melchizedek and get back to our ascension status. Gabriel of Sedona's book is called *The Divine New Order*. What do you think about all this? Hope to hear from you. I thought I loved *CWG*, but maybe we're still Luciferian dupes. Best, Bill, Sante Fe, NM.

Dear Bill, No, I have not heard about Gabriel of Sedona, and I'm not aware of the teachings in the book which he has apparently produced. I have no opinion on what you are telling me in your letter whatsoever, and even if I did, it would be pointless to share it with you, because the entire idea behind the teachings in *Conversations with God* is that you are not to listen to anyone else, but to turn within and find your truth there. Therefore, whatever I would have to say on this subject would be, or should be, irrelevant to you.

If you loved *CWG*, I am glad, and if you do not love *CWG*, or have decided now that it has something to do with being duped by Lucifer, so be it, and that is okay with me as well. I have no need for you to love it or not love it, nor does God. Your experience of *Conversations with God* will be whatever you choose for it to be, nothing more, nothing less. You can decide whether your experience will be colored by what others are telling you that it should be, or whether you will allow your experience to be the pure experience of your own soul.

It is up to you whether you choose to believe in a being called Lucifer, much less in the alleged power that he is supposed to be exerting on the course of human affairs. Believe what you will, but always remember this: as you believe, so will it be done unto you.

That is not my teaching, that is not even Gabriel's teaching, that is the teaching of every god who has ever existed anywhere. Every organized religion, every spiritual tradition, every highly placed philosophy, every human potential movement, every growth group, every philosophy of higher intent known to man holds true one single principle, and it is this: as you believe, so will it be done unto you. Therefore, Bill, choose to believe what you wish, and simply know that what you believe will become your reality.

I wish you well in the belief structure that you create, and hope that you feel comfortable and joyous inside of it. I honor you for your willingness to continue creating your experience exactly as you choose. Whatever that experience is, and whatever your belief system turns out to be, I hope you will treasure it as the grandest gift of your own creation. I send you my highest thoughts and my best wishes for a joyful and celebratory experience of life.

What Is This about Everybody's Spouse?

> Dear Neale: I wish to thank you so much for your excellent book, *Conversations with God, Book 1*. Whoa! It's great! But there is one point I don't understand: Commitment 9. "Nor shall you covet your neighbor's spouse, for why would you want your neighbor's spouse when you know all others are your spouse?" All women/men not married? Can you help me with this please? Thank you, and God bless you! Frederick, Palmira, Colombia.

Dear Frederick, The statement is a figurative truth, not a literal one. It means that we are all married to each other; that we can all love each other openly, and should be able to do so without fear. With this kind of ability to love one another, whom would we covet, and why? We are invited by *CWG* to learn to love each other in whatever way is appropriate to the moment. When we are open to the highest kind of love, to that kind of sharing, to that kind of intimacy, to that kind of emotional truth, to that kind of sensitivity to the feelings of all others, then it is virtually impossible to act in a way which is inappropriate. We covet nothing and no one, for all else is ours to steward, and all others are ours to love.

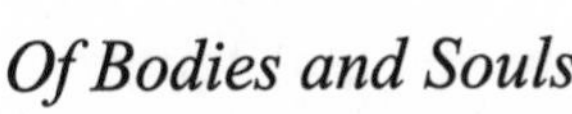

Of Bodies and Souls

Dear Mr. Walsch: I want to thank you for having the courage to write this precious book and bring it to the public. It has changed my life. One question still bothers me. I've heard it said that there are more people alive today than all the people that have died throughout history. If this is true, how is it possible for any of us to be living a second, third, 463rd incarnation? Most of those *alive* today would have to be on their first incarnation, wouldn't they? Kathy, Honey Brook, PA.

Dear Kathy, No. That would only be true if each soul embraces only one body at a time. You have left yourself closed to the possibility that just the opposite may be true. Which it is. (For more on this, see CWG-3.)

A Finite Number of Souls

Dear Neale: God created all the souls at the time of the Big Bang. With the increase in population, where are all the souls coming from to fill these lives? Marilyn, by E-mail.

Dear Marilyn, while there may be a finite number of souls, there is not a finite number of parts into which the soul may divide itself. It would be a mistake to think that any soul was confined to one being. In fact, I have been caused to know that any soul may include and encompass more than one so-called human being or living being. That is to say, it is not one body per soul. It might be 35 bodies per soul, or 72 bodies per soul, or 100,000 bodies per soul. This was given to me directly, and I was caused to know that that's what soul partners and soul brothers and soul mates are all about.

So while there may or may not be a finite number of souls, of one thing we are certain. There is an infinite number of individual expressions of each soul. That is to say, there is no limit on the number of parts into which a soul may divide itself. Therefore, it is entirely possible that 100,000 souls could produce 100,000 bodies in the year 1, and 100,000,000 bodies in the year 1999.

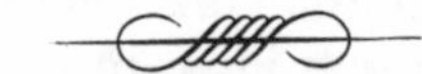

Trouble with the Hitler Material

Dear Neale: At the completion of your second book, you state that some of us may be uncomfortable with the ideas presented, and that they should not be accepted as "gospel." I have a real serious problem with that statement! If you cannot believe the word of God, what else is there? Doesn't that one sentence contradict everything you have written? God says one of our problems is that we don't believe Him . . . HELP! I am confused!

Also, I took everything I read very seriously until I came upon page 42 of *Book 2*, where God says, "The mistakes Hitler made did no harm or damage to those whose deaths he caused." Excuse me? After all, Hitler did cause many thousands to be unmercifully tortured, used for incredibly painful medical experiments, separated young children from their mothers. To me, that would be unbearable mental anguish. Perhaps had he chosen to immediately shoot everyone, one might be able to make an argument that it was merciful, but as we know, that most certainly was not the case.

And what about those who have lived after such suffering? Not to mention the fact that he significantly reduced specific populations (e.g., Jewish). Please help me to understand, because this has presented a barrier for me in continuing with the trilogy. I am obviously missing a very important lesson. I very much look forward to your response. Thebev, by E-mail.

Thank you, Thebev, for your heartfelt and sensitive letter. I deeply appreciate your willingness to engage the question, and to stick with the process of inquiry, rather than turning from it and running, as so many do, when something is encountered with which we disagree, or which we do not understand. So I want to honor you, because you are one of the spiritual warriors.

Thebev, I have stated in all three of my books that I am an imperfect filter. I do not pretend to be able to bring through the wisdom of God in perfect form. I hope only to be able to add to the discussion—to the "conversation," if you will—about God by sharing what I have come to understand about God through my own process, which I have described in my first book. This is important to understand, Thebev. If you believe that I imagine myself to be a prophet of God, a man who speaks the Word of God without flaw or error, then you believe erroneously, my friend. I wish that my book was flawless, but it is not. I wish that the Bible was flawless, but it is not. I wish that the Talmud was flawless, but it is not. I wish that the Bhagavad Gita was flawless, but it is not. Here we go again, you see? There have been many books claiming to contain "the word of God." And they do, Thebev, they do. But this "word" has been brought through the imperfect filters, the not fully developed minds, of men and women. We should not take any of it as "gospel," Thebev. That is, we should not assume that any of it is infallible.

Oh, Thebev, don't you see? The moment I make a claim that my book is infallible is the moment that I become dangerous. So don't do it, Thebev. And don't even have a need to do it. Don't try to make *CWG* the infallible Word of God. Yet, on the other hand, don't lose faith in every single word of the book, simply because I acknowledge that some of the words may be imperfect. Rather, take from the text whatever feels good and valuable and true and real to you, Thebev. And bless it for bringing you that.

Now, as to your comments on Hitler, Thebev, I, of course, deeply understand your difficulty with the passage you have quoted. This is the most challenging passage in the entire *CWG* trilogy, and I, myself, have struggled to understand its deepest meaning.

I do not believe that God meant to say or to imply, Thebev, that in the human sense the actions of Hitler caused no damage or hurt to anyone. I believe that God was speaking in the spiritual sense of all those souls involved. The trilogy makes the point elsewhere that there is not such a thing as death, and that, as divine beings, we cannot, any of us, be damaged or destroyed. It is within this context, Thebev, that the statement which you have quoted should be considered.

I am very sensitive to the fact that many people have been offended by certain other statements in the *Conversations with God* trilogy surrounding this subject, particularly the assertion that "Hitler went to heaven."

I certainly understand why this comment, too, taken on its surface, could be deeply wounding. I believe that only those who have had the opportunity to study the trilogy thoroughly and to examine the entire cosmology from which the statement emerges could find it non-offensive. They may still disagree with its theology, but they would see clearly that no trivializing of the Holocaust takes place in the *Conversations with God* books.

While *Conversations with God* does say that Hitler went to heaven, it does not say that he, or anyone else, ever escapes the consequences of actions while on Earth. Indeed, the books make exactly the opposite point. They indicate clearly that all souls, after death, undergo a process in which they are allowed to experience every moment of the life they have just lived, but from the point of view of every person who was impacted by their decisions. In other words, they experience what they have caused others to experience.

The point of this, however, is not to bring a soul to "justice," but to bring it to awareness; not to provide punishment, but to provide insight. Thus, the experience does not last forever. It is not about eternal damnation, it is about the soul's evolution.

CWG makes the statement that there is no such thing in God's kingdom as eternal damnation. Hell, it says, does not exist as a place where we are sent to endure everlasting torture. Thus, Hitler could not have gone there. Yet one thing is very certain. It is a universal law, and *CWG* states it very succinctly: "Whatever you cause another to experience, you will one day experience."

In the *CWG* dialogue, it is made clear that this is part of a process by which souls become fully evolved—or, as we might put it, "go to Heaven."

The most important point the dialogue makes on this topic, however, is that the Hitler experience was only possible because of group consciousness. "Hitler could do nothing without the co-operation and support and willing submission of millions of people," the books say. "Hitler seized the moment, but he did not create it."

The dialogue says that "it is important to understand the lesson here. A group consciousness which speaks constantly of separation and superiority produces loss of compassion on a massive scale, and loss of compassion is inevitably followed by loss of conscience. A collective concept rooted in strict nationalism ignores the plights of others, yet makes everyone else responsible for yours, thus justifying retaliation, 'rectification,' and war."

The trilogy goes on: "The horror of the Hitler experience was not only that he perpetuated it on the human race, but that the human race allowed him to. The astonishment is not only that a Hitler came along, but also that so many others went along. The shame is not only that Hitler killed millions of Jews, but also that millions of Jews had to be killed before Hitler was stopped."

Finally, *Conversations with God* says that "the purpose of the Hitler experience was to show humanity to itself." The dialogue makes the point that there is a little bit of Hitler in all of us, and it is only a matter of degree. It argues that "wiping out a people is wiping out a people, whether at Auschwitz or Wounded Knee." And, I might add here, Kosovo.

"Hitler was not sent to us, he was created by us. That is the lesson. The consciousness of separation, segregation, superiority—of 'we' versus 'they,' of 'us' and 'them'—is what creates the Hitler experience."

The dialogue concludes: "Hitler thought he was doing good for his people. And his people thought so, too! That was the insanity of it. The largest part of the nation agreed with him." It observes, "If you float out a crazy idea, and ten million people agree with you, you might not think you're so crazy," and asks us, "who, then, to condemn?"

Some critics of *Conversations with God* have said that the books portray Jews as simply having been "liberated from their Earthly troubles" by the Holocaust, and that since return to the Creator is a joyful experience, there is nothing to complain about.

This alludes somewhat to your earlier point, Thebev, and I have heard this comment from others. Yet while the books do state that life is eternal, that death is nothing to fear, and that returning to God is joyful, I do not believe that any reasonable interpretation of the material could fairly portray God as condoning the killing of human beings—or brushing it off as if it were of no importance or consequence. The trilogy does not make light of the acts of Hitler, or seek to justify them. It seeks only to explain those acts, and the lessons that we can all learn—must all learn—if we are to create a better world.

I hope this helps you, Thebev, understand some of the most difficult material in this trilogy. And I want to emphasize again, my friend, that I have only done my best to bring through some very challenging and complex truths. I am sure, I am certain, that I have failed to convey in every case the highest meaning, the deepest wisdom, the grandest truth. But I have never failed to try.

And so, my good friend, the exploring goes on. The questioning continues. The conversation with God never ends. Always we seek clarification. Always we seek correction when we have set the wrong course. Always we seek guidance in taking us all to where we say we want to go. And always God is there to guide us, to nurture us, to love us. Always.

And all ways.

About Collective Consciousness

Dear Sir: In *Book 2*, page 52, there is this exchange: "The events which occur on your planet—which have occurred regularly for 3000 years—are, as I've said, a reflection of the collective consciousness of 'your group'—the whole group on your planet." Can you provide any more meaning to this? With the millennium approaching, should this be tied into those prophecies from so many sources of significant changes in all areas of our existence? John, Spartanburg, SC.

John, my friend, the statement to which you refer means simply that human beings experience on this planet what human beings, collectively, think about themselves, about life, and about how it should be with us. We are the sum total of our collective story. That is, our myths and legends and ideas about ourselves as a species, handed down from generation to generation, and perpetuated in the present moment by the lot of us. Myths such as: "To the victors go the spoils," "survival of the fittest," and so forth. The biggest, most damaging myth, is the idea that we are somehow "better" than the next person, the next tribe, the next nation, the next religion.

The events which occur on our planet, *Book 2* says, are a result of this collective consciousness, or what I would call this group idea of who we are and how life is. What happened in Yugoslavia is a perfect example of this. So is what happened at Columbine High School in Littleton, Colorado. We are going to have to change our idea about ourselves, and about how life is, if we are going to change any of this, John.

The prophecies of changes in all areas of our existence are really predictions John, that we will "change our story," that someone or something will come along to make us change our minds about "how things are" in this world, and in this universe, and in our relationship to God.

Perhaps *Conversations with God* is part of that. Perhaps this is a portion of what will help us create a quantum shift in our ideas, and then, in our realities of life on the Earth.

How Do You Explain That Error in Book 3?

Dear Neale: In *Book 3*, page 185, "God" refers to Judith Schucman as the channel for *A Course in Miracles*. The actual author/channel's name was Helen Schucman. How do you explain the loss of integrity that this error places on your dialogues? RSW on the Internet.

Neale: I'm sure by now it's been brought to your attention that on page 185, *Book 3*, you've confused Helen Schucman and Judith Scutch. Still, I wonder, sir, how it got so far before it was detected? (Was it you or God who made the error?) Now, sir, there is no way

> I can fault *CWG* or you, but how strange: Judith Schucman? If you or an associate might explain a bit, I would count it satisfactory. Your books are, for me, delicious. I'm a "student." Please explain this glitch. Yours, Curtis, Amarillo, TX.

Thanks, both of you, for asking about this. Actually, I have received a number of letters about this, and it is a perfect example of what happens when you don't "trust the Source." Let me explain.

When the material now appearing in *Book 3* about *A Course in Miracles* came through me, I "heard" the name correctly, but—and I remember this moment so clearly—I questioned myself almost immediately and "second-guessed" the voiceless voice. I thought I'd heard it wrong, and that I knew better! So I wrote in "Judith" instead. Somewhat astonishingly, no one at the publishing house caught the error, either. Until the letters started coming in. Now everyone wants to know how "God" could have gotten this wrong, and some have gone so far as to say that now they do not feel that they can rely on anything else in the *CWG* books.

For my part, I see it all as perfect. I know now why I was "allowed" to make this mistake—and why no one at a normally astute publishing house caught the goof either. The error simply points out, glaringly, what I have been saying all along in these books: Do not make this your "Bible." I am not infallible, and this material has been brought through an imperfect filter. My continued commentaries to this effect notwithstanding, people were beginning to put far too much emphasis on the "perfection" of these writings, and to elevate me to the level of infallible messenger.

Because of the symmetry of this design, I sometimes wonder whether my error was a "mistake" at all. This "error" may have been allowed to happen as a means of pricking the balloon, bursting the bubble, and telling people yet one more time: there is no such thing as the infallible Word of God. Your God, and your wisdom source, will be found within. Do not give your power to any source outside of yourself. Not to a book, not to a religion, not to anyone or anything that does not originate within you—for that is where the Holy Spirit dwells, that is where God will be found, and is where God's Son is once again made flesh, in, as and through you.

Whatever the reason, I have learned one thing on a very personal level. I will never second-guess the voice within again.

CHAPTER 14

CWG and Neale

I have been doing a lot of thinking lately. I've been trying to figure out how to better use the wisdom in the extraordinary books which have come through me. I've been trying to understand how to render that wisdom functional in my everyday life.

I've not had an easy time with this. Earlier in my life I at least had an excuse for my behaviors. I didn't know any better. I had no idea what life was about, and so I couldn't make any part of it work for me. In my utter desperation I cried out, and the result was my conversation with God.

Now I've had the conversation, and been given the answers to life's most difficult questions. There is only one question remaining. Will I live them?

This is the question that I have lately been asking my audiences to put to themselves, and the other day it dawned on me that I have no right to ask my audiences to do anything that I am not prepared to do myself. So I took a look at my own life to see if I was living the message of *CWG*. I am sorry to say that I am not.

If I was I would treat everyone as I want to be treated—and I am absolutely not doing this.

If I was, I would eliminate from my life any worry about how I'm going to meet the challenges which confront me—and I am not doing this, either.

If I was, I would stop making myself or others wrong when things are said or done that I don't like. I would step outside of judgment—and here, too, I have failed.

You may think that this very pronouncement is a self-judgment, but I don't see it that way. I think there is a difference between judgment and simple observation, and I believe these observations about myself are very helpful, even if they are a bit discouraging.

Over the last five years, Nancy and I have traveled all over this country in answer to invitations from churches and other organizations to personally share the message of *Conversations with God.* In these lectures around the nation I have said that there are three main messages in the CWG books:

1 We are all one.

2. There's enough.

3. There's nothing we have to do.

I call these the triune truths. If we lived these truths, I've said to my audiences, we would change the world.

I stand by those statements. Now I see that my challenge is to live them. I want you to know that I thought I was, of course. I thought I had dropped many of my old behaviors, changed many of my unwanted habits, altered my course, taken a new path. I see now that this was the hubris of the newly converted. I see now by frankly and truthfully observing my daily behaviors that I have a long way to go.

That's okay, mind you. That's all right with me. Because at least I am on the path. I know which way I'm trying to go. I know where I want to be headed. That's more than I could have said a few years ago. But I've got to be honest with myself about how far I've traveled. The first step towards enlightenment is the step into self-honesty.

Last week I was very sharp-tongued again with a friend and co-worker, and I realized this isn't at all the way I would want to be treated. Yesterday I caught myself being very impatient with my wife, and I'm sorry to say that we were with friends. I know that if she had been so publicly impatient with me, I would not have felt good about it. She could not have felt good, either.

These are not the actions of a man who is living the truth, We Are All One.

A few days ago I passed a man on the street who clearly needed some help. I had some folding money in my pocket, and I passed right by without offering him some. I had this thought that I "needed" all my cash for when I got downtown. It was ridiculous. My credit cards would have gotten me anything I wanted there—including more cash out of the ATM!

Last Sunday Nancy and I visited a church in a far away community and we liked the minister and the message very much. When the collection plate came around I dropped a twenty in it, and felt good about myself. Only when I paid the bill for the after-church brunch we enjoyed did it hit me. I paid thirteen dollars more for food for my body—food that would last four hours—than I gave for the marvelous food for the soul I'd received in that church—food I expect will nourish me a great deal longer.

These are not the actions of a man who is living the truth, There's enough.

And the list of things I have been trying to "do" lately would fill the Manhattan telephone directory!

These are not the actions of a man who is living the truth, There's nothing we have to do.

And so all of this has made me stop and think. What does it take to live the message of the book which is changing the world? What is being asked here? What is being required?

The answer keeps coming down to one word.

Commitment.

What I need is an ironclad agreement with myself. An agreement to use my life as an arena within which to recreate myself anew in the next grandest version of the greatest vision I ever held about Who I Really Am.

This commitment cannot be half-hearted. (I suppose the phrase half-hearted commitment is an oxymoron in any event. One is either committed or one is not, no?)

All of which reminds me of the story of the chicken and the pig. The two were walking down the road one day when they came upon a huge billboard. On it was a picture of ham and eggs, with the legend:

America's Favorite Breakfast.

The chicken turned to the pig and said, "Look at that! Doesn't that make you proud?" To which the pig replied, "Well, yes and no. You see, for you it's partial involvement, but for me it's total commitment."

So I guess the moral of that story is that if you're wanting to move toward enlightenment, you're going to have to be a pig about it.

Really.

I mean, you're going to have to want the whole enchilada. I know I've already tasted a portion of what I'm after. I really have tamed my absolutely worst behaviors. It's the second level offenses, and the third, that I've got to work on now.

Well, actually, I don't have to do anything. Nothing is really being asked of me, nothing is being required. God requires nothing of us in order to love us, and we will not be "punished" if we do not "meet up" to some mythical standard. The choice is ours, and always ours, as to Who We Really Are. So working on those second and third levels is what I seek to do, not what I have to do.

That's why I don't "beat myself up" for not living the message of *CWG*. Or at least, not living it fully. Rather, I'm grateful that I've moved as far as I have down the path. And grateful, too, that I can now even see the path.

For once I was blind, but now I see . . .

In the end what it truly takes is amazing grace. The grace to see not only what is not working in my life, but what is working as well. The grace to bless myself—to allow myself to be blessed—for all that I am, rather than condemn myself for what I am not. For it is out of the blessed part of me that the grandest version of Who I Am will emerge.

I invite you, too, to do the same. Bless yourself for all that you now are. That's the first message of *CWG*. It may very well be the most important. For if you know yourself as blessed, you will surely bless others. Therefore, blessèd be.

The Nitty-Gritty

Dear Neale: How long did it take you to write this book, and how did it "come through"? Phyllis, Eugene, OR.

Dear Phyllis, the process began around Easter, 1992 and continued, sporadically, until February, 1993. What would happen is that I would get an "urge" to write . . . to go to the yellow legal pad and put something down. I had no idea what it was that I was going to write, just that I "had" to write if you can understand what I mean. It was like being hungry for "something," but not knowing what you want, so you just get up out of bed and start rummaging around in the refrigerator. Your spouse says, "What do you want?" and you answer honestly, "I don't know. I just know that I'm hungry for something." It's that sort of thing.

Of course, usually when I got to the paper, I found where I'd left off the last time (often in the middle of a paragraph or thought), and I'd put pen to paper and the dialogue would just pick right up again as if I'd never stopped to begin with.

Were there any "gaps" in the material coming through? Time-wise, yes. Subject-wise, never. That's what was so interesting. In terms of time, there were sometimes weeks, even months, between transcribing sessions. But there were never gaps in the material. Neither the sequence nor the context nor the content. Everything flowed as if there had never been a stop, at all in the process. I would simply get an "urge" to get to that legal pad again, and, presto! everything picked up right where it left off.

It was usually very early in the morning when these urges would hit, around 4:20 a.m., and I'd climb out of bed and try to find someplace quiet to be alone with the pen and paper. But I couldn't count on it returning every morning. It wasn't like that. Not that regular at all. So it was in some ways kind of frustrating.

The important thing, I've learned, is not to try to force it. I can't just go to the legal pad and say, "Okay, start sending, damn it." It just doesn't work that way. I've tried that, believe me. But then I can feel myself start "making it up," and I have to stop immediately. There's a qualitative difference between what comes off the pen when I'm "forcing it" and when it's "flowing." Stuff that came out feeling forced I just tore up and threw away. It was never placed in the dialogue.

Do I ever worry that what I'm putting out there may be "wrong"?

Now that's a very good question, one that I've been asked many times, and the honest answer is, yes, I sure do. Some of the stuff in the book is real controversial, and when I see it in print, especially, it starts to look real scary . . . like, "What if this is all crazy?"

But I can't stop the process because of that, and I can't hold back what's coming through because of that. Finally, I should say that I'm learning to question the process and doubt the material less and less.

Okay, Neale . . . Tell Us Everything!

Dear Neale: Did the *CWG* books give you the freedom to choose a whole new way? Did the books change your relationships, your way of life, and your former path? Have you redefined yourself? Do you wish you hadn't published the first book? Was releasing that book in conflict with who you really are? I, too, have had *Conversations with God*, filled journals with revelations, and decided ultimately that making them public would change the energy of my life in a way I did not choose. Are you in dialogue with God in an ongoing way, beyond your books? I am more interested in your process as a person, in how this has affected you, and in what ways you have grown toward God. Thank you for risking, and for sharing your own sacred experience. Naomi, Waterloo, IA.

Dear Naomi, Did the book give us the freedom to choose a whole new way of life? Yes. But that way of life is not what you might expect. While I must acknowledge that our financial worries are a thing of the past, Nancy and I have now fashioned a life for ourselves in which we spend six months a year, and in some months almost every weekend, on the road, traveling from Los Angeles to Toronto, Atlanta to Korea, British Columbia to Denmark, taking the wonderful message of *Conversations with God* to all who wish to hear it. Soon, we will be opening CWG Centers all over the world to help respond to the growing requests for more explanation and teaching of this material.

To your next questions, yes, I have redefined myself. I have chosen to move to the grandest version of the greatest vision I ever had about myself. I don't always reach that level of expression, but now I have the target set, the path defined, the goal established, and that feels very good—very much better than the aimlessness and essentially non-beneficial, pointless behaviors of the past. I consider myself to be a messenger, and I take that role (if not my life) very seriously.

No, I do not wish that I had never published the books. Quite to the contrary, I am extraordinarily happy as a result of my decision, fulfilled and enriched beyond measure. Not to have published *Conversations with God* would have been the biggest sadness of my life.

Yes, my dialogue with God continues in an ongoing way, outside of my experience of the books. I talk with God every day, and many times throughout each day. She is my best friend, my closest confidant. His advice is always warm and wonderful and perfect. The book has caused me to grow closer to God than I could ever have imagined, and I am decidedly the better for it.

The Greatest Thing I Learned from My Conversations with God

> Dear Neale: Thank you for your wonderful book! I have read it again and again, and given it to so many friends that the lady at the bookstore must think I own stock in the publishing company! I am wondering about something. I know what I've gotten out of the book but I'm curious to know what you got out of it! Would you give us your personal experience of this? Thanks! Mary, Detroit, MI.

Hi, Mary! Well, you've asked a question that is just about the most frequently asked of all. Every talk show host who has interviewed me has asked me that question, and every newspaper reporter. You're the first reader, though.

First, let me tell you that I read the book nearly every day. To me, it is like a book written by someone else. I often read it and feel no sense of connection with it at all, in the sense of an author re-reading his work. It has been that way from the very beginning. Always it has felt as it I had very little to do with this process, except to be there for whatever was supposed to happen. So the book has taught me a great deal, and been a source of continued inspiration to me.

I think the most important thing I got out of the book was a deep sense of God's abiding love. I learned in an extraordinary way of God's unremitting, unconditional love and total acceptance of us, even the worst of us. This came through to me even as I was "writing" the book by the bare fact that I was writing it. I mean, by the earthly standards of many people (including my own), I am the last person who deserves to have been chosen to put this information into a book. Yet I was chosen, and I have put it into book form. So by that measure alone, I am clear that God loves without condition, that God rejects not even the least or the worst of us, and that all we need do to understand and experience that salvation is to accept it, claim it, honor it, and hold it as true.

Now, there are those who disagree with me, Mary. Many, in fact, do. They say that God's word and God's law and God's love is worthless and pointless if there was no such thing as the possibility of God's rejection. They say that the only way to God is through obedience to God's commands, adherence to God's laws, and, in some theological constructions, acceptance of God's Son. Failure to do any or all of these things means certain damnation, they say, and we'd better be aware of that, and ready for it, because we'll get what's "coming to us" if we don't watch out.

In fact, we not only had better watch out, we'd better not cry. We'd better not pout, I'm tellin' you why . . .

Oh, sorry . . . that's a different myth.

You see, Mary? Every myth we create, we create around a system of judgment, around a construction of reward and punishment. It is inconceivable to us that there is a being in the universe, in realty or in mythology, who could accept us just the way we are, and just the way we choose to be. That is because we cannot believe in the ultimate purpose of life. We believe that the purpose of life is to follow God's law, do as God wants, and, essentially, please God. Yet pleasing God is not the purpose of life. Only an egomaniacal deity would create beings whose essential purpose was to please Him. And only an insane egomaniac would then add such treachery and misery to the mix as life contains in order to make it virtually guaranteed that his created beings would stumble and fall. And only an incredibly cruel insane egomaniac would go further, saying it doesn't matter whether they fall or not, because they have already fallen! Before birth!

As improbable as this scheme might seem, that is the theological construction which millions upon millions of people have laid upon their so-called "loving" God. So I think the most important thing the books did for me, and do for me daily, Mary, is free me from the shackles of a belief in an angry, vindictive, judgmental God. I am now more open to creating my life as I want it, not as I imagined it had to be.

The ironic part of all this is that I am now acting more in accordance with what the old teachings asked of me than I was when I was told to act that way, or else. In other words, I am finding that "being good" (whatever "good" means) feels, well . . . good, when it isn't having to be done because I'll be condemned if I don't.

Put another way, I tend to rise to higher expectations of me, and aspirations for me, when those expectations and aspirations are mine, not someone else's. This is a great secret which God understands, but which man refuses to believe: we are basically good, not basically bad. We do not need an angry, vindictive, punishing God to scare us into doing what is "right," act in the interests of others, or "show up" grandly. Our basic nature—human nature—is loving, and kind. We are taught greed. We are taught fear. We are taught ugliness, prejudice, violence. We are love, and we are taught to be something else!

The second most important thing I learned from the books is that there is only one reason to do a thing—anything—and that is to be and to decide, to create and to fulfill Who I Really Am, and Who I now Choose to Be. You see, I thought there were all sorts of reasons that I was supposed to do this or that. My father told me. The world expects it of me. God demands it of me. Whatever. Now I'm clear that God demands nothing, the world's expectations are distorted and misplaced, and my father's orders no longer need to be followed.

We are in this cosmic game of golf, and there's no one keeping score but us. Who we are, and who we turn out to be, is a matter between us and our selves. No one else cares. No one else even knows. Not really. And God, who does know, simply observes, without judgment, all the while, of course, making all of His power available to us, if we will but use it. We are left to our own choices. No instructions, no orders, no commandments. That makes us wholly responsible, completely in charge, and totally at cause in the matter of Who We Turn Out to Be.

This can be empowering, or terribly scary, depending upon a lot of other thoughts a person might have about the universe and how it works. For me it was terrifically empowering.

So the book has served me in these two important ways, and many other ways, of course, too, but in these ways in particular. I hope that has answered your question.

Stop Putting Yourself Down

Dear Neale: *Conversations with God, Book 1* has made a huge impact in my life and in the life of my clients. I am a psychologist working from a psychospiritual perspective. I encourage clients to speak directly with their angels and receive help with their problems. Your book has opened up many doors for clients and has helped me in furthering my work with them. I thank you.

I am most concerned about how you continually put yourself down. In your efforts to not be coming from ego, you are somewhat contradicting the teachings that come through from God in your book. I would encourage you to recognize that you are worthy, as we all are, of God's love and attention. It might help others more if you would forgive yourself for past problems of this life. I send you this message with love. "Angelhol" by E-mail.

Dear "Angelhol," I received your message with love. Thank you. I am working on this. One of the things I experience in my life is my deep regret over my past. And I don't mean the distant past, either. I'm talking about my actions of just a few years ago. I made some choices and decisions in my life of which I am not proud, and through which others have experienced damage. I know that God has encouraged me to forgive myself for that, and move on. Still, when those decisions involve people who declared their love for you, and even your own children, it is not something for which one easily forgives oneself. At least, not in my case. And the fact that I committed these transgressions repeatedly, not just once or twice, makes it even worse. Still, I hear your advice. I get what you are saying. And, truth be told, this is just one area of many where I would do well to heed more closely the wisdom in *CWG*. In fact, the toughest job I have given myself in this life now is to try to live up to the teachings in my own book! Thanks for your encouragement.

Thanks for the Thunder

> Dear Neale: I wonder if you understand—no, I wonder if you appreciate how much your book, *Conversations with God, Book 1*, has and will change the lives of so many people, and therefore the consequence of the grand and glorious twenty-first century. I challenge you to know your greatness by the thunder you have started. Because in your humility you may have missed the joy you have created and by being aware of your greatness and at the same time staying centered in your humility you are the all that is, contained by all that is not. And through my eager arrogance I hope to offer some joy in return for the thunder you have started in my life. And as I grew and awakened with the "being and knowing" of line 20, page 20, thunder did shake my house and bring forth the fresh and heavenly rains to a thirsty land. Layered on the windy rains, jasmine blossom and lemon scented gum trees placed a smile on a tear stained face. In the ancient I Ching, thunder is the most significant indicator of change. Thank you for the thunder. Tracy, Australia.

Dear Tracy, Thank you for your gentle and generous letter. I want you to know that I do not consider that I have done anything which others could not have done, and have not done, for that matter. I am very clear that people have been inspired by God always, and that what has happened to me has been happening all over the world. Our mail here proves that. Each month we receive letters from people who have been receiving the same kinds of inspirations from God I have received.

And, having said that, I am very happy you have been so positively touched by the material which I produced as a result of the process which I experienced. Now I want to invite you to allow the "thunder" to continue. Start writing down your own most magnificent thoughts and grandest inspirations. You'll surprise yourself with the depth of your wisdom.

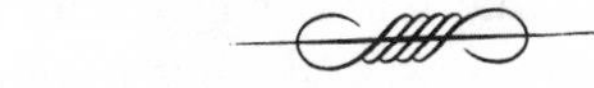

Are You a "Channel" for Divine Information?

> Dear Neale: I have read *CWG Books 1* and 2 carefully. It is not clear where the information is coming from. A person I met at a party commented, "That man sure is on an ego trip!" My own feeling is it doesn't matter where the information came from. Does this information ring true for me? Does it simply re-mind me of what I already know inside? Yes, it does. My own suspicion is that the person who made the above comment cannot see beyond his own ego to allow for the possibility that an "ordinary" person could be selected as a channel for divine information. And once again—it doesn't matter! Does this information serve us, each of us? That is all that matters. Thank you for having the courage to publish the books. Jean, Newtown Square, PA.

Well, Jean, thank you for the letter, and for your sentiments. May I quibble with just one word? I cringe when I hear the word "channel." I have been very careful not to represent myself as a "channel" for God. What I have done is not "channeling." What I have done is a little "inspired writing." Channeling is a whole different experience, and that is not the experience I claim to have had. But I do believe that this information which was given to me through the direct inspiration of the Holy Spirit has enormous implications and wonderful benefits for the whole human race. So I do believe it serves all of us. And if that is the measure of its value, as you suggest it should be, then I believe the *CWG* books to be an extraordinary treasure. (And that is not someone on "an ego trip" talking, because I am very clear that I had nothing to do with this material except to have been the one to "take the dictation.")

Thanks for Your Loving Concern

Dear Mr. Walsch: Yesterday, my wife and I received a gift package in the mail. Among the gifts inside was your book, *Conversations with God, Book 1.* And that is why it happens that I have written to you today.

Sir, first allow me to say with all sincerity that I believe without a shadow of a doubt that you had the conversations which are recorded in the volume mentioned above, and that you had them with a being from the spiritual world which surrounds us. I am not requesting your monthly letter, sir, but I am concerned for you, Mr. Walsch, out of sincerity and a genuine love which is rooted in the Lord Jesus Christ. Please let me share with you why that is.

Mr. Walsch, the being who had a dialogue with you was not God, but either a demon or Satan himself, trying to masquerade as God. Satan is good at deception, and he is going to continue to use you to deceive many others through the second and third books the spirit being spoke about. But only if you continue to allow it.

Let me pause to say that you seem to have a sincere desire to share with people for the purpose of helping all who will listen. But you are sincerely wrong in this message you are bringing. P.D.B., Killeen, TX.

Dear P.D., Thank you so very much for your kind and gentle letter of Christmas Day. I can't tell you how much it means to me to receive from you such a sincere and wonderful communication. I can only tell you that I wish that all the peoples of the world felt as strongly about their personal convictions and spiritual understandings as you do about yours. If each of us acted forthrightly and with honor and integrity in responding to our deepest inner convictions, the earth would become a glorious and wondrous place in which to live. That does not mean to condemn others, however, or to harm them physically or emotionally because they don't agree with us. This you have not done, but merely expressed your opinion and your human concern, and that is something I will always welcome and appreciate.

I want you to know, P. D., that I honor your point of view. I understand how much it means to you. I know that you deeply feel committed to upholding the tenets of your theology, and I encourage you to continue to do so. It was generous of you to take the time to communicate with me at such length, and it was wonderful of you to have the concern which has sponsored your communication. I hope that you will grant me a continuing generosity and allow me to hear your words and receive the wonderful emotion and human concern which underscores them without necessarily having to agree with the conclusions to which you have come. I will always hold you as a friend of the heart who wishes the best for me, and I am grateful for your willingness to act on your highest ideas. I know that we both wish God's greatest blessings for each other, and in this we have found a common ground. And so I close my response to you with my continuing wish that God will grant you ongoing love and goodness as a rich experience in your life.

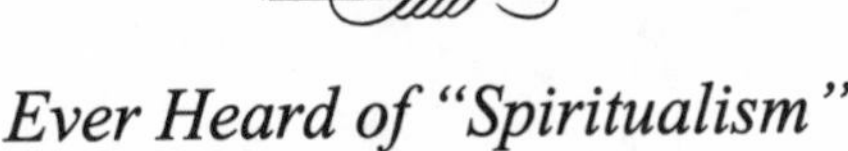

Ever Heard of "Spiritualism"?

Dear Mr. Walsch: Thank you for transcribing *CWG*. It is a magnificent work. Are you familiar with the religion of Spiritualism as taught by the National Spiritualist Association of Churches (NSAC)? My reason for asking the second question is that much of the dialogue is very similar to the Spiritualist writings. Christine, Alexandria, VA.

Dear Christine, I am not familiar with the NSAC, but I have heard of spiritualism, and a very old book from that discipline jumped into my hands about a year ago. I think I was in one of those wonderful used book stores found so often in tiny slivers of buildings on old streets in small towns.

Browsing the theology and philosophy section (the first place I go when I'm in a store surrounded by old books), I chanced upon some writing by an author whose name I've, frankly, forgotten. But I seem to recall the word spiritualist appeared all over this document. And I know I was struck by the similarity between what was written on the pages of that book—sixty years ago or more—and *CWG*.

What this and other experiences—such as the already noted similarity of *CWG* and *A Course in Miracles*—has made me aware of is an old saying I've heard many times in the past: Truth is truth, no matter what the source.

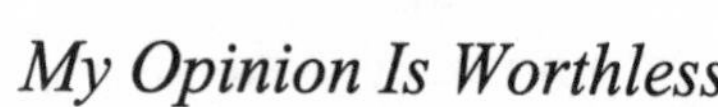

My Opinion Is Worthless

Dear Mr. Walsch: Reading *Conversations with God* has been a watershed in my spiritual development. Until your books came into my life I didn't love God; I feared God. Now I am challenged only to love, and for the first time I am beginning to feel God's love. If possible, I would enjoy reading what you understand to be the purpose (if any) of the book of Revelation in the Bible. Is it purely bunk? Bless you, Mr. Walsch. I hope someday that everyone touched by your book will enjoy the pleasure of meeting you in person. Tom B., TN.

Dear Tom: My opinion on the purpose of the book of Revelation in the Bible is irrelevant. You ask if it is purely bunk, and I can only answer you that that is something you must decide. Remember that nothing has any meaning at all except the meaning that you give it. The meaning that I give it should be irrelevant to you.

It is what you understand that should be important to you. I have been trying these many months since this book has been completed to avoid the temptation of rendering my own personal opinion on any subject whatsoever because I am clear that people will take what I say as being somehow meaningful. This would be the grandest mistake that anyone could make. Nothing I have to say on any subject is meaningful—except perhaps to me, and even then, it has only the meaning that I give it. So I think that is the whole message of *Conversations with God*, and for me to stand here now and pontificate on every subject under the sun would be in direct contradiction of the *CWG* message. Look inside your heart, Tom, and listen to what your soul is saying to you about these things. Therein lies your truth, and therein lies your path.

Do not question the highest understandings that occur to your soul. Do not downplay your own wisdom.

Are You Becoming a "Slick Cult"?

Dear Neale: I am one of those readers who recently discovered *CWG* by its falling off the shelf onto my head: "thank God!" Actually, I have been on "the path" for a number of years (lifetimes) and I have read many books from all angles, but I must tell you that this book was (and continues to be) a real knockout. I gobbled down the book over the Christmas holidays and have not been able to read anything else since (very unlike my personal habit . . .).

Anyway, I got to thinking about this change in my behavior and began to wonder if others were affected in the same manner. My question: Is this turning into a "cult thing"? The book really moved me in a profound way and it makes me happy that sooo many people are "searching," but it's beginning to look a little "slick" with its having a website, study groups, intensive workshops, etc. I, like all the people out there who are getting involved, may be too vulnerable and susceptible to its gravitational pull. Can you address these questioning "feelings"? Tom, Blacksburg, VA.

Dear Tom, I'm going to admit here to being a bit sensitive to your kind of question. I notice I often get my "shackles up" when someone says something like this. Not for long. Just for an instant. Still, my mother would say, "Are you sure that's not because there's a bit of truth to it?" Somehow I don't think so. I think it's because I just haven't yet gotten over the reaction I have to certain negative, unhealed thoughts which roam the universe. For instance, the thought that to do something—anything—which gets the word out to a larger audience about God's magical, magnificent love is somehow besmirching the message or despoiling the process.

What I notice is that today even churches have websites. It's what's happening. A website today is rapidly becoming like the telephone of yesterday—a simple, fast, expedient form of communication, an absolutely essential apparatus, a means of getting and staying in touch. What's "wrong" with that? Why does having a website suddenly render us "slick"? I think it renders us smart.

Does "smart" mean "slick"? If, in fact, our intention is to help as many other people as possible hear more about, and benefit from, the extraordinary message in *Conversations with God*, are we being too "slick"?

We could, of course, simply surrender the mass media and the Internet to the people who really are being slick: to the purveyors of silliness and pornography; to the sellers of trinkets and the hawkers and gawkers. But somehow it seems that it should be okay for people who have a good message to send out to also use these avenues of communication. What do you think?

Now, about those study groups. We have had nothing to do with their formation. They have been forming spontaneously all over the country and around the world without any input or any request from us. Some of the groups have written to us telling us of their existence, and asking us to let others in their area know of their existence through our newsletter. We thought of demanding that these groups disband at once because they would be seen as "a cult thing," but we dropped that idea as too reactionary . . . .

Finally, our workshops, seminars, and 5-day intensives. Well, now, there you have us, Tom. You've caught us red-handed. Surely any organization or movement based in fundamental truth and motivated by a sincere and pure desire to simply share that truth in a way which it hoped would bring help to others would never hold a class or a retreat or a workshop. It is shameful. It does have a high sleaze factor. It is "slick," there's no question about it. Imagine, holding an actual five-day retreat to help people get more closely in touch with the powerful message in these extraordinary books. We should have known better than to try to get away with something like this.

I guess I should stop with the humor and just address your question head on. Tom, the whole point of *Conversations with God* is that we are each responsible for ourselves. You talk about you and all the other people out there who are "getting involved" in *CWG* being "too vulnerable and susceptible" for its "gravitational pull." Do you seriously advance this as a reason for us to stay off the web, prohibit study groups, and never give another workshop? Shall we make ourselves responsible for you, Tom, and make sure we don't do anything that might "pull you into our clutches"? Perhaps a better way for us to proceed, Tom, is to put together a program and make information available which teaches people how to stop being so "vulnerable and susceptible."

As my teenager would say, "Now there's a concept!"

This we have now done, Tom. It is called *CWG* In Action, and it involves establishing *CWG* Centers in cities and towns wherever there seems to be an interest in creating one, and programs in those centers for teens and seniors and all people who yearn to make *CWG*'s wisdom functional in their daily lives.

We are now inviting those who wish to take an active role in this outreach program to become study group facilitators, certified instructors, or *CWG* master teachers. This was mentioned before, on page 231, and I want to strongly reiterate it here. Please see that earlier reference if you would like more details.

CHAPTER 15

General Questions

How can I impact the world?

There's a lot you can do. You can (a) seek to live the principles in *Conversations with God* every hour, every day, and so wipe fear and guilt from the face of the earth, replacing it with unconditional love; (b) form a Conversations study group and get together with four or five people each week to discuss the material chapter by chapter, subject by subject. Debate it. Pull it apart and see if it's real for you. Put it to the test. This is a great way to have fun with the book, fun with people, fun with your own mind, and fun with God. This is a God game. Play it! (c) Bring a CWG Community Center to your community. What we're up to here is spreading the healing opportunities, spreading the love. Become part of a team that is changing the world. Join *CWG* In Action. Do all that you can to make those principles part of your life, and the life of the planet!

Whew! That's more than you asked for, right? More than you want to do? Okay, fine. Don't do any of it. As God says, life is about opportunity, not obligation. See in this whatever opportunity you want to place there. See in our new friendship whatever opportunity you want to create. Or none at all. Just have fun. Have fun with life! And spread joy. Wherever you go, and whatever you do, seek to do that first, and above all.

Because when you spread joy, you give others an experience of Who They Really Are. Because that is Who They Really Are! And you can help them see that in themselves, by helping them feel that in themselves.

That is what we are up to at ReCreation, the Foundation for Personal Growth and Spiritual Understanding, which I should tell you a little bit more about here.

I formed ReCreation in 1993 because I wanted to have a way to put the truth and the meaning and the values I found in

Conversations with God into practice every day. I wanted to make the book real. I wanted its truths to be functional.

As you know, the main thrust of the truth which came through in this book is that life is not a process of discovery; it is a process of creation. We are told that the purpose of life is to recreate ourselves anew in the "highest version of the grandest vision" we ever had about ourselves. When that message came through, I was so inspired! I got up the next day and said, "That's it! That's what I'm going to do for the rest of my life!" And so was born ReCreation.

Since I was a little child, I've always wanted to be doing "God's work." I hope that doesn't sound too "precious" for me to say, because it's true. My only problem was, I didn't know what God's work was. I didn't understand what God was up to. I've spent most of my life trying to find out.

When I was 12, I thought that surely I was going into the priesthood. Raised a Roman Catholic, I was immersed in the theology of the Church. I'd become an altar boy, and I was very devout and very sincere in my deep love of God. The only thing I couldn't figure out was why I seemed to love so much a God who seemed to need everyone else to be so scared of Him. I couldn't image that God would really send anyone to hell, and I used to ask questions in our catechism class that drove all the priests crazy, like, "Father, if God really loves us, why would He condemn us to the everlasting fires of eternal damnation just because we made a mistake?" Things like that. The priests never really liked to call on me, and when they did they seldom had satisfactory answers to my questions. In fact, very few sources had until *Conversations with God*. And I've spent forty years searching.

I read every book, attended every seminar, enrolled in every class, listened to every cassette, prayed to every God I ever heard about, and still I could not get answers that rang true in my soul. Then on January 8, 1980, I had an out-of-body experience which changed my life, and which I'm sure was instrumental in preparing me for all of the events in the years which followed, including the eventual receiving of the material in *Conversations with God*. Now I know what God's work is, and I can finally do it!

The work of the soul is to wake yourself up.

The work of God is to wake everybody else up.

No more do I have to toil at meaningless labor. No longer do I have to spend the days of my life enmeshed and embroiled in the "game of survival," trying to find a way to make enough money to make the rent, pay the electric bill, and put gas in the car . . . so that I can stay on the merry-go-round another day. And no longer do you.

Life now invites you to play a different game. Sing a different tune. Join a different chorus line and dance a different dance. Dance the dance of joy and of truth, of a love which knows no condition, nor requires any limitation in the expression thereof. Life now invites you to "recreate your self anew" in the "greatest version of the grandest idea you ever had about yourself." And if your idea about Who You Are is that you are one of those who wishes, as Robert Kennedy put it, to seek a newer world, then you are aligned with us, and we can work together, if that serves you.

During the next five years we expect to see *CWG* Centers in cities throughout the world. In this way we hope to join hands with you in recreating ourselves anew on this planet. In this spectacular undertaking, we may or may not "succeed." It really doesn't matter. What does matter—and what brings us the greatest joy—is that we spend all the days and times of our lives divorced from irrelevancies, and married to our mission. And our mission at Re- Creation is simple: to give people back to themselves.

Now here are some answers to frequently asked questions:

Why Did You Start a Newsletter?

The main reason I established the newsletter was to offer those of you who have read *Conversations with God* a chance to dialogue about its contents, seek help or inspiration in a time of need, find insight or guidance as you face a particular challenge or question—or maybe simply have "another ear" to listen to the problem. And, as well, I want to give you all a chance to see how others across the country are reacting and responding to the material, so that our experience can be a shared experience. That is the same reason I published this book.

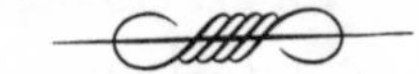

Does God Talk to Everyone?

God talks to everyone, but not everyone believes that. As *CWG* says, "This is the root of every problem you experience in your life—for you do not consider yourself worthy enough to be spoken to by God." How about you? Do you consider yourself worthy enough? Ask yourself this question. If your answer is yes, begin this month to listen more closely for the words of God as guidance in your life. If your answer is no, look to see why you do not think you are sufficiently worthy to receive God's direct guidance.

What about The Little Soul and the Sun*?*

Now I want to tell you how excited all of us at ReCreation are that we've had a chance to make the largest message of *CWG* available and accessible for children. If you haven't yet seen the wonderful job Hampton Roads Publishing has done with our children's book, *The Little Soul and the Sun*, you're really missing something. This story, written for seven to twelve year-olds, is based on the parable by the same name found in two parts in the trilogy, *Book 1* and the conclusion in *Book 3*.

It's an amazing story that explains to the young mind why, sometimes in life, "bad things happen to good people," and makes it clear that there are no victims and no villains. This is one of the major teachings in *Conversations with God*, and it is exciting to see it come to life through the breathtaking illustrations of master artist Frank Riccio.

It is difficult, at best, to find really enlightened literature for children these days. This book is a wonderful answer to that problem. It is perfect for children or grandchildren and I am really happy that we have found a way to bring these wonderful truths to the next generation at a time when they can most easily absorb them.

The *Little Soul and the Sun* is also being made into a story on CD and cassette, with music and singing, and that pleases me as well. Both the book and the audio versions are available from ReCreation. The money from these sales goes directly to support the work of the Foundation.

What Have Been the Effects of CWG on You?

I have never been happier before in my life. I have a relationship which is extraordinarily functional and wonderfully rewarding. My health is better now, in terms of long-term afflictions with which I had been previously bothered, than it ever was before. I have a level of financial security that I never would have dreamed of.

Has *CWG* caused me to change my behavior? Yes, of course. I hope that I have become much more loving, much more compassionate, and much more transparent with others than ever I was before. I also hope that I have become much more kind, much more patient (well, perhaps we should forget about the patient part for now), much more open, much more accessible, much more sensitive to others, and much more aware of my actions and their consequences than I was prior to the *CWG* experience.

I have also learned, at last, to trust. When I finished reading *Conversations with God* the first time, it was impossible not to trust anymore. The book simply put me in a place of deep trust, and I felt so good there, and so glad to have found my way there at last, that I have no desire to remove myself from that place. Many of you have asked how my fears were allayed—my fear that this was truly God talking to me and not an impersonation—and the answer is: I simply read and re-read the book many times. And my wife, Nancy, asked me the following question whenever I doubted that this may have been God talking—"What would happen if all the world behaved according to the teachings of this book beginning tomorrow morning? Would it be a better place, or would the world be worse off for it?"

That was a very good question and I am glad that Nancy asked it, because with that inquiry the entire experience was placed into a context that my mind could understand. I do believe the world would be a better place if everyone lived according to the teachings in *CWG*, and therefore I can't imagine that it really matters much whether the words came from God or from some other source. As God himself said, what's the difference?

I am very much okay right now. I am living the life of my dreams, I am on the road thirty weeks a year lecturing and workshopping with people all over the world on this subject, hoping to bring them a better understanding, and make them more able to embrace a truly loving and non-fearful God. It is my function in life now to give people back to themselves, and I am doing it with relish and with great good energy. I am still having *Conversations with God*, and I know that you are as well.

I think I have changed in many ways, including a vast increase in my tolerance and patience with and for other people, a much higher level of knowingness with regard to the abundance that will flow into my life, and the movement into a greater sense of mission than ever I had before.

The key for me in all of this was not only reading the truths that were given to me in *Conversations with God*, but living them. Of course, no one can live these kinds of truths every minute of every day unless they have achieved an extraordinary level of mastery—and I haven't met anyone like that for a very long time. But the goal should be that we try, now that we know the direction in which we seek to go. And so I would suggest that you stop beating yourself up for your failures, or what you call your failures, and begin to congratulate yourself on your successes, which are many.

Do You Ever Get Embarrassed with Yourself?

Learning not to be embarrassed about oneself is a pinnacle moment in one's development, I think. I am not any longer embarrassed about how I look, how I sound, how I feel, or how I am. Let others be embarrassed if they wish, let others be uncomfortable, I refuse to be anymore. When I am no longer uncomfortable with myself, I find that I can become comfortable at last with God. Because, obviously, myself is God. And so, when I make friends with myself, I make friends, at last, with God Herself. And She smiles, wondering how long it would take me to get this, and rejoicing in celebration that I have finally made it.

So it is all about being comfortable with yourself, and then allowing each person in your life to be comfortable with themselves. If this sounds suspiciously like unconditional love, that is because that is exactly what it is. Some people are getting all of this one day a week, and then going through the rest of the week like a robot. Still, they are trying. They are stepping off on the path. Now, if you are doing this twenty-four hours a day, you are in the front line, you are in the advance guard, you are way ahead of the pack. Wherever you are on this scale, I think, once again, you ought to be congratulating yourself and not beating yourself up so much.

How Can There Be No Such Thing as Right and Wrong?

One of the most controversial concepts in the *CWG* Trilogy is the idea that there is no absolute right and no absolute wrong in God's universe.

The human mind finds this difficult to accept. If there is no absolute right, how can we know when we are on the path to God? By what measure shall we estimate our progress? By what determination shall we know what our actions should be in any given circumstance? How shall we create our laws? What shall constitute our values? And how shall we justify the meting out of our punishments?

The difficulty some people have with the "no right or wrong" message in *CWG* is that they assume the book to be saying that we need to eliminate "right" and "wrong" from our ways of doing things, and they do not see how we can proceed with any kind of orderly society if we do that. Regarding the first assumption, they are mistaken. Regarding the second, they are correct. We cannot, given our current stage of development as a species, have an orderly society if we abandon our ideas of "right" and "wrong." Yet the *CWG* trilogy does not ask us to do that. It does not even suggest that this would be a good thing for us to attempt. Indeed, it does exactly the opposite. It suggests that we hold tight to our values, so long as we see that they serve us.

There is the key point. Values are only values so long as they are value-able. That is, able to be of value. We once thought it value-able to burn witches at the stake in this country, and we did so. Since then, our values have changed, and we don't do that anymore. We may shoot doctors at abortion clinics, and we may electrocute murderers, but we no longer burn witches. So one presumes our society has made a step up.

The dialogue says that "every act is an act of self-definition." It is precisely through our choices about what we currently call "right" and "wrong" that we define ourselves as individuals, and as a society. So the *CWG* statement that "there's no such thing as right and wrong" is not an argument for abandoning our current notions about what is right and wrong. It is an argument for being clear that our notions are precisely that. Our notions. They represent our current idea about things. This has nothing to do with objective reality. In other words, it would be inaccurate to suggest that the reason we should make these our values is because these are God's values.

God has no values. In the sense that God thinks that one course of action is "right," and another "wrong," God has no values. He has no preference in the matter. She does not sit in judgment saying, "You did this, and I wanted you to do that, so now you must be punished." Repeatedly, *CWG* makes the statement that "your will for you is God's will for you." This is difficult for many people to accept. It means, quite literally, that you may do whatever you wish, without recrimination from the Lord.

What we must do to make some sense out of the "no such thing as right and wrong" message of *CWG* is decide to stop using force (economic, spiritual, physical, emotional) in our attempts to get others to accept and adopt our point of view on things. What allows us to use such force now, and to do so with impunity, is our thought that, after all, "right is on our side," and so, we are justified in whatever we are doing to get others to see that.

And let's be clear on something, or else even this discussion will be bogged down in misunderstanding. The reason for not using force is not that using force is "wrong." The reason to stop using force is that it doesn't work. War doesn't work. Fighting and killing don't work. Economic blackmail doesn't work. Not for a society which says it wishes to live in peace and harmony.

Book 3 makes the point that Highly Evolved Beings (HEBs) living in advanced civilizations are different from human beings in two ways. First, they observe what is so, and, second, they do what works. Among the largest number of humans, observing what is so and telling the truth about it, is not common, and doing what works is even more rare.

The point here is that HEBs do not have a value system based on artificial concepts such as "right" and "wrong," but rather, on what "works" and what "does not work" for their health, welfare and happiness. If we applied such a rule-of-thumb here, everything would change overnight.

CHAPTER 16

The Only Question That Matters

In the end, in a book filled with questions, there is only one question that really matters. Everything else hinges on our answer to this question, and nothing else makes any sense until the answer is given.

The most interesting thing about this question is that a new answer has to be created in every moment. We can never be through answering the question—and, in truth, we should never wish to be through, because if we are, the game of life is over.

The second-most interesting thing about the question is that we are already answering it. We have never stopped answering it from the moment it was asked—which was the moment of our birth—and we will be answering it until our last day on earth. And even beyond. Indeed, we have been answering it always (and all ways), and we will be answering it even forevermore.

The question?

Who am I?

This is the question that God is asking. It is the question that life asks. It is the question that you must consciously ask yourself, and to which you must consciously provide the answer, if you are to jump off, at last, what you imagine to be a karmic wheel that keeps you caught up in experiences which you neither choose, nor prefer.

Now the first sentence in that last paragraph may seem unbelievable to you. How can God have any questions about anything at all? Isn't God the source of everything? All wisdom, all knowledge, all understanding, and, especially, all of the answers?

Well, yes and no.

God is the source of all of the answers to every question there is, ever was, and ever will be—and God knows, those answers will be known by God when God knows them.

Clear?

Yeah, right. Well, okay, let's go at it this way. God is in the act of deciding who and what God is. Life is a process by which God is "becoming." You are a part of that process. In fact, you are the process itself, playing itself out. Even as you decide who and what you are, and who you choose to be, so is God making the same decision—for God is the sum total of what everything is. And God will be the sum total of what everything becomes.

Now, to make matters even more complicated, I should tell you that all of this has already been decided. That is, everything that ever was, is now, and ever will be, is, right now. It already exists, has always existed, and always will exist, and it never, ever cannot be. (That is why it is impossible for you to "die.")

As explained in *CWG Book 3*, ultimate reality can be explained using, as an analogy, something familiar to all of us—the CD-ROM. On the disc of computerized games is every outcome that can be imagined. You can sit down and play the game any way you like. You make a move, and the computer responds. The response is certain and it is predictable. Every time you make that move, under those exact same circumstances, the computer will respond in exactly the same way. Yet there are an infinite number of possible moves, and, therefore, possible outcomes—all of which already exist on the disc, ready to be played out.

This is a very rough analogy, but it works, in that it helps us to understand how it could be possible for every outcome in the universe to already exist, and yet remain to be chosen and experienced. If you think that modern computer technology is incredible, wait until you see the technology of the universe.

What remains to be understood is the mechanism by which the "game" is played. How do we choose, and produce, our outcomes? And all of that is explained in great detail in the *Conversations with God* trilogy. If that material is read carefully, you will know and understand how you are answering, right now, in every single moment, whether you are doing it consciously or unconsciously, the only question in life that really matters.

Who am I?

Sometimes it helps, to get you into the swing of this, to ask the question after, rather than before, a particular experience or event. Take a look at three things you did, said, or thought today. Ask yourself, Is this who I really am? Is this who I choose to be?

As you get better at this, you will start to close the gap between the time you think, say, or do something and the time you ask the question. Soon, you will feel yourself asking the question even in the midst of what you are thinking, saying, or doing. Finally, you will find yourself stopping in the split-second before you think, say, or do something, and asking the question ahead of time. Then you will answer the question by whatever behavior you exhibit.

At this point, you will have achieved mastery.

Every other question in this book will then become irrelevant, because you will have known yourself, if only briefly, as the creator of your own experience. Once that happens, there can be no more questions. There will only be answers, flowing from you every moment. And you will be a master, indeed. Not just in thought, not just in word, but in deed.

And what you do will change the world.

In Closing

The process of answering the specific questions of readers continues. In each issue of our newsletter I continue this open dialogue as part of my commitment to provide ongoing opportunities for *CWG's* energy to be present in people's lives. Many people have expressed to us the wish that their experience of this life-changing material did not have to end with the finishing of the books. At first, Nancy and I tried to answer every letter that came in. When that become no longer possible, we decided on the newsletter as a way that the most commonly-asked or humanly interesting letters could be answered.

The newsletter also contains selections from the trilogy itself (as well as excerpts from not-yet-published manuscripts now being written), together with comments on how to apply the spiritual principles described there, in everyday life. Persons wishing to obtain a copy may do so by sending $35 for 12 issues ($45 in U.S. currency for addresses outside the United States), to:

ReCreation Foundation
PMB #1150
1257 Siskiyou Blvd.
Ashland, Oregon 97520

Scholarship subscriptions are available. In addition to the regular newsletter, our foundation produces one-day seminars, weekend workshops, and five-day retreats revolving around the messages of *CWG*. These programs are presented at locations throughout the United States. Information on them is always published in the newsletter, or may be obtained separately by sending a self-addressed, stamped envelope to the above address. Twenty percent of the seats at all of our foundation-sponsored programs are set aside for full or partial scholarships, and inquiries are welcome.

Finally, I want to mention as a resource a booklet which I have written, called *Bringers of the Light*, which explains in wonderfully clear language the difference between what I call "beingness" and "doingness," and focuses on how to find Right Livelihood in one's life, so that we can express, in our working hours, the spiritual truths that live inside us always.

Just forty pages long, it can be read in thirty minutes, but is deceptive in its simplicity. It's readers tell me that they received an enormous "aha" from the manuscript, suddenly understanding far more deeply how to apply the wisdom of "coming from being" which pervades the *Conversations with God* material.

We use the income from these booklets to fund our newsletter and workshop scholarships. The booklet is available by sending $10, with your request for *Bringers of the Light*, to the above address.

I am humbled by the response that *Conversations with God* has received around the world. I only hope that I can always be deserving of the job that God has given me, and the trust that you have placed in me. Above all, though, I hope and pray that you will place the greatest trust in yourself. You are the magic, you are a marvelous work, and a wonder. You are the source and the wisdom, the highest understanding, and the grandest love. The message of *CWG* is that this is what you are. *So be it.*

You are the blesséd one, and so...blesséd be.

With love, always,
Neale

Index

A

B

D

E

H

M

N

O

P

Q

R

S

T

V